From Clerks to Corpora: essays on the English language yesterday and today

Philip Shaw, Britt Erman,
Gunnel Melchers & Peter Sundkvist

Essays in honour of Nils-Lennart Johannesson

STOCKHOLM UNIVERSITY PRESS

Stockholm English Studies 2

Published by
Stockholm University Press
Stockholm University
SE-106 91 Stockholm
Sweden
www.stockholmuniversitypress.se

Supporting Agencies (funding): Department of English, Stockholm University

First published 2015
Cover Illustration: MS Wellcome 537, f. 15r.
Reproduced by permission of © Wellcome Library, London.
Cover designed by Karl Edqvist, SUP

Stockholm English Studies (Online) ISSN: 2002-0163

ISBN (Hardback): 978-91-7635-004-1   ISBN (PDF): 978-91-7635-005-8
ISBN (EPUB): 978-91-7635-006-5   ISBN (Kindle): 978-91-7635-007-2

DOI: http://dx.doi.org/10.16993/sup.bab

Erratum: 2 weeks after publication the following text was added to the title page
of chapter 20 (p367): 'Based on an unfinished manuscript, posthumously edited by
Cecilia Ovesdotter Alm.'

Suggested citation:
Shaw, P., Erman, B., Melchers, G. and Sundkvist, P. (eds) 2015. *From Clerks to
Corpora: essays on the English language yesterday and today.* Stockholm: Stockholm
University Press. DOI: http://dx.doi.org/10.16993/sup.bab

To read the free, open access version of this book online,
visit http://dx.doi.org/10.16993/sup.bab or scan this QR code with
your mobile device.

Stockholm English Studies

Stockholm English Studies (SES) is a peer-reviewed series of monographs and edited volumes published by Stockholm University Press. SES strives to provide a broad forum for research on English language and literature from all periods. In terms of subjects and methods, the orientation is also wide: language structure, variation, and meaning, both spoken and written language in all genres, as well as literary scholarship in a broad sense. It is the ambition of SES to place equally high demands on the academic quality of the manuscripts it accepts as those applied by refereed international journals and academic publishers of a similar orientation.

Titles in the series

1. Begam, R. and Soderholm, J. 2015. *Platonic Occasions: Dialogues on Literature, Art and Culture*. Stockholm: Stockholm University Press. DOI: http://dx.doi.org/10.16993/sup.baa

2. Shaw, P., Erman, B., Melchers, G. and Sundkvist, P. (eds) 2015. *From Clerks to Corpora: essays on the English language yesterday and today*. Stockholm: Stockholm University Press. DOI: http://dx.doi.org/10.16993/sup.bab

Contents

Acknowledgements

We are grateful, first of all, to the Department of English, Stockholm University for generously sponsoring this publication. We are also grateful to many people for help and advice: to Christina Lenz for prompt and friendly advice throughout the publication process; to David Minugh for help with proof-reading; and to Ingrid Westin for knowledge and help. We are also grateful to all those who attended and presented at the symposium for Nils-Lennart in February 2013 and to all our contributors.

Introduction

This volume reports studies of English past and present, all based on empirical work and illumined by a variety of theoretical and methodical approaches. Its range and eclecticism makes it a fitting tribute to Nils-Lennart Johannesson, Professor of English Linguistics, Department of English, Stockholm University, on the occasion of his 67th birthday. In addition to knowing him as a wise and supportive colleague, we have all experienced him as a dedicated teacher and some of us even as a brilliant fellow-student.

Nils-Lennart first came to our department in the late 1960s as an undergraduate student. After proceeding quickly through the undergraduate as well as the graduate courses, and having spent a fruitful period of study at Yale University under the wings of Professor Sydney Lamb, he was ready to present his doctoral dissertation, *The English Modal Auxiliaries: A Stratificational Account,* in 1976. After a brief period as Research Fellow at Lund University, he returned to our department in 1978, first as Research Fellow, then as Docent and Senior Lecturer. In 1991 he left the department for the University of Trondheim, where he served as Professor of English Linguistics for almost a decade. In the year 2000 he returned to Stockholm, having been appointed to the Chair at our department in succession to Magnus Ljung.

It is a daunting task to describe Nils-Lennart's multi-faceted contributions to the department: as a distinguished and productive scholar, committed teacher, organizer of symposia, editor, administrator, and mentor to students as well as colleagues. The following text does not presume to do justice to his complete oeuvre and achievement.

His scholarly work has above all been concerned with historical linguistics, culminating in a passionate, long-standing commitment to the Middle English twelfth century homily collection *Orrmulum,* written by the Augustinian canon Orm from Lincolnshire. The ultimate aim of Nils-Lennart's research on *Orrmulum* is the production of a new text edition, based on a new transcription of the existing manuscripts. Since nobody can improve on the creator's own account of the project, the reader of this preface is referred to the excellent website www.orrmu-lum.net. Over the years Nils-Lennart has delighted the language semi-nar at our department with glimpses of his ongoing research within the Orrmulum project, characterized by linguistic stringency, wide-ranging use of all technical support, and rich cultural and historical depth.

It should not be forgotten, however, that this is just one of many interests. Above all, he is a leading expert on Old English syntax, regu-larly presenting papers at international conferences. He has contributed greatly to studies on dialect in fiction, with special reference to J.R.R. Tolkien, and he takes a great interest in linguistic as well as literary aspects of figurative language, which is reflected in his active role as co-organizer of our department's annual 'Metaphor Festival' and an editor of the festival's proceedings.

He has been a model for us not only as a researcher but also as a teacher and supervisor. His students are always impressed by his conscientiousness and creativity, marked by the production and con-stant improvement of challenging text material for his courses. He is a painstaking and selfless editor and the co-producer of most handbooks, festschrifts and conference volumes published by our department (with the obvious exception of the present volume).

We all know him to be unusually knowledgeable in a number of other fields: he is a fine musician, known to play the bagpipe as well as the flute; he is extremely well read, often quoting Galsworthy and Dorothy Sayers by heart, and has published beautiful translations of works by the Orcadian writer George Mackay Brown. To at least one of us he is even known to be very knowledgeable about the intricacies of traditional knitting.

For a number of years Nils-Lennart served as Head of Department – a complicated and strenuous function which he carried out in a demo-cratic spirit with fairness, care and great commitment. Many of his colleagues and students are deeply grateful for his help and advice in difficult situations, personal as well as academic.

The common thread of the volume is empirical work on English based on actual data, often from corpora and often diachronic. The first five chapters deal with Old and Middle English phonology, syntax, lexis and text editing, forming an overview of current issues in the study of older stages of the language. Cole shows, very much in the spirit of Johannesson's close examination of the *Orrmulum* manuscript, that the glosses in the Lindisfarne gospels provide evidence of linguistic change in progress. Stenbrenden examines a corpus and challenges aspects of the established phonological history of English. Dahl suggests that the unexpected similarities between standard Scandinavian languages and English are evidence for 'reverse' influence of English on Old Norse under Canute's empire. Calle Martin provides an edition of a previously unedited text. Moreno questions the established interpretation of a plant name in a Middle English text.

The next six contributions look at Early Modern and Modern English from a historical point of view, using the variety of methods associated with Nils-Lennart's work. Wright looks through everyday texts for early references (going back to the sixteenth century) that illuminate the etymology of the place-name *Isle of Dogs*. Smitterberg and Kytö discuss the complexity of the notion of genre, which they show is central to historical corpus design. The others all adopt a corpus approach to samples of more or less literary texts. Tottie and Johansson examine the development of a non-standard structure in the drama section of the *Corpus of English Dialogues, 1560–1760*. Melchers looks at representations of dialect in nineteenth century novels while Dossena and Shaw both use corpora and closer reading to examine attitudes to respectively, the Scottish landscape, and foreign languages in nineteenth-century writing.

Nils-Lennart has for many years been interested in the work of J.R.R. Tolkien and the next two chapters describe aspects of Tolkien's scholarly work. Kuteeva looks at Tolkien's concepts of myth and myth study while Zettersten draws on his own personal friendship with Tolkien to illuminate the work.

The remaining chapters discuss aspects of Modern English, the first four once again using corpora, one of the tools which Nils-Lennart pioneered in the 1980s. Minugh examines aspects of register as revealed by corpora of different genres. Aijmer and Egan both make use of parallel multilingual corpora. Aijmer looks at developing meanings of *must*, and Egan examines a central topic in comparative language studies, the expression of the components of motion, here in English and French. Peter Sundkvist shows how a phonological topic which cannot be examined via available corpora can nevertheless be elucidated using the affordances of the internet.

The last three chapters also cover topics related to Nils-Lennart's many-faceted work. He began his career working with Sydney Lamb on the non-generative modelling of syntax, and this theme is taken up by Ursini, who shows how preposition-stranding can be handled in type-logical syntax. Later he became interested in pragmatics, and Erman and Lewis take this up in their paper on the vocabulary use of advanced second-language users of English, including their use of pragmatic markers. Finally, along with the late Christina Alm-Arvius, Nils-Lennart was a founder and organizer of Stockholm University's annual Metaphor Festival, and it is fitting that the book closes with a chapter based on her unpublished work.

In view of the richness and quality of the contributions, inspired by Nils-Lennart's interest and erudition in various fields of linguistic and literary studies, this volume will be of interest to a wide academic audience. Many – if not most – of the contributions offer new and challenging approaches to English studies and linguistics in general, such as reassessments of the dramatic sound change known as the Great Vowel Shift and new theories concerning the complicated English–Scandinavian language contact situation. The importance of English literature as data for linguistic studies is brought to the fore in many articles, most of which demonstrate the value of new and ambitious corpora. The internet, another topical source of linguistic data, is used in innovative and sophisticated ways by some of the contributors.

It is our hope that this collection of texts – in addition to serving as a tribute to a much–esteemed colleague – may contribute to inspiration, discussion and research in a number of linguistic fields, such as historical linguistics, variationist studies, sociolinguistics/dialectology, syntax, phonetics/phonology, pragmatics, corpus design and studies, and language typology.

Stockholm, February 2015

Philip Shaw
Britt Erman
Gunnel Melchers
Peter Sundkvist

A Personal Tribute to Nils-Lennart Johannesson

What a pleasure it is to recall Nils-Lennart Johannesson and to learn that he and his admirable scholarly career are being honored by this Festschrift. It has been many years now since I have seen him, but I remember him well from the time he spent with me at Yale working on his dissertation during the year 1975–76. I recall being repeatedly impressed by his insight and his diligence as he delved into the rich complexities of the English auxiliaries, and by his cogent portrayal of their behavior, enlivened by his well-chosen textual examples, whose humor often lightened the reader's load. Although I was the mentor and he the mentee, he taught me many things about the English auxiliaries, and he was in fact one of the best students I ever had the pleasure of working with in my half-century teaching career.

Sydney Lamb

1 The Middle English Development of Old English ȳ and Lengthened y: Spelling Evidence

Gjertrud F. Stenbrenden
University of Oslo

1. Introduction[1]

The 'Great Vowel Shift' is the term used about a set of changes in the phonetic realisation of Middle English (ME) long vowels, which took place around 1400–1750 according to the handbooks. In this shift, the non-close vowels /eː/, /ɛː/, /aː/, /oː/, /ɔː/ were raised one step in the vowel space, and the close vowels /iː/ and /uː/ were diphthongised (Jespersen 1909: 231 ff.; Luick 1914–40: §§479–488; Dobson 1957 *passim*).

In the late Old English (OE) and early ME periods, changes happened to the long vowels /yː/, /ɑː/, and /oː/, as described by e.g. Luick (1914–40: §§287, 369–370, 406) and Jordan (1968: §§39–42, 44–46, 53–54). However, these changes are not regarded as part of the 'GVS', because (i) they are said to have been completed before the earliest stages of the 'GVS' took place (the changes to /yː/ and /ɑː/), and/or (ii) did not take place in those dialects which later contributed to the phonology of StE (the fronting of /oː/ in dialects north of the Humber). Critical voices have been raised, suggesting that the 'GVS' started earlier than textbooks suggest, most notably by Stockwell & Minkova (1988a, 1988b). This paper treats the ME development of OE ȳ and lengthened y, for convenience called 'eME ȳ', seeking to establish (a) its phonetic

---

[1] A very early and unfinished version of this paper was read at the conference *Historical Language and Literacy in the North Sea Area*, Stavanger, 26–28 August 2009. I am grateful for valuable comments by Meg Laing, Roger Lass and Merja Stenroos, and for suggestions from an anonymous reviewer. Any remaining shortcomings remain my responsibility.

How to cite this book chapter:
Stenbrenden, G. F. 2015. The Middle English Development of Old English ȳ and Lengthened y: Spelling Evidence. In: Shaw, P., Erman, B., Melchers, G. and Sundkvist, P. (eds) *From Clerks to Corpora: essays on the English language yesterday and today*. Pp. 1–16. Stockholm: Stockholm University Press. DOI: http://dx.doi.org/10.16993/bab.a License: CC-BY.

developments in the dialects of ME, (b) the approximate dates at which its various developments started, and (c) whether the said changes were in fact completed before the 'GVS' set in. The answers to these questions may have far-reaching consequences for our interpretation of the Shift.

2. Handbooks on the development of OE ȳ/y

According to standard handbooks, the reflexes of OE /y:/ and /y/ in lengthening contexts were unrounded to [i:] in late OE or early ME in "all northern counties", in parts of the East Midlands, "including Lincolnshire, Norfolk, and the districts bordering on these counties", and in parts of the South-West, "especially Devonshire, Dorsetshire, and Wiltshire" (Wright & Wright 1928: §57 1; cf. Jordan 1968: §41). They became [e:] "in Kent and parts of Middlesex, Sussex, Essex, and Suffolk during the OE period" (Wright and Wright 1928: §57 2; cf. Jordan 1968: §40). In the remaining areas, i.e. parts of the South and the West Midlands, the ȳ remained until the late fourteenth century, when it was unrounded to [i:] (Jordan 1968: §§39, 42–43; Luick 1914–40: §§287–288; Wright & Wright 1928: §57 3). Thus, the changes to the reflexes of eME /y:/ and lengthened /y/ are believed to span a period of at least three hundred years, even by conventional accounts.

In those dialects where late OE /y:/ was unrounded to [i:], this [i:] later participated in the 'GVS', yielding PDE /aɪ/; an example is OE *hwȳ* WHY, RP /waɪ/. In those dialects where the /y:/ was unrounded and lowered to [e:], this [e:] also participated in the 'GVS'. For instance, OE *mȳs* MICE became *mēs* in Kentish, and, after the 'GVS', is reflected as [mi:s] in the modern dialect (Wright & Wright 1928: §57). It should therefore be possible to infer something about the probable ME reflexes of eME ȳ from its modern dialectal pronunciations.

3. Middle English spellings and dialect material

Dialect material in the form of spellings has been extracted from the *Linguistic Atlas of Early Middle English* (*LAEME*), which covers the period c. 1150–1325 for all of England, as well as from the *Survey of Middle English Dialects 1290–1350* (*SMED*), and the *Linguistic Atlas of Late Mediaeval English* (*LALME*), which covers the period c. 1350–1450. All tokens for the lexical items listed in the Appendix were abstracted from all *LAEME* source texts; from *SMED* and *LALME*, material was extracted for all relevant lexical items.

However, ME spelling is not phonetic transcript, so the implied sound value can only be inferred. Traditionally, <i> and <y> for eME *ȳ* are taken to indicate unrounded [i:]; <u> and <ui/uy> are believed to correspond to a retained front rounded [y:], whereas <e> and <ee> imply lowering and unrounding to [e:].[2] When OE *ȳ*-words are spelt with <i> in late OE or early ME, it seems safe to assume that such spellings do indeed indicate unrounding, especially if the modern dialect shows /aɪ/, which is the 'GVS' output of ME *ī*. This assumption is strengthened if spellings with <y> for etymological *ī* also appear in the same ME dialects. However, it would be a mistake to view the continued use of <y> to simply represent [i:] *a priori* in dialects where the *rounded* vowel is believed (in hindsight) to have been retained. In such cases, <y> *could* correspond to [y:], although such an interpretation would be highly improbable if <y> also appears for etymological *ī*.[3] In other words, the scribe's entire orthographical system must be taken into account before his likely pronunciation is inferred, since occasional spellings are by definition deviations from the scribe's norm, and may reveal something about his spoken system.

In those dialects where the OE *ȳ* remained front and rounded, i.e. in parts of the South, and in the West (and Central) Midlands, this vowel is usually represented by <u>, <ui/uy> in ME – and not by <y> alone – from around 1100 onwards (Wright & Wright 1928: §57). The use of <u> for this purpose was made possible when OE *ū*, traditionally spelt <u>, started to be spelt <ou/ow> during the ME period, due to French spelling practice (Stenbrenden 2013).

Gradon (1962) cites spellings indicating late OE unrounding of the reflex of OE *y*, as well as conditioned rounding of the reflexes of OE *i* and *ī*, in the SW Midlands. Forms with <y> for etymological *i* in a set of Exeter documents "are probably to be regarded merely as back-spellings" (1962: 66), based on the merger between OE *y* and *i* at [i], but a number of other such spellings in ten Winchester texts cannot be so dismissed. More specifically, Gradon claims that OE *ī* after *w* seems

---

[2] Anderson (1988) argues convincingly that in Kentish, the reflexes of OE *ȳ/y* must have lowered to [ø(:)] first, before unrounding to [e(:)].

[3] For instance, the latter part of the account of Ohthere's voyage in the OE *Orosius*, which is found only in the later, eleventh-century MS (MS Cotton Tiberius B.1), shows numerous back spellings with <y> for etymological OE *ī/i*, which suggests that in late WS, etymological *ȳ/y* had already been unrounded. Examples of back spellings are <swyþe> for OE *swīþe* 'very', <scypa> ship gen.pl., <swyna> swine gen.pl. Such back spellings are absent from the earlier Lauderdale MS, which has been dated to the first half of the tenth century.

to have undergone rounding. Besides, there is evidence that OE *y* was unrounded before palatals even in the SW Midlands, whereas it was retained in other phonetic contexts (1962: 72).

4. Discussion

The extracted *LAEME* material shows a variety of spellings for eME *ȳ*: <i>, <y>, <e>, <ee>, <eo>, <ey>, <u>, <ui>, <uy>, <yu>, <ou>. Again, it must be stressed that spellings cannot simply be interpreted as transcriptions of sounds. However, interaction between written norms and spoken systems must be assumed, resulting in hyper-adaptations, back spellings, and the like, and when the material is systematised, patterns emerge. Most *LAEME* sources show a mixture of spellings for etymological *ȳ* which seem to contradict each other in terms of their implied sound value. A case in point is the text with index number 1300, whose language has been localised to Suffolk and dated to the second half of the twelfth century: it has dominant <i> (indicating unrounding), a secondary variant <u> (implying a retained front rounded vowel), and minor variants <ui> (implying retained [y:]) and <e>, <eo> (implying lowered and unrounded [e:]). Thus, it is difficult to draw any definite conclusions from the material. Nevertheless, the following observations can be made.

  Unrounding of OE *ȳ/y* to [i:] started in late OE and is indicated in source texts whose language has been localised to Essex, Suffolk and perhaps Hampshire from the late twelfth century; in sources localised to Oxfordshire, Kent, Northamptonshire and Worcestershire from the early thirteenth century; in texts localised to Cumberland, Cheshire, Somerset and Surrey from the mid-thirteenth century; in sources localised to Lincolnshire, Norfolk, Devon, Gloucestershire and Herefordshire from the late thirteenth century; and in texts localised to Ely, Huntingdonshire and the North Riding of Yorkshire from the early fourteenth century. Thus, unrounding seems to have started in the South-East and South-West, and to have spread northwards, which goes against the assumption that the unrounding originated in the North (Jordan 1968: §41). However, the paucity of ME texts from northern England from the early ME period precludes any definite conclusion regarding the locus of this change.

  Lowering and unrounding to [e:] is indicated in sources whose language has been localised to Essex and Suffolk from the late twelfth century; in texts localised to Kent from the early thirteenth century; in texts localised to Somerset and dated to 1240; in sources localised to Gloucestershire and Wiltshire from the second half of the thirteenth century; and in a text whose language has been localised to Lincolnshire from the early fourteenth century. Hence, eME ȳ > [e:] seems to have started in the South-East (Kent, Essex, Suffolk), but also to have taken place independently barely a half-century later in the South-West. Forms with <e> are dominant in sources whose language has been localised to Kent (the texts with index nos. 8, with a second-ary variant <i>, and 142, with minor variants <éé> and <ie>), Essex (no. 160), Gloucestershire (no. 161), Somerset (no. 156, with <y> co-varying with <e>), and Lincolnshire (no. 169, also with <y> co-varying with <e>).

Retained [y:] is indicated in sources whose language has been local-ised to Berkshire, Essex, Suffolk and Worcestershire from the latter half of the twelfth century; in texts from Northamptonshire, Herefordshire and Shropshire from the early thirteenth century; in texts localised to Cheshire, Gloucestershire, Wiltshire and Surrey from the mid-to-late thirteenth century; and in sources from Oxfordshire, Ely and Huntingdonshire from the late thirteenth or early fourteenth century.

The <u> spellings from Berkshire, Essex, Suffolk and Surrey are early, but they seem to suggest that Wright & Wright (1928: §57) may be wrong in stating that the reflex of OE ȳ had become [e:] in Essex and Suffolk in the late OE period; <e> forms do indeed occur in Essex (text nos. 4, 64, 1200) and Suffolk (text no. 1300), but they are not dominant. Sussex is poorly represented in the early ME material, but text no. 67 (1200–50), shows <i>, not <e>, for eME ȳ. Surprisingly, <u>-type spellings also lin-ger on in the East (Ely, Huntingdonshire) as late as the early fourteenth century, although the <u> forms here are minor variants.

Regarding retained [y:], the *LAEME* material seems to also run coun-ter to Wright & Wright's explicit claim concerning the development of ȳ in Wiltshire: dominant <u> in text no. 280 (1250–74) suggests that ȳ had *not* been unrounded in Wiltshire in late OE, but remained rounded. The same text shows dominant <ou> and <u> for the reflex of eME *ū*, and interestingly shows one <ou> for the reflex of eME ȳ as well, which indicates a rounded vowel.

Lass & Laing (2005) suggest that, despite what is traditionally claimed, western ME did *not* have front rounded vowels, i.e. [y(:)] and [ø(:)] from OE ȳ/y and *ēo/eo* respectively.[4] Instead, they maintain that ȳ

---

[4] Lass & Laing's claims regarding the reflexes of OE *ē/eo* will not be addressed here.

became [i:] or [e:] or merged with the reflex of eME $\bar{u}$ in different areas. That $\bar{y}$ changed to [i:] and [e:] is no more than the traditional account, but Lass & Laing's claim that it merged with the reflex of eME $\bar{u}$ in the SW Midlands certainly needs closer examination. Lass & Laing use material from *LAEME* texts 277 (Worcestershire), 272 (Shropshire), and 280 (Wiltshire) to back up their claims, which is why spellings for eME $\bar{y}$ in these three texts must be investigated in some detail.

The extracted *LAEME* material for text 272 shows dominant <u>, and a secondary variant <v> for eME $\bar{u}$; and dominant <u>, and secondary <i>, <e> for eME $\bar{y}$. Likewise, text 277 shows dominant <u> and secondary variants <ou>, <v>, <o> for eME $\bar{u}$; and dominant <u>, and minor variants <i>, <eo> for eME $\bar{y}$. Text 280 shows dominant <ou>, <u>, and minor variants <v>, <o>, <ow> for eME $\bar{u}$; and dominant <u>, and minor variants <i>, <ou>, <eo> for eME $\bar{y}$. Lass & Laing also claim that there are no instances of <y> for eME $\bar{y}$ in the SW Midlands. Close inspection of all *LAEME* source texts localised to the W Midlands reveals that there are, but only for WHY, in text nos. 246 and 1100 from Herefordshire, 2002 from Gloucestershire, and 1600 from Oxfordshire.

Table 1 provides a complete list of **all** *LAEME* texts whose language has been localised to the W Midlands, and their spellings for eME $\bar{y}$ and $\bar{u}$. It seems to be true that many W Midlands texts show <u> for both eME $\bar{u}$ and $\bar{y}$, but most of them also show different secondary and minor spellings co-varying for each reflex. For instance, <ou/ow>, <o>, <uu>, <v>, <ov>, <w> are not infrequent as non-dominant variants for eME $\bar{u}$, whereas such spellings are rare for eME $\bar{y}$. For eME $\bar{y}$, non-dominant spellings such as <ui/uy>, <e>, <eo>, <i> are more frequent. In some W Midlands texts, the two reflexes appear to be kept apart; in these, the spellings suggest unrounding (and sometimes lowering) of eME $\bar{y}$. Such sources are no. 232 (Oxfordshire, 1175–1224), no. 189 (Herefordshire, 1200–24), no. 273 (Herefordshire, 1225–49), as well as no. 161 (Gloucestershire), no. 248 (Herefordshire), and no. 3 (Worcestershire; all 1275–99). Again, most of the W Midlands sources show a mixture of spellings which often contradict each other in terms of their implied sound value.

LAEME spellings for lengthened OE *y* may prove helpful. Most of the source texts whose language has been localised to the W Midlands show dominant <u> for the reflexes of OE *y* in lengthening contexts, though quite a few show minor <i>, particularly for OE *yht*, and particularly towards the later period. In other words, lengthened OE *y* seems to have remained rounded in most of the W Midlands in the ME period.

Table 1. LAEME spellings for eME *ȳ* compared to spellings for eME *ū*; W Midlands texts only.

Text no.	Date	County	OE *ȳ*	OE *y*; -*yht*	OE *ū*
63	12b‡	Brk	u	Ø	u, ou
170	12b2	Wor	u	Ø	u ((o))†
5	c.1200	Wor	u ((i*))	u	u
2000	c.1200	Wor	u (i*)	u; -uht/uct	u ((o, ow, v))
2001	c.1200	Wor	u	-uht/iht	u ((o))
232	12b2–13a1	Ox	i	Ø	u
189	13a1	Hrf	i* ((u))	u	u ((o))
260	13a1	Sal	u (i*)	ey; -uht/uh	u
261	13a1	Sal	u ((i*, ui))	-uht	u ((v, e))
262	13a1	Sal	u ((i*))	-uht	u
1000	13a1	Sal	u ((i*))	u; -uht	u ((v))
6	13a	Wor	u (i)	i	u
7	13a	Wor	u ((i*))	i, u	u ((v))
1900	13a	Wor	u ((i, ui))	u; -urht/iht	u ((v, o, ?eo))
245	13a2	Wor	u (i*) ((ui))	u; -uht	u ((v, o, uu))
272	13a2	Sal	i*	Ø	u ((v, o, uu))
273	13a2	Hrf	i*	Ø	u (v) ((o, uu))
275	13a2	Hrf	u (i*)	u	u ((v))
1800	13a2	Wor	i* (u) ((uu, ei))	u; -uht	u ((w))
118	1240–50	Chs	u ((i, ui))	-iht/uht	u ((v, o))
122	1240–50	Chs	u, ui	u; -uht/iht	u
124	13b1	Chs	Ø	ui	ou, u
158	13b1	Gl	u, i*	e, u	ou ((u, o, ow))
276	13b1	Wor	u ((i*))	u; -ucht/ugh	u ((v, i, o))
280	13b1	Wlt	u ((ou, i*, eo))	u, i; -iþ(t)/iht	ou, u ((v, o, ow))
271	13b	Gl	u, ui, i*	Ø	ou (u) ((o, ow))
2	13b2	Wor	u (i*)	-iȝt	u ((o, v, w))
3	13b2	Wor	i*	u	u ((ou, o, uu))
136	13b2	Chs	Ø	-it	u, ou, ow, ey
161	13b2	Gl	e	ey; -eyt/eȝt	ou ((o, u))
229	13b2	Gl	u	Ø	u ((o))
246	13b2	Hrf	u (ui, y*, i*)	u, i; -ist	u ((ou, o, v, oi, uu, w, eo, eþ))

Table 1. Continued

Text no.	Date	County	OE ȳ	OE y; -yht	OE ū
247	13b2	Hrf	u, ui, i*	u, uy; -it	ou ((ov, o, u))
248	13b2	Hrf	i (u)	Ø	u ((ou, o))
249	13b2	Hrf	u	Ø	u ((o, ou, e))
277	13b2	Wor	u ((i*))	u; -iht/uht/(ih)	u ((v, ou, o))
278	13b2	Wor	u ((i, v))	u, i; -ih(t/uht)	u ((ou, o, v, eo, eu, eou, uo, e, u-u))
1100	13b2	Hrf	u (i*) ((y*))	u; -iht/yht/uht	u ((v, w, ow/ou, o, uo, uw, e, ey))
2002	13b2	Gl	ui (i*) ((y*, u))	ui, u, ey; -iȝt/ uiȝt	ou ((o, ow, u, e, ei))
187	c.1300	Wor	uy	Ø	ou
10	13b2–14a1	Gl	u, i	u, ei	u ((o))
126	13b2–14a1	Wrk	u	Ø	ou
1600	13b2–14a1	Ox	u, uy ((i, y, yu))	u, uy (ui); -iȝht	ou (o) ((u, ov, ow, v, uy))
125	14a1	Hrf	ou	Ø	ou, o
140	14a1	Wlt	u	Ø	ov ((u, v, o))

‡ Suggested dates for source texts follow *LAEME*: the first number refers to century; 'a' and 'b' refer to the first half and the second half of the century, respectively; and '1' and '2' refer to the first and second quarter of each half-century.
† Use of round brackets to enclose non-dominant spellings follows *LALME* practice: single brackets enclose secondary variants, and double brackets enclose minor variants.
* An asterisk indicates that the text has <i> or <y> for *why* and/or OE *bȳsen* only.

Exceptions are found in the following sources: no. 260 (Shropshire, 1200–24) has dominant <ey> for lengthened OE *y* other than *yht* (for which <uht>, <uh> are found); no. 158 (Gloucestershire, 1250–74) has <e> as well as <u>; no. 161 (Gloucestershire, 1275–99) shows only <ey> for lengthened OE *y*; no. 10 (Gloucestershire, 1275–1324) has <u> and <ei>. All of the preceding forms may point to lowering and unrounding of ȳ to [e:]. However, generally speaking, the reflex of OE *yht* appears to be in the process of merging with the reflex of OE *iht*.

Thus, examination of spellings from **all** *LAEME* sources localised to the W Midlands corroborates at least two of Lass & Laing's claims: (a) there is no "neat geographical tri-partition for /y/", and (b) not "only are the symbol-to-sound mappings more multiplex than is suggested, but there is a strong element of lexical specificity in the set of reflexes" (Lass & Laing 2005: 281). In other words, certain lexical items seem to be spelt in certain ways, which supports the theory of change by lexical diffusion (Phillips 2006a, 2006b): sound changes seem to start in certain phonetic contexts, and/or in very frequent words, whence they spread from context to context, and from frequent to less frequent words. Their third claim, that there are no "particular spellings uniquely associated with OE /y(:)/" (*ibid.*), is not entirely correct, as <ui/uy> seem to be used for the reflex of eME ȳ only.[5] It is their assumption that the reflex of eME ȳ fell in with the reflex of eME ū in the SW Midlands which is the most difficult to prove. ME spellings seem to lend support to their view: Table 1 shows clearly that <u> remains dominant for the reflexes of both eME ȳ and ū in the SW Midlands up until the last quarter of the thirteenth century, although <ou/ow> slowly take over as the dominant spellings for eME ū from c. 1250. A very few examples of <ou> for the reflex of eME ȳ appear to support the merger hypothesis also.

Evidence from the modern dialects may settle the issue: if present-day SW Midland accents show a merger between the reflexes of eME ū and ȳ, the ME spellings may be taken to indicate just that; if not, the same spellings simply show a lack of distinct representations on the orthographic level, but not phonetic or phonological merger. The *Survey of English Dialects* (Orton & Dieth 1962) yields material for the lexical items listed in the Appendix for the W Midlands, and for Wiltshire and Berkshire. This phonological material from the modern dialects implies that there was no merger between the reflexes of eME ȳ and ū in the W Midlands, since generally eME ȳ is reflected as a number of diphthongs with *unrounded* off-glides, and eME ū is reflected as a series of diphthongs with *rounded* off-glides. However, exceptions are found in some localities in Cheshire and Staffordshire:

Cheshire
Locality 1: merger in [aɪ] or [ɑɪ];
Locality 2: merger in [æɪ] for some words;
Locality 3: merger in [ɛɪ] for some words;
Locality 4: merger in [aɪ];
Locality 5: merger in [ɛɪ] or [aɪ].

Staffordshire
Locality 2: merger in [ɛɪ];

---

[5] Only text no. 1600 (Oxfordshire, 1275–1324) has <uy> for the reflex of eME ū.

Localities 7–9: merger in [DI];
Locality 10: minimal distinction between [ɑ:ɪ] and [a:ɪ];
Locality 11: merger in [aɪ].

That is, in these localities, there is sometimes a diphthong with an *unrounded* off-glide for the stressed vowel of *cows/kyes* (OE *cȳ*), *mouse, house, mouth, drought, thousand, clouds* (all with eME *ū*), as well as for *dry, hide, fire, wright, why* (all with eME *ȳ*). Interestingly, these have converged on the 'normal' reflex for eME *ȳ* and not for eME *ū*. Thus, the ME spellings from the SW Midlands likely indicate merger of *spellings*, but not of *sounds*, as otherwise it would have been impossible for the reflexes of the two sounds to be distinguished again later on an etymologically correct basis. The only way in which merged sounds could unmerge would be if two different systems co-existed, one of which kept the reflexes apart, and the distinction was re-introduced into the system in which merger had taken place. But such a scenario remains speculative and unlikely.

Interestingly, even in many *LAEME* source texts with dominant <u> for eME *ȳ*, there is only <i> for the lexemes WHY and OE *bȳsen* 'example'. This seems to suggest that if the unrounding of *ȳ* started in any one word, that word is most likely WHY, although it should be noted that there was an OE variant *whie*.[6]

5. Summary of early ME material

The material from *LAEME* suggests the following developments for the reflex of eME *ȳ*:

1. It was unrounded to [i:] across the country, and this process seems to have started in the (South-)East and the W Midlands.
2. It was lowered and unrounded to [e:] in Essex, Suffolk and Kent in the late twelfth or early thirteenth century; in Somerset, Gloucestershire and Wiltshire in the latter half of the thirteenth

---

[6] Likewise, if the lowering and unrounding of *ȳ* to [e:] started in a specific word, it may have been in the OE word *þȳster* 'dark, gloomy' and cognates, since there are frequent <e> and <eo> for these lexemes even in texts with dominant or exclusive <u>, <ui/uy> for all other words with eME *ȳ*. However, OE *þȳster* and cognates also appear with OE *ie, eo*, so ME <e>, <ie> etc. for these probably go back to forms which did not have OE *ȳ*, since they show a very distinct pattern in the extracted material. For this reason, ME spellings for OE *þȳster* and cognates have not been included in Table 1.

century; and perhaps in Lincolnshire in the early fourteenth century.[7]

3. It remained as [y:] in the W Midlands and parts of the South-West, as well as in Ely and Huntingdonshire (at least as a minor variant) in the late thirteenth or early fourteenth century.

With regard to Lass & Laing's hypothesis concerning the phonetic nature of the ME reflex of OE *ȳ*, the modern material does not support their claim that the reflex of eME *ȳ* had merged with the reflex of eME *ū* in the ME dialects of the W Midlands, even though <u> is the dominant spelling for both in ME in the area in question.

6. The later ME material

The *LAEME* material for eME *ȳ* needs to be tied up with the later material from *SMED* and *LALME*. Conclusions based on analysis of this material are briefly summarised below.

Kristensson (*SMED 1–5*) finds that, in the fourteenth century, all the Northern counties except two were [i:]-areas. The case for the West Riding of Yorkshire and Lancashire is less straightforward: Kristensson concludes that they most likely had [i:], but that [y:] was also used in Lancashire south of the Ribble. As for the W Midlands, [y:] was found in Cheshire, Staffordshire, Shropshire, Herefordshire, Worcestershire, Warwickshire, Gloucestershire and Oxfordshire. Derbyshire also had [y:], except in the easternmost tip, which had [i:]. Leicestershire seems to have had [y:] in the west and [i:] in the east and south. Nottinghamshire had [i:]. In the E Midlands, Rutland, Huntingdonshire and Norfolk had [i:], Bedfordshire, Hertfordshire, Middlesex and Buckinghamshire had [y:], Suffolk and Essex had [e:]. Northamptonshire had [i:] in the northern half, [y:] in the southern half. Kristensson thinks Cambridgeshire had [i:] north of the city of Cambridge (including Ely); south of it, it had [e:] to the east and [y:] to the west. In the South, Devon seems to have had [i:] and [y:]; Somerset, Dorset, Wiltshire, Hampshire, Berkshire and Surrey had [y:] (although Surrey may have had [e:] in the easternmost tip). Sussex had [e:] in the east, [y:] in the west; Kent had [e:].

The development of eME *ȳ* before palatals appears to have been different from that in other contexts: in this environment, *ȳ* was unrounded

---

[7] Perhaps more likely, lowered and unrounded [e:] spread occasionally to Lincolnshire from Suffolk through Norfolk, although in that case, one would expect <e>-type spellings in Norfolk too. That is, however, not the case.

to [iː] in Hampshire and Dorset, and also in Berkshire, Wiltshire and Somerset. There are traces of such a development in Surrey also, but not in Sussex or Kent. Finally, Devon shows a tendency to unrounding regardless of phonetic context.

Ek (1972) investigates the ME development of OE $\bar{e}o$ and $\bar{y}$ in the South-East, using onomastic material which partly overlaps with that of *SMED*, although much of Ek's material is earlier. His conclusions differ somewhat from Kristensson's, particularly regarding the extent of the [eː]-area. However, Kitson (1998: 170) concludes that since Ek's material is earlier, "what the two investigations show between them is a retreat of the *e*-reflex in favour of the *u*-reflex as well as, further north, the *i*-reflex".[8] In other words, Ek's and Kristensson's data demonstrate change in progress.

The *LALME* material suggests that the reflexes of eME $\bar{y}$ had been unrounded to [iː] in the East and the North in the late ME period. Retained [yː] is implied by spellings from the West and the South, and from the West Riding of Yorkshire, whereas <e>-type spellings linger on in most of the East, and in parts of the West (Gloucestershire, Worcestershire, Oxfordshire), the South-West (Devon, Dorset, Hampshire, Wiltshire) and the South-East (Kent, Sussex, Surrey). That is, <i>-type and <e>-type forms co-vary in the East, but whether these systematically correspond to [iː] and [eː] is an open question.

7. Conclusions and implications

The three corpora exploited all contain spellings which seem to indicate that the 'GVS' started much earlier than 1400, perhaps around 1250 or 1300 (Stenbrenden 2010). For eME $\bar{y}$, for instance, *LAEME* text 142 (1275–99), whose language has been localised to Kent, shows dominant <e>, but has one <i-hierde> for the 3.pres.sing. of OE *hȳran* HIRE v. (beside three tokens with <e> for the same), which may indicate raising of $\bar{e}$ to [iː]. Source text no. 2002 (1275–99), whose language has been localised to Gloucestershire, has dominant <ui> and a secondary variant <i> as well as minor variants <y> and <u>. It has <flei> for FLY (noun); this may however go back to OE *flēoge* or *flȳge*. For OE *y* in lengthening contexts, text no. 137 (Cambridgeshire, 1275–99) has <bein> for OE *bycgan*

---

[8] Wyld's two articles (Wyld 1913–14a, 1913–14b) on the dialectal development of eME $\bar{y}$ are classics, but have not been included in the discussion in the present paper. For a full account, see Stenbrenden (2010).

BUY (verb); this text has <i> for the long vowel, so vowel-shift may be inferred. Text no. 269 (Norfolk, 1275–1324) likewise shows <beyn> for OE *bycgan*, but there are no tokens for the long vowel in this source text, so it is difficult to assess whether this form indicates vowel shift or not.

Generally, there are more irregular spellings which may indicate vowel shift for the lengthened OE *y* than for the etymologically long vowel, which may suggest that the vocalisation of post-vocalic *–h, –g* in late OE produced a minimal diphthong [ɪi] (rather than a long monophthong). This diphthong would have been an allophone of /iː/ (since words with OE *–iht, –ig* and *–yht* subsequently had the same development as OE *ī*-words), and may have triggered the vowel shift, as suggested repeatedly by Stockwell (1964, 1972, 1978), and by Stockwell & Minkova (1988a, 1988b). *LAEME*, *SMED* and *LALME* also contain irregular spellings indicating early vowel shift of eME *ū*, *ē* and *ō* (Stenbrenden 2010), lending support to this 'Early Vowel Shift Hypothesis'.

It must be concluded, therefore, that there is a long temporal overlap between the constituent 'GVS' changes and the assumed earlier set of changes. Consequently, the two sets of changes cannot be treated separately: the changes to early ME *ȳ* must be seen as part of the Shift, as must the changes to OE *ā* (south of the Humber) and OE *ō* (north of the Humber). This points to a very lengthy period of long-vowel shifting, from c. 1100 (or earlier) to c. 1750, which raises the question, Is it possible for one unitary and coherent 'Great Vowel Shift' to take place over 650 years or more? Clearly not. Rather, Stockwell seems right when he states that "the series of changes of which the GVS is a part have been going on at a remarkably steady rate for more than 1500 years" (Stockwell 1969: 93), a claim which has not received much support until now.

Appendix

A. *LAEME*: lexical items with OE *ȳ/y* searched for in all source texts

For OE *ȳ*:

    4scȳte, ālȳfedlīc, ālȳman, ālȳsedness, ālȳsend, ālȳsendness, behide, bride, bridegift, bridegroom, bȳsen, bȳsnian, cȳpan, dry (adj., v.), *drȳ* (n.), *dryfoot, fire, fireburning, hide* (n. and v.), *hire* (n. and v.), *hireman, lȳt, lȳþerlīce, lȳþerness, lȳþre, lȳtlian, lȳtlum* (adv.), *pride, þwȳrian, þȳfel, þȳster, þȳsterness, þȳstrian, þȳstrig, why*

For lengthened OE *y*:

  bitight, buy, buyer, crockwright, flight, forbuy, fright, frighten, frighty, frightyhood, frightyly, hyht, hyhtan, hyhtlīc, kind (n.), *mankind, offrighten, wright*

B. The *Survey of English Dialects*: questionnaire items examined for the W Midlands, and for Wiltshire and Berkshire

For OE *ū* and lengthened *u*:

  plough, cow(s), sow, snout, mouse, boughs, house, mouth thousand, clouds, drought

For OE *ȳ* and lengthened *y*:

  dry (III.1.9), *hide* (noun), *fire, dry* (VII.6.19), *wright, why*

References

Anderson, J. (1988). The great kEntish collapse. Kastovsky & Bauer (eds) 1988: 97–107.

Dobson, E. (1957). *English Pronunciation 1500–1700, Vol. I.* Oxford: Clarendon.

Ek, K-G. (1972). *The Development of OE ȳ and ēo in South-Eastern Middle English.* Lund: Gleerup.

Gradon, P. (1962). Studies in Late West-Saxon Labialization and Delabialization. Davis, N. & Wrenn, C.L. (eds), *English and Medieval Studies Presented to J.R.R. Tolkien on the Occasion of his Seventieth Birthday*: 63–76. London: George Allen & Unwin.

Jespersen, O. (1928). *A Modern English Grammar, Part I.* (4th ed.) Heidelberg: Carl Winters Universitätsbuchhandlung.

Jordan, R. (1968). *Handbuch der mittelenglischen Grammatik: Lautlehre.* (3rd ed.) The Hague: Mouton.

Kastovsky, D. & Bauer, G. (eds). (1988). *Luick Revisited.* Tübingen: Gunter Narr.

Kitson, P. (1998). Review of Kristensson 1995. NOMINA 21: 169–178.

Kristensson, G. (1967). *A Survey of Middle English Dialects 1290–1350. The Six Northern Counties and Lincolnshire.* Lund: CWK Gleerup.

———. (1987). *A Survey of Middle English Dialects 1290–1350: the West Midland Counties.* Lund: Lund University Press.

———. (1995). *A Survey of Middle English Dialects 1290–1350: the East Midland Counties.* Lund: Lund University Press.

———. (2001). *A Survey of Middle English Dialects 1290–1350: the Southern Counties I. Vowels*. Lund: Lund University Press.

———. (2002). *A Survey of Middle English Dialects 1290–1350: the Southern Counties II. Diphthongs and Consonants*. Lund: Lund University Press.

LAEME: Laing, M. (2008). *A Linguistic Atlas of Early Middle English*. University of Edinburgh. URL: http://www.lel.ed.ac.uk/ihd/laeme1/laeme1.html.

LALME: McIntosh, A., Samuels, M., Benskin, M. *et al.* (1986). *A Linguistic Atlas of Late Mediaeval English, Vols. I–IV*. Aberdeen: Aberdeen University Press. URL: http://www.lel.ed.ac.uk/ihd/elalme/elalme.html.

Lass, R. & Laing, M. (2005). Are front rounded vowels retained in West Midland Middle English? In Ritt, N. & Schendl, H. (eds) *Rethinking Middle English: Linguistic and literary approaches*: 280–290. Frankfurt am Main: Peter Lang.

Luick, K. (1914–40). *Historische Grammatik der englischen Sprache, Vol. I*. Oxford: Basil Blackwell.

Orton, H. & Dieth, E. (1962). *The Survey of English Dialects*. Leeds: Arnold.

Phillips, B. (2006a). *Word Frequency and Lexical Diffusion*. Basingstoke: Palgrave Macmillan.

———. (2006b). Word Frequency Effects in the Great Vowel Shift. Paper read at the 14th International Conference on English Historical Linguistics, Bergamo, Italy, 21–25 August 2006.

SMED: see Kristensson 1967, 1987, 1995, 2001, 2002.

Stenbrenden, G.F. (2010). The Chronology and Regional Spread of Long-Vowel Changes in English, c.1150–1500. PhD dissertation, University of Oslo.

———. (2013). The diphthongisation of ME ū: the spelling evidence. Andersen, G. & Bech, K. (eds) *English Corpus Linguistics: Variation in Time, Space and Genre: Selected Papers from Icame 32* (*Language & Computers*): 53–67. Rodopi.

Stockwell, R.P. (1964). On the Utility of an Overall Pattern in Historical English Phonology. *Proceedings of the Ninth International Conference of Linguistics*: 663–671. The Hague: Mouton.

———. (1972). Problems in the Interpretation of the Great English Vowel Shift. Smith, M.E. (ed.) *Studies in Linguistics in Honor of George L. Trager*: 344–362. The Hague: Mouton.

————. (1978). Perseverance in the English vowel shift. Fisiak, J. (ed.) *Recent Developments in Historical Phonology*: 337–348. The Hague: Mouton.

Stockwell, R.P. & Minkova, D. (1988a). The English Vowel Shift: problems of coherence and explanation. Kastovsky & Bauer (eds) 1988: 355–394.

————. (1988b). A rejoinder to Lass. Kastovsky & Bauer (eds) 1988: 411–417.

Wright, J. & Wright, E.M. (1928). *An Elementary Middle English Grammar*. Oxford: Oxford University Press.

Wyld, H.C. (1913–14a). The Treatment of OE. $\bar{y}$ in the Dialects of the Midland, and SE. Counties in ME. *Englische Studien* 47: 1–58.

————. (1913–14b). Old English $\bar{y}$ in the Dialects of the South, and South Western Counties in Middle English. *Englische Studien* 47: 145–166.

2 Linguistic Mysteries Around the North Sea

Östen Dahl
Stockholm University

Everyone who knows anything about the history of the Germanic languages knows that English was influenced by Scandinavian around the Viking Age. The question I will raise in this paper, without giving any definite answer, is: Did the contacts across the North Sea have any effect on the Scandinavian languages? As far back as ten years ago, Maria Koptjevskaja Tamm and I asked the same question in a conference presentation that never resulted in a published paper (but see Dahl 2010a, 2010b for some discussion). Our point of departure was the striking similarities between the possessive constructions called "*s*-genitives' in English and the Scandinavian languages, and the observation that in Scandinavia, *s*-genitives are by and large found only in standard Danish, standard Swedish, and some Danish-influenced varieties of Norwegian. Moreover, it seemed that the origin of *s*-genitives was in western Denmark, next to the North Sea.

In this connection, two papers by the Danish Scandinavianist Kristian Ringgaard seemed relevant (Ringgaard 1986, 1989). Ringgaard argues against the common view that the simplification processes that took place in the Danish inflectional system in the Middle Ages were due to the intensive contacts with Low German in the Hanseatic period. Referring to earlier work by Anders Bjerrum, he argues that these processes started much too early to be triggered by the influx of German merchants, whose culmen was in the second half of the 14th century. He also argues that there were significant differences within the Danish-speaking area as to the strength and chronology of these processes, with a cline Jutland>Island Danish>Scanian. In the second paper, Ringgaard focuses on *Jyske Lov* 'The Jutlandic Law', one of the provincial Danish laws, signed by King Valdemar II in 1241. Ringgaard's textual source is

How to cite this book chapter:
Dahl, Ö. 2015. Linguistic Mysteries Around the North Sea. In: Shaw, P., Erman, B., Melchers, G. and Sundkvist, P. (eds) *From Clerks to Corpora: essays on the English language yesterday and today*. Pp. 17–34. Stockholm: Stockholm University Press. DOI: http://dx.doi.org/10.16993/bab.b License: CC-BY.

the Flensburg manuscript, which was at the time considered the oldest version, dated to 1300; later, another manuscript, *Codex Holmiensis*, has been reliably dated to 1271. Ringgaard describes the language in *Jyske Lov* as having among other things the following features – all innovations relative to the language found in Runic inscriptions:

two genders for nouns (residual feminine gender)
no nominative-accusative distinction
generalized *s*-genitive
dative only in lexicalized expressions
definite articles are rare and always postposed
no case inflections in adjectives
participles tend to lack a neuter form
examples of singular verb forms with plural subjects occur

No exact date for when the law was formulated can be given; Ringgaard notes that the version that existed in 1241 would have been written by people born around 1200, even if they may have relied on earlier legal rules. He notes that modern dialects in western Jutland show features that mark it off as a "radical innovation area". What we see then is that a language with a surprisingly "modern" grammar must have been spoken somewhere in western Denmark well before Hanseatic contacts could have had an effect on the language.

Ringgaard is himself slightly baffled by his findings; he wonders why innovations would spread from western Jutland, which was not the centre of the realm in historical times, and speculates that in fact the changes started much earlier, perhaps as early as the period 100–500 CE. But perhaps part of the explanation could rather be found on the other side of the North Sea.

The story of the Scandinavian presence in Britain has been told many times, but much of what really happened is still in dispute. Viking raids began already in the 8th century; they were undoubtedly spectacular but had hardly any bearing on linguistic developments. Towards the end of the 9th century, more ambitious attempts of military takeover began, and in 886 the Danes and the kingdom of Wessex made an accord in which the Danes were given control over a large part of northern and eastern England (the "Danelaw"). During the period that followed, there was considerable migration from Scandinavia to the Danelaw areas, the extent and nature of which have been much debated, as we shall see later. What is not being questioned, however, is that the Scandinavian settlements in the Danelaw were the basis for the impact that Scandinavian languages have had on English. Around the middle of the 10th century, the Danes had lost their political control of the Danelaw, and the Scandinavian parts of the population were presumably being integrated with the Anglo-Saxon elements, although it is not possible to judge how fast this process was.

Towards the end of the century, the Danes renewed their attacks on England, as a result of which the English were forced to pay large tributes ("Danegeld"). On November 13, 1002 ("St. Brice's Day"), the English king Æthelred "the Unready", in his own words, sent out a decree "to the effect that all the Danes who had sprung up in this island, sprouting like cockle amongst the wheat, were to be destroyed by a most just extermination" (as translated in Whitelock 1996: 545). From the modern point of view, this seems like a surprisingly candid admission of ethnic cleansing. It is unlikely that it was directed against the population of the Danelaw; rather, it concerned recently arrived Danes, but it indicates that they must have been present in significant numbers. Æthelred did not attain the goal of ridding England of Danes; on the contrary, after a decade of continued raiding, the Danish king Sweyn Forkbeard managed to secure the English throne in 1013, but died shortly thereafter. After three years of political unrest, his son Cnut became King of England and ruled it together with Denmark and Norway until his death in 1035, when he was succeeded by his son Harthacnut whose death in 1042 marked the end of Danish rule in Britain. The epilogue came 25 years later, after the Norman invasion, with "the Harrying of the North", another campaign, the character and extent of which are controversial, but which is claimed by contemporary sources to have laid large parts of the Danelaw waste, with possibly as many as a hundred thousand people killed.

Turning now to the main issue of the paper, the first observation to be made here is that there is a similarity between the histories of English and East Nordic (Danish and Swedish) in that there is a hiatus in the beginning of the second millennium CE, during which there is very little written documentation of the languages. Furthermore, when the languages started being used in writing after the hiatus, they seem to have undergone, or started to undergo, quite similar simplifications in their morphology. It is also during and around this period that contacts across the North Sea are at their peak.

The extent to which Scandinavian was spoken in England, as well as its impact on English, has been much disputed. To start with, there are different views on the length of the migration period. Thomason and Kaufman (1988: 267) say that "Norse speakers settled in the North and East of England during the period from 865 to 955 (though not in the East after 920)". Baugh and Cable (1993: 96), quoted approvingly by Emonds and Faarlund (ms.), say that "[u]p until the time of the Norman Conquest the Scandinavian language in England was constantly being renewed by the steady stream of trade and conquest..." and consequently, "many of the newcomers ... continued to speak their language at least as late as 1100". Emonds and Faarlund agree that "we can say with some certainty that at the outset of Norman rule, the Danelaw contained many speakers of two distinguishable languages, one of them being Norse". Thomason and Kaufman (1988: 288), on the other hand, think that Norse had disappeared from large parts of the Danelaw before the end of the first millennium although it was spoken in present-day Yorkshire until about 1015. Similarly, they say (1988: 302) that the influence of Norse on English "was pervasive, in the sense that its results are found in all parts of the language; but it was not deep, except in the lexicon". For Emonds and Faarlund (ms.), on the other hand, "influence" is the wrong word, since Old Norse is in their view the mother language of Middle and Modern English.

For the understanding of what happened to English and the North Germanic languages during and around the Viking age, it is important to keep apart two major types of contact-induced change: one is transfer of features, leading to increased similarity between languages; the other is simplification due to imperfect learning by second-language speakers. The latter type is of particular interest since both English and Mainland Scandinavian underwent quite significant simplification processes in their morphology. As noted above, the breakdown of the old inflectional system in Mainland Scandinavian has been attributed to contact with Low German, but Ringgaard argued that this would be the wrong time and the wrong place. For English, three possible culprits have been proposed: Norman French, Celtic, and Old Norse. Trudgill (2010) invokes what he calls "sociolinguistic typology" and the suggestion that the structure of a language may be at least partly determined by the type of social environment and social structure in which it is spoken. Thus, he claims, long-term contact situations influencing child language acquisition will tend to lead to complexification through the addition of features from other languages, whereas short-term contact involving adult language learning tends to lead to simplification, due to the problems adults have in coping with irregularity and nontransparency.

Norman French, like Low German in the Scandinavian case, can be acquitted since it would be the wrong time – the changes begin earlier – and the wrong place – the changes start in the north, where there were few Normans. As for the choice between Celtic and Old Norse, several scholars have recently suggested that Brittonic Celtic may have survived much longer than was earlier thought (Tristram 2002, 2004; Schrijver 2006; Laker 2008; Trudgill 2010). Furthermore, the sociolinguistic situation makes simplification much more probable in the case of the contact between the Anglo-Saxons and the Celts than in the contact between the Anglo-Saxons and the Vikings. In the former case, a large population submitted to a relatively small group of intruders; in the latter case, the situation would be the reverse. Tristram (2004) hypothesizes that there was a long period of diglossia, in which the majority of the population spoke "Brittonic English" and only the aristocracy the "purer" variety of Old English. The variety that the Norse immigrants mainly met could well be Brittonic English, in which categories such as gender and case would already have disappeared due to imperfect learning. The role of the contact with Norse would then be at most to strengthen the processes that had already been initiated earlier.

Against this background, let us now consider what happened at roughly the same time or a bit later in Scandinavia. As already noted, many linguistic changes in the Middle Ages seem to have originated in western Denmark (Jutland) and progressed east. In fact, some of them continued beyond what was then considered as Denmark (that is, including the southernmost Swedish provinces). However, as we get further away from the point of origin, changes tend to be later and weaker. The regions in Mainland Scandinavia that show most resistance are Norway, northern Sweden and the trans-Baltic areas. Island Scandinavian (Icelandic and Faroese) were often not reached at all. The striking observation is now that in a number of cases, these developments have close parallels in Britain. Let us look at the most important of them.

Reduction of unstressed vowels and apocope

This is a type of phonological change that took place in large parts of the Germanic-speaking area and also has parallels in some Romance languages. It has been blamed on earlier prosodic changes (initial word-stress) and has also been used to explain the general simplification of the inflectional systems in West European languages. There are basically two possible outcomes of this process: (1) unstressed vowels (particularly final ones) are reduced to *e* or schwa; (2) these vowels disappear altogether (apocope or "schwa loss"). During the Middle Ages, the first possibility was realized generally in West Germanic and in western and central Danish – but only to a limited extent in Peninsular Scandinavian; the second outcome is found in a smaller area, according to Thomason and Kaufman (1988: 319): "English, Dutch, some Frisian, some Low German, and some High German". Crucially to our discussion, "some Danish" should be added to this list, more specifically West Jutlandic. In English, the reduction process started already in the OE period. The apocope started in the north and was already spreading to the south in the period 1100–1250 (Minkova 1991: 30). According to Perridon (2005: 1023), all unstressed final vowels were reduced to *æ* or *e* in western and central Danish as early as "in the 12th century, or even earlier". Loss of final vowels is attested in early manuscripts such as *Jyske lov* – that is, more or less simultaneously with the spread to southern England – and has been generalized in modern Jutlandic dialects. The timing of the process in Danish would allow for influence from the south for the vowel reduction but hardly for the apocope, which seems to have taken place later in the neighbouring languages, to the extent that it took place at all (Ringgaard 1986: 182).

The case system

As noted above, the breakdown of the old noun case system had already gone quite far in the language of 13th century western Denmark as represented in *Jyske Lov*. The distinction between nominative and accusative had disappeared almost wholly, with some remnants in adjectives, and the dative was used almost exclusively in lexicalized prepositional phrases (Bjerrum 1966: 58). (The genitive will be discussed below.) In Peninsular Scandinavian, the process was much later, and has not yet been brought to completion in some dialects in the north.

Looking at Middle English, we find that the situation in *Jyske Lov* comes very close to the way the mid-12th century text in the *Peterborough chronicles* is presented in Burrow & Turville-Petre (1991: 29), where the nominative and accusative have no endings, and the dative in *-e* of strong nouns is said to sometimes occur after prepositions, "but is as often uninflected" and "...in later texts the inflexion is dropped altogether except in a few phrases". Likewise, case inflections in adjectives were preserved only in the South "to a limited extent".

It is interesting to contrast this with the Old Danish letter from late 14th century Halland (then part of Denmark, now a province of Sweden) quoted in Ringgaard (1986: 181), where "there is not much to object to the inflectional system", that is, the old system is more or less fully preserved – as it also was in Middle Low German (a distinction nominative-oblique is still alive in present-day Low German). In other words, 13th century western Danish aligns more closely with 12th century Midland English than with 14th century eastern Danish and with its neighbours to the south.

The genitive

In many Germanic languages, the genitive case has undergone developments that set it off from the rest of the case paradigm. Thus, one single case suffix, -(e)s, which originally marked the genitive singular of non-feminine nouns, has survived even in the languages where the case system has otherwise broken down but is used in innovative possessive constructions and has been generalized to feminine and sometimes plural nouns. As noted above, the s-genitives of English, Danish and Swedish share a number of properties, in particular: a uniform suffixed marker -s which (i) can be used with all types of noun phrases; (ii) is added to the last word of the possessor NP (rather than to the head noun); (iii) always precedes the head noun of the possessee NP; (iv) is used with a possessee NP which lacks definiteness marking. Properties (i–ii) make these s-genitives different from similar constructions in West Germanic, which tend to be restricted to proper and kinship nouns and mostly do not appear in complex NPs. Properties (iii–iv) distinguish them from constructions found in some Swedish traditional dialects, where the possessee NP takes a definite suffix and the genitive phrase may follow the head noun of the possessee NP. It should be noted that s-genitives are virtually non-existent in the traditional dialects of Northern Scandinavia, where a plethora of other possessive constructions are used instead (Delsing 2003; Dahl 2010a).

Ringgaard's statement about *Jyske Lov*, "the s-genitive was generalized", has to be modified – it was rather "generalizing". Perridon (2013) made a thorough investigation of a number of manuscripts and found a rather complex pattern of variation. In particular, the genitive is sometimes zero-marked, as in *sankte knut sun* 'St. Cnut's son'. In definite nouns, forms such as *landæns* 'the land's' competed with forms with double genitive marking like *landzæns*. In a later development, a "linking pronoun construction" – parallel to the much debated English type *John his house* – gained ground in western Denmark and is preserved in modern Jutlandic, while the *s*-genitive was further generalized in more eastern varieties.

Middle English is usually said to have a single genitive ending *-es* but zero marking is also found. A particularly striking attestation is found on the Kirkdale sundial, dated to 1060, which contains the phrases *in Eadward dagum* 'in Edward's days' and *[i]n Tosti dagum* 'in Tosti's days'. Thomason and Kaufman (1988: 289) note that this is one trait found in the sundial text that characterizes Northern Middle English although "the writers of the text were evidently trying to write Standard West Saxon". Klemola (1997) argues on the basis of modern dialect data and quotations from earlier scholars that there was a loss (apparently general) of the genitive endings in a northern area including Yorkshire. Zero marked genitives are one of the traits that are mentioned as characteristic of Yorkshire speech. As the *s*-genitive has been generalized in Standard English, this means that the similarities across the North Sea are today greater in the standard languages than in the dialects in the areas where the original contact took place. As for the development of the *-s* marker from an affix to a clitic (or "phrasal affix") in English and Scandinavian, it is hard to say if they have a common origin, since unequivocal attestations of "group genitives", that is, *s*-genitives marked on the last word of the NP rather than on the head noun, are relatively late. Allen (2008: 153) provides an example from 1387 of an *-s* attached to a postmodifier: *þe kyng of Fraunces men*. Perridon (2013: 142) cites as the first comparable example from Danish *pana hans allar rigens aff Danmarks wegna* 'on behalf of him or the kingdom of Denmark' from 1410.

Summing up, the story of the *s*-genitive is a complex one: on both sides of the North Sea we see a competition between generalized *s*-genitives, zero-marked genitives and linking pronoun constructions, but and even if the parallels are striking, it is not possible to construct a coherent narrative that would show how the developments are linked together.

Gender

In standard Danish and Swedish and conservative Bokmål Norwegian the original Germanic three-gender system – which is still preserved in most non-standard varieties in Peninsular Scandinavian and even in some Danish traditional dialects – has been reduced to a distinction between common and neuter gender. In general, these varieties use the erstwhile demonstrative *den* to refer to non-neuter inanimates. According to Ringgaard, (1989: 163), the two-gender system is found already in *Jyske Lov*, meaning that the simplification process must have started no later than the 13th century and probably earlier. In large parts of Jutland, the common:neuter distinction has also been abolished or (mainly for pronominal reference) been transformed into a semantically-based count: mass distinction. Even this more radical state-of-affairs may be reflected in the earliest texts to some extent (Perridon 2005: 1021).

The three-gender system was more or less intact in Old English but had already gone in the earliest texts in Early Northern Middle English and was also on its way out in other varieties of Early Middle English. In the choice of pronouns, however, there was a certain tendency towards "natural gender" already in Old English (Curzan 2003).

Gender, especially of the "non-natural" type not motivated directly by semantics, is often thought of as a quirk that languages will tend to get rid of as soon as possible. However, gender systems are astonishingly stable overall. (For a more detailed discussion, see Dahl (2004: 196–202), and for a survey of earlier views on gender, see Kilarski (2007)). Only a small number of Indo-European languages have lost their gender systems altogether – outside Germanic it has happened in some Iranian languages and Armenian. According to McWhorter (2002: 230), the loss of NP-internal gender in English makes it unique "among *all the languages of Europe*" except for "a few nonstandard dialects of particular languages". He mentions two non-Germanic examples, both said to be due to language contact, and two Germanic ones, "Western Danish" and "Ostrobothnian Swedish" – which he labels as "cases of internal loss". The references to the varieties in question are not quite exact – "Western Danish" is the area in Jutland referred to above, and "Ostrobothnian Swedish" is not all of the Swedish speaking area of Ostrobothnia but only the northernmost part of the Swedish speaking area of Finland. Given the proximity to Finnish, a genderless language, an account in terms of language contact would seem natural here too, which leaves English and Jutlandic as the only cases to be explained – which makes one wonder if they are really independent of each other.

"Direction of case levelling"

As an argument for their position that English is a North Germanic language, Emonds and Faarlund (ms.) mention that both English and

Danish/Norwegian (but not Swedish) share the tendency to use the object forms of pronouns in all positions other than uncoordinated subjects of overt finite verbs, as in *It's me* or Danish *Det er mig*. Prima facie it looks as if English could have been influenced by French on this point, since in French the pronouns used in those positions are derived from Latin accusative forms. However, French makes a distinction that English lacks, namely between the clitic pronouns used with uncoordinated direct objects, e.g. *me* 'me' or *te* 'you', and the "full' pronouns used e.g. in *C'est moi* 'It's me'. Basing themselves on this difference, Emonds and Faarlund (ms.) reject the possibility of French influence.

Timing is critical here. Emonds and Faarlund's formulation "some kind of extension of either subject or object forms took place in all Germanic languages in which case distinctions are restricted to pronouns" suggests that they assume a connection between the loss of case distinctions on nouns and the extension of subject or object forms. But this seems to imply that either (i) the nominative-accusative distinction had already disappeared in the last common ancestor of English and Scandinavian or (ii) the similarity is due to later contact between Scandinavia and England. In fact, Emonds and Faarlund say that they do not exclude this possibility even if their preferred hypothesis seems to be that "ME pronominal case patterns simply continued those of Old Danish". But if the change is due to contact, there is not really any reason why it could not equally well go from west to east.

The definite article

Most Scandinavian varieties have one postposed and one suffixed definite article whose distribution varies according to slightly complex patterns (Dahl, 2003). West and South Jutlandic varieties also have two definite articles, with basically the same distribution as the standard Danish ones, but the one that corresponds to the suffixed article, that is, the one that is used when there is no modifier before the head noun – is an invariable marker *æ* which always precedes the noun, as in *æ by* 'the town'. This has been claimed to be due to influence from Low German. Perridon (2005: 1019) argues that the isomorphism between the Danish and the Jutlandic systems speaks against this. He also argues against the possibility that the Jutlandic dialects have replaced an earlier suffixed article by a prefixed one, and hypothesizes that Jutlandic *æ* and the definite suffix arose at the same time, in the 11th or 12th century, in spite of the fact that *æ* is only attested from the 16th century onwards.

He attributes the difference in position to the timing of the change from postposition to preposition attribute-noun order, which was earlier in South and West Jutland. Yet, if Perridon is right about the time of the change, it coincides with the period when influence from English could be expected. Furthermore, the Jutlandic and the English articles share a feature not found elsewhere in Germanic languages at this time – they are invariable, not only in gender and case but also in number. The invariable article þe is another of the innovations in Middle English that were established early in the North and then spread to the south. White (2002) and Tristram (2004) invoke influence from Brittonic Celtic, where there was also an invariable definite article which, as they argue, was older than the English one.

Verb morphology

In the present indicative, Old English distinguished all persons in the singular and none in the plural. By contrast, Old Norse distinguished all persons in both the singular and the plural except for the second and third singular. Both Northern Middle English and Old Danish had virtually the same simplified system in which there were no person distinctions except that the first person singular was optionally different from the second and third persons (although there seems to have been a difference in the extent to which this distinction was made).

It thus seems that the systems have converged in that distinctions that were not made in both Old English and Old Norse were abandoned. However, this convergence was at least initially restricted to NME and Old Danish; other varieties of Middle English and Medieval

Table 1. Verb endings in Old English, Northern Middle English, Old Danish, and Old Norse.

	OE	NME	Old Danish	ON
1sg	-e	-e/-es	-e/-er	-a
2sg	-est	-es	-er	-ar
3sg	-eþ	-es	-er	-ar
1pl	-aþ	-e	-e	-um
2pl	-aþ	-e	-e	-ið
3pl	-aþ	-e	-e	-a

Scandinavian kept the old systems to a much larger extent. The system of Modern Icelandic is identical to that of Old Norse and in Swedish, three persons were distinguished in the plural at least in the written language for many centuries, and Elfdalian still keeps this system.

Possessive reflexives

Older forms of Germanic made a distinction in the third person between (i) the reflexive pronoun *sīn* which agreed with its head noun and (ii) the non-reflexive, non-agreeing genitive pronouns. In the modern languages, this distinction is retained only in North Germanic. In West Germanic, two different developments have taken place, both leading to the disappearance of the distinction. In Continental West Germanic, the process seems to have been one of fusion between the two types of pronouns, resulting in a generalization of the agreeing type. In English, on the other hand, the non-reflexive forms were generalized and the reflexive pronoun disappeared without trace already in the course of the Old English period.

As an exception to the general retention of the reflexive possessive in North Germanic, Danish uses the possessive reflexive *sin* only in the singular, and in West and South Jutlandic the distinction between reflexive and non-reflexive pronouns has generally been lost; *sin* is retained as a general non-human possessive, for human referents the ordinary, non-agreeing possessive pronouns are used. Perridon (1999: 185) rejects the possibility of Low German influence, as Low German does not have non-agreeing possessives. I am not sure how strong this objection is, but it can be noted that it could not be used against the alternative hypothesis that we are dealing with influence from English, where, as mentioned above, the non-agreeing pronouns were generalized.

Other phenomena

There are a few other points where there is a split between Danish and some or all Peninsular Scandinavian varieties, and the Danish pattern is also found in English, but where I have not found sufficient information about the historical development. These will just be briefly mentioned here with Swedish as representing the other side of the split:

- In presentational sentences ('There is beer in the fridge'), Swedish uses a neuter pronoun (*det*) as an expletive but English and Danish use an original adverb (*there* and *der* respectively);

- In Swedish, pronominal objects normally follow a verb particle, in English and Danish they normally precede it;
- In Danish possessive pronouns consistently precede the head noun; in Swedish they optionally follow kin terms, and in many Swedish and Norwegian varieties postposed possessives are the norm.

Thus, we have seen that the grammatical changes that have shaped the modern standard Scandinavian languages, in particular standard Danish and Swedish, largely originated in western Denmark, and that many of them have been more strongly implemented in Denmark, especially the western parts. We have also seen that a significant part of the changes had already made their way into Old Danish as it was written in western Denmark in the mid or late 13th century. Furthermore, many of them closely parallel what happened in the transition from Old English to Middle English, while resemblances to Continental West Germanic are considerably weaker, and parallel changes in those languages are often later.

These observations fairly strongly suggest that Old Danish, and later on and more indirectly, other Scandinavian varieties were influenced by English or Anglicized Norse, or both, during the transition period from Old to Middle English. There are some major stumbling blocks here, though.

One is that the influence appears to be essentially restricted to grammar and phonology. There are a number of words in the Scandinavian languages that are usually regarded as loans from Old or Middle English (although usually originally from Latin or Greek), but they tend to be connected with religion (such as Swedish *ängel* 'angel' and *kyrka* 'church') and are assumed to have arrived with Anglo-Saxon missionaries. It should be added that the number may be a bit larger than is usually thought, since it is not always possible to see which West Germanic language a word comes from, and there may be a tradition to routinely ascribe a continental origin to such cases. Quak (2005: 569) notes a number of presumed loans from Old Frisian which could equally well be from Old English. However, the absence of a larger number of clear loanwords from Old or Middle English in Scandinavian can be seen as a serious problem for the hypothesis that Scandinavian was under influence from the British Isles, especially if we assume that England was the culturally and economically more advanced part. (Compare the large number of Low German loanwords in Scandinavian and French loanwords in English.)

The second stumbling block is how to find a credible account of how the influence took place. The result of the changes that have been discussed here was a major restructuring of the grammar of the Scandinavian languages, in particular of the inflectional system. An explanation in terms of contact-induced change demands that the contacts were more than superficial. We know that there were intimate contacts between Scandinavian and English in Britain, even if the intensity and length of the contact is controversial. It is a common assumption that this led to a mutual convergence of the languages, possibly including morphological simplification due to imperfect learning. For instance, Braunmüller (2005: 1033) speaks of a "transition from focused bidialectalism to the use of diffuse, jargon-like interdialectal variants in the next generation(s)". Thomason and Kaufman (1988) think that "there must have been heavy borrowing between the two languages before the Norse speakers in the end switched to English" and that "[if] the Norse had survived we would have seen a Norse equally riddled with English traits". But maybe the Norse survived after all, in some sense. If Danelaw Scandinavian was still around when the Danes took control of England after the millennium shift, it might have been strong enough to become some kind of prestige dialect in Cnut's empire, including Denmark.

Not much seems to have been said about language at Cnut's court. However, Frank (1994: 108) says in her paper on the poetry of the Scandinavian "skalds" there that there was a "casual use in the verse of Old English words, idioms, and syntax", as if

> the skalds were composing for a Norse-speaking community enisled in a sea of Anglophones; at times the language seems almost Anglo-Danish, a dialect as distinct from Old Norse as Québecois is from metropolitan French.

She bases this statement on Hofmann (1955), one of the very few works that look seriously at the possible influence of English on Viking Age Scandinavian. Hofmann analyzed a number of poems by Norse "skalds" and indeed finds quite a few Anglicisms in them; it has to be admitted, however, that as examples of code-mixing they are not so impressive in comparison to what has been documented in the rich literature on such phenomena (see e.g. Muyskens 2000). Still, Frank's picture does not sound too unrealistic. In the enumeration of Cnut's earls in Keynes (1994) we find 12 Scandinavian earls and 9 English ones, giving the impression of a relatively even distribution of both groups in the ruling élite. There would have been a considerable linguistic diversity in these circles. On the other hand, the period of Danish control was probably too short for the linguistic situation to stabilize.

It is clear that being part of Cnut's empire also had an impact on Denmark. Two areas where Cnut had clear ambitions are often mentioned in the literature: religion and coinage (Lund 1994; Jonsson 1994). There were mints in all major regions of Denmark during Cnut's reign, and the Anglo-Saxon influence on the Danish church "was also more than traceable, it was massive" (Lund 1994: 39). Already Cnut's predecessor Sweyn Forkbeard replaced the German bishops with English and Norwegian ones, and Cnut continued this policy. What this means from a linguistic point of view is that there will have been significant numbers of speakers of various forms of English and/or "Anglo-Danish" in Denmark – although it may be questioned how much this would influence the language spoken in Denmark in general.

One important but obscure point is to what extent there was remigration of Scandinavians from England. It seems likely that part of the Danes in England, particularly those who had arrived recently, would move back to Denmark when the Danes lost the political control. It may also be speculated that the harsh treatment of the population in the north after the Norman invasion may have driven some of them to seek refuge on the other side of the North Sea.

The ruling élite seems to have been quite mobile during this period. Among royals, marriages across ethnic and linguistic borders seem to have been the rule rather than exceptions, although this may of course have been less pronounced further down in the hierarchy. Cnut himself may have had a Slavic mother and possibly a Slavic paternal grandmother; his wives Ælfgifu and Emma were Anglo-Saxon and Norman, respectively. His nephew Sweyn Estridson, who was King of Denmark between 1047 and 1074, had a Norwegian father and was born in England; he married two Swedish women and one Norwegian woman.

All this may still seem a bit thin as a basis for the assumption that Old Danish was shaped in a decisive fashion by contacts across the North Sea. On the other hand, the alternative hypothesis is that the similarities we see between Early Middle English and Old Danish are due to parallel but independent developments – and that it is a pure coincidence that these parallels are strongest between the Danelaw area and western Jutland. For the time being, I think the linguistic mysteries around the North Sea will remain.

References

Allen, C.L. (2008). *Genitives in Early English: Typology and Evidence*: Oxford/ New York: Oxford University Press.

Baugh, A.C. & Cable, T. (1993). *A History of the English Language*. London: Routledge.

Bjerrum, A. (1966). *Grammatik over Skånske lov: efter B 74*. Copenhagen: Københavns Univ. Fond til Tilverjebringelse af Læremidler.

Braunmüller, K. (2005). Language contact during the Old Nordic period I: with the British Isles, Frisia and the Hanseatic League. O. Bandle, L. Elmevik & G. Widmark (eds) *The Nordic Languages: An International Handbook of the History of the North Germanic Languages* (Vol. I). Berlin: Mouton de Gruyter, 1028–1039.

Burrow, J.A. & Turville-Petre, T. (1991). *A Book of Middle English*. Oxford: Blackwell.

Curzan, A. (2003). *Gender Shifts in the History of English*. Cambridge: Cambridge University Press.

Dahl, Ö. (2003). Competing definite articles in Scandinavian. B. Kortmann (ed.) *Dialectology Meets Typology*. Berlin: Mouton de Gruyter, 147–180.

———. (2004). *The Growth and Maintenance of Linguistic Complexity*. Amsterdam: Benjamins.

———. (2010a). *Grammaticalization in the North: Noun Phrase Morphosyntax in Scandinavian Vernaculars*. Stockholm: Department of Linguistics, Stockholm University.

———. Review of C. Allen: Genitives in early English: Typology and evidence. *Diachronica* 27:3, 489–496.

Delsing, L.-O. (2003). Syntaktisk variation i nordiska nominalfraser. L.-O. Delsing, Ø.A. Vangsnes & A. Holmberg (eds) *Dialektsyntaktiska studier av den nordiska nominalfrasen*. Oslo: Novus.

Emonds, J. & Faarlund, J.T. (ms.). *English as North Germanic*.

Frank, R. (1994). King Cnut in the verse of his skalds. A.R. Rumble (ed.) *The Reign of Cnut, King of England, Denmark and Norway*. London: Leicester University Press, 106–124.

Hofmann, D. (1955). *Nordisch-englische Lehnbeziehungen der Wikingerzeit*. Copenhagen: Munksgaard.

Jonsson, K. (1994). The coinage of Cnut. A.R. Rumble (ed.) *The Reign of Cnut: King of England, Denmark and Norway*. London: Leicester University Press, 193–230.

Keynes, S. (1994). Cnut's Earls. A.R. Rumble (ed.) *The Reign of Cnut: King of England, Denmark and Norway*. London: Leicester University Press, 43–88.

Kilarski, M. (2007). On grammatical gender as an arbitrary and redundant category. D.A. Kibbee (ed.) *History of Linguistics 2005: Selected papers from the Tenth International Conference on the History of the Language Sciences (ICHOLS X), 1–5 September 2005, Urbana-Champaign, Illinois*. Amsterdam: Benjamins, 24–36.

Klemola, J. (1997). Dialect evidence for the loss of genitive inflection in English. *English Language and Linguistics* 1:2, 349–353.

Laker, S. (2008). Changing views about Anglo-Saxons and Britons. H. Aertsen & B. Veldhoen (eds) *Six Papers from the 28th Symposium on Medieval Studies*. Leiden: Leiden University Press, 1–38.

Lund, N. (1994). Cnut's Danish kingdom. A.R. Rumble (ed.) *The Reign of Cnut. King of England, Denmark and Norway, Leicester*. London: Leicester University Press, 27–42.

McWhorter, J.H. (2002). What happened to English? *Diachronica* 19:2, 217–272.

Minkova, D. (1991). The History of Final Vowels in English: The Sound of Muting. Berlin: Walter de Gruyter.

Muysken, P. (2000). *Bilingual Speech: A Typology of Code-Mixing*. Cambridge: Cambridge University Press

Perridon, H. (1999). Review of A. Torp. 1998. Nordiske språk i nordisk og germansk perspektiv. *Tijdschrift voor Skandinavistiek* 20:2, 182–186.

———. (2005). Dialects and written language in Old Nordic II: Old Danish and Old Swedish. O. Bandle, L. Elmevik & G. Widmark (eds) *The Nordic Languages: An International Handbook of the History of the North Germanic Languages* (Vol. I). Berlin: Mouton de Gruyter, 1018–1027.

———. (2013). The emergence of the *s*-genitive in Danish. *Language Sciences* 36, 134–146.

Quak, A. (2005). Nordic and North Sea Germanic relations. O. Bandle, L. Elmevik & G. Widmark (eds) *The Nordic Languages: An International Handbook of the History of the North Germanic Languages* (Vol. I). Berlin: Mouton de Gruyter, 568–572.

Ringgaard, K. (1986). Flektionssystemets forenkling og middelnedertysk. *Arkiv för Nordisk Filologi* 101, 173–183.

———. (1989). Fleksionssystemets forenkling i dansk. *Arkiv för Nordisk Filologi* 104, 160–165.

Schrijver, P. (2006). What Britons spoke around 400 A.D. N.J. Higham (ed.) *Britons in Anglo-Saxon England*. Woolbridge: Boydell, 165–71.

Thomason, S.G. & Kaufman, T. (1988). *Language Contact, Creolization, and Genetic Linguistics*. Berkeley: University of California Press.

Tristram, H.L. (2002). Attrition of inflections in English and Welsh. M. Filppula, J. Klemola & H. Pitkänen (eds) *The Celtic Roots of English*. Joensuu: Joensuu University Press, 111–49.

———. (2004). Diglossia in Anglo-Saxon England, or what was spoken Old English like? *Studia Anglica Posnaniensia* 40, 87–110.

Trudgill, P. (2010). *Investigations in Sociohistorical Linguistics*. Cambridge: Cambridge University Press.

White, D.L. (2002). Explaining the innovations of Middle English: What, where, and why. M. Filppula, J. Klemola & H. Pitkänen (eds) *The Celtic Roots of English*. Joensuu: Joensuu University Press, 153–174.

Whitelock, D. (1996). *English Historical Documents: Volume 1*. London: Routledge.

3 The Late Middle English Version of *Practica Urinarum* in London, Wellcome Library, MS 537 (ff. 15r-40v)[1]

Javier Calle-Martín
University of Málaga

1. Introduction to the edition

Mediaeval uroscopic treatises have been traditionally underestimated in the last decades, to such an extent that they can be safely deemed to be the Cinderella of the subject categories of Medicine, especially if compared with Herbals, Remedybooks and Leechbooks (Keiser 1998: 3661; Calle-Martín 2012: 243). Using Voigts and Kurtz's electronic database of *Scientific and Medical Writings in Old and Middle English* (2000), Tavormina has found that the subject field 'Urine and Uroscopy' contains 408 texts, representing "the fourth largest in the entire database, preceded only by 'Recipes', 'Alchemy', and 'Herbs and Herbal Medicine'" (Tavormina 2005: 40; 61). Unfortunately, however, many of these uroscopic treatises are hitherto unedited and, more importantly, they are still waiting for a patient scholar to investigate the textual tradition of the extant witnesses (Tavormina 2009: S33–S41). According to Tavormina, there is a scholarly gap in the field and further research is needed in the following three areas: a) the publication of more uroscopic treatises in the vernacular; b) the complete taxonomy of the texts in Middle English; and c) the relations of these texts to their Latin/English sources (2005: 41).

---

[1] The present research has been funded by the Spanish Ministry of Science and Innovation (grant number FFI2011–26492) and by the Autonomous Government of Andalusia (grant number P11-HUM7597). These grants are hereby gratefully acknowledged. This Festschrift article is dedicated to Prof. Nils-Lennart Johannesson, a keen attender of *Selim* conferences in Spain (The Spanish Society for Medieval English Language and Literature), on the occasion of his retirement.

How to cite this book chapter:
Calle-Martín, J. 2015. The Late Middle English Version of *Practica Urinarum* in London, Wellcome Library, MS 537 (ff. 15r-40v). In: Shaw, P., Erman, B., Melchers, G. and Sundkvist, P. (eds) *From Clerks to Corpora: essays on the English language yesterday and today*. Pp. 35–52. Stockholm: Stockholm University Press. DOI: http://dx.doi.org/10.16993/bab.c License: CC-BY.

Our analysis then falls within Tavormina's first area and contains the semi-diplomatic edition of the Middle English version of *Practica Urinarum*, a small uroscopic treatise instructing the mediaeval practitioner on the examination of urine in the light of the following three elements: substance, colour and sediment. The text also reports what must be considered for the treatment of the patient, i.e. his/her age, duration of illness, the time of greatest suffering together with "further questions regarding the time of the specimen and the diet of the patient" (Keiser 1998: 3662). As far as we have been able to investigate, the text has been preserved (completely or partially) in seven different witnesses (Keiser 1998: 3852):

- London, Wellcome Library, MS Wellcome 537, ff. 15r-40v (c. 1460).
- Cambridge University Library, Gonville and Caius College, MS 336/825, ff. 132v-136r (1480–1500).
- Cambridge University Library, Trinity College, MS O.1.77, ff. 21r-29v (c. 1460).
- British Library, MS Sloane 2320, ff. 4r-9v (c. 1458).
- British Library, MS Sloane 3566, ff. 24r-33v (1450–1475).
- Boston Medical Library, MS Countway 19, ff. 14r-18v (c. 1460).
- Yale University Library, Takamiya 33, ff. 24v-37r (1480–1500).

MS Wellcome 537 has been used as the source text for the present edition, which is hitherto unedited. With the title *Miscellanea Medica VII*, MS Wellcome 537 is a relatively small volume written in octavo size, measuring approximately 14.5 x 11 cm. The volume houses a collection of eight anonymous treatises, both in English and Latin, on medical astrology, weather prediction, uroscopy together with a collection of medical receipts. The following collation relies on Moorat's accurate description of the volume (1962: 394–395):

- [Anon.] Canon pro medicinis dandies (in Latin), ff. 6r-12r.
- [Anon.] Menses per circulum anni (in Latin), ff. 12v-14v.
- [Anon.] Seeing of Urines (in English), ff. 15r-40v.
- [Anon.] Medical receipts (in English), ff. 40v-46v.
- [Anon.] Practica medicinae (in English), ff. 48r-310v.
- [Anon.] Table of Golden Numbers and Dominican Letters, ff. 315v-318v.
- [Anon.] De cursu lunae (in Latin), ff. 318v-325r.
- [Anon.] On the Changes of the Moon (in English), ff. 326r-333r.

Even though the volume had been previously dated by Francis Douce (1757–1834) to the first half of the 15th century, Moorat reports that there is an autograph letter to Dr Joseph Frank Payne (1840–1910) from Thomas Wright (1810–1877), proposing to date the composition of the volume to the year 1462 because "the whole of it is written in the hand which is common enough throughout the reigns of Henry VI and Edward IV" (Moorat 1962: 395). The palaeographic analysis of the scribe's handwriting confirms it to be a hybrid script composed in the second half of the 15th century in the light of the overwhelming prefer- ence for the Secretary script, with just sporadic tinges of the Anglicana (Petti 1977: 15). Fig. 1 below reproduces the inventory of letterforms used in MS Wellcome 537 where the letters have been numbered for reference purposes. As shown, the Secretary script is witnessed in the use of distinctive letterforms, which sharply differ from the conventional cur- sive hand of the Anglicana. Among others, the following stand out: the single-lobed <a> with a pointed head (1); two-lobed <b> (2); the letter <d> with a looped stem (4); the letter <k> with its characteristic right- arced headstroke (10); the letter <l> with a lobed arm (11) (Clemens and Graham 2007: 167–168); the right-shouldered <r>, footed and sitting on the script line (17); the heavy ascender of the letter <v> (24); and the letter <w> already resembling a double v (25).

Already in the second half of the 15th century, "the two compet- ing Gothic *cursiva* scripts often seem so intermingled as to have pro- duced a new cursive book script, typically Secretary in ductus, but using Anglicana round *e* and sigma-shaped *s* as cursive features and liable to adopt other Anglicana letterforms" (Roberts 2005: 212–213; Derolez 2003: 162; also Denholm-Young 1954: 28–29; Hector 1966: 58). In this fashion, the Anglicana script is limited to the use of the following four distinctive letters in MS Wellcome 537: the round <e> (5);

Figure 1. Inventory of letterforms in MS Wellcome 537.

the two-compartment figure 8 form of <g> (7); the sigma-like <s> (20); and the letter <w> consisting of a double <l> together with a 3 (26).

The principles of a semi-diplomatic edition have been adopted in the present edition so as to render an accurate reproduction of the source text, complying with the following guidelines, partially adapted from Clemens and Graham (2007: 75–81; also Calle-Martín and Miranda-García 2012: 67–68): a) the spelling, capitalization and punctuation of the original have been retained; b) abbreviations have been expanded with the supplied letter(s) italicized;[2] c) insertions, both of single letters and words, have been inserted in their proper sequence in the body of the text;[3] d) word separation has been normalized, regardless of whether words are run together without separation or whether a gap is left within a word; and e) lineation and paragraphing have been disregarded for reasons of space.

2. The Middle English text[4]

{f. 15r} . ihc .

¶ here begynneþ þe practise of the sighte of vrynes . HIt is to vndurstonde þat who so wille loke an vryn ꞉ him behoueþ to considere þre þinges / Firste he muste aske þe age of þe pacient or seke body . and how longe his sekenes haþ holde him . and what tyme hit toke him furste . and whiche tyme of þe day or of þe ny3t hit greueþ him moste . Also if þe vryn were made and brou3te in a clene vessel . and þat hit were þe furste water after mydny3t Also þe dyete of þe seke body {f. 15v} wheþer he haþ vsed highe metis and drinkes꞉ or ellis lowe . Also hit behoueþ to consider þe substaunce of þe vryn wheþer hit be þicke or þynne . and þe qualite wheþer it be highe or lowe of coloure . and þe quantite wheþer it be litil or moche . and þe contentis . and þe cloudes þat ben þeryn . And in whiche regioun þey ben yn ꞉ and if þey be oueral in liche colourid . or if hit be more remise in oon regioun꞉ þan in anoþer . or if hit be of twoo colouris ꞉ or if hit be oueral in liche colourrid . boþe intencioun and remissioun . {f. 16r} Than hit behoueþ principally to wyten by consideracioun of þe vryne and by askyng also what þe maledy is . wheþer hit be a feuer or anoþer maledy . and wheþer hit be

---

[2] Superior letters are lowered to the line, as in wᵗ > *with* or þᵉ > þe. Superfluous brevigraphs and otiose flourishes, in turn, have been disregarded.

[3] Insertions above the line and in the margin have been noted with the use of slashes (/ \) and double slashes (// \\), respectively.

[4] (c) Wellcome Library (London) as the owner of the manuscript.

in þe begy*nn*ny*ng* . or ell*is in* state . or *in* þe endi*ng* . Also whe*n* þu hast
vndirstonde . al þis . *and* þe vryn*e* of þe pacient . is brou3te to þe ꞉ þu
muste co*n*sider*e* þre þingis *in* euery vry*n* . þat is to sey . þe substau*n*ce .
þe coloure *and* þe sedyme*n* . Oon is cause of colo*ur* . ano*þ*er is cause of
substau*n*ce . þe þirde is cause of sedyme*n* . Now *in* euery man is body
is foure qualitees . hete *and* colde . moyste {f. 16v} *and* drye ꞉ hete *and*
colde ꞉ þey be*n* causers of colours . Drynes *and* moystenes ꞉ þey be*n*
cause of substau*n*ce . /hete\ is cause of rede coloure . drynes is cause
of þyn substau*n*ce . moystenes is cause of þycke substau*n*ce . As þus .
if þe vryn of þe pacient be rede *and* þicke ꞉ it signifieþ þat blode haþ
more do*m*inacioun þan an o*þ*er . Why ꞉ For blode is hote *and* moyste .
If it be rede *and* þynne ꞉ hit sheweþ þat colere haþ do*m*inacioun . For
why . colere is hote *and* drye . If þe vryn appere white *and* þicke ꞉ hit
betokeneþ fleume . For fleume is colde *and* {f. 17r} moyste . If þe vryn
shewe white *and* þynne ꞉ it sygnifieþ malencoly . For malencoly is colde
and drye . Whe*n* þu hast co*n*siderid wel as þis ꞉ þen beholde þe diu*er*site
of colours of þe vryns *and* þe cercles of he*m* . whiche now folowen .

Karapos . is an vryn *in* coloure ꞉ like to kamellis flesshe . whiche is a
colo*ur* white douny . *and in* substaunce hit is þyn . The whiche sweweþ[5]
and signifieþ þe droppesy . or a wynde vndur þe syde . þe stone . þe hede
ache . a posteme *in* þe longis . or a {f. 17v} or elles a fleume . ¶ Plu*m*bea ꞉ is
an vryn *in* colo*ur* lyke to lede . whiche signifieþ þe falli*ng* yuel . or membris broken . or a palsy . or a feuer t*er*tian . or difficulte of wat*er* maki*ng*
. or wo*m*ma*n* is floures ¶ Pallida ꞉ is an vry*n* /*in* colo*ur*\ like to flesshe
halfe sode*n* þe iuse not putte oute . which signifieþ a feble hede . or a
feu*er* . or a colde stomake . or a bre*n*ny*ng* vndur þe lyuer . or wastyng
of longes . ¶ Plu*m*bea ꞉ is an vry*n in* coloure {f. 18r} like to lede . as
hit write*n* tofor*e* of colo*ur* pallida ¶ Viridis ꞉ is an vry*n* þat is gre*n*e *in*
colo*ur* like to þe caule leaf . whiche betokeneþ wasti*ng* of kynde/li\ hete .
þe morfu . or þe hede ache . or þe iaundyse . or chasi*ng* of þe luy*er and*
wasti*ng* of ky*n*deli hete . ¶ Inopos ꞉ is an vry*n in* colo*ur* like to a man is
lyuer . or to olde rede wyne ytu*r*ned *in*to blackenes . whiche betokeneþ
þat þe galle brenneþ þe lyuer . *and* þerof co*mm*eþ þe iau*n*dise . or hit
signifieþ a veyne rote*n* /or broken\ of the /r\eynes . or to myche delynge
wiþ a womman . {f. 18v} ¶ Subpalida ꞉ is an vry*n in* coloure /like\ to iuse
of flesshe halfe soden . *and* þe iuse yputte oute . The whiche betokeneþ
a posteme *in* þe ri3t syde . or a tysike . or hardenes to make water ¶

---

[5] Probably an erroneous form for <sheweþ>. The *e-MED* notes a similar form (ie.
swewe) which is identified as an error.

Rubicunda ⁚ is an vryn in colour like to a flaume of fyre sentte oute . The whiche betokeneþ a feuer acute and sharpe . and vndursette at þe herte . defaute of wynde and a drie coughe . ¶ Subcitrina ⁚ is an vryn in colour . like to þe iuse of an appel orynge . whiche betokeneþ a feuer agu . and þe same as doþe cytryne {f. 19r} coloure but not so myche . ne so perfite . ¶ Subrufa ⁚ is an vryn in colour like to golde and siluer medelid togedir . whiche betokeneþ a feuer tertian . or a posteme vndur þe ribbes . or þe goute . or a tisike . /or\ shortenes of wynde . and simple bitternes in taste and grete dryness ¶ Subricunda ⁚ is an vryn in colour like to a flaume of fyre not sente oute . This betokeneþ as doþe subrufa . but þat þe yuel is more greuous in þis ⁚ þan hit is in þat other . {f. 19v} ¶ Rubea ⁚ Rede vryn is in coloure like to safron in dorte . whiche beto-keneþ a feuer þoroughe chafyng of þe lyuer . or a feuer quarteyn . or ellis a posteme of þe longis . begynnyng of a dropesy . or of a morfu . ¶ Citrina ⁚ is an vryn like to þe coloure of an appelle of an orynge . whiche betokeneþ wasting of þe splene and of þe lyuer . commyng of þe frenesy . and hete aslaked in a feuer tercian . ¶ Subrubea ⁚ is an vryn in colour like to safron belynge . whi{f. 20r}che betokeneþ a feuer of corrupte blode /in þe veynes\ . or a veyne broken in þe backe . or ellis þe floures of wommen . ¶ Rufa ⁚ is an vryn in colour like to pured golde . The whiche betokeneþ þe emoyraudis . or þe dropesy . or passing of floures . ¶ kaynos ⁚ is an vryn in colour like to blacke wyne or to blacke water . And hit betokeneþ a crampe in þe veyne of þe herte . or a posteme in þe stomake . or ellis þe goute .

¶ Lactea ⁚ is an vryn in coloure {f. 20v} like to whey of coughe mylke and hit betokeneþ deþe if þe paciente slepe not . or ellis a frenesy . or a longe /during\ feuer . ¶ Subuiridis ⁚ is an vryn in colour clere as þe welle water . And hit betokeneþ þe same as doþe þe rede coloure. but not so perfitly . ¶ Alba ⁚ is an vryn in colour as clere welle water . and hit betokeneþ wasting of þe splene . or þe dropesy . or þe stone and greuaunce in pissyng . or pissing ageyne wille . or þe emoyraudis . or stopping of floures . cha{f. 21r}fyng of þe lyuer . wodenes . and in axces and feuer ⁚ hit is deþe . ¶ Nigra ⁚ is an vryn in colour like to blacke ynke or to a brent horne . And hit betokeneþ a feuer quarteyn . or a blacke iaundise . peryl of deþe in shorte tyme . ¶ Glauca ⁚ is an vryn like in colour to a shenyng horne . And hit betokeneþ a posteme in þe riȝt side . or a feuer etike . or /a\ bladder on the longis .

¶ Her endeþ þe significacioun of /þe coloures\ of vryns Now we wille {f. 21v} declare and telle of þe Cercles of vryns and begynne at þe hede of man A Cercle þat is grete shevweþ þe feblenes of þe hede and moche akynge þeryn . ¶ A . cercle þat is white *and* þycke . signifieþ þat fleume haþ duraciou*n* i*n* þe hynder parte of þe hede . for þat is his resti*n*g place . ¶ A . cercle white *and* clere . signifieþ þat malencoly haþ duraciou*n* on þe lifte syde of þe hede . for þat is his sete . ¶ A . cercle þat is rede *and* þicke . signifieþ þat blode haþ duraciou*n* i*n* þe forehede . for þat is his sete . ¶ A . cercle r*e*de *and* clere ⸗ signifieþ þat colere haþ duraciou*n* . {f. 22r} i*n* þe ri3te side of þe hede . for þat is his restyng place . ¶ If a cercle shewe or appe*re* grene ⸗ hit betokeneþ gr*e*te ache i*n* þe hede . *and* vnd*er* þe ri3te side . ¶ If a cercle appe*re* white ⸗ hit signifieþ gr*e*te ache i*n* þe hynder party of þe hede . ¶ If a cercle appe*re* rede ⸗ hit betokeneþ ache i*n* þe forehede . And if hit appe*re* blacke ⸗ hit signifieþ þe falli*n*g yuelle . ¶ If þ*er* be i*n* a cercle smale bollis as þey we*re* of reyne wat*er* ⸗ hit betokeneþ a wynde i*n* þe {f. 22v} hede . risy*n*g oute of þe stomake . ¶ If þ*er* be i*n* a cercle mottis as be*n* i*n* þe su*n*ne ⸗ hit betokeneþ a reume of þe hede . or þe pose . or deffenes . or heuynes . ¶ If þ*er* appe*re* i*n* a cercle a tree ⸗ hit betokeneþ a posteme i*n* þe bladder . or ell*is* i*n* þe lyuer . ¶ If þ*er* appe*re* i*n* a cercle fattenes ⸗ hit signifieþ a feuer . or ell*is* streittenes at /þe\ breste . ¶ If blode appe*re* i*n* a cercle ⸗ hit betokeneþ breki*n*g of a veyne i*n* þe backe . If þe /vryn\ appe*re* blac{f. 23r}ke ⸗ hit betokeneþ deþe . which is causid of þe blacke iau*n*dise . or ell*is* of þe feu*e*re quarteyn . ¶ Wat*er* ful of smale þredis ⸗ betokeneþ dry complex-iou*n* . or ell*is* a posteme i*n* þe ri3te side . ¶ White gr*a*uel appering i*n* a cercle signifieþ þe stone i*n* þe bladd*er* . Rede gr*a*uel ⸗ betokeneþ ache i*n* þe reynes . *and* also a spice of þe stone . Blacke gr*a*uel betokeneþ ache i*n* þe rigge bitwene þe kidneys . Shales as hit we*re* of fysshes betokeneþ stoppi*n*g of floures . *and* a scabbe i*n* þe matrice .

¶ here endiþ þe cercles {f. 23v} of vryns w*ith* her significacions *and* now foloweþ þe co*n*tent*es* of he*m* . *and* þe passing excesse of hem . *and* þe oþ*er* declary*n*g of which ben gode *and* holsu*m* and co*m*mend-able . Eche vryn is clensi*n*g of blode . as hit is pr*o*purly pr*o*ued of two þi*n*ges significatife . or forsoþe hit signifieþ of þe lyuer *and* of þe veynes . or of þe bladd*er* *and* of þe reynes . Of oþ*er* þi*n*ges hit is yppirliche significatyfe . ¶ But i*n* vryn lokeþ *and* beholdeþ diu*erse* þinges . þat is to wite . substau*n*ce . coloures . regions . *and* þe co*n*tent*es* . Anoþer is because {f. 24r} of substau*n*ce . Anoþ*er* is because of coloure . Anoþ*er* is becau⁶ of residens . Now i*n* eu*er*y ma*n* is body is foure qualitees . hete *and* colde . moystenes *and* drynes . hete *and* colde ⸗ þey be*n* cause of

---

⁶ An erroneous form instead of <because>. The scribe does not provide the full form of this conjunction probably because the word is broken at the end of the line.

coloures . Drynes *and* moystenes ꞉ þey be*n* cause of substau*n*ce . As þus
hete is cause of rede coloure . Colde ꞉ is cause of white coloure . Drines
꞉ is cause of þyn substau*n*ce . moystenes ꞉ is cause of þicke substaunce
. ¶ An vryn is deuided i*n* foure parties . þe on*e* p*ar*ty ꞉ is þe cer{f. 24v}
cle . þe secu*n*de ꞉ is þe body of þe eyre . þe þridde ꞉ is p*er*foraciou*n* . þe
fourþe ꞉ is þe grounde . ¶ By þe cercle ꞉ is see*n* þe sekenes of þe hede
and of þe brayne . By þe body ꞉ alle yuelis *and* sekenes of þe spirituel
me*m*bris *and* of þe sto*m*ake . By p*er*foraciou*n* ꞉ sekenes of þe lyuer *and*
of þe splene . By þe grounde ꞉ we shewen accident*es* of þe reynes *and*
of þe matrice . *and* of þe p*ri*ue me*m*bris / ¶ An vry*n* haþ þre regions .
þat is . þe neþereste bygy*n*neþ fro þe grounde of þe vrynal *and* dureþ
{f. 25r} by þe space of two fyngers / þe myddel regiou*n* begy*n*neþ þer
as þe neþer endeþ ꞉ *and* dureþ to þe cercle . þe whiche cercle is þe ouermeste regiou*n* . And whe*n* þer is i*n* þe ouermeste regiou*n* as fome ꞉ hit
signifieþ ventosite bulny*n*g vppe i*n* þe veynes of þe vryn . or elli*s* i*n*fla-
ciou*n* . or oþer vices or sekenes of þe lungis . ¶ If /so be þat\ þe cercle be
þicke ꞉ hit signifieþ to moche repleciou*n* i*n* þe hede *and* doloure or ache
. A . white cloude appering i*n* þe myddel regiou*n* ꞉ i*n* hole me*n* is an yuel
signe . but i*n* me*n* þat haue þe feue{f. 25v}res . hit signifieþ digestiou*n* of
þe mat*er* *and* of þe yuel . In þe neþ*er*meste regiou*n* if þer app*er*e grauel
or litil stones . hit sheweþ /þat\ þe paciente is ful of litil stones . *and* is
greued w*ith* þe vice of þe stone . Oþ*er*while þe r*e*sidence is blacke ꞉ if þat
falle i*n* a feuer q*u*arteyn . or for kyndely hete yquenchid ꞉ hit is a signe
of deþe . If it be for expulsiou*n* of venomous mat*er* whiche is putte oute
by þe vry*n* ꞉ hit is a toke*n* of helþe / ¶ If an vryn be white at morwe *and*
brovne aft*er* mete ꞉ hit {f. 26r} signifieþ gode helþe *and* welle . ¶ If an
vryn be fatte *and* trobely ꞉ hit betokeneþ wat*er* in þe bowwelis / ¶ If an
vry*n* be riȝt rede *and* clere . hit signifieþ a bre*n*nyng feu*er* / ¶ If an vry*n*
be oueral rede *and* þicke w*ith* a blacke cercle ꞉ hit signifieþ grete sekenes
and feru*ent* . *and* but if he swete ꞉ hit is deþe / ¶ If an vry*n* be white
and þy*n*ne *and* a litil dy*m*my ꞉ hit signifieþ a coldenes i*n* þe body . ¶ If
an vry*n* be dy*m*me *and* su*m*del rede . w*ith* a blacke cercle ꞉ /it\ signi{f.
26v}fieþ a badde sto*m*ake . do medisy*n* . ¶ If an vry*n* be cler*e* *and* haþ
a blacke cercle ꞉ hit is deþe . ¶ If an vry*n* be þy*n*ne . *and* grene abouen ꞉
hit signifieþ a colde complexiou*n* . *and* if i*n* þe casting be blode aboue*n*
꞉ it is a tisike . ¶ If an vry*n* be dy*m*me *and* blacke aboue*n* . or vndir þe
cercle i*n* þe casti*n*g ꞉ hit betokeneþ luste of kynde . *and* he wolde haue
a woman to pley / ¶ If an vry*n* be þicke *and* trobely like horse pisse .
hit signifieþ grete hede ache . do to hi*m* medisyne . {f. 27r} ¶ If an vry*n*
be fatte i*n* þe botty*m* . *and* white i*n* þe mydd*es* . *and* rede aboue*n* . hit

is a feuer quarteyn . ¶ If an vryn appere flessheli *and* haue drestis *in* þe bottu*m* as shauyng ⁝ hit is a dropesy . Also if hit be as whey aboue . *and* clere *in* þe myddis . *and* shadweþ beneþe ⁝ hit is þe colde dropesy . ¶ If an vryn haue dreste*s* *in* þe bottu*m* like gobetti*s* of coles *and* be*n* depa*r*tid asou*n*der *and* not to grete ⁝ hit signifieþ a worme *in* þe body . do medis*ine* / ¶ If an vry*n* haue blacke co*n*tente*s* *and* smale as motte*s* stondi*n*g *in* {f. 27v} þe mydde*s* of þe wat*er* . hit signifieþ a posteme *in* þe side . ¶ If an vry*n* haue *in* þe bottu*m* like gobetti*s* of flesshe of smale shawyng ⁝ þ*at* is a token of stoppi*n*g of þe reynes *and* also of þe pipis of þe lyuer . do to hi*m* medis*ine* ¶ If an vry*n* /be\ blacke *and* grene wi*th* longe co*n*tente*s* like to þe sparme of ma*n* . hit is þe palsy . *and* hit be frotthi *and* like lede *in* þe mydde*s* ⁝ it is þe same / ¶ If an vry*n* haue greynes vndir þe side*s* of þe cercle ⁝ hit signifieþ a stomake ful of {f. 28r} humours . *and* bre*n*nyng at þe breste . do to hi*m* medisyne . ¶ If an vry*n* haue askes aboue ⁝ hit /is\ harme *in* alle þe spiritual p*ar*ties of al þe body . do medis*ine* / ¶ If an vry*n* haue co*n*tente*s* white *and* blacke *in* þe bottu*m* ⁝ hit is costifnes / ¶ If an vry*n* abide longe lefti*n*g þi*n*ne ⁝ hit signifieþ swelli*n*g *in* þe body . *and* moche reume *and* humou*r*s þeryn . ¶ If an vry*n* be þycke *and* litil *in* qua*n*tite ⁝ hit is toke*n* of þe ston*e* / ¶ If an vry*n* be froþthi *and* clere *and* litil *in* qua*n*tite *and* also rede ⁝ {f. 28v} hit signifieþ peyne *in* þe riȝt side ./ ¶ If an vry*n* haue grete froþe aft*er* þe casti*n*g . hit signifieþ wynde *in* þe bowel/l\is *and* peyne vndir þe sides *and* bad stomake / ¶ If an vry*n* be rede as bre*n*ning golde ⁝ hit is þe dropesi of deþe / ¶ If an vry*n* be as bre*n*nyng cole ⁝ hit is a posteme on þe lyuer . do to hi*m* medisyn*e* .

URyn as flaume of fyre sente oute / Vryn as safro*n* belyng*e* / Vry*n* as safron dorte / Vryn as flavme of fyr*e* not sente oute / These four*e* signifien excesse of digestio*n* / {f. 29r} ¶ Vryn of þe coloure of a ma*n* is lyuer / Vryn of þe coloure of blacke wat*er* / Vryn þat is grene as a caule lefe / These thre . signifien moche adustiou*n* and brennyng*e* . ¶ Vryn þat is pale of colo*ur* as is lede / Vryn þat is blacke *in* colo*ur* of adustion . as is ynke / Vry*n* þat is blacke *in* colo*ur* as blacke wat*er* . or as a blacke horne / These þre ⁝ betoken mortificaciou*n* /*and*\ sleing*e* / ¶ Vryn þat is cler*e* as welle wat*er* / Vryn þat is shenyng as a horne / {f. 29v} ¶ Vryn *in* colo*ur* as whey of mylke / Vryn þat is white douny as is þe flesshe of a camel / These four*e* signifien i*n*digestiou*n* / ¶ Vryn like to iuse of flesshe halfe soden . þe iuse yput oute / Vryn like to flesshe sode*n* þe iuse not yputte oute / These ij° signifien þe begynnyng of digestiou*n* / ¶ Vryn þat is as þe colo*ur* of þe iuse of an orynge appel / Vryn þat is like to þe appel of orynge /rinde\ / These ij° signifien myddel digestiou*n* / {f. 30r} ¶ Vryn

þat is as golde *and* siluer meddelid togeder / Vryn þat is as golde purid
. þese ij° signifien parfite digestiou*n* / And þis vryn rufa ⁒ betokeneþ
helþe *and* gode disposiciou*n* of ma*n* is body / Vryn subrufa signifieþ
gode helþe ⁒ but not so p*er*fitely i*n* ony ma*n*er as doþe rufa . ¶ Vryn þat
is of þe colo*ur* of an orynge appel . Wha*n* hit is white *and* a myddel
substau*n*ce . *and* whe*n* þe cercle is of þe same coloure ⁒ hit is praisable /
Vryn þat is of colo*ur* as is þe iuse of an appel orynge ⁒ is not so {f. 30v}
p*er*fite as is colo*ur* citrine ⁒ for citrine is best colo*ur* / ¶ Vryn þat is of coloure as is þe rede rose betokeneþ a feu*er* ⁒ þat is callid effimera . *and* if a
ma*n* pisshe co*n*tynuelly ⁒ hit signifieþ a feu*er* co*n*tynuel . ¶ Vryn þat is of
colo*ur* as blode i*n* a glasse ⁒ betokeneþ a feuer of to moche blode . *and*
þa*n* anoon a ma*n* muste be letid blode . but if þe mone be i*n* þe signe of
geminor*um* . ¶ Vryn þat is grene as is þe caule lefe whe*n* hit is pissid ⁒
and afterwarde appereþ rede ⁒ {f. 31r} hit betokeneþ adustiou*n and* sore
barny*n*g . *and* hit is mortal *and* deþe / ¶ Vryn þat is rede i*n* al maner .
remeued fro cleernes ⁒ betokeneþ declyny*n*g of þe yuel . and amendyng
of þe sekenes . ¶ Vryn þat is rede meddelid sumwhat *with* blackenes ⁒
betokeneþ þe yuel of þe lyuer . *and* of þe herte . ¶ Vryn þat is pale as
flesshe halfe soden ⁒ betokeneþ defecciou*n* or feblenes of þe stomake .
and letting of þe secou*n*de digestioun . ¶ Vryn þat is white as is welle
{f. 31v} wat*er* i*n* hole me*n* ⁒ hit betokeneþ rawenes of humours . *and* i*n*
sharpe feuers ⁒ hit is deþe / ¶ Vryn i*n* colo*ur* as whey of mylke w*ith* þicke
substau*n*ce . if hit falle i*n* a wo*m*ma*n* ⁒ hit is not so p*er*ilouse as hit is i*n*
a man / for þe i*n*ordenau*n*ce of þe matrice . but neu*er* þe late i*n* sharpe
feueres ⁒ hit is deþe / ¶ Vryn i*n* coloure aboue ⁒ as whey of mylke . *and*
byneþe shadueþ aboute*n* þe myddel regiou*n* clere . hit betokeneþ þe
dropesy / Also if þe vry*n* of him {f. 32r} þat haþ þe dropesy be rufa . or
subrufa . hit betokeneþ deþe / ¶ Vryn þat is white douny . as is camell*e*
flesshe ⁒ betokeneþ multitude of corrupte humours . which befalleþ i*n*
fleumatike*s* . ydropeke*s* . podagr*es* . *and* so of oþer . ¶ Vryn þat is blacke
⁒ may be of kyndely hete yquenchid . *and* þa*n* hit is mortale *and* deþe /
Or hit may be for expulsiou*n* of venomou*s* mat*er* . whiche is putte oute
by þe vry*n* . *and* þa*n* hit betokeneþ helþe . In a feu*er* q*u*arteyn ⁒ hit is
eu*er*more deþe / {f. 32v} ¶ Vryn i*n* colo*ur* as /a\ sheny*n*g horne betokeneþ
yuel disposiciou*n* of þe splene . *and* disposicion of þe feu*er* q*u*arteyn / ¶
Vryn i*n* colo*ur* as safron i*n* dorte w*ith* þicke substau*n*ce . *and* stinkyng
and fomy . betokeneþ þe iau*n*dise . ¶ Vryn i*n* colo*ur* as purid golde .
and vry*n* as golde *and* siluer meddelid togedir . hauyng byneþe rounde
resoluciou*n and* white aboue ⁒ *and* su*m*what fatty . betokeneþ þe feuer
etike . ¶ Vryn i*n* þe grounde of þe vessel vnto þe myddil clere {f. 33r}

after þicke *and* þynne betokeneþ harme i*n* þe breest ¶ Vryn þ*at* is fomy
and clere ∴ *and* i*n* colou*r* as safron belinge ∴ betokeneþ mor*e* harme i*n*
þe riȝt syde ∴ þe*n* in þe lifte side / ¶ Vryn if hit be white *and* fomeþ ∴ hit
betokeneþ mor*e* harme i*n* þe lifte side ∴ þen in þe riȝt side . for þe lifte
side is more colde þen þe riȝte side . ¶ Vryn þ*at* is þinne *and* pale *and*
also cleer ∴ betokeneþ acetosu*m* fleuma / If þe cercle of þe vryn be not
resti*n*g but tre*m*blyng ∴ hit betokeneþ re*n*nyng of fleume {f. 33v} *and* of
oþer humour*e*s fro þe hede . by þe necke to neþer p*ar*ties / ¶ Vryn þicke
and mylky *and* litil i*n* qua*n*tite *and* fatte byneþe wi*th* shalis ∴ betokeneþ
þe stone / *and* if þe vry*n* be wi*th*oute shalis *and* be þicke *and* mylky
and litil i*n* qua*n*tite ∴ hit signifieþ þe fluxe i*n* þe wombe / Vryn þicke
and mylky *and* haþ meny dropes i*n* þe ou*er* p*ar*ties ∴ signifieþ þe goute
i*n* membris of þe body . ¶ Vryn þ*at* is pale bineþe i*n* men ∴ betokeneþ
harme i*n* þe reynes Vri*n* in whiche litil gobettis appere*n* . if hit be litil
and trobelid {f. 34r} hit signifieþ bre*n*nyng of a veyne aboute þe reynes
in þe bladd*er* / ¶ Vryn in whiche quitoure appereþ i*n* þe grou*n*de of
þe vessel ∴ betokeneþ roti*n*g of þe bladd*er* . or elli*s* a posteme / And if
þer appere quitoure þoroughe alle þe vry*n* ∴ hit betokeneþ roti*n*g of al
þe body / Vryn i*n* whiche frustis appere*n* litil *and* brode ∴ hit signifieþ
excoriaciou*n* of þe bladd*er* / Vryn motty ∴ signifieþ by longe tyme þe
stone i*n* þe reynes / ¶ Vryn þ*at* is white wiþouten feuer boþe i*n* man *and*
wo*m*man oþer{f. 34v}while hit signifieþ harme i*n* þe reynes . *and* oþer-
while i*n* wo*m*men hit signifieþ i*m*pregnaciou*n* . *and* cesyng of childe
berynge / ¶ Vryn of he*m* þat be*n* wi*th* childe / If þey oon moneþe or
two or iij*e* florisshe so ∴ þeyr vry*n* shal be ful cleer . *and* hit shal haue a
white ypostasy i*n* þe grou*n*de / And if þey haue four*e* moneþes þe vryn
shal be cler*e* . *and* haue a white ypostasi *and* a þicke i*n* þe grou*n*de . Hit
was wo*n*te an ymage to apper*e* in þe glasen vessel / If þilke vri*n* be of
a wo*m*man ∴ hit signifieþ þe co*n*cepciou*n* to be made . *and* {f. 35r} if þe
ymage of hi*m* þat shewiþ appereþ i*n* þe vrin of a seke man ∴ hit signifieþ
feuers i*n*terpolatas . or elli*s* sekenes of þe lyuer . or drawyng of lengþe
of þe sekenes / ¶ Vryn fomy ∴ signifieþ ventosite of þe stomake i*n* wom-
me*n* . or hete fro*m* þe nauyl to þe þrote *and* grete dryness *and* þurste /
Vryn of a meyde shal be as þe iuse of an orynge appel . wher*e* vri*n* liuida
and ful cler*e* declareþ þe meyde stedfaste / Vrin trouble i*n* þe whiche
sede appereþ i*n* þe grou*n*de ∴ hit signifieþ þe wo*m*man to be wi*th* a man
{f. 35v} late / Vryn of a wo*m*man þicke ∴ declareþ hir to be corrupte . þe
foreseide vri*n* namely tr*o*bul i*n* whiche sede appereþ i*n* þe grou*n*de of
þe vessel / For if suche vrin be i*n* a ma*n* ∴ hit declareþ hi*m* to haue delite
wi*th* a wo*m*man / Vryn of a wo*m*man þat is me*n*struate makeþ a blody

vryn / If þis blode be cruddid in a womman ː she shal seme with childe
til hit be dissolu/e\d . as it is shewid in Antidoda .

Here endeþ þe tretise of þe cercles of vryns with her significacions
. and also also þe propirtes {f. 36r} of vryns . and /þe\ ouer passing
excesse of hem . and nowe foloweþ remedy and medysyn for meny of
hem þat ben rehersid .

MEdisyn for colour as camelle flesshe / Take þe croppe of sauge . and
drinke trisandala . and auente þe in þe leggis / Or ellis take þe ynner
barke of eldryn tree and grynde hit with ale and clense hit . and drinke
hit seuene sponeful at ones and vse hit / al liuida ¶ Plumbea vrina .
For þis . take scamonie and do hit in a pere and roste hit and vse hit /
Also make a poudre of þe rotis of pyony and persil rotis and þe barke
of an {f. 36v} oke and vse hit daily til þu be hole / ¶ Pallida vrina . For
þis . take mirabolane . indi . aloes . epatice . cene . sugur . of alle þes a
dramme and make a poudre of hem and vse in þy potage or in drinke /
¶ Viridis vrina . For þis . take gynger . canel or synamon and sene . and
tempere hem with clarified hony . and vse þis at morwe and at euen .
¶ Inopos vrina . For þis . take osemounde . saueyn . and gromel . and
boyle hem in white wyne and a litil hony and streine it {f. 37r} and vse
þis drinke erly and late / ¶ Subpallida vrina . For þis . take poudre of
grete toonecrasses sede . and vse hem in þy potage . ¶ Rubicunda vrina .
For þis . take vynegre . mustarde and boyle hem togedir . þen take talwe
as moche as a notte and do þerto . and ete þis when þe sekenes takeþ þe
/ vse also dyacameron and trisandala . ¶ Subcitrina vrina . For þis . take
polipodium . anes . alloe . epatice . meddele hem with sugre . and make
a poudre of þes ː and vse in þy potage . {f. 37v} ¶ Subrufa vrina . For þis
. take poudre of elenacampana . turmentille medle hem with hony clarified and boyle hem togedre and make þerof a confeccioun and use hit
day by dai / al subrubia . ¶ Subrubicunda vrina . For þis . / vse þe same
medisyn þat longeþe to subrufa . as it is nexte afore . ¶ Rubea vrina .
For þis . take triacle and boyle hit in þe iuse or water of moleyne and
vse hit daily / Also take cassiafistula . tamarindes and triasandali and
medle hem togedir and vse þe medisyn daily / {f. 39r} ¶ Citrina vrina .
For þis . take fyges . licoris . ysope . elenacampana . horehonde . yliche
moche . boyle hem in a galoun of water into þe halfe be wastid . and
vse þis drinke . at euen and at morwe vij sponful warme . ¶ Subrubea
vrina . For þis take water crasses and grynde hem smale and boile hem
in wyne . and vse it / ¶ Rufa vrina . For þis take hony and seþe hit til hit
be harde and do þerto poudir of sene and gynger . and make a plaster
of dewete and of wyne / If it be þe flores ley it on þe nauyl . {f. 39v} ¶

Kaynos vrina . For þis . take þe bone of an hertis herbe *and* make þerof /a\ poudir *and* medle hit w*ith* diacameron . *and* vse þis poudir /in\ þy potage or ellis i*n* þy dri*n*ke . ¶ Lactea vri*n*a . For þis . take þe sede of white popy *and* bray he*m* smale *and* putte he*m* i*n* letuse wat*er* or i*n* þe iuse þerof . *and* medle he*m* toged*er and* drinke þat licoure . *and* vse hit . And anoynte þy te*m*plis w*ith* þis onyment made of henbane . letues . popi *and* mandrake . *and* vse hit daily . ¶ Subuiridis vri*n*a . For þis . {f. 4or} lete þe seke blede vnd*er* þe ancle . or i*n* þe veyne of þe arme . *and* lete hi*m* take a pynte of white wyne . *and* þeryn boyle a dra*m*me of alloes *and* anoþ*er* of epatice *and* drinke of þat a sponeful /at\ morowe and anoþ*er* at eue*n* . first *and* last / ¶ Alba vri*n*a . For þis . take saxifrage . gromel . persile . *and* sage . yliche q*u*antite *and* boyle he*m* i*n* gode stale ale . *and* vse þat dri*n*ke on þe morowe *and* at eue*n* . and also make of þes herbes a poudir *and* vse hit daily i*n* þy potage . ¶ Nigra vri*n*a . For þis . dri*n*ke {f. 4ov} þe iuse of celidon *and* of moleine *and* triacle w*ith* wyne . *and* dri*n*ke hit at morwe *and* at eue*n* . ¶ Glauca vri*n*a . For þis take þe iuse of tansy . þe /ribbe\ worte *and* boyle he*m* i*n* /white\ wyne w*ith* a litil hony *and* vse hit <u>And þus þis practif of fisike endeþ</u> /

¶ Of eu*er*y sekenes thre tymes þer be þat muste be obs*er*ued *and* tendrid . þat is to wite . þe begy*n*nyng . þe state *and* þe ending / If a ma*n* sekele of þe axes *and* be i*n* þe begy*n*nyng {f. 41r} þerof ∴ take for hi*m* p*er*celly *and* fenel . an handful of eche . *and* seþe he*m* i*n* a galou*n* of welle wat*er* vntil halfe be almoste wat*er*i . þen take halfe an handful of violettis *and* putte þerto . *and* let/t\e al /þis\ seþe til hit be i*n*corpor- ate *and* of oon streng þe . þen streyne hit þoroughe a lyne*n* cloþe *and* close hit i*n* a close vessel . *and* vse þis dri*n*ke fyue daies co*n*tynuelli vij spoonful at morwe *and* at eue*n* as moche luke warme . *and* sanab*er*is ∴ or su*m*what more of almondis . *and* a gode handful of violett*es* ∴. {f. 41v} ¶ For hi*m* þat is i*n* þe axes i*n* state . Take sage . meyntis . foþeþistil . *and* lady þistil *and* sorel yliche moche . *and* wasshe he*m* clene *and* bray he*m* i*n* a mort*er and* take þe iuse of he*m and* putte i*n* a potel of mylke . þen sette hit ou*er* þe fire *and* lete hit seþe til þe mylke may take þe v*er*tu of herbes . þen take a q*u*arte of gode stale ale *and* put þer to . or þre peynt*es* if hit so nede . *and* make a possette *and* vse þe dri*n*ke ix daies i*n* al dryness *and* hetis ny3t *and* day as ofte as þu wilt . *and* þu shalt be hole by þe g*ra*ce of god . {f. 42r} ¶ For hi*m* þat is t*ra*uelid w*ith* þe feuers daily or oþ*er* . eiþ*er* day . Take camylmelle *and* stampe hit . þen streyne oute þe iuse þorough a ca*n*ues . /þen\ take þat *and* sette /it\ ou*er* þe fire *and* lette hit seþe . *and* alwey scome awey þe fome til hit be clere . *and* if þu wilt þu may put a q*ua*ntite of sugur

þerto to make hit þe more liking *and* when /it\ is clere . take hit doune
and lette hit kele . þen put hit *in* a close vessel . *and* vse þe drinke ix
daies . vj or vij sponful at ones *in* þe mornyng *and* in þe euenyng luke
warme . And þe þenke camelmyl ouerbitter ⁖ þu may take sorel . *in* þe
selfe wise . {f. 42v} ¶ For to swage *and* abate þe malice of þe hote axes /
Take mandrake . sorel . syngrene *and* dauntlyoun yliche moche . *and*
seþe he*m* in barly mele *and* vynegre *and* make of þis a plaster . *and* ley
hit to þe sid*es* of þe seke *and* to h*is* breste *and* to þe stomake *and* to þe
powes of þe hand*es* and of þe fete *and* he shal be be hole *in* short ty*me*
¶ For hi*m* þat pisseþ blode / Take wilde sage . saxifrage . *percely yliche*
moche *and* stampe he*m* . *and* put þe iuse *in* a potel of mylke *and* lette hit
seþe a while . þen streyne hit . *and* vse þe drinke ¶ For dy*m*nes of yen .
take cen{f. 43r} tuary *and* planteyn yliche moche . seþe he*m* in white
wyne *and* put a litil qua*n*tite of pip*er* þerto . þen streyne al þorough a
clene cloþe *and* drinke þis medisyn luke warme last whe*n* þu goest to þy
bedde / ¶ For þe coughe / Take elemini fenel sede . longe pip*er* . com*myn*
. *and* hony as sufficeþ . Of elemini take . *dragme* . 1 . 3 . handful of fenel
sede *and* longe pip*er* an*a* . *dragme* vj . of com*myn* halfe an vnce . *and*
seþe al in a qua*n*tite of hony as nedeþ *and* vse þe drinke . first *and* laste /
¶ Electuary for þe coughe / Take cynamu*n* . spice . gyng*er* . {f. 43v}
galangal . aneys . longe pip*er* . dra/ga\gante . an*a* . *dragme semis* . þe
kernel of pyne clene clensid . *dragme* . drie figes . *dragme* ij . *and* clarified hony as nedeþ *and* make electuari *and* vse hit ¶ Sargarismus . for
*p*urgyng of þe hede / Take mustard staffeacre . pellet*er* . cokil . com*fery*
spiconarde . hony . vinegre . or white wyne menge al toged*er* *and* take
ij° sponful þerof *and* holde *in* þy mouþe *and* rense hit wel þerwith . vntil
þe fleume descende . þen spet oute þat *and* take more . so ofte . til þu be
esid ¶ For a collerike ma*n* þat is dissesid w*ith* þe axes þat is caused of
{f. 44r} brenny*ng* coler *and* hete . *and* also for to ease þe grete dryness
þat he haþ by þis sekenes / Take borage . violett*es* . sorel . letwis . endif
. souþeþistil . stra/u\bery leues . mary gold*es* . þe tendrons of vynes .
dauntlyon . pety morel . malowis . sengryn . *p*ersely . langedebef . an
handful of eche w*ith* þre or iiij*e* stick*es* of likeris ybrusid . to poud*er* .
and al yput *in* a galou*n* of welle wat*er* *and* yconsumed *and* sode*n* vntil
halfe be wastid . þen take hit doune *and* streyne hit *and* put hit *in* a glas
. or *in* a cle*n*e erþen pot wel closid . *and* vse þerof at morwe *and* at eue*n*
vj or {f. 44v} vij sponful luke warme *and* sanab/is\ Gargarismus . for þe
hede þat is stoppid w*ith* reugme *and* viscous fleume .

{f. 45r} ¶ Ther be*n* iiij ages *in* whiche eu*er*y humoure haþ h*is*
duraciou*n* to her likenes . þat is childehode . bachelerhode . manhode .

and fadirhode / Childehode is fro þe begynnyng of birþe into xv ȝere /
bachelerhode . fro xv /ȝere\ vnto xxx . ȝere / manhode fro xxx ȝere vnto
lx ȝere / faderhode *and* olde age fro lx ȝere vnto þe ende of man is lyfe
/ ¶ And þer ben iiij cesons in þe ȝere apriped to þe foure complexions
of men / ver . sommer . haruest *and* wynter / Ver . is hote *and* moyst /
sommer is hote *and* drye / haruest is colde *and* drye / wynter is colde
and moist / ¶ Collerike men ben wel in vere . *and* yuel in sommer / *and*
wel in haruest *and* in wynter beste at ease / Sanguyne folke ben ywel
in ver . *and* better in sommer *and* haruest *and* wynter best at ease /
Fleumatike folke ben wel in ver in haruest best *and* sommer best . *and*
worste in wynter / Malencolious folke ben best in ver *and* somer .
{f. 45v} *and* worste in haruest . *and* wynter is not gode / Also þer ben
iiij wyndes . eest wynde is moyst *and* hote / souþe wynde is hote *and*
drye / west wynde is colde *and* moyst / Norþe wynde is colde *and* drie /
And þes ben þe iiij parties of þe worlde . eest . west . souþe *and* norþe /
¶ Collerike folke ben wel while þe sonne *and* þe wynde ben eest . west
. or norþe / *and* þey ben yuel . while þe sonne *and* þe wynde ben souþe
/ for þat is her quarter / Sanguyne folke ben yuel when þe sonne *and*
þe wynde ben eest . for þat is þeir quarter . *and* þey ben wel when þe
sonne *and* þe wynde ben souþe . west or norþe / Fleumatike folke ben
wel when þe sonne *and* þe wynde ben eest . souþe or norþe / *and* þei
ben werste when þe sonne *and* þe wynde ben west /for þat is þeir quar-
ter\ / Malencolious folke ben werst when þe sonne *and* þe wynde ben
norþe {f. 46r} *and* þey ben wel when sonne *and* þe wynde ben souþe .
est . *and* west / souþe is þeir quarter / Nowe folweþ þe reignyng of þe
iiijᵉ humours in euery man or womman . ¶ Fro þe iij of þe clocke after
mydde nyȝt vntil ix of þe clocke before no/u\ne . regneþ sanguyne / *and*
from ix of þe clocke afore none vntil þre after no/u\ne . regneþ coler-
ike / *and* from þre of /þe\ clocke after noune vntil ix before mydnyȝt .
regneþ fleumatike / *and* from ix of þe clocke before mydnyȝt vntil iij
. after mydnyȝt . regneþ malencoly / And euery man in þe tyme of þat
humoure þat is most regnyng in him / *and* in þe tyme . þat his humour
regneþ . is most greued ∴ ¶ For þe morfu . wasshe al þy body with
water þat stampid garleke is soden yn . *and* þy body is dried *and* clene
. rubbe al þe morfu with garlike *and* affadile stampid togeder . *and* vse
it so a while *and* drinke federfoy . eldren fumetory *and* rede docke rotes
made in {f. 46v} tysane . *and* euery morwe erly drinke a gode draugte .
and vse þis medisyn ix daies *and* þu shalt be clene of þe morfu with yn
and wiþoute . if þe medisin be wel vsid ¶ For þe iavndise take greynes
clowes mases galenga notemygges of eueryche of þes an halfe peny

worþe / of ysope of hertistonge of celidon ylichemoche *and* seþe al i*n* þre quartis of white wyne vnto þre pynt*es* . *and* vse þ*is* medisyn warme at morwe /*and*\ at euen . vj or vij sponeful at ones.

Appendix 1

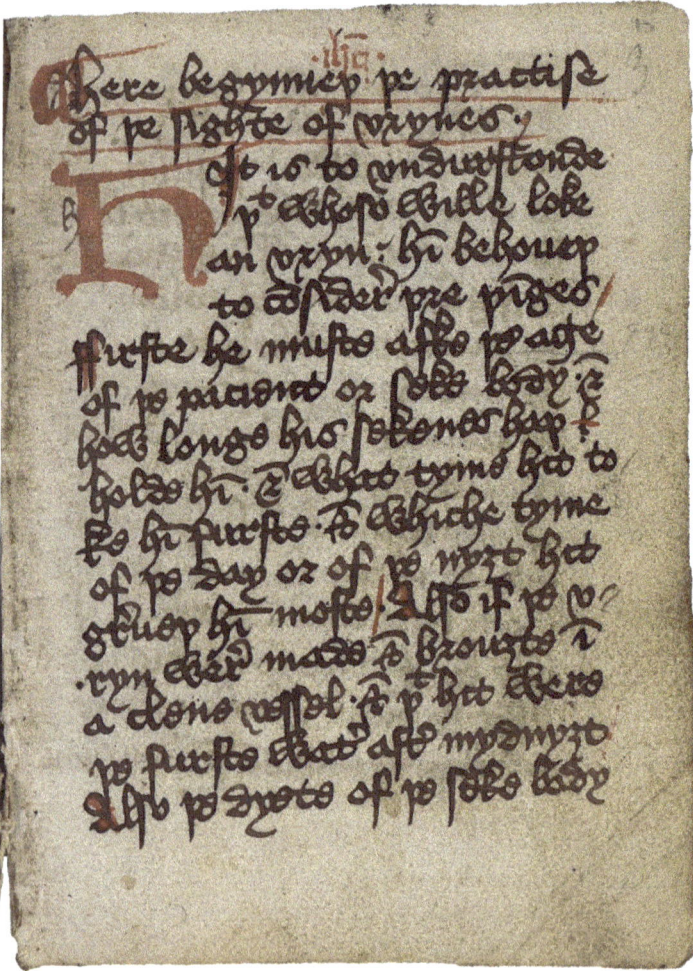

Figure 2. MS Wellcome 537, f. 15r.
© Wellcome Library, London, as the owner of the manuscript.

References

Calle Martín, J. & Miranda García, A. (2011). From the manuscript to the screen: Implementing electronic editions of mediaeval handwritten material. *Studia Anglica Posnaniensia* 46:3, 3–20.

Calle Martín, J. & Miranda García, A. (2012). *The Middle English Version of De Viribus Herbarum (GUL MS Hunter 497, ff. 1r-92r)*. Bern – Berlin – Bruxelles – Franfurt – New York – Oxford – Wien: Peter Lang.

Calle Martín, J. (2012). A late middle English version of *The Doom of Urines* in Oxford, MS Rawlinson C. 81, ff. 6r-12v. *Analecta Malacitana* 35:1–2, 243–273.

Clemens, R. & Graham, T. (2007). *Introduction to Manuscript Studies*. Ithaca and London: Cornell University Press.

Denholm-Young, N. (1954). *Handwriting in England and Wales*. Cardiff: University of Wales Press.

Derolez, A. (2003). *The Palaeography of Gothic Manuscript Books. From the Twelfth to the Early Sixteenth Century*. Cambridge: Cambridge University Press.

Hector, L.C. (1966). *The Handwriting of English Documents*. London: Edward Arnold.

Keiser, G.R. (1998). *A Manual of the Writings in Middle English 1050–1500. Volume X. Works of Science and Information*. New Haven, Connecticut: The Connecticut Academy of Arts and Sciences.

Lewis, Robert E., Kurath, H., Sherman, M.K. & Reidy, J. (eds) (1952–2001). *Middle English Dictionary*. Ann Arbour: University of Michigan Press. (Electronic dictionary: <http://quod.lib.umich.edu/m/med/lookup.html>).

Moorat, Samuel A.J. (1962). *Catalogue of Western Manuscripts on Medicine and Science in the Wellcome Historical Medical Library. Vol. I. Manuscripts Written before 1650 AD*. London: Publications of the Wellcome Historical Medical Library.

Moreno-Olalla, D. and Miranda-García, A. (2009). An annotated corpus of middle English scientific prose: aims and features. J.E. Díaz Vera and R. Caballero (eds) *Textual Healing: Studies in Medieval English Medical, Scientific and Technical Texts* (123–140). Bern – Berlin – Bruxelles – Frankfurt – New York – Oxford – Wien: Peter Lang.

Petti, A.G. (1977). *English Literary Hands from Chaucer to Dryden*. Cambridge, Mass: Harvard University Press.

Roberts, J. (2005). *Guide to Scripts Used in English Writings up to 1500*. London: The British Library.

———. (2005). The Twenty Jordan Series: an illustrated middle English uroscopy text. *ANQ: A Quarterly Journal of Short Articles, Notes and Reviews* 18:3, 40–64.

Tavormina, M.T. (2009). Practice, theory and authority in a middle English medical text: 'Barton's urines which he treated at Tilney'. *Origins of Nephrology* 22, S33–S41.

Voigts, L.E. & Kurtz, P.D. (2000). *Scientific and Medical Writings in Old and Middle English. An Electronic Reference.* Ann Arbor: Michigan University Press.

4 Is Plant Species Identification Possible in Middle English Herbals?

David Moreno Olalla
Universidad de Málaga

Brother Cadfael tucked up his habit and ran for the shelter of the cloister, there to shake off the water from his sleeves and cowl, and make himself comfortable to continue his reading in the scriptorium. Within minutes he was absorbed in the problem of whether the 'dittanders' of Aelfric was, or was not, the same as his own 'dittany'.

Ellis Peters, *The Devil's Novice* (1983), Chapter 1.

The problem

The transmission of the classical textual corpus during the Middle Ages was complicated because the oldest volumes that served as exemplars for the medieval manuscripts were copied and recopied at monasteries, universities and private scriptoria. The sad result was that many MSS present gibberish fragments due to the many scribal mistakes and hypercorrections that accumulated in them during the several copying processes. This is of course an academic truism, which we may call the *universal* cause of error as it was at work in virtually every medieval textual tradition regardless of its actual subject. But in the case of texts dealing with the Natural Sciences, and very acutely in pharmacological treatises, a second, *particular* cause should also be taken into account. This has to do with the fact that Western phytography, i.e. plant description, was still in its infancy, having receded rather than proceeded since Graeco-Roman times. In fact the opinions held by the likes of Dioscorides or Pliny the Elder in their fundamental treatises

How to cite this book chapter:
Moreno Olalla, D. 2015. Is Plant Species Identification Possible in Middle English Herbals? In: Shaw, P., Erman, B., Melchers, G. and Sundkvist, P. (eds) *From Clerks to Corpora: essays on the English language yesterday and today*. Pp. 53–70. Stockholm: Stockholm University Press. DOI: http://dx.doi.org/10.16993/bab.d License: CC-BY.

(*De materia medica* and *Naturalis historia*)[1] were still taken as law without much ado fifteen centuries after they were first put down in writing.

This *argumentum ab auctoritate* moved in two directions. On the one hand, it seems to have hampered any real development in botanical field-work, and so the descriptions appearing in medieval treatises remained vague. On the other hand, the desire to interpret the Classical texts correctly led the medieval scribes to collect all possible synonyms from all accessible sources, forgetting that the same species may/will be known under different names in different places and oppositely that different species may be designated with the same name,[2] which in practice meant the sloppy application of syllogisms ('A is B and B is C, therefore A is C;' in relation to this, see Moreno Olalla 2013a: 398–399). This (mis)treatment of plant-names is behind the well-known problem that it is very difficult sometimes to be certain as to the actual species being mentioned in a medieval text: more often than not, at least two or three different species are theoretically possible. Of course the problem is most acutely felt with laconical texts such as synonyma, which seldom provide a physical descriptions of the plants, but it can also usually be detected in more verbose texts such as receptaria and even medical herbals.

In the particular case of medical and botanical treatises composed in Atlantic countries such as England, the above confusion became worse, since those species that did not grow in the Mediterranean milieu were ascribed as a matter of course to plant-names already used by the Greeks and Romans. The Middle English plant-name and the Latin synonym therefore do not necessarily tally. This last hindrance is still very well alive in Contemporary English and examples abound: think for instance of the *acacia*, which according to the Classical evidence (*MM* i 101; *NH* xxiv 109) probably meant a species of the genus *Acacia* Willd. (so García Valdés 1998: 201, fn. 201), or perhaps some *Mimosa* spp. (André 1956: *s. v.*; Simpson & Weiner 1989: *s. v.* acacia[1]), but which is

---

[1] These will be indicated respectively as *MM* and *NH* henceforward. I ignore the information from Theophrastus's Περὶ φυτικῶν ἱστοριῶν as this work was virtually unavailable to Western scholars until its 1483 translation into Latin (*De historia et causis plantarum*). Note that Dioscorides, just like Galen, was in fact best known in Western Europe through Latin translations and the works of epigones, but for the sake of convenience his work will be here quoted in the original Greek.

[2] Prior 1863: xx mentions the well-known case of the Bluebell, which refers to *Hyacinthoides non-scripta* L. in England and to *Campanula rotundifolia* L. in Scotland—and, one may add, to sundry species in the US (*Mertensia virginica* (L.) Pers. ex Link, *Eustoma russellianum* Salisb., *Phacelia campanularia* A. Gray, *inter alia*), the Caribbean (*Clitoria ternatea* L.) or Australia (*Wahlenbergia gloriosa* Lothian).

commonly understood in English today as the *Robinia pseudacacia* L., a species brought from the New World (Prior 1863: 1).

The outcome of all these factors is that we cannot always know for a fact which plants are *really* being treated by the writer of a Middle English treatise: frequently a very broad identification by genus is the nearest we can get, while in some cases we must rest content if we can identify the family to which some obscure plant-name refers. But a more precise identification by species is occasionally possible. In the following pages I intend to (*a*) comment on problems, both medieval and contemporary, that are often encountered in connection with plant identification, (*b*) show how the meanings usually given to plant-names in dictionaries, even in the most scholarly ones such as the *Middle English Dictionary* (*MED*), are sometimes vitiated because of those very problems and do not withstand a careful textual analysis, and hence the species provided by general lexicographical works should never be accepted at face value, and (*c*) suggest that despite all odds, it is sometimes possible to identify the species meant by the writer—or, at least, to provide very educated guesses.

I will draw my examples from *Lelamour's Herbal* (*LH* hencefor-ward). This is a medicinal collection of 214 plant species,[3] alphabetically arranged by their English names and kept in London, British Library, Sloane MS 5, ff. 13ra–57ra (*S* for short). Although in its *explicit* the piece purports to be a Middle English translation of Macer Floridus's *De Viribus Herbarum* made in 1373 by an otherwise unknown Hereford schoolmaster called John Lelamour, the version preserved in *S* was actu-ally composed in the 1460s near or in London and it is best described as an assortment of entries drawn from different ME traditions.[4] It would be a moot question even to decide whether Lelamour translated some entries himself: the *Rue Herbal* and *Agnus Castus*, the two main detec-ted sources for *LH*, were already in English in MSS older than *S*.[5] Apart from the substantial number of entries, which makes it one of the most

---

[3] It would be more accurate to say that there are 214 entries but no more than 211 species, for at least three of them were treated twice (Moreno Olalla 2007: 120).

[4] The only 14th-century piece in the MS is a brief botanical trilinguale (ff. 4r–12v), which was bound together with the rest of the volume at a later date: the wear and tear and the dirt on ff. 4r and 13r suggest that these pages were left uncovered for quite a long time. On f. 3r–v there is a late 13th-century medical fragment in Latin on urines.

[5] See Moreno Olalla 2007: 122; 2013b: 948 about the *Rue Herbal*. *Agnus Castus* was edited in Brodin 1950.

important herbals in Middle English (Hunt 1989: ix), *LH* is actually quite an average work; as is usually the case with vernacular herbals, there are no illustrations, and whenever the text provides a physical description of the species, this is by no means detailed. Broad remarks on the size and colour of leaves and flowers, and sometimes the presence of bulbs and seeds, is about all one can wish to find there. A detailed comment on the usual habitat of the species is the exception and not the rule.

I will reference my quotations from this source using a folio/line system, since *LH* remains unpublished even though it has been known since the late 17th century and used as a source text since the 1840s at least.[6] It has been the subject of two theses as well. The first of them was an M.A. completed in the late thirties (Whytlaw-Gray 1938), which was used by the editors of the *MED*. Whytlaw-Gray's editorial and lexicographical approach to the text was considered dated and inaccurate at times, and so a fresh edition, following more modern criteria, was included as part of a Ph.D. dissertation a few years ago (Moreno Olalla 2002).

Scribes behaving badly: *Carthnote*

I would like to begin with perhaps the most simple form of distortion: scribal mistakes and overzealousness through the ages and their modern consequences. On f. 20va/6–19, in the section of the herbal for plant-names beginning with the letter ‹C›, we read the following:

Cidanum

Carthnote, that is an erbe that haþe levis like to fenell and wiþ flouris and smale stalkys. He growiþ in wodis, also in medis. The vertu of this erbe is þis: that, and he be stampid *and* laid to a sore, he will feche a-wey all dede fleshe and helpiþe renewe the quyck fleshe. Also stampe this erbe and put hi*m* to þat place þat lackiþ here: he shall restore hit a-gayne w*ith*-in schorte tyme of plast*er* layeng.

According to *MED* (Kurath *et al.* 1954–2001: *s. v.*), *carthnote* is a *hapax legomenon* vaguely defined there as '[s]ome medicinal plant'. It is certainly possible to go further than that just by reading the whole entry: the text itself provides us with several clear clues, beginning with

---

[6] Sloane 5 was catalogued already in Bernard 1697: ii.251. To my knowledge, *LH* was first quoted in Halliwell-Phillipps 1889: i.xx. The excerpt chosen was the entry *Mowsere*, i.e. Mouse-ear (*Hieracium pilosella* L.). The MS was also perused by contributors to the *NED/OED*, as witnessed by several quotations contained therein (see Moreno Olalla 2007: 119 for a list of entries).

the accompanying Latin heading. *Cidanum* is not recorded in any text or glossary I know of, but *Cidamum* is (the faulty reading in *S* can be easily explained as a scribal misreading/mispelling of the original cluster of minims). This word appears in another important medical herbal, *Agnus Castus* (*AC* henceforward), which offers almost a twin entry of *S*, although it also provides a collection of synonyms that is missing in *LH*: 'dilnote or slyte or haylwourth' (Brodin 1950: 216).

The lists of synonyms provided in *AC* and other sources such as *Alphita* (see next paragraph) make it clear that *cidamum* must be taken as a mistake for **Ciclamen*, while *carthnote* is obviously another error, for **earthnote* this time (cf. *AC corhnote* < OE *eorðnut*) due to the Lombardic initial ‹E› in the exemplar, which probably had a round shape. *Cyclamen* was used to refer to the name-sake genus and especially to the Sow-bread (*C. purpurascens* Mill.), and indeed both virtues of *carthnote* mentioned in *S* (against wounds and alopecia) are also reflected in Dioscorides's account of the Sow-bread (*MM* ii 164).

Still, there is an important detail in the English text that seems to gainsay this identification: according to Dioscorides 'the cyclamen has leaves similar to those of ivy' (κυκλάμινος φύλλα ἔχει ὄνομα κισσῷ)[7] while the author of *LH* wrote that '[e]arthnote [...] haþe levis like to fenell'. The connection between both texts can, nevertheless, be maintained. Cf. the following definition from *Alphita*: '[c]iclamen uel ciclamum, sive citeranum, panis porcinus, malum terre idem. angl. dilnote' (Mowat 1887: 39). The synonym *panis porcinus* restitutes the lost link between both texts again, cf. '[p]anis porcinus, ciclamen, malum terre idem. a[nglic]e dilnote uel erthenote' (Mowat 1887: 134). The identification of *erthenote* with *cyclamen* is assured as well by the translation of the original L. *succum ciclaminis* as 'þe Iuse of erþenote' in the *Cyrurgie of Guy de Chauliac* (taken from Kurath *et al.* 1954–2001: *s. v. ērthe*).

Yet another problem remains, not only in *LH* but in many medieval texts including *Alphita* or *AC*. OE *eorþnut* did not refer to the Sowbread, but was an umbelliferous species, identified as some *Bunium* sp., especially the Earth-chestnut (*B. ferulaceum* Sibth. & Sm.), or else the Pig-nut (*Conopodium majus* (Gouan) Loret = *B. flexuosum* Stokes). This is confirmed by the explicit mention of the similarity of this species with dill and the resemblance of its leaves to those of fennel. I think that the confusion between both plants ultimately lies in a mistaken

---

[7] Translations from Greek are my own.

reading in *NH* xx 21, where Pliny confused the Greek plant-name βουνιάς (L. *napus* = OE *næp*) with βούνιον (L. *bunium* = OE *eorþnut*; see André 1956: *s. v.* nāpus). *Napus*, on the other hand, was also called *rapum* in some Post-Classical sources; and finally, *rapum* was also a name for *cyclamen* (*vid*. André 1956: s. vv. cyclam*i*–nos, nāpus, rāpum). The tiresome scribal thirst for synonyms, which is so frequently encountered in medieval glossaries, equated both plants even though they were clearly distinguished in the Classical literature. The misidentification seems to have passed unnoticed to scribes perhaps because all those plants present a big edible bulb which swine craved after.[8]

As a short excursus, I would like to highlight here that misreadings are not peculiar to medieval scribes only, but are shared by modern researchers and unsuspectingly transmitted by serious scholarly works sometimes. Drawing from *LH*, *MED* includes an entry *ara-wŏrt*, which is laconically defined as '[a] Flowering plant of some kind', and even given a tentative etymology: '[c]p. *wŏrt* plant, & *?arwe* arrow'. The word is presented as a *hapax* taken from the entry *Pes columbe* (probably, the Soft Cranesbill, *Geranium molle* L.) in *LH*: 'Coluyr-fote is an herbe, his levis beþ like to araworte'. This should in fact be put down as a ghost entry, for it is due to a faulty reading by Whytlaw-Gray that crept into the dictionary. The manuscript actually reads ‹Maworte›, i.e. some Mallows (*Malva* sp.). Comparison of the flowers of the Cranesbill with those of the Mallows was traditional: it is used already in *MM* iii, 116: καλεῖται δὲ ὑπ' ἐνίων καὶ ἕτερον γεράνιον, ἔχον [...] φύλλα μολόχῃ ἐμφερῆ 'Some call another species "Cranesbill", one that has [...] leaves like those of the Mallows'.

---

[8] This also explains why several fungi of the genus *Tuber* L. (i.e. the truffles), the arachis, etc. were also called 'earth-nut'. Already in *NH* xxv 114, *rāpum, tūber* and cyclamīnos are said to be similar plants, providing with an early instance of quasi-confusion between them. This mistake was transmitted to the late OE *Durham Glossary of the names of worts*, which seems to be the first instance in English where cyclaminos is equated with some plant different from the Sow-bread: 'Cyclaminos, Eortheppel, slite, attorlathe' (Cockayne 1864–1866: iii-301). Judging from the English names (see Bosworth & Toller 1898: *s. v.* átorláþe), the Cyclamen was apparently confused here with the Mandrake. Note that the Mandrake was called *malum terrae* (André 1956: *s. v.* mandragoras), but this name was also applied to the *Cyclamen* sp. (André 1956: *s. v.* cyclamīnos), thus providing a bridge between both plants: *cyclamen* ‹---› *malum terrae* ‹---› *mandragoras*.

Habits die hard: *Horse-þistill*

Another common mistake in modern works is to accept uncritically the identification of a ME plant-name suggested traditionally or on the basis of a single scholarly work, even though the context in another treatise may be against that equation. On f. 22vb/28–23ra/18, for example, we can read the following:

Endiuia
Endyue ys an erbe that som men calliþ horse-þistill. Þis erbe haþe prykkys with-oute. Þe lefe ar longe and when he is brokyn he dropiþ mylke, and he haþe a litell yelow flour and his sede blawiþ a-waye with þe wynde as doþe dent de lyon. The vertu of him is þis: take þe juis þere-of and medill hit with hote water and drynke hit, and þat heliþ þe stoppinge of þe mylte and þe lyuer. Also þis erbe is gode y-dronke for þe jaundys and for þe feuer tercian and for þe hote postem. Also þis erbe a-swagith þe grete hete of þe lyuer and of þe stomake, for he is colde *and* moiste.

In Present-day English, *Endive* is a common name for two species of Chicory, a family of Compositae (*Cichorium* spp.): *C. intybus* L., indigenous to Europe, and *C. endivia* L., which was imported from China as early as the 16th century. Obviously only the former could fit in here; but the description does not fit at all: *C. intybus* bears bright blue flowers,[9] and its leaves do not have 'pricks', as stated in the text.

The editor of *AC* (Brodin 1950: 221), a text which shares this entry with *LH*, was evidently aware of the impossibility of accepting a *Cichorium* species, so in the accompanying glossary he suggested, perhaps on account of the yellow flowers, that the plant intended here might be some wild lettuce, *Lactuca virosa* L. or else *L. scariola* L. This identification was accepted by *MED*, where the text of *LH* is actually quoted (Kurath *et al.* 1954–2001: *s. v.* thistle n., sense *b*). Still, this identification should be rejected since the general look of these species is not reminiscent of a thistle at all, see Figure 1 for details.[10]

Again, reading closely the physical description provided in the actual ME text—which is uncharacteristically detailed—will not go unrewarded. The comparison of this species with a thistle, implicit in the ME designation and explicit in the mention of a dandelion, and the colour

---

[9] 'Blue daisy', 'blue dandelion', 'blue-sailors' are modern synonyms for this species.
[10] The engravings used in this chapter were taken from Bauhin 1598, and kindly provided by the Missouri Botanical Garden.

Figure 1. Θρίδαξ ἀγρία–*Lactuca sylvestris* (after Bauhin 1598: 400).

of the flowers make me think that the plant actually intended here may well be some *Helminthotheca* sp., a genus akin to *Cichorium* that normally displays yellow flowers. There is one species in particular of this genus, the Bristly Ox-tongue (*Helminthotheca echioides* (L.) Holub) that fulfills the physical description in *LH* quite well. Its leaves and bracts are noticeably covered with white bristles that very much resemble small 'prikkys', just like any other Liguliflorate Composite this species yields a white latex when the stem is broken ('when he is brokyn he dropiþ mylke'), and its pappused achenes are easily blown away with the wind ('his sede blawiþ a-waye *with* þe wynde'). It is interesting also to note here that the distribution of this plant in Britain seems to be the south-west counties (Martin 1965: 50), and this is exactly the same area where, to judge from the linguistic evidence, the text may have been originally composed (Moreno Olalla 2007: 126–132). Since the description of the species seems not to have been recorded in the Classical literature, could this support the hypothesis that the author of *LH* did some field work after all?

One size fits all: *Affodil*

I would like to stress further the pitfalls of accepting uncritically the meanings provided by modern lexicographical works through the case posed by the species called *Centum capta* in the Latin heading and *affodill* in the ME text. The fragment where this plant is described in *LH* (f. 14va/1–29) runs as follows:

> Centu*m* capta
>
> Affodill is an herbe þat beriþe a faire yolewe floure and at þe toppe he haþe ronde coddys, in þe whiche he berith sede and his levis beth smale and longe. The vertu of hi*m* is that þe branchis of this erbe ben gode to hele þe dropesy. Also drynke þe juis of þe flourys of the[s][11] erbe in wyne and that will sle byti*n*g of venymo*us* wormys. Also take þe more of this erbe and þe juis of his leuys and a litell safar, lat this boyle to-gadrys w*ith* swete wyne streyned fayr: hit is gode for renynge eyen. Also þe more j-brent and made to poud*er* temp*er* þat w*ith* a litell oyle, a-noynte that place wher that lackyth here and hit shall make hit to growe a-yene. Also, and a harde sharpe cloþe be wette in þe juis of this erbe, let rubbe the morfue w*ith* that cloþe and hit shall fall a-way, for this erbe is hote and drye in the secund deg*re*.

At least three different species from three different genuses can be proposed as the plant referred to here, depending on which authority we accept. *MED* (Kurath *et al.* 1954–2001: *s. v.* affodil, sense *a*) states that this plant-name normally stands for the Ramsons (*Allium ursinum* L., also called Wild, Bear or Wood Garlic; an image is given below as Figure 2), and provides thirteen illustrative quotations. The meanings 'asphodel' (sense *b*, three quotations, two of them taken from synonyma) and 'rhododaphne' (sense *c*, a single quotation) are preceded by a question mark, which denotes that these senses are uncertain— all in all a sensible editorial policy: we have just seen how compilers were not too particular when it came to the gathering of synonyms and so, their equivalences should be taken with a big pinch of salt. In the same vein, Tony Hunt identified three *Allium* spp. as the species behind Latin "Centum Capita": *A. ursinus*, *A. vineale* L. (Crow Garlic) and *A. schoenoprasum* L. (Chives). It is worth mentioning that, even though other ME synonyms are given in Hunt's glossary (*ramese, crowgarlyk, wilde garlek, civys* and *maudefeloun*), *affodill* stands out as the most usual ME plant-name to refer to this Latin species (Hunt 1989: *s. v.*).

---

[11] ‹s› added over the line.

Figure 2. *Allium ursinum* (after Bauhin 1598: 422).

It is only natural therefore that one would assume that the entry in *LH* deals with Ramsons too.

Still, the physical description provided in the entry may point to a second candidate: the species referred to by the medieval author could also be the daffodil (*Narcissus pseudo-narcissus* L.; see Figure 3). Indeed, the confusion between the *Asphodelus* and the *Narcissus* species in England can be traced at least to the 1550s, as recorded by William Turner in his *New Herball*: 'I could neuer se thys herb [ie. *asphodelos*, 'ryght affodill'] in England but ones, for the herbe that the people calleth here Affodill or daffodill is a kynd of narcissus' (Turner 1551: B.iij verso); in fact, the very word 'daffodil' is etymologically connected with 'affodill' (see Simpson & Weiner 1989: *s. v.* daffodil for details). This possibility is not contemplated in Kurath *et al.* 1954–2001: *s. v.* affodil, but in view of the description and the post-medieval evidence, it may be worth speculating whether the entry in *LH* may be after all devoted to some *Narcissus*.

So far we have paid attention to lexicography and phytography. Yet if we turn to the list of healing properties proposed in the

Figure 3. Νάρχισσος–*Narcissus* (after Bauhin 1598: 858).

text, we will notice that the entry in *LH* fits extremely well with the Dioscoridean entry ἀσφόδελος (*MM* ii 169). Compare the following Greek excepts with the virtues given in *LH*: ὁ δὲ χυλὸς τῆς ῥίζης προσλαβὼν οἴνου παλαιοῦ γλυκέος καὶ σμύρνης καὶ κρόκου συνεψηθέντων ἐπὶ τὸ αὐτὸ ἔγχριστον γίνεται ὀφθαλμοῖς φάρμακον 'Adding old sweet wine, myrrh and saffron to the juice of the root and boiling all together, one makes a healing ointment for the eyes', καεῖσα δὲ ἡ ῥίζα, τῆς τέφρας ἐπιπλασσομένης, ἀλωπεκίας δασύνει 'having burnt the root, and anointing [the bald place] with the ash, it brings back the hair', and ἀλφόν τε λευκὸν προανατριφθέντα [ἐν] ὀθονίῳ ἐν ἡλίῳ καταχρισθεῖσα ἡ ῥίζα σμήχει 'The root, used as a salve, wipes off white leprosy if rubbed with a linen cloth in the sun'. The virtue of *affodill* against poison mentioned in *LH* also appears in *MM*, although the wording is somewhat different.

The Dioscoridean species has been tentatively identified as some *Asphodelus* spp., perhaps *A. aestivus* Brot. or *A. fistulosus* L. (García Valdés 1998: 346, fn. 208), but I think that we can attempt a

different species identification. There is indeed a yellow-flowered species (*Asphodeline lutea* L.),[12] but this was at the time a native of the
Eastern Mediterranean only and, as such, apparently unknown to the
Classical and medieval authors. If the Latin heading in *LH*, *Centum
capta* (for *capita, meaning 'a hundred heads') and the mentioning of
'ronde coddys' at the top of the stalk is taken into account, *Asphodelus
aestivus* Brot. is a very attractive candidate (cf. the capsules at the end
of the stalk of Figure 4). This is the third, and last, possibility.

Identification of the species treated in *LH* with the Ramsons presents two almost insurmountable problems. To begin with, the general
description of the plant in the ME entry is very much against this idea:
the leaves of the Ramsons are long indeed, but also rather broad, as seen
in Figure 2 above, while their flowers are conspicuously white. Second,
the pharmacological virtues proposed for this species, which are apparently the same as those of the common garlic (*Allium sativum* L.; see

---

[12] See www.botanic-garden.ox.ac.uk/asphodeline-lutea.

Figure 4. Ἀσφόδελος–*Hastula regia* (after Bauhin 1598: 450).

NH xix 116), do not match at all with those appearing in *LH*. Since neither the physical nor the medical description favour this identification, we can, I think, safely reject this candidate *MED* notwithstanding. Note moreover that *A. ursinum* is not a Mediterranean species, and this runs counter to the other entries in *LH*, which ultimately derive from Classical sources.[13] We have then to decide between the *daffodil* (as suggested by the general physical description), and the *asphodel* (as suggested by the matching virtues with Dioscorides's account and, partially, also by its physical description). Two factors should be taken into account before deciding which is likely to be the actual species in the ME text.

As mentioned above, *LH* is a *compilation* of several Latin sources: this means that as a rule those works by Dioscorides, Pliny or Galen were the ultimate sources of information, rather than the reflection of any personal fieldwork undertaken by Lelamour himself—or indeed any other English contemporary botanist. Therefore, that particular entry in Pliny's *Natural History* or Dioscorides's *Materia Medica* that fits the Middle English text best will probably be the plant that the original ME translator intended to describe and extol in his text. And it happens in this case that the virtues offered in the Middle English match perfectly those of the asphodel, having nothing to do with those of the daffodil, as they are given in *MM* iv 158 or *NH* xxi 128.

The second factor to bear in mind is purely pharmaceutical, and has to do with the chemical constituents present in those species. There is only one property of the daffodil worth mentioning: it contains an alkaloid, called *narcissine* after the plant, which is emetocathartic and phlogogenetic (i.e., induces vomit and causes inflammation; see Felter & Lloyd 1905: *s. v.* narcissus). Moreover, narcissine has strong stupefacient properties as well: cows avoid the plant, for eating it could paralyse them for some minutes (Font Quer 1987: 911). This feature was already known to the Greeks—although, contrary to *NH* xxi 158, the plant-name is apparently unrelated to the root meaning 'numbness'

---

[13] Ramsons, in fact, is not recorded in the Dioscoridean entry for Garlic (*MM* ii 152), nor appears in Mattioli, 1558; the image used for Figure 2 is actually an addition by Caspar Bauhin (that is why there is no Greek name in the caption), who included it in his edition of Mattioli together with the description and an image of 'Allium Anguinum' (i.e. *A. victorialis* L.), another *Allium* sp. that he found in the Sudetes ('montes qui Bohemiam à Silesia disterminant') in 1573 (Bauhin 1598: 423).

that we can also find in *narcotic*.[14] These two virtues were of course recorded in *MM* and would not fail to appear in any medieval treatise, but they are missing in *LH*. A lacuna in the text is highly unlikely, since *AC*, which again runs parallel to *LH* here, does not record such properties in any of the several extant MSS either.

These reasons seem to support that the *asphodel* (*Asphodelus aestivus* Brot.) is the plant treated here, but the question remains as to why the general description of the plant is that of a daffodil. Is is an addition in *LH*, or else was something taken from his exemplar? The latter is a more sensible option, if only because this is also stated in *AC*. The description of the plant in this textual tradition (161/26·30; Brodin 1950: 124–125) is in any case fuller and different in some minor details:

Affadilla is an herbe þat men clepe affadille or belle blome. It is lyke to lek *and* it hath a ʒelwʒ flo*ur*, *and* in þe crop a round codde q*ua*nne þe flo*ur* is falle. In quyche is seed lyke to onyou*n* seed.

Be that as it may, the description of the plant should not be used as compelling evidence. We should never forget that the plants described by Greeks and Romans did not always grow on an Atlantic island. This is in fact a case in point: the asphodel does not grow naturally in Britain, but the daffodil does. What we have here seems to be a case of *name shift*: the original name is used to refer to another species, and in fact *daffodil* is but a by-form of an original *affodil* (see Simpson & Weiner 1989: *s. v.*). The second phase of this identification is that of *virtue shift*: the medicinal properties of the former are also assumed for the latter, to such a degree that the early English botanists came to think that the plant that they were then holding was the same one described by Dioscorides many centuries before.

We can logically deduce from here that the ME author's purpose was to translate the uses of the plant *Centum capta*, which cannot but be the Asphodel and, probably, the *Asphodelus aestivus* Brot., and he described physically the English plant that he honestly thought was the asphodel. He actually never intended to talk about a daffodil; had he known that the plant that he had in front of him as he was writing this entry was the *Narcissus* of the Greeks and Romans, not the *asphodelus*

---

[14] 'A narce [i.e. νάρκη] narcissum dictum, non a fabuloso puero.' Similar remarks can be found in Plutarch's *Questiones conviviales* 647b. Cf. Chantraine 1999: *s. v.* νάρκισσος: 'il ne peut s'agir que d'une étymologie populaire'.

or *centum capita*, it stands to reason that he would have written a very different entry.

Quis custodiet ipsos custodes?: Conclusions

Is plant species identification possible in Middle English herbals? I think that for many cases the slightly disappointing answer is: 'yes, but…'. Twisted textual transmissions, recurrent scribal crazes for synonyms (at least since Greek times), and misapplication of the same names and virtues to species growing in separate areas of the world but sharing some feature are conspicuous dangers in this journey. I have provided a few examples that will hopefully demonstrate that close reading can and must be instrumental for the job of defusing (albeit just partially) such minefields.

Perhaps the main problem here is that trustworthy literature on this topic is scarce in comparison with the attention paid to the same matter among Classicists (see André 1956, 1958, 1985; Fortes Fortes 1984a, 1984b *inter alios*). Tony Hunt's stab at a solution (Hunt 1989) must be taken as a thoroughly scholarly yet preliminary work, since he provides no discussion on the whys and wherefores that motivated his decision to equate Middle and Contemporary English plant-names. Carole Biggam's initiative, the ASPNS (*Anglo-Saxon Plant Name Survey*),[15] and the articles by her collaborators and herself (for example Biggam 1994, 2003) do hit the mark fully, but they deal by definition with Old English names only.

Historically, moreover, there has been a perceptible scholarly habit towards passing the buck and—if one is allowed to continue with clichéd idioms—leaving the proverbially drowsy dogs safely tucked inside their kennels when it comes to equating ME plant-names and the modern binomial nomenclature. While this is perhaps a bit of a foregone conclusion (see McCarren 1998 for similar caveats but with a more general scope), the examples analyzed above, which are in no way unique to *LH* or any other ME herbal that I know of, teach us that when it comes to plant-identification we simply should never trust the information fed to us by dictionaries.

It would, however, be very unfair to put the blame on dictionaries and glossaries. We are dealing here with a lexicological, not a

---

[15] http://www.arts.gla.ac.uk/STELLA/ihsl/projects/plants.htm. The project seems sadly discontinued.

lexicographical, problem. Therefore it is neither Tony Hunt nor the editors of the *MED*, but their colleagues working on manuscripts, who are ultimately responsible for the current situation. In the particular case of *LH*, for instance, *MED* was misled by the work of Whytlaw-Gray, which was poor by any scholarly standard. Reliable editions must be done of the many treatises, big and small alike, that still await publication on the shelves of libraries scattered over the world, while critical revisitations of those treatises already edited and discussed will be much appreciated. Text glossaries remain an absolute need in any edition indeed, but no more than ample textual and linguistic notes that should accompany them, discussing at length why the editor deems that this or that particular species is the one referred to in that particular text.

References

André, J. (1956). *Lexique de termes de botanique en latin*. Paris: Klincksieck.

———. (1958). *Notes de lexicographie botanique grecque*. Paris: Honoré Champion.

———. (1985). *Les noms de plants dans la Rome antique*. Paris: Les Belles Lettres.

Bauhin, C. (ed.) (1598). *Petri Andreæ Matthioli medici Cæsarei et Ferdinandi Archiducis Austriæ, Opera quæ extant omnia*. Francofurti: Officina Nicolai Bassæi.

Bernard, E. (1697). *Catalogi librorum manuscriptorum Angliæ et Hiberniæ in unum collecti, cum indice alphabetico*. Oxoniæ: Theatro Sheldoniano.

Biggam, C.P. (1994). *Hæwenhnydele*: an Anglo-Saxon medicinal plant. *Botanical Journal of Scotland*, 46:4, 617–22.

Biggam, C.P. (ed.) (2003). *From earth to art: the many aspects of the plant-world in Anglo-Saxon England*. Amsterdam-New York: Rodopi.

Bosworth, J., & Toller, T.N. (1898). *An Anglo-Saxon dictionary based on the manuscript collection of the late Joseph Bosworth*. Oxford: Oxford University Press.

Brodin, G. (ed.) (1950). *Agnus Castus. A Middle English herbal, reconstructed from various manuscripts*. Upsala-Copenhagen-Cambridge (Mass.): A.-B. Lundequistska Bokhandeln-Ejnar Munksgaard-Harvard University Press.

Cockayne, O. (ed.) (1864–1866). *Leechdoms, wortcunning, and starcraft of early England*. London: Longman.

Chantraine, P. (1999). *Dictionnaire étymologique de la langue grecque. Histoire des mots.* (2nd ed.) Paris: Klinksieck.

Felter, H.W., & Lloyd, J.U. (1905). *King's American dispensatory.* (19th ed.) Cincinnati: The Ohio Valley Company.

Font Quer, P. (1987). *Plantas medicinales. El Dioscórides renovado.* (10th ed.) Barcelona: Labor.

Fortes Fortes, J. (1984a). Fitonimia griega I. La identificación de las plantas por los fitónimos griegos. *Faventia,* 6:1, 7–29.

———. (1984b). Fitonimia griega II. Las fuentes del vocabulario fitonímico griego. *Faventia,* 6:2, 7–15.

García Valdés, M. (ed.) (1998). *Plantas y remedios medicinales (De materia medica).* Madrid: Gredos.

Halliwell-Phillipps, J.O. (1889). *A dictionary of archaic and provincial words, obsolete phrases, proverbs and ancient customs from the fourteenth century.* (11th ed.) London: Reeves and Turner.

Hunt, T. (1989). *Plant names of medieval England.* Cambridge: D. S. Brewer.

Kurath, H., Kuhn, S.M., Reidy, J., & Lewis, R.E. (eds) (1954–2001). *Middle English Dictionary.* Ann Arbor: University of Michigan Press.

Martin, W.K. (1965). *The concise British flora in colour.* London: Ebury Press and Michael Joseph.

Mattioli, P.A. (1558). *Commentarii secundo aucti, in libros sex Pedacii Dioscoridis Anazarbei De medica materia.* Venetiis: Ex Officina Erasmiana, Vincentij Valgrisij.

McCarren, V.P. (1998). Editing glossographical texts: to marrow and to marrow and to marrow. V. P. McCarren & D. Moffat (eds) *A guide to editing Middle English.* Ann Arbor: University of Michigan Press, 141–55.

Moreno Olalla, D. (2002). *Lelamour's Herbal (MS Sloane 5, ff. 13–57). Critical edition and philological study.* (Ph.D. University of Málaga PhD dissertation), Universidad de Málaga, Málaga.

———. (2007). *The fautys to amende.* On the interpretation of the *explicit* of Sloane 5, ff. 13–57, and related matters. *English Studies,* 88:2, 119–142.

———. (2013a). A plea for ME botanical synonyma. V. Gillespie & A. Hudson (eds) *Probable truth. Editing medieval texts from Britain in the twenty-first century.* Brussels: Brepols, 387–404.

———. (2013b). The textual transmission of the *Northern Macer* tradition. *English Studies,* 94:8, 931–957.

Mowat, J.L.G. (1887). *Alphita. A medico-botanical glossary from the*

Bodleian Manuscript, Selden B.35. London-Oxford: Henry Frowde-Oxford University Press.

Prior, R.C.A. (1863). *On the popular names of British plants, being an explanation of the origin and meaning of the name of our indigenous and most commonly cultivated species*. London: Williams and Norgate.

Simpson, J.A., & Weiner, E.S.C. (eds) (1989). *The Oxford English dictionary*. (2nd ed.) Oxford: Oxford University Press.

Turner, W. (1551). *A new herball, wherin are conteyned the names of herbes in Greke, Latin, Englysh, Duch Frenche, and in the potecaries and herbaries Latin, with the properties degrees and naturall places of the same*. London: Steven Mierdman.

Whytlaw-Gray, A. (1938). *John Lelamour's translation of Macer's Herbal*. (M.A. University of Leeds MA dissertation), University of Leeds, Leeds.

5   The Periphrastic Subjunctive in the Old English Multiple Glosses to the Lindisfarne Gospels

Marcelle Cole
Utrecht University

The recessive nature of the subjunctive as a formal category in Old English is witnessed in the use of alternative grammatical structures other than inflectional subjunctives in contexts of non-fact modality. An increasing analytic reliance on grammatical devices signalling non-fact modality (e.g. *gif* 'if', *sua hua* 'whoever', etc.) both fostered and facilitated the occurrence of the indicative in such contexts. The modal verbs *magan*, **sculan* and *willan* served as fully independent verbs in Old English, but even during the Old English period there appears to have been a 'modern' tendency to use modal constructions involving a (subjunctive) modal + infinitive construction, instead of an inflectional subjunctive, with little (or no) underlying sense of non-modal notional meaning.[1]

In the Old Northumbrian (ONbr) interlinear gloss to the Latin text of the *Lindisfarne Gospels* (British Library, MS Cotton Nero D.iv; henceforth *Li*), the increasing lack of direct correspondence between contexts of non-fact modality and the subjunctive in Old English is attested in the widespread tendency for present-indicative forms in *-s* and *-ð* to supplant subjunctive forms, e.g. *7 swiðe bebead him þætte hia ne æwades l mersades hine* L *et uehementer comminabatur eis ne manifestarent illum* 'And he very much commanded them that they should not make him known' MkGl (Li) 3.12, or for indicative forms to alternate with subjunctive forms, which in ONbr ended in *-a/-e/-o* in both

---

[1] For detailed discussion of the semantics of the Old English modal verbs see Standop (1957: 18–66, 94–132, 133–155), Visser (1963–1973, iii §1483, §1562, §1653), Mitchell (1985, §§1012–1015, §§1019–1020, §§1021–1022), and the dictionaries.

How to cite this book chapter:
Cole, M. 2015. The Periphrastic Subjunctive in the Old English Multiple Glosses to the Lindisfarne Gospels. In: Shaw, P., Erman, B., Melchers, G. and Sundkvist, P. (eds) *From Clerks to Corpora: essays on the English language yesterday and today*. Pp. 71–85. Stockholm: Stockholm University Press. DOI: http://dx.doi.org/10.16993/bab.e License: CC-BY.

the singular and plural, e.g. *gif gie* **habbas *l* hæbbe** *leafo* L *si habueritis fidem* 'If you have faith' MtGl (Li) 21.21 and *þætte gie* **eta** 7 **drincga** [...] 7 *gie* **sittað** *ofer heh sedlo* L *ut edatis et bibatis* [...] *et sedeatis super thronos* 'That you may eat and drink [...] and sit on high thrones' LkGl (Li) 22.30 (see Cole, 2014 for extended discussion).[2] Periphrastic modal verb + infinitive constructions also occur in *Li* to translate the Latin subjunctive mood, as in *7 sohton ða hehsacerdas 7 ða uðuuto huu hine mið facne* **gehealdon *l* mæhton** *hia* **gehalda** *7 ofslogon l hia* **mæhton ofslaa** L *et quaerebant summi sacerdotes et scribae quomodo eum dolo tenerent et occiderent* 'and the chief priests and the scribes sought how they might with wile lay hold of him and they might kill him' MkGl (Li) 14.01.[3] The glossator's reliance on structures other than the inflectional subjunctive is possibly all the more surprising given the requirements of the glossing process to render the Latin as atomistically and faithfully as possible in the target language.

The present paper examines the glossator's use of the modal + infinitive construction in *Li* in relation to that of the inflectional subjunctive and indicative simple verb forms. The strategy of using modal + infinitive structures in the translation of Latin subjunctives in *Li* has long been noted (Bosworth & Toller 1898, *magan*), yet data drawn from the ONbr glosses are not included in any of the major studies on Old English modal verbs (cf. Gorrell 1895; Standop 1957; Ogawa 1989). Modal + infinitive constructions in *Li* occur frequently (though not exclusively) in multiple glosses whereby a single Latin lemma is rendered using at least two Old English glosses, separated by Latin *vel* 'or' (abbreviated to *l* in the manuscript). Multiple glosses conveniently facilitate the comparison of the forms that occur in identical contexts of non-fact modality in ONbr. Certain properties of the multiple glosses

---

[2] The abbreviations used in this paper to refer to the *Lindisfarne Gospels* (*Li*) and the *West Saxon Gospels* (*WSCp*) are those employed by the *Dictionary of Old English Web Corpus* (*DOEC*) and identify gospel, chapter and verse. The *DOEC* relies on Skeat's (1871–1887) edition of the Gospels. Citations are taken from the *DOEC*, checked against the online facsimile of *Li* available at <http://www.bl.uk/manuscripts/FullDisplay.aspx?ref=Cotton_MS_Nero_D_IV>. Biblical translations translate the Old English text as opposed to the Latin and are my own. Multiple glosses in the Old English text are provided with one Modern English translation.

[3] Northern variants of *uton* + infinitive also occur in *Li* to translate the Latin hortative subjunctive, e.g. *gæ we l wutum geonga* L *eamus* 'Let's go!' but this usage will not be dealt with in this paper.

may also function as a diagnostic for evaluating the status of modal + infinitive constructions in Old English.

The periphrastic subjunctive in Old English

The extent to which modal + infinitive constructions functioned inter- changeably with inflectional forms as periphrastic expressions of mood is a vexed question that has received a great deal of attention in the lit- erature (Gorrell 1895; Standop 1957; Krzyszpién 1980; Mitchell 1985; Goossens 1987; Ogawa 1989). The need for caution in too readily inter- preting modal verbs as grammatical circumlocutions for the inflectional subjunctive has been reiterated in the literature: modal verbs often pres- ent little loss of primary meaning and occur in the subjunctive under the same circumstances that trigger its use with other verbs (Mitchell 1985, §§2971–2980). The terms 'modal' and 'modal auxiliary' are in themselves problematic, given that these verbs functioned as independ- ent lexical items in Old English and the issue of whether *magan*, *scu- lan* and *willan* expressed mood at this early stage is controversial. I follow Mitchell (1985, §991) in using the label 'modal auxiliary' for want of a better term, but in full awareness of the potential prolepsis involved in employing the terms 'modal' and 'auxiliary' with regard to the function of these verbs in Old English.

From a historical point of view, it has been argued that in the initial (Old English) stage of the history of the subjunctive and the 'modal aux- iliaries' in English, modal verbs with an infinitive were treated as gram- matical equivalents to inflectional subjunctive forms (Gorrell 1895). The growing tendency in the language to use auxiliary constructions was triggered and propagated by the breakdown in the formal distinc- tion between the indicative and subjunctive inflectional forms of verbs. Gorrell's examination of the frequency of Old English 'modal auxilia- ries' in relation to that of inflectional subjunctives in indirect discourse indicates a striking increase in the use of the periphrastic construction with a distinct tendency to occur when the corresponding inflectional forms of verbs would prove ambiguous (1895: 458).

Observations in the literature that the use of a periphrastic subjunctive was fostered by the breakdown in the formal distinction between the indicative and subjunctive mood is particularly pertinent to the ONbr gloss. One of the main characteristics of the ONbr texts is the advanced state of morphological simplification across the verbal system caused by various processes of reduction and levelling, including the proliferation of the northern present-tense marker *-s* at the expense of *-ð*, and the early loss of final *-n*, most notably in the infinitive and present-plural subjunctive, but also in the preterite-present plural verbs and preterite indicative and subjunctive (see Cole 2014). The preterite subjunctive and indicative are more often than not indistinguishable from each other as the preterite plural subjunctive shows preterite-indicative *-on* endings rather than *-en* and indicative forms occur with subjunctive *-en*, which suggests the coalescence of the endings in [-ən].

The view of the history of the modal auxiliaries as a simple chronological development whereby modal + infinitive constructions increasingly occur as a subjunctive equivalent as the Old English period progresses is belied, however, by the textual variation that the incidence of modal verbs exhibits in the Old English period. Ogawa's (1989) survey of Old English texts indicates a varying incidence in the use of the periphrastic construction across different text types and time periods that challenges what he terms the 'substitution theory', the notion of the history of the English subjunctive as characterised by the use of modal auxiliaries to compensate for the loss of inflectional morphology. His analysis of the meanings of the modal verbs in subjunctive contexts does not show the degree of loss of semantic meaning which would be expected if the verbs were being used as auxiliaries. Instead modal verbs are employed to convey a particular shade of meaning as required by the context: their use adds a nuance that is not explicit in the inflectional subjunctive. The suggestion that the periphrastic construction is not a mere grammatical alternative to the inflectional subjunctive but expresses instead a semantic nuance not found in the simple subjunctive is in line with Standop (1957: 169) and Krzyszpién (1980). The latter argues that periphrastic *magan* + infinitive and the inflectional subjunctive were not wholly semantically interchangeable. The use of one form or the other was determined by a difference in meaning: inflectional subjunctives denoted general non-fact modality whereas the periphrastic *magan* + infinitive expressed a particular aspect of non-fact modality, objective possibility. When *magan* itself occurred in the subjunctive inflectional form "general non-fact modality was 'superimposed' on the narrower meaning of objective possibility" (Krzyszpién, 1980: 51).

Ogawa's findings, in particular, emphasise the relevance of text type and stylistic factors in determining the occurrence of the modal verbs; there is a preference for poetry as opposed to prose to favour the use of modal verbs across the entire Old English period, probably as a stylistic poetic device that added emphatic detail (Ogawa 1989: 231–232;

Gorrell 1895: 458). In prose, modal verbs are favoured in argumentative religious and philosophical writings and homiletic literature rather
than in narrative prose. Text type and subject matter are also found
to affect the individual incidence of each modal verb, e.g. *magan* and
*sculan are common in didactic and religious writings where the latter commonly serves to emphasise commands, whereas narrative prose
works show a preference for *willan* (Ogawa 1989: 235). Interestingly,
the *West Saxon Gospels* (Corpus Christi College Cambridge MS, 140;
henceforth *WSCp*) exhibit an "almost entire neglect of the periphrastic
[modal] forms" (Gorrell 1895: 458). The low incidence of modal verbs
in *WSCp* is attributed by both authors to the translator holding "slav-
ishly" to the Latin original (Gorrell 1895: 458; see also Ogawa 1989:
225, 236). Verse translations in the *Paris Psalter* and the *Kentish Psalm*
reflect a similar reluctance to employ periphrastic forms (Ogawa 1989:
236), which tells in favour of a close degree of dependence on the Latin
source inhibiting the use of periphrastic [modal] forms. The avoidance
of periphrastic forms involving modal verbs found in *WSCp* does not,
however, find a parallel in the interlinear ONbr glosses in *Li*; despite
the glossarial nature of the text type, the glossator's language is not as
subjugated to the demands of atomistic glossing as might be expected.[4]

Modal + infinitive and the subjunctive mood in *Li*

Li is consistent with general Old English usage in its employment of
the modal + infinitive compound instead of an inflectional subjunctive form of the verb in indirect discourse after verbs of thinking and
believing and in the employment of *willan* with expressions of prom-
ise (Gorrell 1895: 449–455), exemplified in (1a) and (1b), respectively.
Such usage overlaps broadly with the future-in-the-past employment of

---

4   It should be borne in mind, nevertheless, that neither the Old English translation in
WSCp nor *Li* is consistent in its attitude towards the Latin original. The effect of
Latin influence is at times blatantly obvious in *Li*; for instance, the Latin negative
imperative construction *nolite* (plural) / *noli* (singular) + infinitive is categorically
translated using a contracted negative form of the verb *willan* followed by an infinitive in an attempt, no doubt, to render the Latin construction as atomistically as
possible, e.g. *nallaðgie g[e]wyrce* L *nolite facere* 'make not!' JnGl (Li) 2.16 and
nælle gie gedoema L *nolite iudicare* 'judge not!' JnGl (Li) 7.24. Contrastively, the
continuous prose translation in *WSCp* diverges from the Latin in its rendering of
negative imperatives and follows a more native OE *ne* + V + Spro structure compared with the literal counterparts found in *Li*, as in *ne wyrce ge* Jn (WSCp) 2.16 or
ne deme ge Jn (WSCp) 7.24.

the preterite subjunctive (Mitchell 1985: §646) found in (1c). It should be noted that (1d) is the only instance in which *sculan* is used periphrastically to translate a Latin subjunctive in *Li* (Kotake 2006: 44). Ogawa's (1989: 235) observation that *sculan* commonly serves to emphasise commands would seem to find exemplification here.[5]

(1)a. *wiste forðon huoelce uoere seðe* **salde hine ł ualde** *hine sealla*
   'for he knew which one it was who would betray him'
   sciebat enim quisnam esset qui traderet eum

   JnGl (Li) 13.11

   b. *ðona ł forðon mið að gehatend wæs hir þæt* **sealla walde** *suæ huæt wælde giwiga ł giuiade from him*
   'therefore with an oath it was promised to her that he would give whatsoever she would ask of him'
   unde cum iuramento pollicitus est ei dare quodcumque postulasset ab eo

   MtGl (Li) 14.7

   c. *7 forhuon ne saldes ðu feh meh to wege ł to disc 7 ic miððy cuome mið agnettum ł uutedlice ic* **giude ł walde** *giuge þæt*
   'and why did you not give my money to the bank, and when I came, with usury indeed I would have exacted it?'
   et quare non dedisti pecuniam meam ad mensam et ego ueniens cum usuris utique exigissem illud

   LkGl (Li) 19.23

   d. *7 huu auritten is on sunu monnes þætte feolo* **geðolas ł scile** **ðoliga** *7 gehened ł geniðrad ł geteled*
   'and how it is written about the Son of man that he must suffer many things and be despised'

---

[5] *sculan* is more widely used in *Li* to translate the Latin future tense where it approximates a modern periphrastic future on occasions, e.g. *from hernise gie geheras 7 ne oncnæugie ł ne cuðon ge 7 gesegende ge sciolon gesea ł ge geseas 7 ne geseað ł ne sciolon gesea* L *auditu audietis et non intelligitis et uidentes uidebitis et non uidebitis* 'By hearing you shall hear, and shall not understand: and seeing you shall see, and shall not perceive' MtGl (Li) 13.14; *in caelo geong sua huæt ðu hæbbe bebyg 7 sel ðorfendum 7 hæfis ł ðu scealt habba gestrion in heofne* L *uade cumque habes uende et da pauperibus et habebis thesaurum* 'Go, sell whatsoever you have and give to the poor and you shall have treasure in heaven' MkGl (Li) 10.21; *7 gie geseað ł scilon gesea sunu monnes to suiðrom sittende ðæs mæhtes* L *et uidebitis filium hominis a dextris sedentem uirtutis* 'And you shall see the Son of man sitting to the right of the power of God' MkGl (Li) 14.62

et quomodo scribtum est in filium hominis ut multa patiatur et contempnatur

MkGl (Li) 9.12

The construction *magan* + infinitive is used in *Li* in both the present and preterite in clauses of purpose, a usage that is not peculiar to *Li*, but which differentiates it from *WSCp* where *magan* is never used in purpose clauses: there is a preference for *willan* instead (Ogawa 1989: 236). In the case of (2a) and (2b), the inflectional subjunctive *gesii* alternates with (subjunctive) *magan* + infinitive. Behre (1934: 92, fn. 1) states that the subjunctive form of *magan* + infinitive is the only way of unambiguously expressing subjunctive mood in the first-person singular given the lack of formal distinction between the first-person present-indicative and subjunctive. In ONbr *gesii* is a subjunctive form (Ross 1937: 133), which effectively eliminates morphological ambiguity as a motive for including *mæge* + infinitive alongside *gesii* in the double gloss. Standop (1957: 60–61) suggests that *magan* expresses a different kind of uncertainty from the subjunctive of a simple verb. Similarly, as previously mentioned, Krzyszpién (1980: 51) argues that subjunctive *magan* + infinitive is not a mere circumlocution for the subjunctive but contributes semantic precision by expressing a particular aspect of non-fact modality, that of objective possibility. The inclusion in *Li* of both an inflectional subjunctive and *mæge* + infinitive would seem to corroborate this view. Behre's hypothesis may hold nonetheless in preterite contexts where the simple verb form is formally indicative but indistinguishable from the subjunctive in speech (example 2c).

(2)a. *huæd wilt ðu ðe þæt ic gedoe se blinde uutedlice cuoeð him laruu god þætte ic **gesii** ɫ þæt ic **mæge sea***
'what (do) you want that I do to you? The blind man indeed said to him: master, that I may see'
quid uis tibi faciam caecus autem dixit ei rabboni ut uideam
MkGl (Li) 10.51

b. *cuoeð huæd ðe wilt ðu þæt ic doam ɫ gedoe soð he cuoeð la drihten þætte ic **gesii** ɫ **gesea mæge***
'he said: what (do) you want that I do to you? Indeed he said: Lord, that I may see'
dicens quid tibi uis faciam at ille dixit domine ut uideam
LkGl (Li) 18.41

c. *monigo forðon he gehælde ðus þætte hia raesdon on him þætte hine hie **gehrindon ɫ hrina mæhtæs***
'for he healed many, thus that they pressed upon him that they might touch him'
multos enim sanabat ita ut inruerent in eum ut illum tangerent

MkGl (Li) 3.10

Clauses of indefiniteness involving *sede* and *sua hua, sua huelc* 'whoever', *suæhuælc* 'whatever', etc. generally required a subjunctive verb form in Old English, although the indicative became increasingly common as the period progressed (Visser 1963–1973, i. §886). Indicative and inflectional subjunctive forms both occur in indefinite contexts in *Li*, e.g. *in suahuelcum hus gie inngae* L *et in quamcumque domum intraueritis* 'in whatever house you enter' LkGl (Li) 9.4; *on sua huelcne hus gie ingæeð* L *in quamcumque domum intraueritis* 'in whatever house you enter' LkGl (Li) 10.5. There is also one instance of a double gloss consisting of both an inflectional subjunctive and an indicative, e.g. *sua huelc iuer hæbbe ɫ hæfeð friond* L *quis uestrum habebit amicum* 'whoever of you has a friend' LkGl (Li) 11.5. The *Li* glossator also avails himself of a further strategy in double glosses and renders the Latin subjunctive using a (subjunctive) modal + infinitive construction. In double glosses present indicative *ɫ welle* + infinitive is the particular combination of grammatical forms that is employed in *Li* to translate the Latin subjunctive mood in clauses of indefiniteness. This strategy is illustrated in (3):[6]

(3)a. *seðe soðlice **ðerhwunes ɫ ðerhwunia wẹlla** wið ɫ in ende ðes hal bið*
'he that truly perseveres until the end, he will be saved'
qui autem perseuerauerit in finem hic saluus erit

MtGl (Li) 10.22

b. *7 sua hua dringe **selles ɫ sealla wẹlle** anum of lytlum ðassum cælc ɫ scenc wætres caldes [...] ne loseð meard his*
'and whosoever gives drink to one of these little ones a cup of cold water [...] he loses his reward'
quicumque potum dederit uni ex minimis istis calicem aquae frigide [...] non perdet mercedem suam

MtGl (Li) 10.42

---

6 See 1b in the present paper for the same combination of grammatical forms used in a multiple gloss in an indefinite clause, but in the preterite: *suæ huæt wælde giwiga ɫ giuiade*. The occurrence of unambiguous indicative forms in the present tense, illustrated in (3), suggests that *giuiade*, though formally indistinguishable from the subjunctive preterite, was intended as an indicative form.

c. *7 sua hua* **cueðes ł cueða wele** *word wið sunu monnes forgefen bið him*
'and whosoever speaks a word against the Son of man, it shall be forgiven him'
et quicumque dixerit uerbum contra filium hominis remittetur ei

MtGl (Li) 12.32

d. *7 seðe suæ huælc* **wælla suerige ł** *seðe* **suerias** *on wigbed noht is seðe sua huelc uutedlice* **wælla sueria** *in gefo þæt is ofer ðæt is rehtlic*
'and whosoever swears on the altar, it is nothing; indeed whosoever swears by the gift that is on it is a debtor'
et quicumque iurauerit in altari nihil est quicumque autem iurauerit in dono quod est super illud debet

MtGl (Li) 23.18

e. *7 cuoeð to him sua hwælc* **forletas ł forleta welle** *wif his 7 oðer laede derneleger efnesende ł geendade ofer hia ł bi hir*
'and he said to them: whosoever puts away his wife and marries another, commits adultery against her'
et dicit illis quicumque dimiserit uxorem suam et aliam duxerit adulterium committit super eam

MkGl (Li) 10.11

f. *seðe* **welle losige ł loses ł fordoes ł forfæras** *sawel his fore meh onfindes hia ł ða ilco*
'he that loses his life for me, shall find it'
qui perdiderit animam suam propter me inueniet eam

Mt (Li) 10.39

In double glosses, therefore, there is a preference for the modal periphrastic construction, as opposed to an inflectional subjunctive, to occur alongside a present-indicative form in clauses of indefiniteness. Clearly, both forms were acceptable grammatical alternatives in this context, although it should be noted that the subjunctive modal form *welle* is used and *willan* here retains an implied element of volition, intention or acquiescence. Given that the indicative also occurs in this context, the use of *welle* + infinitive may be an attempt to vivify the sense of modality inherent in clauses of indefiniteness as to the person, place, time referred to in the clause. The modal's primary meaning has not been eliminated, but such usage provides an insight into an intermediate stage in the development of the English periphrastic subjunctive.

The apodosis of a hypothetical condition in ModE requires a preterite modal: in fact its occurrence in this environment serves as a test of modal status (Denison 1993: 313). In Old English the preterite inflectional subjunctive generally occurred in this context, e rally 'if God were your father indeed you loved me' Jn (WSCp) 8.47, where *lufedon*, though formally preterite indicative, is to be understood as a subjunctive. In *Li*, however, preterite forms of *willan* + infinitive occur in the apodosis of a hypothetical proposition, compare, *gif god faeder iuer woere gie ualde lufiga uutedlice mec* 'if God were your Father, you would indeed love me' L *si deus pater uester esset diligeretis utique me* Jn (Li) 8.42. Visser (1963–1973, §1532, §1607, §1672) records such usage in Old English with *should* and *might*, but cites no examples of *would* for Old English, apparently dating the emergence of *would* in the apodosis of a hypothetical proposition to the early ME period. Instances of *wolde* in the apodosis of a conditional would appear to exist in Old English, however: Ogawa (1989: 131) identifies an example of *wolde* used with an inanimate subject in *Ælfric's Lives of Saints* (*ÆLS* 31.672) that "may well serve as a pure expression of an imaginary event in the past". The examples in (4) illustrate the occurrence of *walde* in the apodosis of a hypothetical condition in *Li*.

(4)a. *gif nere ðes yfeldoend ne ðe ue **gesaldon ł nalde** ue **gesealla** hine ðe*
'if he were not this evildoer, we would not have delivered him up to you'
'*si non esset hic malefactor non tibi tradidissemus eum*
JnGl (Li) 18.30

 b. *gif ðu gegiuuedes from ðæm 7 **gesalde** ðe ł æc **ualde gesealla** ðe uæter cuic ł lifwelle   uæter*
'if you had asked of him, and he would have given you living water'
petisses ab eo et dedisset tibi aquam uiuam
JnGl (Li) 4.10

Here *willan* serves to express an intermediate idea between simple volition and an imaginary past result: it cannot be said that *walde* is entirely non-volitional in nature, but it does approximate 'modern' usage in conveying the probable past results of an unreal past condition. The examples also succinctly exemplify the lack of formal opposition between the indicative and the subjunctive in the preterite that may well have contributed to the glossator's decision to signal non-fact modality more explicitly using a periphrastic form.

As previously noted, periphrastic subjunctives occur frequently in double glosses in *Li*, which, given the preference for multiple glosses in *Li* is not in itself significant.[7] Nonetheless, the double-glossing translation technique provides a unique insight into what type of grammatical units co-occurred in identical contexts. Multiple glosses in *Li* generally involve two items, though triple and even quadruple glosses also occur (see examples 1d and 3f in the present paper, in which the triple glosses *gehened ꝉ geniðrad ꝉ geteled* and *loses ꝉ fordoes ꝉ forfæras* translate Latin *contempnatur* 'scorn, despise' [3sg pres.subj.pass.] and *perdiderit* 'lose, destroy' [3sg perf.subj.act.], respectively). The multiple glosses vary with regard to the type of information that they supply; some provide lexical alternatives for a single Latin lemma, involving the use of synonyms or near-synonyms, e.g. *berað ꝉ bringeð* L *adferte* 'bring!' JnGl (Li) 21.10. Other double glosses provide grammatical alternatives for a single Latin lemma, e.g. *geseað ꝉ geseas* L *uideritis* 'you see' LkGl (Li) 21.20, *ne habbas ꝉ nabbas* L *non habent* 'they do not have' MtGl (Li) 14.16, or supply both a grammatical and a lexical alternative, e.g. *gæ we ꝉ wutu[m] geonga* L *eamus* 'Let's go!' MkGl (Li) 1.38.

In double glosses translating the subjunctive mood the preferred strategy in *Li* is to juxtapose an indicative with a (subjunctive) modal + infinitive, rather than an inflectional subjunctive. It would be an oversimplification to infer that the occurrence of the periphrastic construction alongside simple forms in double glosses is in itself proof that the modal + infinitive structure is a mechanical substitute for the inflectional subjunctive. Double glosses in *Li* clearly provide alternatives that are equally acceptable in a given context but they convey differing nuances. Double lexical glosses generally involve an item that introduces a semantic nuance, such as *berað ꝉ bringeð* L *adferte* 'bring!' JnGl (Li) 21.10, cited above, or a contextualised nuance. Pons-Sanz (forthc.) cites the rendering of L *puella* as *dohter ꝉ mægden* at MkGl (Li) 5.41. The Latin lemma *puella* would normally be translated using OE *mægden* 'girl, maiden', but here, Pons-Sanz argues, OE *dohtor* 'daughter' is included because the girl referred to is the daughter of the leader of the synagogue mentioned a few lines previously. Even alternative grammatical glosses, such as *geseað ꝉ geseas* L *uideritis* LkGl (Li) 21.20 and *ne habbas ꝉ nabbas* L *non habent* MtGl (Li) 14.16, which appear to present simply morphological variants, provide an additional form that is more idiomatic or colloquial, such as the dialectal ONbr second-person plural form *geseas*

---

[7] Kotake (2006: 37, fn. 4) gives the total occurrences of multiple glosses in *Li* at 3159, of which 466 are grammatical glosses.

alongside *geseað* 'you see' at LkGl (Li) 21.20, or *nabbas* instead of *ne habbas* at MtGl (Li) 14.16. Similarly, the double glosses under scrutiny involving 'modal auxiliary' constructions are a complex case that do not necessarily involve grammatically interchangeable forms with no difference in meaning. Careful analysis suggests that the periphrastic modal subjunctive is a grammatically acceptable – if somewhat stylistically different – alternative to the inflectional subjunctive.

With regard to the ordering of the items in double grammatical glosses in *Li*, i.e. whether the glossator chooses to place a term in first or second position, Kotake (2006) identifies a considerably consistent pattern in the ordering of the alternative grammatical glosses, including those that translate Latin verbs forms conveying future tense and subjunctive mood. In the majority of cases, the double glosses consist of a simple form in first position followed by a periphrastic construction. He attributes this ordering preference to the glossator placing the Old English grammatical category that is morphologically closest to the Latin first, followed by the "more morphologically marked" periphrastic construction (2006: 44–46). I interpret the grammatical unit that most deviates from the Latin original as the more idiomatic or colloquial item in the doublet. The translation technique of double glossing provides the glossator with the scope to include one Old English translation that is atomistic and closely parallels the Latin morphologically and another that distances itself from the original Latin text and provides a more concrete or colloquial rendering. Such an interpretation both corroborates and finds support in Ogawa's contention that the modal verb phrase probably reflects colloquial Old English usage. Ogawa notes the tendency for modal verbs to occur more readily at the colloquial rather than literary level of Old English prose and in direct speech and suggests that "the colloquial level of style favours the use of modal verbs in its endeavour to make description vivid and concrete" (1989: 237–238). The colloquial sphere of usage is also a locus of grammatical change where the 'modern' periphrastic future and subjunctive forms would be expected to make their first appearance.

Summary

The data in *Li* provide further insight into an intermediate stage in the history of the periphrastic subjunctive whereby modal verbs were used initially to emphasise a particular aspect of non-fact modality that an inflectional subjunctive could only do more generally and which indicative forms left unexpressed. The notion of the history of the English subjunctive as characterised by the use of modal auxiliaries to compensate for the loss of inflectional morphology only tells part of the story of the English periphrastic subjunctive: stylistic factors were of considerable importance. In a succinct summary of the Old English state of affairs, Ogawa (1989. 223–234) highlights that the varying distribution of modal verbs across text types

> points to no clear tendency for them to form the 'periphrastic subjunctive' when the corresponding simple verb form would be ambiguous with respect to mood. [...] Although the distinction between the modal verb construction and the simple verb form is not always easy to explain, the former can be generally shown to stand for clearer, more concrete expressions, emphasizing and specifying, by the appropriate choice of a relevant modal verb, a particular nuance of desired relationship as the context requires it

The status of the modal verb construction as a clearer, more concrete expression that emphasises and specifies is also in line with the double glossing technique found in *Li*. Double grammatical glosses generally provide one translation that is morphologically closer to the Latin and an additional gloss that is more idiomatic or colloquial, in this case, the modal verb construction.

Nevertheless, the type of grammatical structures that alternate in double glosses alongside modal verb constructions also suggest that the breakdown in formal opposition between the indicative and subjunctive played a role in the history of the subjunctive and the 'modal auxiliaries' in English. Double glosses such as *þætte ic gesii ł þæt ic mæge sea* L *ut uideam* MkGl (Li) 10.51 indicate that *mæge sea* is not a mechanical grammatical circumlocution for the subjunctive form *gesii*. But in cases such as *ne ðe ue gesaldon ł nalde ue geseall a* L *tradidissemus* JnGl (Li) 18.30, the lack of formal opposition between the indicative and the subjunctive in the preterite may well have fostered the use of the periphrastic structure as a more distinctive means of signalling non-fact modality; after all, *walde* + infinitive is the only way of unambiguously expressing non-fact modality given the coalescence of the preterite indicative and subjunctive. It is also important to bear in mind that even in the present where unambiguous subjunctive forms were retained for longer, modal + infinitive constructions co-occur mainly with indicative forms in double glosses rather than the inflectional subjunctive. The lack of direct correspondence between contexts of non-fact modality and the subjunctive (inflectional or periphrastic) in Old English and the increasing occurrence of present-indicative (or of morphologically ambiguous preterite) forms would also have fostered the use of periphrastic subjunctive forms. The glossator's preferred strategy in *Li* of juxtaposing an indicative with a (subjunctive) modal + infinitive, rather than an inflectional subjunctive militates in favour of Krzyszpién's (1980: 62) view that one of the functions of modal verb compounds was to serve as "a more distinctive and productive means of signalling non-fact modality" [be it a particular aspect of non-fact modality] left unexpressed by indicative forms.

References

Behre, F. (1934). *The Subjunctive in Old English Poetry*. (Göteborgs Högskolas Årsskrift 40). Göteborg: Elanders.

Bosworth, J., & Toller, T.N. (1898). *An Anglo-Saxon Dictionary Based on the Manuscript Collection of the Late Joseph Bosworth*. Oxford: Oxford University Press.

Cole, M. (2014). *Verbal Morphosyntax in Old Northumbrian and the (Northern) Subject Rule*. (NOWELE Supplement Series). Amsterdam & Philadelphia: John Benjamins.

Denison, D. (1993). *English Historical Syntax*. London & New York: Longman.

[DOEC =] *Dictionary of Old English Web Corpus*. (2007). Antonette diPaolo Healey et al. (eds) Toronto, ON: University of Toronto. <http://www.doe. utoronto.ca/pages/pub/web-corpus.html>.

Goossens, L. (1987). The auxiliarization of the English modals: a functional grammar view. In M. Harris & P. Ramat (eds) *Historical Development of Auxiliaries*. Berlin & New York: Mouton de Gruyter, 111–143.

Gorrell, J.H. (1895). Indirect discourse in Anglo-Saxon. *PMLAA*, 10, 342–485.

Kotake, T. (2006). Aldred's multiple glosses: is the order significant? In M. Ogura (ed.), *Textual and Contextual Studies in Medieval English: Towards the Reunion of Linguistics and Philology*. Bern: Peter Lang, 35–51.

Krzyszpién, J. (1980). The periphrastic subjunctive with *magan* in Old English. *Studia Anglica Posnaniensia* 11, 49–64.

Mitchell, B. (1985). *Old English Syntax*, 2 vols. Oxford: Clarendon.

Ogawa, H. (1989). *Old English Modal Verbs: A Syntactical Study*. (Anglistica, 26). Copenhagen: Rosenkilde & Bagger.

Pons-Sanz, S. (Forthcoming). A study of Aldred's multiple glosses to the Lindisfarne Gospels. In J. Fernández-Cuesta & S.M. Pons-Sanz (eds) *The Old English Glosses to the Lindisfarne Gospels: Language, Author and Context*. Berlin: Mouton de Gruyter.

Ross, A.S.C. (1937). *Studies in the accidence of the Lindisfarne Gospels*. Leeds School of English Language Texts and Monographs 2, Kendal.

Skeat, W. W. (ed.) (1871–1887). *The Holy Gospels in Anglo-Saxon, Northumbrian, and Old Mercian versions*. Cambridge: Cambridge University Press.

Standop, E. (1957). *Syntax und Semantik des modalen Hilfsverben im Altenglischen: 'magan', 'motan', 'sculan', 'willan'*. (Beiträge zur Englischen Philologie, 38). Pöppinghaus, Bochum-Langendreer.

Visser, F. T. (1963–1973). *An Historical Syntax of the English Language*, 3 parts, 4 vols. Leiden: E. J. Brill.

6   On the Place-Name *Isle of Dogs*

Laura Wright
University of Cambridge

1. Introduction

In a contribution to the study of the *Ormulum* (Johannesson 2012),
Professor Nils-Lennart Johannesson pinpointed, by means of pictorial
as well as written evidence, the social nuance inherent in Orm's metaphor of hunting with nets and dogs to represent the disciples' catching
of men's souls for their Lord. Professor Johannesson showed how trap-
ping deer in nets for use as food was the workaday task of servants, as
opposed to the lordly pursuit of hunting as a pastime by giving chase.
Orm's net metaphor (*spelless nett* 'net of preaching'), therefore, aligned
his rendition of the Gospels with the servant class: the disciples serve
their master. Professor Johannesson notes that Orm's hunting dogs were
not present in his Latin source texts but were his own invention, and
presumably reflect twelfth-century Lincolnshire reality, where his audience would have expected dogs to accompany hunting (Johannesson
2012: 237–238). In what follows I continue with the theme of dogs, the
dogs in question being not literal but to do with word-play.

2. Explanations for the place-name *Isle of Dogs*

The place-name *Isle of Dogs* refers in Present-Day English to the land
within a meander of the River Thames in East London. In high Victorian
style, B.H. Cowper tells us that the Isle of Dogs is "embosomed, by
our noble river, which describes a magnificent curve in the form of a
horseshoe from Limehouse to Blackwall" (Cowper 1853: 1). The land
embosomed by this magnificent curve was not, historically, an island.
It was artificially made into an island when the West India Docks were

How to cite this book chapter:
Wright, L. 2015. On the Place-Name *Isle of Dogs*. In: Shaw, P., Erman, B., Melchers, G.
and Sundkvist, P. (eds) *From Clerks to Corpora: essays on the English language yesterday and today*. Pp. 87–116. Stockholm: Stockholm University Press. DOI: http://dx.doi.
org/10.16993/bab.f License: CC-BY.

created in 1802, by means of the narrow channels of the West India Dock Canal at Limehouse and Blackwall, but this was almost three hundred years after the place-name *Isle of Dogs* came into use. Strype (1720), Cunningham (1849: vol 2, 417) and Mills (2004: 121) list the following explanations for the name *Isle of Dogs*:

1.

> Next is the Isle of Dogs; being a low Marshy Ground, so called, as is reported, for that a Waterman carried a Man into this *Marsh*, and there murthered him. The Man having a Dog with him, he would not leave his Master; but Hunger forced him many times to swim over the *Thames* to *Greenwich*; which the Waterman who plied at the *Bridge* observing, followed the Dog over; and by that means the murthered Man was discovered. Soon after the Dog swimming over to *Greenwich* Bridge, where there was a Waterman seated, at him the Dog snarled, and would not be beat off, which the other Watermen perceiving, (and knowing of the *Murther*) apprehended this strange Waterman; who confessed the Fact, and was condemned and executed.
>
> (Strype (ed.) 1720: Vol 1, Book 1, 43)

My objection to this explanation is that there is no supporting evidence, and the date of 1720 is two hundred years after the date of the first attestation of the name *Isle of Dogs*. Plus, only one dog is mentioned.[1]

2.

> The fertile Soil of the Marsh here is much admired, usually known by the Name of *The Isle of Dogs*: So called, because, when our former Princes made *Greenwich* their Country Seat, and used it for Hunting, (they say), the Kennels for their Dogs were kept on this Marsh; which usually making a great Noise, the Seamen and others thereupon called the Place *The Isle of Dogs*: Though it is not an Isle, indeed, scarce a *Peninsula*, the Neck being about a Mile in length."
>
> (Strype (ed.) 1720: Vol 2, Book 6, 102)

This explanation was given to John Strype by the Reverend

[1] My grateful thanks to Prof Richard Coates, who asked me about the *Isle of Dogs* in the first place – and who noticed the singularity of dogs in the first explanation, which I had overlooked. I am also grateful to Prof Ian Donaldson, Peter Guillery, Prof Derek Keene and Prof Nicholas Rodger for criticising and commenting on earlier drafts, and to Steve Roberts for supplying the fruiterers' number-system discussed in Section 5.

Dr Josiah Woodward, Minister of the Chapel and Hospital of Poplar. Again, there is no evidence, and the dating is two hundred years after the first attested usage.

3. That *Isle of Dogs* was originally *Isle of Ducks*, or possibly *Isle of Docks*.

    My objection here is that there are no written occasions on which the area is referred to as either of these, so far as I know. Voiced word-final stops do not usually become devoiced in London English, and there is no obvious motivation for the replacement of a semantically-transparent and contextually-relevant word (whether *ducks* or *docks*) with a less relevant one.

4. That *Isle of Dogs* was originally *Isle of Doggers*, from the fourteenth-century fishing vessels known as *doggers*.

    The difficulty with this explanation is that there were no ports, hithes or landing-stages on the land embosomed by the curve of the river.[2] There was nowhere for a fishing vessel to call in, or for fishing vessels to congregate, unlike on the southern side where there were hithes at Greenwich and Deptford. Also, there is no evidence that the land was ever called *Isle of Doggers* by anybody.

5. That there were either wild dogs there, or dead dogs washed up by the tide there.

    We have no way of knowing whether either of these were true, or more true of this part of the Thames than any other.

6. That *Isle of Dogs* alludes to the Canary Islands, because Latin *Insulae Canariae* means 'island of dogs'. The historian Pliny says that these islands were so-named because there were large dogs there.

    This hypothesis lacks evidence or circumstance that would make this likely. *Canary Wharf* appears not to have become

---

[2] I thank an anonymous reviewer for pointing out that the name *Stepney*, earlier *Stebbenhithe* (and spelling variants) implies a hithe or landing-stage. However it is not thought that the hithe in question was situated on the marsh, but at Ratcliff Cross, in present-day Limehouse: "Evidence for Saxon settlement is etymological. The first reference to Stepney is to men of the bishop of London's estate (vill) of Stybbanhythe c. 1000, recording a hithe or landing-place either on the Thames or the Lea. Since the place-names Old Ford and Stratford are associated with the Lea, while the name Stepney has always been linked with the southwest quarter of the parish, the hithe was probably on the gravel at Ratcliff Cross, one of the few sites below London Bridge suitable for landing before the marshes were embanked and wharfed." (Baker (ed.) 1998: 13–19).

so-named until 1936, when the shipping company Fred Dessen & Co., which unloaded fruit from the Mediterranean and Canary Islands, was granted permission to rename the wharf known previously as *West Wood Wharf*. [3]

I conclude that none of these explanations really holds water, with no supporting evidence for any of them.

3. Early attestations of the place-name *Isle of Dogs*

The name *Isle of Dogs* is first attested in 1520. Before 1520, the place we know as the *Isle of Dogs* was called *Stepney Marsh*, for which Mills (2001: 121) has a first attestation date of 1365. Stepney Marsh is relatively well documented: there exists a field survey of the marsh from around 1400, and also wills of several landlords who bequeathed land in Stepney Marsh to their heirs in the late 1300s and early 1400s. There was a settlement in the marsh from at least the second half of the twelfth century; the manor house at the southern end, somewhat inland from the sea-wall, was owned by William de Pontefract, and his manor house, chapel and the hamlet around became known as *Pomfrets*,[4] which manor was ultimately owned by the Bishop of London (Cowper 1853: 16). However this place-name did not last. The manor house was in ruins by the 1360s, and the hamlet was abandoned in 1448 when the river burst through the sea-wall (Dugdale 1662: 72). It seems that the manor of Pomfret became abandoned because of partible inheritance, as none of the descendents of William de Pontefract actually lived at Pomfrets or maintained it or the sea-walls (Currie (ed.) 1998: 1–7, 52–63).

Further place-names of Old English etymology in the marsh are as follows. At the northern perimeter of Stepney Marsh the long street village of *Poplar*[5] runs from foreshore to foreshore, with the lime kilns

---

[3] 'The West India Docks: The buildings: warehouses', *Survey of London: volumes 43 and 44: Poplar, Blackwall and Isle of Dogs* (1994), pp. 284–300. URL: http://www.british-history.ac.uk/report.aspx?compid=46497&strquery=west india docks buildings war. Date accessed: 06 December 2012.

[4] 'The Isle of Dogs: Introduction', *Survey of London: volumes 43 and 44: Poplar, Blackwall and Isle of Dogs* (1994), pp. 375–387. URL: http://www.british-history.ac.uk/report.aspx?compid=46507. Date accessed: 06 December 2012.

[5] AN *popler* 'at the poplar tree', Gover, Mawer, Stenton 1942: 133–134.

of *Limehouse* at the north-western point of the curve[6] and *Blackwall*[7] at the north-eastern point. Moving south around the curve, the western embankment of Stepney Marsh was called *Westwall*;[8] the north-eastern embankment was called *Blakewalle*, present-day *Blackwall* (after which the hamlet was named)[9] and some, or perhaps all, of the embankment round Stepney Marsh was called *Themsewall* and *Longewall*.[10] Further dwellings in the marsh were situated at *Westwall* and at *Newebygynge*.[11]

From various wills we learn that the marshland was called *Stebbenhith mersche*; *Stebbenhithmerssh*;[12] that fields in the marsh were called *Margarusagre atte gate*, 'Margaret atte Gate's acre',[13] *Potterisfeld*, 'Potter's Field' and *Chafcroft*, 'Calves' Croft'.[14] We learn that there was a bridge or jetty called *ffisshbregge*; and that the chapel at Pomfrets was dedicated to St Mary and All Saints in the marsh: *Beate Marie & Omnibus Sanctis*,[15] *Beate Marie de Capelle in le Merssh*,[16] *Capelle Beate Marie in Marischo*.[17] From the Stepney Field Survey of c.1400[18] we learn that *ffysshysbregge*, *ffysshysfeld* and *ffysshyslond* were owned by Thomas ffyssh; that Thomas Edewyne had three rods of land lying by the wall called *Thameswall*; and that John Hamme had one rod lying above *le Throwedych*.[19] The names of hills, fields, walls, enclosures,

---

[6] Gover, Mawer, Stenton 1942: 150; OE *līm* 'lime' + OE *āst* 'oast, kiln'.

[7] Gover, Mawer, Stenton 1942: 135; presumably OE *blæc* 'black' + OE *weall* 'wall, rampart of earth or stone'.

[8] Kew, TNA, SC 12/11/31 fo 12v.

[9] Kew, TNA, SC 12/11/31 fo 16v.

[10] Kew, TNA, SC 12/11/31 fos 17v and 19. Cowper (1853: 4), discussing process of building these medieval embankments, writes "With might and main they toiled, and by might and main they overcame".

[11] Kew, TNA, SC 12/11/31 fo 12. "*wall vocata Newebygynge*" – which might indicate ongoing embanking work as *bigging* meant both 'dwelling' and 'building' (see *OED* bigging, *n.*).

[12] E.g. 1404; London Metropolitan Archives DL/C/B/004/MS09171/002, fo 54v; Will of Roger Grummote.

[13] 1376, LMA DL/C/B/004/MS09171/002, fo 36v. Roman type indicates expansion of abbreviations and place-names have been given initial capital letters.

[14] 1380, LMA DL/C/B/004/MS09171/002, fo 71; Will of Williamo pottere de maresco de Stebunhith.

[15] 1380, LMA DL/C/B/004/MS09171/002, fo 71.

[16] 1402, LMA DL/C/B/004/MS09171/002, fo 26; Will of John Broun of Stebbenhith.

[17] 1405, LMA DL/C/B/004/MS09171/002, fo 51v.

[18] Kew, TNA SC/12/11/31. I have tried to restrict this list to features in the marsh alone, but it is possible that a few may have lain further north. See Croot (1997) for a description and discussion of the Stepney Field Survey.

[19] Kew, TNA SC/12/11/31, fos 17v, 18.

ditches, weirs, hedges, bushes and meadows in the marsh recorded in the Field Survey were:

I have counted 74 place-names in Stepney Marsh in the late 1300s and 1400s, but no mention at all of the name *Isle of Dogs*. If the name had been in use then, one might expect it to show up in these detailed sources. But it does not.

Table 1. Names of hills, fields, walls, enclosures, ditches, weirs, hedges, bushes and meadows in Stepney Marsh (*Field Survey of Stepney*, c.1400, TNA SC/12/11/31).

fo 11	*Sandhell, Battysfeld*
fo 11v	*Westwall, Westyerde, Kalfstokkysfeld, Pylyslond*
fo 12	*Sonderesffeld, Sondereslond, Sonderesthrowe, Wall vocata Newebygynge, Amystonerffeld, le Chekyr*
fo 12v	*Cochysgate, Worlycheslond, Sandhell in South Newelond, Codyneshawe, Kalstokkyslond, Kalstokkyswere, Chapell Lond, Rodeberdeslonde, Coughdesyerde, Long Acre, Karles Acre, Breweresyerde, Schypmade, Gattyswere, Goldyngeslond, ffanneresmade* (belonging to Henry Vannere), *Shyftylcroft*
fo 14	*le ffanneresmade apud le Wylde*
fo 15	*Byllokysland, Northbroke, Elderbussh, Scottysacre, Longemade, le Hyedoune, le Netherdoune iuxta le Hye doune, Crepyneslond in le Hyedoune, Wowehegge*
fo 17v	*Rancesfeld, Rysshcroft par le Rance, Themsewall, Deleswey, Admondeslond in Estnessh*
fo 18	*Le Throwedych in Gabelond, Admondeswere, Madehawys, Deleslond, Boleyffeld*
fo 19	*Nethyr Somerlase, Nokysfeld, Byllokyswere, Southawys, Wereye, Madeye, ffleecroft, Longewalle iuxta Madeye*
fo 19v	*Southmadeye, Schatffletebregge, Chynham*
fo 20	*Brademade, Sandhell in Brademade, le Longeforlond, Est Bryзt Onelond, Colmansyerde*
fo 20v	*Wyseffletdych, Rowynglond, Thornhegge*
fo 21	*Chalfcroft, Grandylhope, Bradecroft in le Hooke*
fo 21v	*Pareshawe apud Pomffret*
fo 22	*Buntynglond, Smythlond*

We next turn to some information provided by Sir William Dugdale in his *History of Imbanking and drayning of divers Fenns and Marshes* of 1662:

> Upon an inquisition taken in 27 H. 6. the Jurors presented, that by the violence of the tides upon the banks of Stebenhithe marsh, a great part of the said banks, adjoining to that marsh, was then ruinous and broken through the neglect of the Land-holders there: And that through the default of one *Iohn Harpour* Gentleman, in not repairing his bank, opposite to Deptford Strond, there was, on the *Monday*, being the Feast of the *Annunciation* of the blessed Virgin, in the 26 year of the reign of the said King H. 6. a breach made in the said bank of the before-specified *Iohn Harpour*, for the length of *xx* Rods, unto the land of *Iohn Fyloll*, in so much as a thousand Acres of land, lying within the said marsh, were drowned.
>
> (Dugdale 1662: 72)

It is significant that the 26 Henry 6 (1448) breach of the banks occurred opposite Deptford Strand, because in 1520 the place-name *Isle of Dogs* occurs, also referring to a specific area of Stepney Marsh opposite Deptford Strand; specifically, opposite the Royal Dockyard at Deptford. It is in *The Boke of thaccoumptte of Costys Ande Charges don & made on the Kinges Schyppes for the transportynge of the kinge & the Qwen to Calyce to the metynge of the frensche kinge & from thence in to Inglond Ageyn*.[20] This is the accounts-book of Henry VIII's Dockyard at Deptford, where warships were built and repaired, and which had been in existence for seven years in 1520. The place-name *Isle of Dogs* is mentioned as a berth:

> "& to John holmes for a hose for the mary George lynge in at doke at theille of dog*ges* afor depford xd"
> (October 1520; Kew, TNA MS E 36/11, fo 117v, calendared in *Letters and Papers of Henry VIII*, volume 3, pp 369–381)

The location of *theille of dogges* is 'afor depford' (the word *opposite* was not available, as it did not carry its present meaning at this date, see Wright 2006). The same ship, the *Mary George*, was again berthed in the same place five years later:

> "vppon the Este side of the ile of doggis" (the leaf is damaged here so there is no more context) … "Item the Mary george beinge of portage / ijC &

---

[20] Kew, TNA E 36/11, fo 104; 'Calyce' is Calais.

L tonne / lythe / vppon the sowthe syde / of the Ile of doggis / and
muste be Calkyd / w'ine the borde & w'oughte / also she must be
seerchyd for wurmehoolys because she hath ben in leevaunte /"
(October 1526; London, British Library Cotton MS Otho E IX, fo
68²¹ calendared in Letters and Papers of Henry VIII, volume 4, pp
757–772)

4. Early map evidence

The first map to show the place-name *Isle of Dogs* is Robert Adam's
map *Thamesis Descriptio*, of 1588, which shows the lower reaches
of the River Thames below the Pool of London.²² Robert Adam was
Surveyor of Works to Queen Elizabeth I. His map was made as part
of the response to the Spanish Armada, the Secretary of State for War
having asked what arrangements had been made for the defence of the
kingdom. It shows the river as seen from on board a vessel, plus the
army's camp further inland at West Tilbury. The map demonstrates,
by means of arcs of sweeping lines, the rakes of gun-fire possible from
the defences positioned on the riverbank. There are tiny horses and
riders depicted on the causeway from Tilbury Fort to the camp "beset
wth twentye & seven ensigns", and rowbarges and small boats at the
barrage or boom between Gravesend and Tilbury Fort. Two batteries
are shown upriver on either side at Lee Ness on the south bank and
Saunders Ness opposite on the north (Saunders Ness lies on the eastern
side of Stepney Marsh). These are the first marked defences downriver
from London, and there is another boom across the river at this point.
The river seems well defended, but the effort was not, in the event,
necessary, as the Armada was blown off course and never attempted to
attack London.

The careful labelling of this map deserves a fuller treatment.²³ There
are three types: labels written perpendicular to the river, labels written
horizontally to the river, and labels written in the river. The first group
contains natural features of the riverbank which enable that part of the
bank to be identified visually from onboard ship, with two non-natural

---

²¹ See *State Papers Online* database:
http://go.galegroup.com/mss/i.do?id=GALE|MC4301001776&v=2.1&
u=cambuni&it=r&p=SPOL&sw=w&viewtype=Calendar
²² London, British Library, Adds MS 44839.
²³ I am particularly grateful to Prof Derek Keene for drawing my attention to the
significance of the orientation of the labelling.

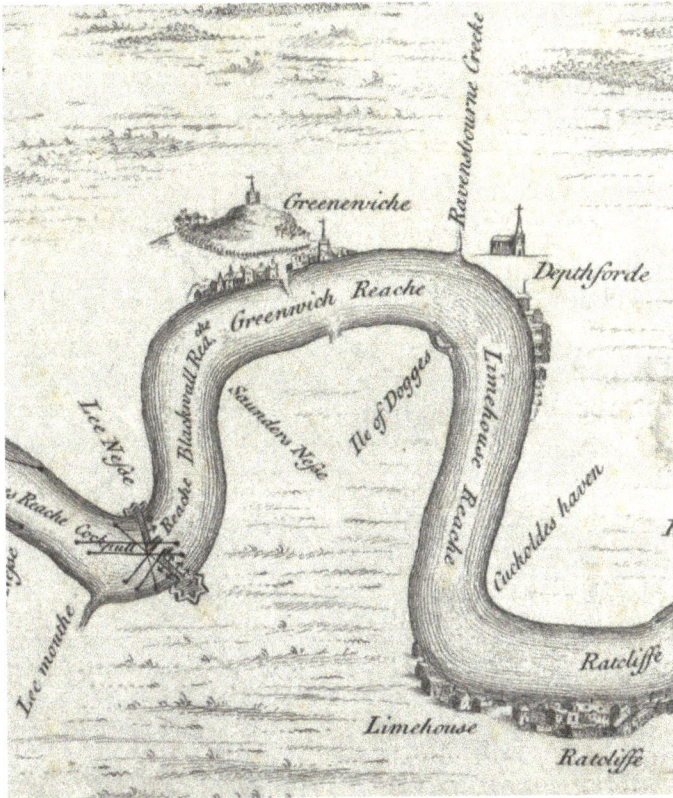

Thamesis Descriptio Anno 1588, surveyed by Robert Adams, 1738. Crace Collection, British Library. Reproduced with permission. (Note: this is a different map to the one described, the same in all essentials but with shipping omitted and slightly different spellings).

(source: http://www.bl.uk/onlinegallery/onlineex/crace/t/largeimage88364.html)

exceptions (*Gallion* and *Tripcotts*, the names of riverside buildings in what was otherwise featureless marsh). Head-nouns are *breache, creeke, elmes, haven, ile, mouthe, nesse, pointe, tree.* The second group, written horizontally to the river, contains place-names. The third group, written in the river, contains the names of stretches of the river that could be viewed from bend to bend. Head-nouns are *checke, hope, poole, reache.*

Group One, written perpendicular to the river, grouped alphabetically according to head-noun, contains:

Ye Litle Breache
Ye greate Breache
Stackie Breache

Barkinge Creeke
Daignâ Creeke
Dartfoorde Creeke
East Ham Creeke
Rainam Creeke
Rauensborne Creeke

Podds elmes
Saunders elmes

Ile of Dogges

Cuckolds haven

Leemouthe

Brode Nesse
Crosse Nesse
Erithe Nesse
Gallion Nesse
Greenhith Nesse
Hooke Nesse
Lee Nesse
Magott Nesse
Northfleete Nesse
Saunders Nesse
Staffleete Nesse
Stone Nesse
Theeves Nesse
Tilberie Nesse

Gilian tree pointe
Middway tree

Gallion
Tripcotts

Saunders Elmes and *Podds Elmes* are marked by trees. *Gallion* and
Tripcotts are marked by small buildings. The breaches are marked by
lesser or greater pools, and the creeks are marked by tributaries entering the river. The features labelled with Group One names all act as

checkpoints in otherwise featureless marsh, either distinguishing one reach of the river from the next, or helping to identify that particular reach. They are navigational aids, especially necessary in darkness or foggy weather.

Group Two, written horizontally to the river, and looking downstream from Westminster, contains place-names:

Westminster, Lambeth, London, Southwarke, Raderife, Ratcliffe, Limehouse, Depthfoorde, Greenewiche, Woolwiche, Erithe, Rainam Marshe, Pourfleete, Stone, St Clementes, Greenehithe, Graies, Northfleete, Grauesende, Tilberie forte, The Campe, Grauesende forte, the olde Blockhouse (marked thus on both sides of the river), East Tilberie, Cliffe.

Group Three labels are written in the river, looking from downstream from London:

the Poole
Ratcliffe Checke
Limehouse Reache
Greenewiche Reache
Blackwalle Reache
Cockpull Reache
Podds elmes Reache
Woolwiche Reache
Gallion Reache
Tripcott Reache
Crosse Nesse Reache
Erithe Reache
Maese
Longe Reache
St Clements Reache
Northfleete Hope
Grauesende Reache
Tilberie Hope

These short stretches of river from bend to bend enable the sailor to identify his position at any one point.

There are two labels written on Stepney Marsh: *Saunders Nesse* at the south-eastern point of the curve and *Ile of Dogges* at the south-western point. The *I* of the label *Isle of Dogges* is located right next to two small islands in the breach opposite Deptford. Both labels are written perpendicular to the river, aligning them with features of the riverbank that could be identified from on board ship as aids to navigation. They are both identifying features, a ness and an isle, in otherwise uninterrupted marshland. It might be argued that there is little room on Stepney Marsh for a label to be written horizontally, and that therefore the certain identification of the label *Ile of Dogges* with the two small islands, rather than the mainland, is not secure. However this is also the case with what appears to be an anomaly in Group Two, *Rainam Marshe*, which, being a natural feature of the riverbank, might be thought to sit better in Group One. However, Rainam Marshe is not an identifying feature – all the foreshore from the estuary up was lined with indistinguishable marshland. This particular marsh is named because it is depicted as an island, created by a small channel slicing the tip of Erith Ness from east to west. The perpendicular label *Erithe Nesse* (the identifying feature) intersects the horizontal label *Rainam Marshe* (the place-name) at right angles. Similarly, the perpendicular label *Greenehithe Nesse* (the identifying feature) intersects the horizontal label *St Clementes* (the place-name) at right angles. The feature salient to shipping – in this case, the ness or bend of the land – is clearly differentiated in each case from the place-name. Had *Isle of Dogs* been a marsh place-name, it could have been positioned horizontally so as to intersect the label *Saunders Nesse*, just as the horizontal label *Rainam Marshe* has been positioned. But it was not, and therefore has to be interpreted as marking the two small islands.

Lastly, let us consider the shipping in the river. There are four separate groups of ships depicted, at the Tilbury Fort/Gravesend boom (4 or 5 rowbarges and several small boats), Ratcliffe Checke (9 ships), the Pool (5 ships), and just upstream of London Bridge (3 large vessels, 6 small). The only other vessel to be depicted is a three-masted ship in the river between Deptford and the Isle of Dogs islands.

Recall the Field Survey of c.1400, where two island names were mentioned on folio 19, *Wereye* and *Madeye*. These are presumably derived from Old English *wer* + *īeg*, 'Weir Island' and *mǣd* + *īeg*, 'Mead Island'. There are only two island names mentioned in the Field Survey and I speculate that they are the pre-1520 names of the two eyots afore Deptford, bestowed by those who worked in the marsh, catching fish in weirs and farming sheep on meadows. Eyots in the Thames are not permanently fixed entities but shift in shape and position over time, and can be unified at low water yet divided into two or more at high water.

Therefore a name of *Isle of Dogs* for two eyots is not inappropriate: the Thames eyots upriver at Brentford now collectively known as *Brentford Eyot* currently fit this description.[24] The foreshore opposite Deptford at this point in the curve is particularly shifting and unstable,[25] and the two Stepney eyots have since disappeared, but B. H. Cowper records that the two eyots were positioned where Messrs Ferguson's mast-pond was situated in 1853, on the south side of the pond adjoining Tindall's dock and the mast house (Cowper 1853: 17) "which pond is an indentation of the river bank, and called Drunken Dock". Apparently one of the eyots was still there at that time. This mast pond was directly opposite the King's Yard at Deptford (Cowper 1853: 19).

To recap so far: the place-name *Isle of Dogs* referred originally not to Stepney Marsh, but to two small islands lying in the river in a breach on the Stepney side opposite Deptford. The eyots may not predate 1448, which was when the river flooded that part of the marsh (they may have resulted from that inundation), and are likely to have been known to marsh-dwellers as *Wereye* 'Weir Island' and *Madeye* 'Mead Island' between 1448 and 1520. The dating and the context make it likely that the name or nickname *Isle of Dogs* was bestowed by workers in Deptford Dockyard, as they were the ones who created a dock out of the Stepney Marsh eyots. In which case, what do we know about the ships that were berthed at this place at this point in time? Can the *Mary George* and her ilk tell us anything about the Stepney Marsh dock?

5. Early Ships at Deptford

We return to the *Book of Accounts of the King's Ships* where the name *Isle of Dogs* is first mentioned:

> "Here Aftyre Ensuythe All Suche Costys Chargys & sundry expenses hade made & done by the Commaundement of the kinge owre moste drade soueren lorde henry the viij from the xijth daye of marche in the xjth yere of his moste nobull Reyngn of fore and apon the kinge is grette barke the lesse barke the newe barke namyd the Kateryn

---

[24] The western end of Brentford Eyot, which at high water becomes a separate islet, is known nowadays as *Smith's Eyot* or *Lot's Eyot*.

[25] Information from Julian Kingston. Prof Derek Keene suggests that the name *Isle of Dogs* denoted the larger island, on later maps marked 'Osier Hope', rather than both of them.

plesaunce The mary & John w^t the ij Rowbarges whiche schippes
were prepared Ryggyd & sett forthe ffor the transportyng of owre
seid soueren lord to Calice and from Calice in to Inglond ageyn"

(October 1520, Kew, TNA MS E 36/11 fo 105)

Table 2. The King's ships in 1525 (Sources: Loades (2002); "Names of the
King's ships at Portsmouth and Thames, 22 Oct 17 Hen 8", *Letters and
Papers, Foreign and Domestic, Henry VIII*, volume 4: 1524–1530. Tonnage
given where specified. Where tonnages vary it is because more than one figure
is given in the source documents. (bark) signifies that a vessel was specified as
such in the source documents.)

Henry Grace A Dieu	(1,500 tons)
Great Galley	(800 tons)
Sovereign	(800 tons)
Gabriel Royal	(650–700–750 tons)
Katherine Fortileza	(700 tons)
Mary Rose	(600 tons)
Great Barbara	(400 tons)
Great Nicholas	(400 tons)
John Baptist	(400 tons)
Peter Pomegranate	(340 tons)
Mary James	(260 tons)
Mary George	(240–250 tons)
Great Bark	(200–250 tons)
Mary and John	(200 tons)
Minion	(180 tons)
Lesse Bark	(160–180 tons)
Hulk	(160 tons)
Mary Gylforde	(160 tons)
Primrose	(160 tons)
Henry of Hampton	(120 tons)
Maudelen of Deptford	(120 tons)
Mary Imperial	(120 tons)
Katherine Bark	(100 tons)

Table 2. Continued

Bark of Bullen	(80 tons)
Griffin	(80 tons)
Trinity Henry	(80 tons)
Sweepstake	(bark, 65 tons)
Bark of Murlesse (Morlaix)	(60 tons)
Swallow	(60 tons)
Great Sabra	(50 tons)
John of Greenwich	(50 tons)
Lesser Sabra	(40 tons)
Bonaventure	
Carvel of Eu	
Jennett of Purwyn	
Katherine Plesaunce	(bark)
Lion	
Margaret	
Mary Fortune	(bark)
Regent	

The king's lesser bark, his great bark, the little bark and his new bark were being repaired or built on the Thames in 1520.[26] In 1495 the peacetime navy had no more than three or four ships. By 1523 it had about thirty, of varying sizes (Loades 2002: 24), as Henry VIII built up the navy. By 1525, the following 40 of the King's ships were listed as being in the Thames, or in the Thames and at Portsmouth:

A *bark* was a smaller, masted, sailing vessel. If we assume that anything greater than 250 tons (the *Great Bark*) was not called a bark, and only include of those without specific tonnage the vessels that were explicitly named as barks, then even at this conservative estimate, more than half of Henry's fleet were known, at the time, as barks.

At this point, let us leave ships and consider other islands in the Thames. Upstream, small islands are known as *eyots* (*Brentford Eyot, Chiswick Eyot, Isleworth Eyot*, also spelt *ait*), from Old English *īeg*

---

[26] Letters and Papers, Foreign and Domestic, Henry VIII, volume 3, October 1520.

'island' with diminutive suffix –*eth* (*OED* ait, *n.*, eyot, *n.*, with fifteenth and sixteenth century attestations spelt *le Eyte, hayte*). Downstream, the far bigger islands came to be known as *isles* (*Isle of Grain, Isle of Sheppey, Isle of Harty, Isle of Thanet*). *Isle* is from Anglo-Norman, ultimately from Latin *insula* (*OED* isle, *n.* 1. a.); *ilde of Wiʒt* is attested from c1320; *jlde off Tenett* (Thanet) from 1473.[27] I argue in Wright (2010) that the Thames term for a tidal eyot found at tributaries' deltas was a *horse* (e.g. *Fobbing Horse, Upper Horse, Lower Horse, Wodeham Horse, Sea Horse, Wyllyspitt Horse* and perhaps *Horse End* and *Horsleydown*) from OE *horsc* 'mud'. I have speculated that the traditional names for the islands opposite Deptford were *Wereye* and *Madeye*, and we might also reasonably expect these islands to have been known collectively as *Stepney Eyot*. Instead, the name *Isle of Dogs* occurs, in the context of ship-building and dock-working. To return to the barks, I wonder whether this is Tudor dockers' word-play. The grandiose downstream *Isle of* – has been applied bathetically to very small islets, and the name *Dogs* bestowed as a pun, the eyot at Stepney harbouring barks.

Does this hypothesis fit what we know of the word *bark*? *OED* bark | barque, *n.* 2 derives *bark* 'small ship with sails' as being "possibly from Celtic"; "a small vessel with sails; the latter was the sense with which the word was taken from French into English". The first attestation in English is by Caxton in 1477. *OED* bark, n. 3 derives *bark* 'the sharp explosive cry uttered by dogs' from the Old English verb *beorcan* 'to bark'. The first written attestation of the noun is not, according to the dictionary, until 1562, but this need not detain us as the attestation is poetical (literature being the text-type most thoroughly scrutinised). As the verb is Old English, the noun could have been derived at any point in the language's history. The present-day quasi-archaic spelling *barque* is a red herring: a search of the *Early English Books Online* database reveals that in the sixteenth century the spelling was always *bark(e*, with the –*que* spelling an innovation of later centuries.

That the pun was possible does not mean that it was certainly the origin of the place-name *Isle of Dogs*, of course; it merely raises the possibility. We next hear of the place-name *Isle of Dogs* on John Norden's map of Middlesex of 1593. This is a map of the whole of Middlesex and so the area is necessarily small and lacking in detail, but two parallel horizontal streams are drawn east-west on Stepney Marsh so as

---

[27] Note that the 'island' element in *Canvey Island* seems to postdate the period under discussion here. It is attested as *Canwaie Iles* in 1586 (Reaney 1935: 148).

to cut the marsh into two horizontal bands, with a meridional stream flowing north-south between the lower horizontal stream and the Thames, and another smaller north-south stream at Saunders Ness (neither *Stepney Marsh* nor *Saunders Ness* is so labelled on the map). Four labels appear in the marsh, with three symbols identified in the key. The labels are *Stepney* at the far north, identified with the symbol for a parish; *Limehouse* in the north-west and *Blackwall* in the north-east, both identified with the symbol for "Hamletes or villages"; and *Isle of doges ferm*, the lettering printed in the middle of the marsh but the identifying symbol placed precisely where Pomfrets was previously situated. This symbol, the key informs us, indicates "Howses of Knightes, Gent. &c.", and indicates that by 1593 the place-name *Isle of Dogs* had superseded the place-name *Pomfrets* for the gentleman's house and hamlet situated on the inland part of Saunders Ness. It does not follow that the whole of Stepney Marsh had become known by that name at that date. In fact all the evidence accrued so far indicates that Stepney Marsh was still known as Stepney Marsh until at least 1600 (and indeed considerably later).

6. On London Workers' Word-Play

If the punning explanation of the place-name *Isle of Dogs* suggested in Section 4 is correct – and we will never know, but it does fit the facts, which no explanation has done hitherto – then dockers' word-play goes back at least to the days of the Tudors. That there is ample evidence that writers of Tudor literature enjoyed word-play perhaps needs no elaboration here.[28] But what about Tudor dock-workers? We cannot

---

[28] I leave it to the reader to decide whether both senses of *bark* are operative in Shakespeare's *Sonnet 80* (1609):

O how I faint when I of you do write,
Knowing a better spirit doth vse your name,
And in the praise thereof spends all his might,
To make me toung-tide speaking of your fame.
But since your worth (wide as the Ocean is)
The humble as the proudest saile doth beare,
My sawsie barke (inferior farre to his)
On your broad maine doth wilfully appeare.
Your shallowest helpe will hold me vp a floate,
Whilst he vpon your soundlesse deepe doth ride,
Or (being wrackt) I am a worthlesse bote,
He of tall building, and of goodly pride.
Then If he thriue and I be cast away,
The worst was this, my loue was my decay.

know whether they too created puns. However, we do know that there
has in more recent centuries been a tradition of London workers using
word-play as an integral part of their working day. I give by way of
illustration here a counting system[29] long in use between (although not
limited to) importers, wholesalers and retailers in the fruit trade:

Table 3. Fruiterers' counting terms, London, 2012.

1	Cherry
2	Bottle
3	Carpet
4	Rofe/Sugar
5	Ching
6	Tom
7	Nevis
8	Garden
9	Clothes
10	Cockle
20	Apple
25	Pony
500	Monkey

Some of these terms are demonstrably over a hundred years old and
must speak to continuity of usage from father to son. Henry Mayhew
attests to numbers four and seven pronounced backwards: "'I'll try
you a "gen"' (shilling), said a coster; 'And a "rouf yenap"' (fourpence),
added the other." (Mayhew 1851: I 17/2, cited in *OED* rouf, *adj.* and
n.; see also neves *adj.* and *n.*). *OED* marks headwords *rouf* and *neves*
as 'now rare' and 'obs. rare', although they have subsequently been
common in the spoken functional variety of market traders.[30] *Carpet*,
from rhyming *carpet bag* with *drag* (*OED* carpet n. II. 6.; carpet bag
n.2; drag n.8 b.), presumably postdates 1830 when carpet bags were in
vogue, but is in reference to *drag* in the sense 'stretch of imprisonment',
attested from 1781. The sense development is from *drag* 'handcart'

[29] Kindly provided by Mr Steve Roberts of Westminster Produce, who is a third-generation Covent Garden fruiterer.
[30] *Sugar* must have come later than *rouf* as *sugar loaf* rhymes with [rəʊf].

to "The drag, is the game of robbing carts, waggons, or carriages.of trunks, bale-goods, or any other property. Done for a drag, signifies convicted for a robbery of the before-mentioned nature" (James Hardy Vaux *A Vocabulary of the Flash Language*, 1819) to Henry Mayhew's "Sometimes they are detected, and get a 'drag' (1851: I. 219/2), in reference to the length of the term of imprisonment, which seems to have been at first six, then three months. *Monkey*, '500', first occurs in *St James's: A Satirical Poem, in Six Epistles to Mr. Crockford*, by someone writing under the pseudonym of 'Westminster St James', first published in London in 1827. The subject is aristocrats gambling away the family inheritance at Crockfords gambling club, so that their children, the heirs, are ruined by the losses of the father. The poem mentions an Earl losing 'ten or twenty ponies' and a footnote explains: "It is not every reader that is aware of the modern title by which, in the Clubs, certain sums of money are recognised. A pony is £25, a rouleau £50, and a monkey £500. The noble Earl in question, who is gifted with two sons, partaking very largely of the latter quality, was accosted by a friend at Crockford's one evening, (when His Lordship had been a loser,) who thought him looking very much out of humour, and asked the cause. 'I have lost a monkey,' replied the Earl." (*OED* monkey, n. IV. 23; St James 1827: 134). *Pony*, '25' (pounds, guineas or sovereigns), is first attested in a novel of 1797 by Mary Robinson, and again the meaning is made clear in a footnote: "There is no touching her even for a poney. [Note. Half a rouleau or twenty-five guineas]." (*OED* pony, *n.1* and *adj.* 3.; Robinson 1797: II, 97). Although I can find no specific supporting evidence or previous discussion, *ching* 'five' would seem to be derived from Anglo-Norman *cinq*, surviving along with *ace*, *deuce*, *trey, quatre, sise*, still in use (or in use until very recently) in the context of card-play (*OED* cinque | cinq, *n.*),[31] and in Channel Islands French. The relevance for our present purposes is that the counting system (or parts thereof) must have been used over several generations in an entirely non-literary, working context. It does not constitute proof that Tudor dock-workers did the same, of course, but it gives a measure of plausibility to the suggestion that they might have done so.

---

[31] For the palatalisation of the first phoneme, cf. ME *chiche* 'chickpea' < AN *chiche* < L *cicer* (*OED* chich, *n.*). Jerriais *chîn, chînq* 'five'.

7. Jonson and Nashe's play *Isle of Dogs*

In the summer of 1597 the place-name *Isle of Dogs* achieved some kind of notoriety, but it is unclear why. The playwrights Ben Jonson and Thomas Nashe (and perhaps members of Pembroke's company) wrote and performed, but did not publish, a satirical comedy called *The Isle of Dogs* (www.lostplays.org; Donaldson 2012: 101). As a direct result, Jonson and two members of the company were imprisoned, and Nashe fled into hiding. Donaldson (2012: 103–107) reconstructs events: in late July or early August, the Queen's inquisitor, interrogator and torturer Robert Topcliffe was instructed by the Privy Council to discover the instigators and perpetrators of the play, and to seek out all copies and their owners. Nashe could not be found, but Jonson and his two fellow players were arrested and imprisoned. They were examined on 15th August by the Privy Council Court at Greenwich, and accused of "lewd and mutinous behaviour,"[32] the play containing "very seditious and slanderous matter". It is likely that they were tortured, but seven weeks later, on 8th October 1597, the three men were set free. Simultaneously, although it is not clear whether the two events were related, the Lord Mayor and Court of Common Council requested on 28th July 1597 that the Privy Council ban all theatrical activity, it being to the detriment of the well-being of the citizens (the Corporation of London had made similar requests on previous occasions). The same day, the Privy Council banned all plays in London throughout the summer, and ordered that theatres be dismantled – although it seems that the second part of this edict was not carried out. Was this prohibition a response to recent productions of *The Isle of Dogs* at the Swan playhouse? The impresario Henslowe recorded a memorandum on 10th August that the current restraint was "by the meanes of playinge the Jeylle of Dooges",[33] so he seems to have thought that it was. Donaldson (2012: 106) summarises the speculations of literary historians about who, exactly, might have found the play offensive. Individuals have been suggested,[34] but Donaldson suggests that the severity of the response seems too great to have been triggered by an attack on a mere individual, and suggests that it may have touched upon matters of national defence (2012: 107).

---

[32] *lewd* meant 'evil, wicked, unprincipled' in this context; see *OED* lewd, *adj.* 5.

[33] http://www.lostplays.org/index.php/Isle_of_Dogs,_The. *Jeylle of Dooges* = Isle of Dogs.

[34] The King of Poland, the late Lord Chamberlain (Donaldson 2012: 106, and references therein).

Following Donaldson's suggestion, if we take the phrase 'Isle of Dogs' to have conveyed a meaning of something along the lines of 'place where warships were fitted out', then the question follows, what was happening to shipping that summer? Wernham (1994: 143–190) describes in detail the movements of the fleet. The Queen's main priority that year was to prevent the Spanish armada[35] from attacking Britain. At the beginning of 1597, relations with France were "about at their lowest" (Wernham 1994: 146), and her two counsellors Sir Robert Cecil and the Earl of Essex were quarrelling with each other. There was rebellion in Ireland, which rebels (it was feared) might seek help from Spain, and the wheat harvest was failing. National security seemed greatly threatened. Elizabeth was persuaded that her best form of defence was attack, and on 10th March, she made Essex Master of the Ordnance. However it was not clear during the spring what his commission would be – whether to attack the armada at Ferrol, to put down the rebellion in Ireland or to attack Calais – and it was not until 9th May that the Privy Council wrote to the Lords Lieutentant and Commisioners of Musters instructing them to mobilise troops for service abroad. In early April, a plan was made to fit out two fleets. The first would lie off the Spanish coast and intercept the armada. The second fleet would follow, and be the striking force. But Elizabeth delayed, and withheld her permission until the 20th May. Immediately thereafter, during the end of May, 28 ships of war were fitted out, plus around 30 flyboats to transport troops.[36] The two-fleet plan was dropped and consolidated into one 'powerful strike force', with Essex in command.

Essex's commission had been sealed on 4th June, that is, 4th June is the date from when it could have been known that a war fleet was being assembled. He received his detailed instructions privately on 15th June: he was to destroy the armada then lying at Ferrol, and afterwards sail to the Azores to intercept the Spanish treasure ships where they revictualled on returning from the East and West Indies, and to return home by winter. He was forbidden to attack either Spain or Portugal. Essex's fleet finally set out on 10th July, but a week of storms caused half the fleet to return, leaking and damaged. The other half

---

[35] Known as the Ferrol armada, from where it spent the summer of 1597.
[36] Cadwallader (1923: 5) specifies 38 vessels and troop-carriers, plus 5/6 small vessels with each of the 4 squadrons, plus 20 voluntary barks on the look-out for plunder. The discrepancy arises, I think, due to differences in classifying the smaller ships.

Table 4. Ships of the 1597 Islands Voyage fleet. (Sources: Wernham (1994), Gorges (1625), Cadwallader (1923). Dating and construction information taken from Colledge and Warlow eds (2006), http://en.wikipedia.org/wiki/List_of_ship_names_of_the_Royal_Navy.)

Ship	Where built	When built	Rebuilt
Adventure	Deptford	1594	
Advice	Woolwich	1586	
Antilope		1546	1577
Ark Royal	Deptford	1587	
Bonaventure		1567	
Defiance			
Dreadnought	Deptford	1573	1592
Due Repulse	Deptford	1595	
Elizabeth Jonas	Woolwich	1559	Deptford 1597
Foresight		1570	
Garland		1590	
Golden Lion		1557	1582
Hope	Deptford	1559	
Marigold			
Mary Rose		1556	1589
Mercury	Deptford	1592	
Merhonour	Woolwich	1590	
Moon	Deptford	1586	
Nonparellia		1556	1584
Rainbow	Deptford	1586	
Roebuck		1585	
St Andrew	Spain		
St Mathew	Spain		
Spy	Limehouse	1586	
Sun	Chatham	1586	
Swiftsure	Deptford	1573	1592
Tramontana	Deptford	1586	
Triumph	Deptford	1562	1597
Warspite/Wast Spite	Deptford	1596	
White Bear		1563	

sailed close to Ferrol, close enough that the armada could see them, arriving there on 25th July. After this show of bravado, the half-fleet sailed back to Plymouth and regrouped on 31st July. Frustrated by bad weather, Essex and Sir Walter Raleigh planned to quit Spain altogether and sail instead to the West Indies to capture treasure ships. But the Queen forbade it: defeat of the armada was the nation's first priority. On 14th August the wind changed, and the fleet duly set out for Ferrol, only to become becalmed. This is the point at which Jonson and his two collaborators were being interrogated. Looking back, on 28th July when the edict against plays and playhouses went out, half the fleet had been lying storm-damaged at Plymouth and Falmouth, and the other half had been taunting – but not destroying – the Spanish armada. In June, Elizabeth had been vacillating, and at the end of May, the dock-yards had been busy fitting ships for war. We cannot know precisely when the play *Isle of Dogs* was written, but if it was topical, it was created and performed during sensitive times for national security. There might be evidence that it predates June 11th: an entry in the *Calendar of State Papers* for that date reads:

> John Chamberlain to Dudley Carleton, attendant on the ambassador at Paris. ... There are great preparations for a voyage, some say for Calais, some the islands of Jersey, some the King of Spain's navy, or the Indian fleet. There are 15 of the Queen's ships, two Spanish ships taken last year and re-fashioned, 22 Holland men-of-war, and 24 fly-boats for carriage of men and victuals. ... There is a new play of humours in great request, but it is great cry for little wool."
>
> (Green (ed.) 1869: 437–8)

Humours at this date meant 'an excited state of public feeling'.[37] If this is our play, then it was composed before June 11th, during the weeks when the Deptford Dockyard would have been fitting out the fleet for war. If national defence was the target, or perceived target, of the play's satire, as Donaldson (2012: 107) hypothesises, then against a background of such threats to national security, any criticism of

---

[37] *OED* humour, *n.* II. 5. c., first attestation 1600: "It was not fitte to stirre up humours in Spaine."

strategy, policy or capability of the fleet could have been interpreted as mutinous and seditious.[38]

Subsequent events are not material to the play, but if *The Isle of Dogs* had criticised national defence, its authors would indeed have been percipient. Never had England been allowed to be so off-guard. Essex's fleet had left Plymouth on 17th August, and again been assailed by poor weather, causing damage to some of the ships. By 27th August the fleet had been scattered and partly blown past Ferrol. Unable to sail back due to an adverse wind, Essex decided to press on and intercept the Spanish treasure fleet returning from the Indies. On 30th August he was misinformed that the armada had set sail for the Azores, and so the fleet arrived there in early September. Raleigh's troops caused damage to one of the islands, and Essex did manage to capture three Spanish cargoes, but on 9th October the fleet set sail for home, arriving separately in the last week of October. They did not know that on 9th October the armada had also set sail, leaving Ferrol bound not for the Azores but for England. The Spaniards had intelligence that Essex was in the Azores and had left England undefended, and their plan was to attack Falmouth and Plymouth, then lie in wait to intercept Essex's fleet as it returned. In the event, the armada got to within 30 to 10 miles off the Lizard when adverse weather set in, storms damaged the ships, and the armada returned to Coruña and Ferrol. There was no attack (Wernham 1994: 183–190; Green (ed.) 1869: 520).

There were two further dramatic uses of the place name *Isle of Dogs* published sufficiently close to 1597 to constitute a possible reference to the events of that summer. The first occurs in Middleton and Dekker's play *The Roaring Girl, or Moll Cutpurse*, published in 1611. As well as a pun on dogs, there is a context of knavery and fighting. The place-name occurs in a conceit of sea-faring, which has nothing to do with the rest of the play, which is set in Holborn.

Moll.   Souldier? thou deseru'st to bee hang'd vp by that tongue
         which dishonours so noble a profession, souldier you

---

[38] A trivial possibility, for example, arises from the detail of Essex's instructions on his appointment to the office of Master of the Ordinance. "We would prevent your falling into the errors of your predecessors" … "You shall keep the quantity of stores a secret from all but our sworn servants, not using your own clerks or strangers, which has heretofore done disservice" (Green (ed.) 1869: 381–3). Apparently the previous Master of the Ordinance, the Earl of Warwick, had pilfered the stores and stolen munitions.

skeldering varlet? hold, stand, there should be a trapdore here abouts.

Pull off his patch

Trap.   The balles of these glasiers of mine (mine eyes) shall be shot vp and downe in any hot peece of seruice for my inu-incible Mistresse.

Iac. Dap. I did not thinke there had bene such knauery in blacke patches as now I see.

Mol.   Oh sir he hath bene brought vp in the Ile of dogges, and can both fawne like a Spaniell, and bite like a Mastiue, as hee finds occasion.

L. Nol.   What are you sirra? a bird of this feather too.

T. Cat.   A man beaten from the wars sir.

T. Long.   I thinke so, for you neuer stood to fight.

Iac. Dap. What's thy name fellow souldier?

T. Cat.   I am cal'd by those that haue seen my valour, Tear-Cat.

Omnes.   Teare-Cat?

Moll.   A meere whip-Iacke, and that is in the Common-wealth of rogues, a slaue, that can talke of sea-fight, name all your chiefe Pirats, discouer more countries to you, then either the Dutch, Spanish, French, or English euer found out, yet indeed all his seruice is by land, and that is to rob a Faire, or some such venturous exploit; Teare-Cat, foot sirra I haue your name now I remember me in my booke of horners, hornes for the thumb, you know how.

T. Cat.   No indeed Captaine Mol (for I know you by sight) I am no such nipping Christian, but a maunderer vpon the pad I confesse, and meeting with honest Trapdore here, whom you had cashierd from bearing armes, out at elbowes vnder your colours, I instructed him in the rudements of roguery, and by my map made him saile ouer any Country you can name, so that now he can maunder better then my selfe.

(Middleton & Dekker, 1611,
The Roaring Girl, or Moll Cutpurse)

The place-name *Isle of Dogs* also occurs in Beaumont and Fletcher's *Thierry and Theodoret*, first published in 1621. Again, there is a pun – this time on cats – and a context of quarrelling and fighting:

Enter Thierry, Theodoret, Brunhalt, Ordella, Memberge, Martell.

Thier.   What villain dares this outrage?

Devitry.	Hear me, Sir, this creature hir'd me with fifty crowns in hand, to let *Protaldye* have the better of me at single Rapier on a made quarrel; he mistaking the weapon, laies me over the chops with his club fist, for which I was bold to teach him the Art of memory.
Omnes.	Ha, ha, ha, ha.
Theo.	Your General, Mother, will display himself.
	'Spight of our Peace I see.
Thier.	Forbear these civil jars, fie *Protaldy*,
	So open in your projects, avoid our presence, sirrah.
Devi.	Willingly, if you have any more wages to earn,
	You see I can take pains.
Theo.	There's somewhat for thy labour,
	More than was promis'd, ha, ha, ha.
Bawdb.	Where could I wish my self now? in the *Isle of Dogs*.
	So I might scape scratching, for I see by her Cats eyes
	I shall be claw'd fearfully.
Thier.	We'll hear no more on't,

Soft Musick.

(Beaumont and Fletcher, 1621,
Thierry and Theodoret, Act II Scene 2)

The place-name *Isle of Dogs* may have been chosen for no other reason than it allows wit about dogs and cats and was part of the zeit-geist.[39] The quarrelsome contexts could be due to coincidence (quarrels being dramatic staples), or there may be some allusion here to the contents of the 1597 play. Duplicity would seem to be relevant to fawning like a spaniel and biting like a mastiff. And it must be borne in mind that the 1597 play may have had nothing to do with Donaldson's suggestion of the Islands Voyage at all, as there were plenty of other sensitivities to probe.

---

[39] Names which catch the zeitgeist can move well outside their original sphere of reference; see Wright (2011) for *waterloo blue* (battle 1815, dye 1823), *magenta red* (battle 1859, dye 1860), *solferino* (battle 1859, dye c.1865), *waterloo bang-up* (a type of cracker, 1826), *waterloo cracker* (1833), *trafalgar chair* (battle 1805, chair 1822), *trafalgar cotton* (1826), *trafalgar coach* (1848). *Gibraltar rock* (1831) and *Wellington pillars* (1851) were types of sweets. In the 1860s the name *Garibaldi* was marketed as the name of a type of blouse, in the 1880s as both a hat and a type of fish, and then from the 1890s to the present as a type of biscuit.

8. Conclusion

It now remains to sort hypothesis from fact. I have hypothesised that the name *Isle of Dogs* may be Deptford dockworkers' word-play on the barks berthed at Stepney Eyot. This hypothesis hinges on the two meanings of the word *bark* on the one hand, and the fact that the place-name is first known to us in the context of the Deptford Dockyard in 1520, just seven years after that dockyard opened, on the other. Were further research to reveal an earlier, pre-1513 attestation, this hypothesis would no longer stand. It is also worth emphasising that just because the pun was possible, it does not follow that it is necessarily the correct explanation. What is certain, however, is that sixteenth-century dockworkers used the name *Isle of Dogs* for the eyots opposite their yard, rather than for the whole of Stepney Marsh as it is known today. Therefore, whatever the contents of the lost 1597 play *The Isle of Dogs*, the reference may have been concerned with that dockyard in some way, if that reference were indeed topical rather than allegorical or fantastical.

References

Manuscripts

Kew, The National Archives MS E 36/11. Accounts Book of the King's Ships. 1520. Calendared in *Letters and Papers of Henry VIII*, volume 3, pp 369–381.

Kew, The National Archives, MS SC 12/11/31. Field Survey of Stepney, c.1400.

London, British Library, Adds MS 44839. Robert Adam, *Thamesis Descriptio*, 1588.

London, British Library, Cotton MS Otho E IX, 1525. Calendared in *Letters and Papers of Henry VIII*, volume 4, pp 757–772.

London, London Metropolitan Archives, DL/C/B/004/MS09171/002, wills, 1380–1405.

Printed Sources

Baker, T.F.T. (ed.). (1998). Stepney: Settlement and Building to c.1700. *A History of the County of Middlesex: Volume 11: Stepney, Bethnal Green*. British History Online. Web. 05 November 2014. http://www.british-history.ac.uk/report.aspx?compid=22733).

Cadwallader, L. H. (1923). *Career of the Earl of Essex 1597–1601*. Philadelphia: University of Pennsylvania.

Colledge, J.J. & Warlow, B. (eds) (2006). *Ships of the Royal Navy: the Complete Record of all Fighting Ships of the Royal Navy from the 15th Century to the Present*. London: Chatham.

Cowper, B.H. (1853). *A Descriptive Historical and Statistical Account of Millwall, Commonly Called the Isle of Dogs; Including Notices of the Founding, Opening, Etc., of the West India Docks and City Canal, and Notes Relating to Limehouse, Poplar, Blackwall, and Stepney*. London: Robert Gladding.

Croot, P. (1997). Settlement, tenure and land use in medieval Stepney: evidenceof a field survey c.1400. *London Journal* 22:1, 1–15.

Cunningham, P. (1849 edition). *A Handbook for London, Past and Present*. Volume 2. London: John Murray.

Currie, C. R. J. (ed.). (1998). *A history of Middlesex. Vol.11, Early Stepney with Bethnal Green*. The Victoria history of the counties of England. Oxford: Published for the Institute of Historical Research by Oxford University Press.

Donaldson, I. (2012). Note on *The Isle of Dogs*, lost play (1597). D. Bevington, M. Butler and I. Donaldson (eds) *The Cambridge Edition of the Works of Ben Jonson*. Volume 1, 1597–1601. Cambridge: Cambridge University Press, 101–109.

Dugdale, W., Sir. (1662). *The History of Imbanking and drayning of divers Fenns and Marshes, both in forein parts, and in this Kingdom. And of the improvements thereby*. London: Alice Warren.

Fletcher, J. & Massinger, P. (1679). *The Tragedy of Thierry and Theodoret*. London: John Martyn, Henry Herringman.

Gorges, A., Sir. (1625). A Larger Relation of the said Iland Voyage. Purchas, Samuel. *Purchas his Pilgrimes*. Book 4. (1938–1969). London: Henrie Fetherstone.

Green, M.A.E. (ed.). (1869). *Calendar of State Papers, Domestic Series, of the reign of Elizabeth, 1595–1597*. London: Longmans, Green, Reader, and Dyer.

Johannesson, N-L. (2012). "Rihht alls an hunnte takeþþ der. /Wiþþ hise ȝæpe racchess": Hunting as a metaphor for proselytizing in the *Ormulum*. R. Dance and L. Wright (eds) *The Use and Development of Middle English: Proceedings of the Sixth International Conference on Middle English, Cambridge 2008*. Frankfurt am Main: Peter Lang, 229–240.

Loades, D. ([1995] 2002). From the King's Ships to the Royal Navy 1500–1642. J.R. Hill & B. McL. Ranft (eds) *The Oxford Illustrated History of the Royal Navy*. Oxford: Oxford University Press, 24–55.

Middleton, T. & Dekker, T. (1611). *The Roaring Girle. Or Moll Cut-Purse.* London: Thomas Archer.

Mills, A. D. ([2001] 2004). *Oxford Dictionary of London Place Names.* Oxford: Oxford University Press.

Norden, J. (1593). *Speculum Britannicae. The First Parte. An Historicall, & Chorographicall Discription of Middlesex. Wherin Are Also Alphabeticallie sett Downe, the Names of the Cyties, Townes, Parishes Hamletes, Howses of Name &c. Wth Direction Spedelie to Finde Anie Place Desired in the Mappe & the Distance betwene Place and Place without Compasses. No Place.*

Reaney, P. H. (1935). *The Place-Names of Essex.* English Place-Name Society, volume 12. Cambridge: Cambridge University Press.

Robinson, M. (1797). *Walsingham: or, the Pupil of Nature: a Domestic Story.* 2 volumes. London: T. N. Longman.

St James, Westminster. (1827). *St James's: A Satirical Poem, in Six Epistles to Mr. Crockford.* London: Ibotson and Palmer.

Strype, J. (ed.). (1720). *A survey of the Cities of London and Westminster: Containing the Original, Antiquity, Increase, Modern Estate and Government of those Cities. Written at first in the year MDXCVIII by John Stow.* London: A. Churchill, J. Knapton, R. Knaplock, J. Walthoe, E. Horne, B. Tooke, D. Midwinter, B. Cowse, R. Robinson and T. Ward. Volume 1.

Wernham, R.B. (1994). *The Return of the Armadas: The Last Years of the Elizabethan War against Spain 1595–1603.* Oxford: Clarendon Press.

Wright, L. (2006). Street addresses and directions in mid-eighteenth-century London newspaper advertisements. N. Brownlees (ed.) *News Discourse in Early Modern Britain.* Selected papers of the Conference on Historical News Discourse 2004. Linguistic Insights Studies in Language and Communication, Volume 30. Bern: Peter Lang, 199–215.

———. (2010). A pilot study on the singular definite articles *le* and *la* in fifteenth-century London mixed-language business writing. R. Ingham (ed.) *The Anglo-Norman Languge and its Contexts.* York: York Medieval Press and The Boydell Press, 130–142.

———. (2011). The Nomenclature of some French and Italian Fireworks in Eighteenth-Century London. *The London Journal* 36:2, 109–39.

Online References

Early English Books Online: http://eebo.chadwyck.com.

Letters and Papers, Foreign and Domestic, Henry VIII, Volume 3: 1519–1523

(1867), pp. 369–381. URL: http://www.british-history.ac.uk/report.aspx?compid=91055. Date accessed: 16 November 2012.

Literature Online: http://lion.chadwyck.co.uk/

OED Online. www.oed.com.

'The Isle of Dogs: Introduction', *Survey of London: volumes 43 and 44: Poplar, Blackwall and Isle of Dogs* (1994), pp. 375–387. URL: http://www.british-history.ac.uk/report.aspx?compid=46507. Date accessed: 15 November 2012.

'The West India Docks: The buildings: warehouses', *Survey of London: volumes 43 and 44: Poplar, Blackwall and Isle of Dogs* (1994), pp. 284–300. URL: http://www.british-history.ac.uk/report.aspx?compid=46497. Date accessed: 16 November 2012.

7 English Genres in Diachronic Corpus Linguistics

Erik Smitterberg & Merja Kytö
Uppsala University

1. Introduction

This chapter is about problems and possibilities associated with using genre as a parameter in corpus-based historical linguistics. We will begin by discussing why genre has become an increasingly central concept in historical linguistics and by defining genre and related terms. Next, we will discuss a number of challenges that corpus linguists need to address when they use genre as a parameter in their research. To begin with, we will discuss potential conflicts between two key desiderata, namely representativity and comparability. We will also take up the problem that not all genres are attested for the whole history of English and that even genres which have a long history may have changed over time. Thirdly, we will discuss how historical linguists have used genre comparisons to access an approximation of past speech. We will then devote a section to two case studies where genre plays a central role. We first look at how additional information can be gained by considering genre differences within the framework of multi-feature approaches to genre variation in the past; this account is followed by an analysis of a single linguistic feature, viz. the units co-ordinated by *and*. The chapter ends with a summary of our main points and some desiderata for future work.

2. The Centrality of the Genre Concept

Even though linguistic variation according to genre was recognized as an important variable before the advent of corpus linguistics, it has become even more central in corpus-based approaches (see Lange 2012: 401).

How to cite this book chapter:
Smitterberg, E. and Kytö, M. 2015. English Genres in Diachronic Corpus Linguistics. In: Shaw, P., Erman, B., Melchers, G. and Sundkvist, P. (eds) *From Clerks to Corpora: essays on the English language yesterday and today*. Pp. 117–133. Stockholm: Stockholm University Press. DOI: http://dx.doi.org/10.16993/bab.g License: CC-BY.

This is so partly because every corpus-compilation project has to take the genre parameter into account. If the researcher is compiling a single-genre corpus, delimiting the genre sampled is crucial in order to reach reliable results. And if the corpus project includes several genres, considering genres in relation to one another is a key issue when the compiler decides what research questions studies based on the corpus can hope to answer.

According to Kohnen (2001: 115), genres can serve as vehicles for spreading language change. That is, while genres themselves may not bring about change, they can certainly affect whether or not a change will spread through a language. For instance, if an incoming informal feature such as the contracted form *can't* instead of *cannot* becomes accepted in informal writing, colloquial written genres can function as "bridgeheads" from which the innovative feature can colonize other forms of writing. Hundt & Mair (1999: 236) note that a new form which arises in speech often "then spreads at differential speeds through various genres until at a very remote point it can be said to have been established in 'the language' ". At the same time, genres may also retard a change that is spreading through a language by preserving conservative and/or fossilized usage; for instance, many legal texts preserve an obligation use of *shall* that is no longer current in everyday communication.

There is a certain amount of terminological confusion in linguistic research that considers the genre parameter. Terms such as *genre*, *register*, and *text type* are sometimes used by different linguists to mean more or less the same thing. In this chapter, we use the term "genre" to refer to categories of texts that are defined on extralinguistic or text-external grounds (the term "register" has also been used to cover such categories in previous work); in contrast, we reserve the term "text type" for categories that are defined based on their linguistic characteristics.

Within this framework, the linguistic make-up of the text itself thus does not determine what genre it belongs to; for instance, a novel may be written in the form of a series of letters or diary entries and still remain a novel. This means that genres are "fuzzy sets": central members of a genre category will have a form that is close to the genre prototype, while more peripheral members of the set will deviate from the prototypical pattern. For instance, a prototypical member of a genre such as academic writing will contain a relatively large number of linking adverbials, prepositional phrases, and passive clauses. However, text types do not have to correlate with genres; it would be fully possible, for instance, to write a novel where the text type was Scientific

Exposition, although it would not be a prototypical member of the genre; Susanna Clarke's 2004 novel *Jonathan Strange & Mr Norrell*, for instance, remains a historical fantasy novel even though it contains numerous footnotes, a feature not usually associated with that genre. Other criteria for genre membership include the function of the texts in the society in which they are used (a novel, for example, may be read primarily for amusement) and audience expectations (members of the audience at a linguistic symposium, for instance, will typically expect a paper to inform them with regard to some aspect of linguistics). What we will mainly focus on in the remainder of this section is a set of problems that historical linguists typically encounter when including genre as a parameter in their research.

We will begin by addressing the issue of representativity. If a corpus is representative, the study of that corpus (or combination of corpora) "can stand proxy for the study of some entire language or variety of a language" (Leech 2007: 135). However, while this notion is simple enough to define, the practical application is problematic, especially with regard to historical texts (see, for instance, Biber 1993 and Leech 2007 for different suggestions on how to operationalize this parameter). Several genres – e.g. everyday conversation – are absent from the historical record even though they were important components of the language variety that researchers wish to represent, and even attested genres contain only a few of the textual witnesses that once existed.

Another desideratum of corpus-based research is comparability, viz. the extent to which sets of material are equivalent except for one single variable (Leech 2007: 141): in the case of historical linguistics, that variable is usually time. A typical example of comparability concerns the "clones" of the LOB corpus with texts from 1961; roughly equivalent publications have been sampled from later years (FLOB) as well as earlier decades (e.g. BLOB-1931) at intervals of approximately 30 years.

However, one important problem in diachronic corpus design is that representativity and comparability may clash. One reason why this happens is that genres develop and change through time, as shown in Figure 1. In Figure 1, the two ellipses represent the textual universes of newspaper English in two different periods. The difference in horizontal position indicates genre development: the textual universe in period 2 is greater, as new genres have been added (e.g. interviews), but a few genres such as shipping news have also all but disappeared during the time that separates the periods. If precedence is given to comparability,

Period 2

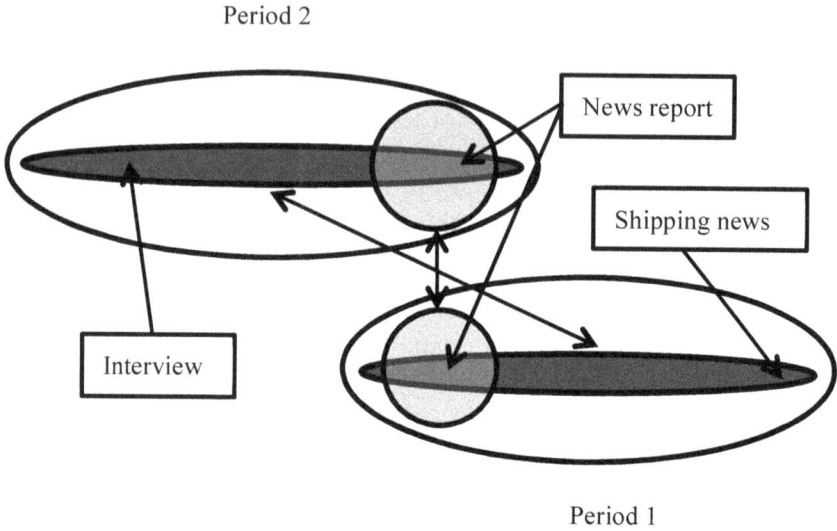

Figure 1. Textual universes of newspaper language in two periods.

only the genres that are present in both periods should be sampled (as illustrated by the two circles); this would make the period samples maximally comparable, but each sample would become less representative of the language of its period. The other strategy would be to make each period sample representative (as illustrated by the two narrow ellipses), which would instead decrease the comparability of the period samples.

Whole genres may even change across time to serve language users' needs. Drama texts included in the Helsinki Corpus (1420–1500) may serve as an example. In the Late Middle English section of the corpus, the Drama texts included are religious mystery plays, while the Early Modern English section contains Drama comedies (this difference between the samples is also recognized by the corpus compilers in that "Drama" has been qualified with different subtitles in these two cases). Both mystery plays and comedies are Drama texts in the sense that they are scripted dialogue texts used for stage performances. However, differences in the intended main functions of these two forms of drama (religious instruction vs. entertainment) may decrease the comparability of such samples from a corpus-linguistic standpoint. On the other hand, including such heterogeneous genres will make the corpus more representative of late Middle and early Modern English.

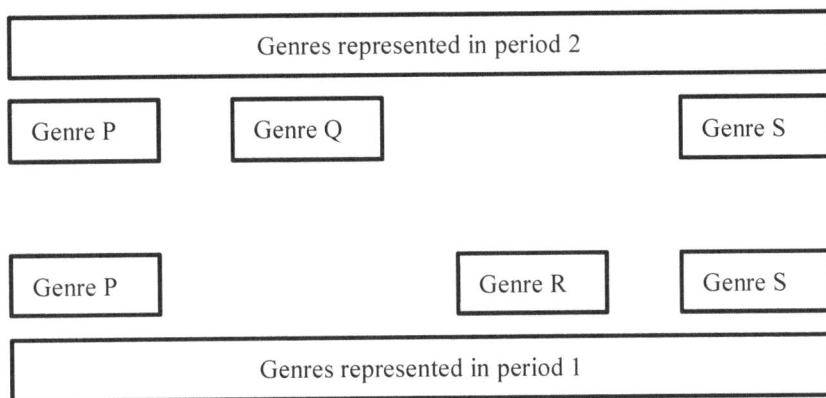

Figure 2. Variation in genre representation between two periods.

In addition, even if genres do not change over time, they may emerge late in the period studied or die out, leading to other representativity and comparability issues. This is illustrated in Figure 2. If the aim is to produce two comparable period corpora, only genres P and S should be included in corpus compilation, as they are represented in both periods. However, this would lead to each period sample being less representative, as genre Q in period 2 and genre R in period 1 would be ignored.

As Figure 2 implies, not all genres have been attested throughout the recorded history of English; for instance, the emergence of some genres is tied to technological developments (e.g. e-mail). The patchy picture that some genres afford researchers is illustrated in Figure 3.

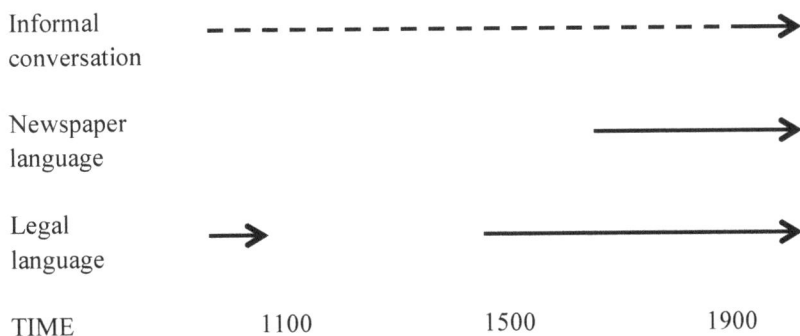

Figure 3. Genre representation in English across time.

Figure 3 illustrates one genre and two genre groups. While informal conversation has of course existed since the beginnings of the English language, it is only recorded from the 20th century on; the line is thus dashed for most of the history of the language. Genres that belong to newspaper language can be said to have existed in English since 1665, when the *Oxford Gazette* was first published, although there were precursors of newspapers before then, such as corantos (see Dahl 1953 and Brownlees 2012 for accounts of the beginnings of periodical news). Finally, genres may disappear at a certain point in the history of a given language only to re-emerge later on. This is the case with law texts in English. They are attested in the Old English period, but are absent from most of the Middle English period, as Latin and, later, French took over in official use in England. However, after a gap of several centuries, law texts written in English re-appeared in the late Middle English period (Claridge 2012: 239–240).

Yet another scenario that may introduce problems for corpus compilers is one in which two or more genres exist in all periods studied, but their relative importance has changed over time. The question then becomes whether this change should be reflected in corpus compilation. Figure 4 illustrates this situation. The news report did exist in seventeenth-century England: as mentioned above, the *Oxford Gazette*, later the *London Gazette*, appeared in 1665, and there were precursors such as corantos. But it was not a central genre compared with the Bible,

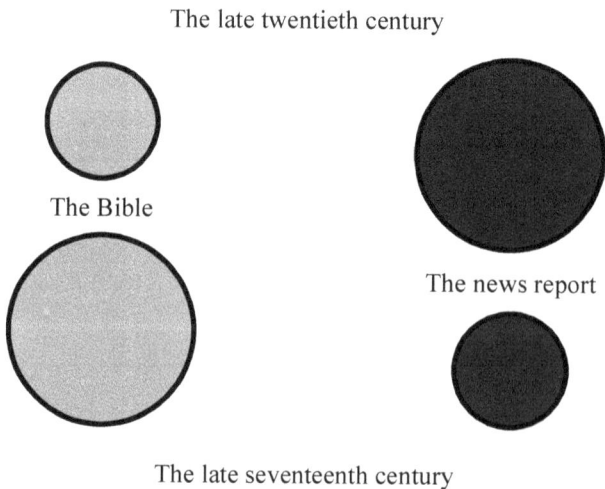

Figure 4. The relative importance of two genres in late seventeenth-century and late twentieth-century English.

which was part of most language users' daily lives. The situation had arguably been reversed by the late twentieth century: the secularized nature of modern Britain means that most speakers have limited contact with biblical texts, while news in some form – newspapers, television, the Internet, etc. – reaches nearly all language users. In addition, multiculturalism has led to the establishment of religions that do not make use of the Bible in Britain, which further decreases the special standing of that text.

There are thus clear difficulties involved both in achieving representativity and in balancing comparability and representativity. Depending on the underlying research questions that the study of a given corpus is intended to help answer, corpus compilers have approached these difficulties from different angles. For instance, the compilers of the BLOB-1931 clone of the LOB corpus gave precedence to comparability over representativity in the selection of newspaper texts (Leech 2007: 143): priority was given to including the same newspapers in BLOB that had been included in LOB, even though a given newspaper may not have been equally representative of its genre around 1931 and in 1961. However, as Leech (2007: 143) notes, in investigations with greater time-depth, complications relating to genre evolution would have made comparability very difficult to achieve. In such cases, varying the granularity of the genre parameter may be useful. When possible, corpus texts may be coded not only for genre, but also for subgenre and/or subfunction. Biber and Gray (2013) argue that keeping subgenres such as newspaper articles and news magazine articles constant may be essential in order to allow researchers to identify and describe language-change phenomena with a high degree of reliability. As regards subfunctions, Kohnen (2007) suggests that coding parts of corpus texts according to the subfunction they fill can help to make texts more comparable; for instance, a genre like religious instruction can be divided into subfunctions such as narration and exegesis, and texts belonging to the same genre can then be compared to see whether they also emphasize the same subfunctions.

Alternatively, grouping several genres together into hyperonymic entities can enable scholars to collect roughly comparable text categories if not all genres are attested in all periods sampled. The prototypical text categories in the Helsinki Corpus can be used as an example of this; for example, the category Imaginative Narration covers genres such as Fiction, Romance, and Travelogue, which suggests that these genres share some features that may make them roughly comparable if one or several of them are missing from some period samples.

In contrast, if priority is given to representativity, some steps have been taken to improve a corpus in this regard. These include covering a wide range of genres, giving precedence to texts that are considered good representatives of their genres, aiming at a proportional representation of the genres included, and simply enlarging the size of the corpus (see Kytö & Smitterberg forthcoming for a fuller discussion). In historical linguistics, the most serious obstacle to achieving representativity is of course the lack of spoken texts. The available material has been preserved in writing, while a great deal of the actuation of change is likely to have taken place in speech and notably in speech used in dialogue situations (see, however, Biber & Gray 2011 for an account of change that has spread mainly in non-speech-related writing). One solution has been to turn to comparisons of texts and genres that stand at different distances from past speech. For instance, written records of spoken language can be assumed to come closer to the actual spoken language of the time than written language that was not based on language taken down in speech situations or created to imitate speech. Even though it is practically impossible to take down speech in writing in all its aspects, previous research indicates that the essence of what was said was relayed in the recorded version. Consequently, it is necessary to look for what have been referred to as "spoken", "oral" or "colloquial" genres. To this end, scholars have compiled genre-specific corpora that focus on speech-related language. For example, in the Corpus of English Dialogues 1560–1760 (CED), past speech can be studied from the perspective of speech-purposed (e.g. Drama) and speech-based (e.g. Depositions) genres (see Culpeper & Kytö 2010 for more detailed information on CED, including case studies). The results of such analyses can then be compared with those based on speech-like genres such as Private Correspondence in order to shed further light on the spoken language of the period.

3. Case Studies: Drama and Science in Focus

We will now consider two actual studies to show how the impact of the genre perspective has affected historical corpus linguistics. Our examples are taken from the Modern English period. One study considers the co-variation of a large number of features, while the other focuses on a single linguistic feature.

One way of looking at linguistic variation is to consider how a large number of linguistic features co-vary in texts. Within this framework, different features load on a number of dimensions of variation. Features that co-occur in texts end up on the same pole on a dimension of variation; features that tend not to co-occur also belong to the same dimension, but will be placed on opposite ends. When genres are positioned on these dimensions, they can be shown to be more or less "involved", "informational", etc., depending on the co-occurrence patterns of the linguistic features that are included in the analysis. Among the pioneers in extending this methodology to historical texts are Douglas Biber and Edward Finegan; we will consider one of their studies here, viz. Biber & Finegan (1997). This study is based on the original version of A Representative Corpus of Historical English Registers (ARCHER), a 1.7-million-word corpus of British and American English which covers the period 1650–1990. The features studied include colloquial features such as contractions as well as features characteristic of impersonal styles, e.g. passives (Biber & Finegan 1997: 258–259).

In their study, Biber and Finegan (1997) demonstrate that not all English genres have followed the same trajectory through Modern English. Whereas specialist expository writing has consistently tended towards more "literate" styles, popular non-expository texts show a reversal of this trend towards more "oral" styles during the Late Modern English period (Biber & Finegan 1997: 272–273). As a result, the linguistic differentiation between different kinds of writing increases during the period studied. For instance, while Drama leads the way towards a more involved style of communication, science writing exhibits an equally clear trend towards the informational end of the same dimension (Dimension 1, "Involved versus Informational Production") (Biber & Finegan 1997: 266).

Another way of considering linguistic variation is from the perspective of a single linguistic feature. The second case study, which concerns the co-ordinator *and* and the linguistic units that *and* can co-ordinate, exemplifies this perspective. Following Quirk et al. (1985), we will refer to these units as "conjoins". *And* can link conjoins on different levels of syntactic structure, from individual morphemes to whole sentences. In the literature, a basic distinction is often made between clausal co-ordination and phrasal co-ordination (see, for instance, Culpeper & Kytö 2010). In example (1) below, the co-ordination is clausal because the two conjoins are main clauses. In example (3), in contrast, the two conjoins are adjective phrases, so we are dealing with phrasal co-ordination. We apply a similar, but slightly modified classification to the data in this study.

The main reason why co-ordination by *and* is of interest is that "oral" and "literate" genres display different preferences as regards phrasal and clausal co-ordination. Biber et al. (1999) show that, while clausal co-or-dination predominates in conversation in Present-day English, phrasal co-ordination is frequent in academic writing. Moreover, Biber (2003) demonstrates that clausal co-ordination and phrasal co-ordination are characteristic of "oral" and "literate" discourse, respectively. We might thus expect expository genres to display more phrasal co-ordination than non-expository genres in Late Modern English.

To investigate this, Smitterberg (forthcoming) retrieved a random subset of *and* in A Corpus of Nineteenth-century English (CONCE), a one-million-word multi-genre corpus of British English from the 1800s. We focus on results for Drama and Science, one stereotypically "oral" and one stereotypically "literate" genre. The analysis is based on 400 randomly selected instances per genre from each of the two periods included, viz. 1800–1830 and 1870–1900. The conjoins of each instance of *and* retrieved were classified according to their syn-tactic make-up. Three categories are recognized in this classification. Smitterberg refers to the first category, which is exemplified in (1) and (2), as "super-phrasal". (Conjoins are given in bold face in numbered examples; speaker identifications and stage directions are enclosed in square brackets and dollar signs in the corpus.)

(1) [$Blunt.$] No. **I came too late,** *and* **I am sorry for it:** [...]
     (CONCE, Drama, Holcroft, 1800–1830, p. 25)
(2) Soon after the application of the heat, a dark line, thin and delicate as a spider's thread, was observed to be **slowly creep-ing down each of the bright sodium lines** *and* **exactly occupy-ing the centre of each.**
     (CONCE, Science, Lockyer, 1870–1900, p. 128)

In order to be included in this category, the conjoins have to meet two criteria. First, both have to contain more material than one syntac-tic phrase. Second, both conjoins have to contain at least part of a verb phrase. For the second category, the traditional term "phrasal" is used; it is illustrated in (3) and (4).

(3) [$MISS T.$] Have those **base** *and* **servile** things called settle-ments been satisfactorily adjusted? [$eating$]
     (CONCE, Drama, Gilbert, 1870–1900, p. 25)
(4) It would undoubtedly be advantageous to the capitalists of England, and to the consumers in both countries, that under

such circumstances, **the wine** *and* **the cloth** should both be made in Portugal, [...]
(CONCE, Science, Ricardo, 1800–1830, pp. 160–161)

In phrasal co-ordination, the conjoins are either on or below the level of a syntactic phrase and do not consist of full verb phrases. Finally, Smitterberg (forthcoming) recognizes an indeterminate category, to which examples (5) and (6) belong. This category contains examples whose conjoins did not meet all criteria for either of the other categories.

(5) [$Mait.$] A vindictive temper is the master passion that **degrades** *and* **ruins** the peace of Mr. Anson: [...]
(CONCE, Drama, Holcroft, 1800–1830, p. 34)

(6) [$Admiral. [More sandwich.]$] If ever there was a jewel of a wife it's Lady Darby. God bless her! Here's her health. [$Drinks.$] I don't deserve her. She's too good for me. When I remember **what an unfaithful rascal I've been,** *and* **the lies I've had to tell** – the awful lies – [$Is overcome with painful reminiscences and weeps.$]
(CONCE, Drama, Jones, 1870–1900, p. 50)

In (5), both conjoins contain one verb phrase but no other material; and in (6), the first conjoin consists of a clause and the second of a noun phrase.

The manual analysis of 400 instances from each period/genre sample led to the exclusion of 116 instances, or c. 7% of the data. These include instances of *and* in stage directions, chapter headings, and numerical expressions such as *four and a half*; a small number of

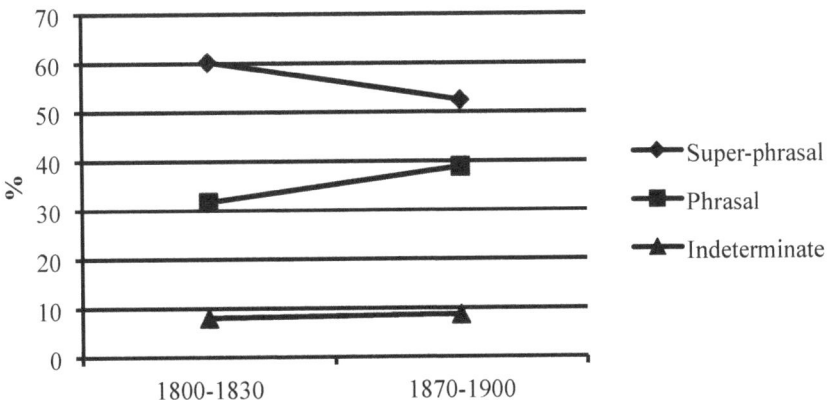

Figure 5. Conjoins of *and* in Drama.

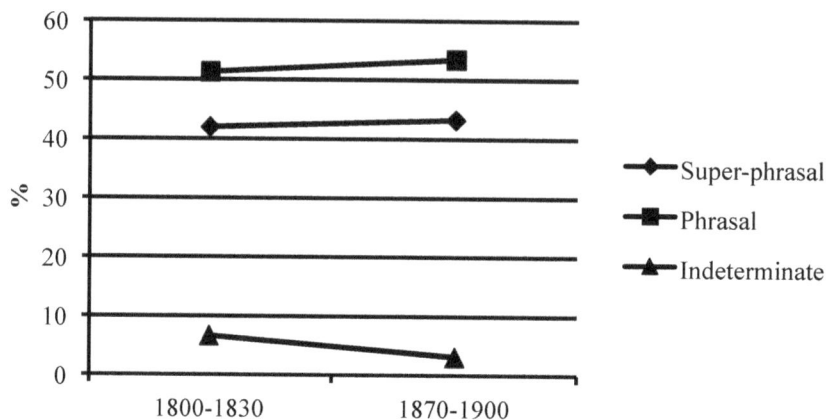

Figure 6. Conjoins of *and* in Science.

instances that resisted classification were also excluded. The total number of instances of *and* included is 347 from Drama, period 1, 378 from Drama, period 3, 376 from Science, period 1, and 383 from Science, period 3. The period/genre distribution is given in Figures 5 and 6.

As Figures 5 and 6 show, the proportion of super-phrasal co-ordination is higher in Drama than in Science; this difference is statistically significant in both periods (for period 1, d.f = 2; χ^2 = 28.9; p < 0.001; for period 3, d.f. = 2; χ^2 = 22.1; p < 0.001). This genre difference tallies well with previous research on spoken and written communication. As mentioned above, Biber's (2003) factor analysis of present-day academic English demonstrates that clausal co-ordination and phrasal co-ordination are characteristic of spoken and written English, respectively. As Drama comes out as a stereotypically "oral" genre in Biber and Finegan's (1997) diachronic factor score analysis of Modern English, the predominance of super-phrasal co-ordination in this genre is to be expected. Likewise, the high percentage of phrasal co-ordination in the "literate" Science genre is in accordance with what would be expected against the background of Biber's (2003) results.

In contrast to the cross-genre differences, there are no clear indications of change across time in either genre. While there are tendencies towards, for instance, more phrasal co-ordination in Drama and less indeterminate co-ordination in Science, these period differences do not reach statistical significance (for Drama, d.f. = 2; χ^2 = 4.72; p = 0.095; for Science, d.f. = 2; χ^2 = 5.06; p = 0.080). Neither the consistent trend towards more literate styles in specialist expository writing nor the reversal towards more oral styles in a popular written genre such as Drama noted by Biber and Finegan (1997: 272–273) is thus mirrored in our results. Regarding the results for Science, Geisler (2002) found that this genre did not change significantly on any dimension in his factor score analysis of CONCE; it is possible that differences in textual selection and/or the time span covered underlie these differences between results found for scientific English in CONCE and ARCHER (cf. Biber & Finegan 1997).

The genre perspective comes across as crucial in two respects in our case study on co-ordination. First, including both "oral" and "literate" writing is necessary to obtain a full picture of co-ordination in nineteenth-century English as a whole; neither genre included could have stood proxy for the entire language variety. Secondly, it is well known that, while language change presupposes language variation, not all variation leads to change; a genre perspective can help to uncover such cases of stable variation in language.

The two approaches exemplified here both yield important information on the development of the English language and on how this development is connected to the genre parameter. For instance, detailed studies of single features can show what features are worth including in multi-feature analyses; at the same time, the overall view afforded by multi-dimensional studies provide single-feature analyses with an overall theoretical framework (see Biber 1988: 62–63 for further discussion).

4. Concluding Remarks

As we hope to have shown in this chapter, genre is an indispensable parameter in historical linguistics. If the language of a period is treated as a monolithic phenomenon, patterns such as genre drift and genre differentiation may go unnoticed. Similarly, factors underlying the distribution of individual linguistic features may escape notice if genre differences in their occurrence are not taken into account.

However, as we have also demonstrated, the limitations imposed by historical material require that attention be paid to methodological issues. Above all, it is crucial that researchers account for their definitions of the genre concept and their criteria for identifying and classifying genres (e.g. the relative importance of linguistic and extralinguistic criteria). Attention must also be paid to the socio-historical contexts of the genres sampled; for instance, factors such as literacy and level of education will have affected the size of the audience of a written genre at any point in the history of English. Conversely, the author perspective is important especially when dealing with genres that have few textual witnesses. A text such as the *Orrmulum*, for instance, can be seen as representing the genre of homily collections in the twelfth century. However, it can also be seen as a concrete representation of the author's own idiolect as against the more abstract genre level.

As we have discussed above, the desiderata of comparability and representativity may clash when corpora are compiled from a genre perspective. Genres have emerged and died out through the recorded history of English, causing gaps in genre representation across time. There are of course also plenty of examples of genre continuity; but even in such cases, attention must be paid to genre evolution and the extent to which what is nominally the "same" genre can be said to occupy the same communicative space in an ever-changing society.

The two case studies we have reported on demonstrate that the genre concept is of central importance in diachronic corpus linguistics. This is of course true of multi-feature studies, which are typically based on contrasting linguistic co-occurrence patterns in several different genres. However, even studies of single linguistic features such as *and* and its conjoins often require a genre perspective, as different patterns may manifest themselves in different genres and genre groups.

As regards future developments, the genre concept is likely to continue to grow in significance in historical corpus linguistics. Above all, genres are likely to become central parameters in a wide range of sub-disciplines, from pragmatics and discourse studies to grammar. (See, for instance, Walker 2007 for a study where the genre concept is crucial for an understanding of pragmatic variation and change in pronoun usage.) Regarding methodology, there is a need for new approaches to studying past language forms on their own terms. In terms of resources, there is plenty to do in, for instance, providing faithful linguistic editions of early manuscripts that can be used as the basis for new historical corpora. We also need to pay better attention to poorly represented speaker groups, for instance the language of women and lower socio-economic strata. In addition to studying British English, we should also consider the development of genres in overseas varieties of the language.

Corpora Referred to

ARCHER = A Representative Corpus of Historical English Registers, originally compiled under the supervision of D. Biber and E. Finegan (modified and expanded by subsequent members of a consortium of universities). For more details, see http://www.alc.manchester.ac.uk/subjects/lel/research/projects/archer/ and http://www.helsinki.fi/varieng/CoRD/corpora/ARCHER/updated%20version/introduction.html.

BLOB-1931 = The BLOB-1931 Corpus, compiled by G. Leech, P. Rayson & N. Smith. For more details, see http://www.helsinki.fi/varieng/CoRD/corpora/BLOB-1931/index.html.

CED = A Corpus of English Dialogues 1560–1760 (2006), compiled by M. Kytö & J. Culpeper. For more details, see http://www.helsinki.fi/varieng/CoRD/corpora/CED/index.html.

CONCE = A Corpus of Nineteenth-century English, compiled by M. Kytö & J. Rudanko. For more details, see Smitterberg (2005).

FLOB = The Freiburg–LOB Corpus of British English (1999), compiled by C. Mair. For more details, see http://www.helsinki.fi/varieng/CoRD/corpora/FLOB/index.html.

Helsinki Corpus = The Helsinki Corpus of English Texts (1991), compiled by M. Rissanen (Project leader) & M. Kytö (Project secretary); L. Kahlas-Tarkka & M. Kilpiö (Old English); S. Nevanlinna & I. Taavitsainen (Middle English); T. Nevalainen & H. Raumolin-Brunberg (Early Modern English). For more details, see http://www.helsinki.fi/varieng/CoRD/corpora/HelsinkiCorpus/index.html.

LOB = The Lancaster-Oslo/Bergen Corpus (1976), compiled by G. Leech, S. Johansson & K. Hofland. For more details, see http://www.helsinki.fi/varieng/CoRD/corpora/LOB/index.html.

References

Biber, D. (1988). *Variation across Speech and Writing*. Cambridge: Cambridge University Press.

———. (1993). Representativeness in corpus design. *Literary and Linguistic Computing* 8:4, 243–257.

———. (2003). Variation among university spoken and written registers: A new multi-dimensional analysis. P. Leistyna & C. Meyer (eds) *Corpus Analysis: Language Structure and Language Use*. Amsterdam & New York: Rodopi, 47–70.

Biber, D. & Finegan, E. (1997). Diachronic relations among speech-based and written registers in English. T. Nevalainen & L. Kahlas-Tarkka (eds) *To Explain the Present: Studies in the Changing English Language in Honour of Matti Rissanen*. Helsinki: Société Néophilologique, 253–275.

Biber, D. & Gray, B. (2011). Grammatical change in the noun phrase: The influence of written language use. *English Language and Linguistics* 15:2, 223–250.

———. (2013). Being specific about historical change: The influence of sub-register. *Journal of English Linguistics* 41:2, 104–134.

Biber, D., Johansson, S., Leech, G., Conrad, S. & Finegan, E. (1999). *Longman Grammar of Spoken and Written English*. Harlow: Pearson.

Brownlees, N. (2012). The beginnings of periodical news (1620–1665). R. Facchinetti, N. Brownlees, B. Bös & U. Fries *News as Changing Texts: Corpora, Methodologies and Analysis*. Newcastle upon Tyne: Cambridge Scholars Publishing, 5–48.

Claridge, G. (2012). Linguistic levels: Styles, registers, genres, text types. A. Bergs & L.J. Brinton (eds) *English Historical Linguistics: An International Handbook*. Vol. 1. Berlin & Boston: Walter de Gruyter, 237–253.

Clarke, S. (2004). *Jonathan Strange & Mr Norrell*. New York & London: Bloomsbury.

Culpeper, J. & Kytö, M. (2010). *Early Modern English Dialogues. Spoken Interaction as Writing*. Cambridge: Cambridge University Press.

Dahl, F. (1953). *A Bibliography of English Corantos and Periodical Newsbooks 1620–1642*. Stockholm: Almqvist & Wiksell.

Geisler, G. (2002). Investigating register variation in nineteenth-century English: A multi-dimensional comparison. R. Reppen, S.M. Fitzmaurice & D. Biber (eds) *Using Corpora to Explore Linguistic Variation*. Amsterdam & Philadelphia: John Benjamins, 249–271.

Hundt, M. & Mair, C. (1999). "Agile" and "uptight" genres: The corpus-based approach to language change in progress. *International Journal of Corpus Linguistics* 4:2, 221–242.

Kohnen, T. (2001). Text types as catalysts for language change: The example of the adverbial first participle construction. H-J. Diller & M. Görlach (eds) *Towards a History of English as a History of Genres*. Heidelberg: Universitätsverlag C. Winter, 111–124.

———. (2007). From Helsinki through the centuries: The design and development of English diachronic corpora. P. Pahta, I. Taavitsainen, T. Nevalainen & J. Tyrkkö (eds) *Towards Multimedia in Corpus Studies*. Helsinki: Research Unit for Variation, Contacts and Change in English (VARIENG), University of Helsinki. Available at http://www.helsinki.fi/varieng/journal/volumes/o2/ kohnen/; last accessed 13 February 2013.

Kytö, M. & Smitterberg, E. (Forthcoming). Diachronic registers. D. Biber & R. Reppen (eds) *The Cambridge Handbook of English Corpus Linguistics.* Cambridge: Cambridge University Press.

Lange, C. (2012). Text types, language change, and historical corpus linguistics. C. Lange, B. Weber & G. Wolf (eds) *Communicative Spaces: Variation, Contact, and Change. Papers in Honour of Ursula Schaefer.* Frankfurt am Main etc.: Peter Lang, 401–416.

Leech, G. (2007). New resources, or just better old ones? The holy grail of representativeness. M. Hundt, N. Nesselhauf & C. Biewer (eds) *Corpus Linguistics and the Web.* Amsterdam: Rodopi, 133–149.

Quirk, R., Greenbaum, S., Leech, G. & Svartvik, J. (1985). *A Comprehensive Grammar of the English Language.* London & New York: Longman.

Smitterberg, E. (2005). *The Progressive in 19th-century English: A Process of Integration.* Amsterdam & New York: Rodopi.

———. (Forthcoming). *Colloquialization in Nineteenth-century English.*

Walker, T. (2007). Thou *and* You *in Early Modern English Dialogues: Trials, Depositions, and Drama Comedy.* Amsterdam & Philadelphia: John Benjamins.

8   *Here is an Old Mastiffe Bitch Ø Stands Barking at Mee:* Zero Subject Relativizers in Early Modern English *(T)here*-Constructions[1]

Gunnel Tottie
The University of Zurich

Christine Johansson
Uppsala University

1. Introduction

There are two kinds of zero relativizers – those where the gap functions as direct object, as in (1), and those where the gap functions as subject in the relative clause, as in (2), henceforth ZSR. [2]

> (1) I have nothing Ø I can call my own…. (Thomas Killigrew, *Chit-Chat*, 1719)
>
> (2) **There** were Seven Horses Ø came in. (The Tryal of Ambrose Rookwood, 1696)

Our purpose here is to throw light on the use of one of the major types, viz. ZSRs in presentative constructions introduced by *there* or *here,* as in (2), in Early Modern English, and to attempt to establish factors that influence the choice of surface or zero variant. The gap will be marked Ø throughout.

---

[1] We are indebted to participants at the symposium in honor of Nils-Lennart Johannesson in February 2013 and at the ICAME 34 conference, Santiago de Compostela, 22–26 May, 2013, for constructive comments, especially Holger Diessel, Uwe Vosberg, Lilo Moessner and Yoko Iyeiri. We are also indebted to Hans-Martin Lehmann and Sebastian Hoffmann for helpful comments and technical support.

[2] Terminology varies here; the term *bare relatives* is used by Huddleston & Pullum (2002: 134, 155). There are also scholars who challenge the classification of zero subject relativizers as relativizers, (e.g. Erdmann 1980, Nagucka 1980 and Lambrecht 1988). We will not enter that discussion here but will use traditional terminology and consider zero relativizers as variants of one relativizer variable.

How to cite this book chapter:
Tottie, G. and Johansson, C. 2015. *Here is an Old Mastiffe Bitch Ø Stands Barking at Mee*: Zero Subject Relativizers in Early Modern English *(T)here*-Constructions. In: Shaw, P., Erman, B., Melchers, G. and Sundkvist, P. and Sundkvist, P. (eds) *From Clerks to Corpora: essays on the English language yesterday and today.* Pp. 135–153. Stockholm: Stockholm University Press. DOI: http://dx.doi.org/10.16993/bab.h License: CC-BY.

2. ZSRs in Present-Day English

ZSRs get scant attention in the major grammars of contemporary English. Quirk et al. (1985: 1250) consider them to be "of doubtful acceptability" or "slovenly," Biber et al. (1999: 619) assert that they occur in "conversational varieties" or "marginally non-standard usage" and Huddleston & Pullum (2002:1055) declare that "they fall at the boundary between very informal and non-standard." However, ZSRs are characteristic of many British and American English dialects, as is clear from e.g. Ihalainen (1980), Hackenberg (1981), van den Eynden (1993: 160) and Kortmann & Schneider (2004).

Moreover, according to a large-scale quantitative and accountable study by Lehmann (2002), based on the spoken demographic component of the British National Corpus (4.2 million words) and on the Longman Spoken American Corpus (5 million words), ZSRs account for 13% of all subject relativizers in British Present-Day English (PDE) but for less, 2.5%, in American PDE.[3] Following Shnukal (1981), Lehmann lists the major types of constructions in PDE as those shown in (3)–(6), adding one residual mixed category of "other" types, listed as (7) (the examples given below are from various sources):

(3) Existential *there*-constructions : **There** was a farmer Ø had a dog (Lambrecht 1988)
(4) Clefts: **It was** he Ø took you out. (Erdmann 1980)
(5) *Be*-constructions: ...they **were** people Ø got in there for the summer...(Lehmann 2002: 171)
(6) *Have*-constructions: We **had** a client Ø came in about two weeks ago (Erdmann 1980)
(7) Other types: *I knew a girl* Ø worked in an office...(Shnukal 1981)

Lehmann found the distribution of the five ZSR types shown in Table 1. In both British and American English, existential *there*-constructions predominate.

---

[3] Accountable studies account for all the constructions where alternative variants could have been used, in this case the relativizers *that* or *which/who* as in *There is a man* who/that/Ø *wants to see you.*

Table 1. The use of ZSR constructions in PDE. Based on Lehmann (2002:172, Table 2).

Types	British English (1581 subject rel. clauses)		American English (3741) subject rel. clauses)	
	N	%	N	%
Existential *there*-constructions	126	61%	27	29%
Clefts	25	12%	24	26%
Be-constructions	8	4%	14	15%
Have-constructions	15	7%	9	10%
Other types	31	15%	20	21%
Totals zero subject relatives	205	13%	94	2.5%

3. ZSRs in some previous studies

Zero relatives have received a fair amount of coverage in diachronic studies of English, but ZSRs have been less well described, although they may be the older type. Both existed in OE, according to several writers (see e.g. van der Auwera 1986) but zero objects increased in frequency and are now very common (see e.g. Johansson 2012; Tottie 1997).

Previous studies have either concentrated on the origin of the ZSR and how it decreased from the Old English period and onwards (see e.g. Erdmann 1980; Nagucka 1980; van der Auwera 1984), or have described its use in written data and in other time periods – see e.g. Dekeyser (1984) and Rydén (1966).

Ukaji (2003) is based on all of Shakespeare's plays, three plays by Ben Jonson, and Nashe's *The Unfortunate Traveller*. In his material, consisting of 303 examples, 40% of all ZSR instances are either *here*- or *there*-constructions, 14% are *it*-clefts, 10% are *have*-sentences, and 23% various other types, thus a distribution not unlike that found by Lehmann for Present-Day English.

Although some earlier historical grammarians have quantified their material, none seem to have carried out accountable studies. Our study appears to be the first diachronic study of ZSRs that is both quantified and accountable. We also aim to pinpoint factors that trigger or constrain the choice of ZSRs, something that has not previously been attempted beyond the basic establishment of the major contexts favoring ZSR, i.e. existential (*t/here-*), cleft, *have-* and to some extent *be*-constructions.

4. Our speech-related data

As the zero relativizer has been described as colloquial and "spoken" in character (see Erdmann 1980; Nagucka 1980; Romaine 1981:94; Dekeyser 1986), we will focus on the use of ZSRs in speech-related texts: Trials and Comedy, which have been deemed the most speech-like (cf. Culpeper and Kytö 2000:186–193).

We studied transcripts of trials and plays from the category Drama/Comedy in the computerized *Corpus of English Dialogues, 1560–1760* (CED) (for a full description of this corpus, see Kytö & Walker 2006). We will use the term Comedy for simplicity. The material is presented in Table 2:

Table 2. Our CED sub-corpus consisting of Trials and Comedy.

CED periods	Trials	Comedy	Totals N words
1. 1560–1599	19,940	47,590	67,530
2. 1600–1639	14,430	47,700	62,130
3. 1640–1679	70,190	47,590	117,780
4. 1680–1719	96,630	47,200	143,830
5. 1720–1760	84,650	48,510	133,160
	285,840	238,590	524,430

As appears from Table 2, our sub-corpus amounted to just over half a million words from five successive 40-year time periods between 1560 and 1760. It is skewed in several respects: The first two periods contain fewer words than the others because of the scarcity of trial transcripts from the 16th and early 17th centuries, but in the following three time periods, Trials account for more material than Comedy, in fact twice as many words in period 4, 1680–1719. This must be kept in mind when the results are presented.

5. Method and first results

We first did a simple lexical search for *there, here, it is,* and *it was* (*it*-clefts); we included *here* because it had been bundled with *there*-examples by earlier writers (e.g. Jespersen 1927: 147; Rydén 1966: 267–268). We then read the whole corpus to weed out irrelevant material and to find additional types less amenable to lexical searches. We ended up with 210 relevant examples, i.e. relativizers in subject function in either *(t)here*-constructions or clefts, with explicit or zero realizations. We also found 17 miscellaneous examples where only zero realizations were collected because of problems of finding alternants with surface subject relativizers, as in example (8).

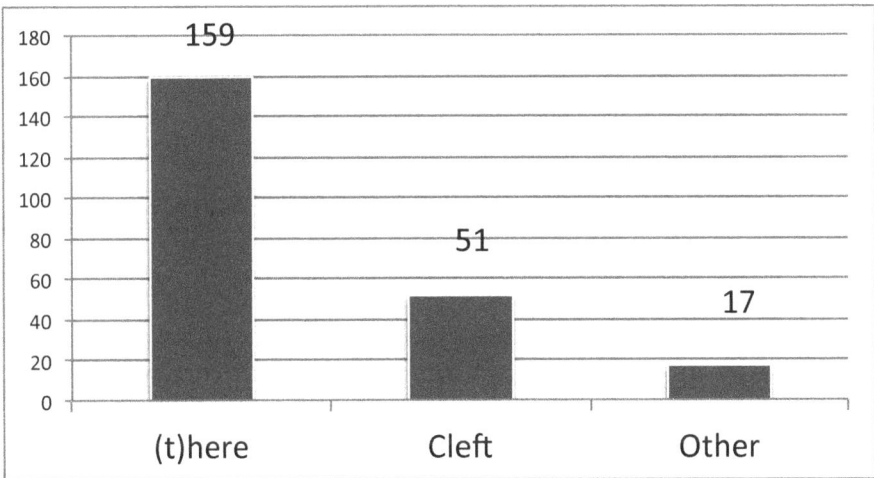

Figure 1. The distribution of constructions capable of taking zero relative constructions in Trials and Comedy in CED.

(8) [Daffodil] Not do it! [hops] Why, I'll get a Chelsea Pensioner Ø shall do it in an Hour, with his wooden Leg.
(David Garrick, The Male-Coquette, 1757)

The different types of constructions were distributed as shown in Figure 1:

The largest category was thus *(t)here*-constructions – 159/210 or 76% of the instances where an accountable analysis was possible, and thus the type most amenable to a quantitative analysis. *(T)here*-constructions will therefore be the focus of our investigation.

Henceforth we will only distinguish between zero or non-zero constructions; the use of *that*- versus *wh*-relatives has been adequately treated in earlier work, such as e.g Johansson (2012), and will therefore not be discussed here. The distribution of zero relatives in *(t)here*-constructions is shown in Table 3.

Table 3. The distribution of zero subject relatives in *(t)here*-constructions in Trials and Comedy in CED.

	Trials			Comedy			Trials+Comedy		
I	II	III	IV	V	VI	VII	VIII	IX	X
Period	Total subj rels	N ZSR	% ZSR	Total subj rels	N ZSR	% ZSR	Total subj rels	N ZSR	% ZSR
1	5	0	0%	5	2	40%	10	2	20%
2	6	1	17%	17	13	76%	23	14	70%
3	31	13	42%	10	6	60%	41	19	46%
4	36	4	11%	7	2	29%	43	6	14%
5	21	2	10%	21	7	33%	42	9	21%
	99	20	20%	60	30	50%	159	50	31%

Table 3 shows the total number and distribution of relevant *(t)here* constructions in the entire sub-corpus. Trials are accounted for in columns II–IV, Comedy in columns V–VII, and the entire corpus in columns VIII–X. The total proportion of ZSRs was 50/159 or 31%, but notice the difference between the two genres: ZSR-constructions amount to 20% in Trials and 50% in Comedy, as appears from columns IV and VII. This discrepancy is itself an interesting finding that will be discussed in section 7.4 below.

The frequency of 50 ZSRs in *there*-constructions in our 524,430-word sample corresponds to 95 instances per million words (pmw). If we exclude 21 instances of *here* and consider only *there*-constructions, we get 29 ZSRs per 524,430 words, or 55 pmw. Lehmann's figure of 126 ZSRs in *there*-constructions in the 4.2 million words of British PDE corresponds to 30 instances pmw, and his figure for American English of 27 ZSRs in *there*-constructions in 5 million words corresponds to 5.4 per million words – we can thus see a sharp decline in the use of ZSRs in these constructions over time. This corroborates findings reported in earlier works (e.g. Erdmann 1980; Nagucka 1980).

6. Factors determining the choice of ZSRs

After gathering the relevant data, we checked a large number of factors for their possible influence on the choice of ZSR. We first cast our net wide, including all those listed below, extra- and intra-linguistic. Only those marked in boldface yielded interesting results and will be discussed in detail below.

EXTRALINGUISTIC
- **Sociolinguistic factors: socio-economic class and gender of speakers**
- **Time period**
- **Text type/genre – Trial or Comedy**

INTRALINGUISTIC FACTORS
- *Here* vs. *there* – constructions
- **Distance between head of antecedent and relativizer slot**
- Antecedent number (There is *someone*.../there are *two men*...)
- Antecedent head: Indefinite noun, definite noun, pronoun, name
- Animacy of antecedent head
- Tense in matrix clause (*There is, there was*...)
- Verb form in relative clause – Finite, Modal, or other Auxiliary
- Polarity – positive or negative matrix clause
- Question or statement in matrix clause
- Prose or meter – convenience of zero in blank verse could be a factor

For coding, we used Goldvarb X, which is useful for establishing basic statistics even when the material inspected is too small to permit a regression analysis, as in the present case.

7. Extralinguistic factors

We begin with socio-economic class as a possible factor favoring ZSR, as the construction has been labeled "non-standard" by grammarians.

7.1 Socioeconomic class

A fine-grained analysis was not possible, but we were able to categorize most speakers as belonging to either a higher class, which we called U(pper class), consisting of nobility, clergymen, judges and attorneys, and a class comprising other speakers, Non-U(pper class), made up of servants, cooks, nurses and most defendants. Three individuals could not be classified, but that still left a total of 156 speakers. As shown in Figure 2, there was no difference between U- and Non-U speakers as measured by the percentages of ZSRs – the proportion of ZSR use was

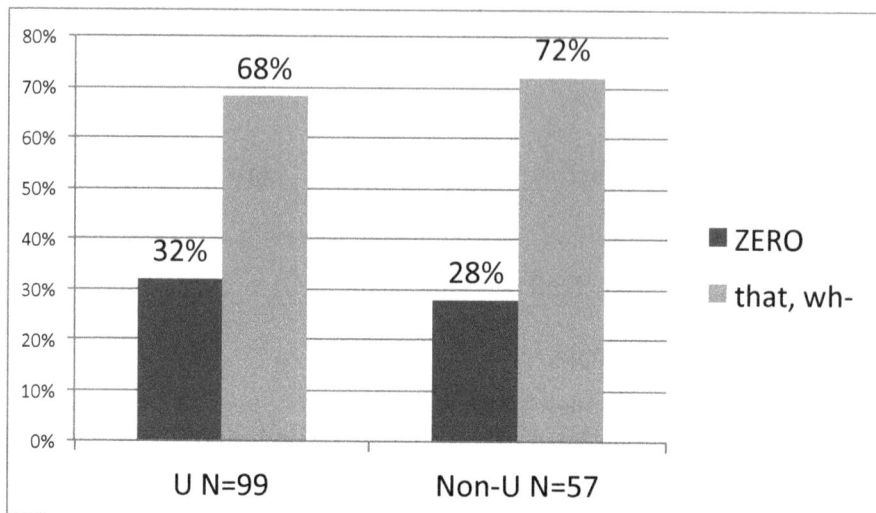

Figure 2. The distribution of ZSR and surface relativizers in the CED subsample.

roughly the same in the two samples, 32% for U speakers, and 28% for Non-U speakers.

The small difference between U and Non-U speakers was not significant. It thus appears that in Early Modern English, the use of ZSRs was not a marker of socio-economic class, but that more educated speakers were as likely to use these constructions as less educated ones. Examples (9) and (10) are from Trials and illustrate *there* + ZSR with U and Non-U speakers, respectively.

(9) [Parson] **There** was a Gentleman Ø fetch'd Me and the Clerk from the Fleet.

(Tryals of Haagen Swendsen, 1702)

(10) [Mr. Baley] My Lord, **there** has been at least 500 people Ø have viewed her.

(Tryal of Mary Moders, 1663)

7.2 Speaker gender

Speaker gender could not be analyzed in the same way as socio-economic class, as there were only 11 observations based on women speakers in the whole sub-corpus, i.e. 7% of the data, as appears from Table 4. But this in itself is an interesting fact that prompted us to investigate whether speech by women actually accounted for only 7% of the total CED sub-corpus.

Table 4. The distribution of zero subject relatives in *(t)here*-constructions in Trials and Comedy in CED.

	Relativizer		
	Ø	that/wh-	Total
Male speakers	46	102	148 (93%)
Female speakers	4	7	11 (7%)
All speakers	50	109	159 (100%)

A representative sample consisting of 20% of our sub-corpus shows that women actually participated very little – the overall proportion of women's speech is about 16% in the whole material.[4] There is a big difference between Trials and Comedy, however: in Comedy, women account for about 28% of all speech, and in Trials for only 4%. Three texts are exceptional in having high proportions of female speech, Farquhar's *The Beaux Stratagem*, the *Tryal of Stephen Colledge* and the *Tryals of Haagen Swendsen*, all from Period 4. A couple of illustrative examples are (11) and (12) from the Haagen Swendsen trials, where two women, Mrs. Rawlins and Mrs. Busby, are very talkative:

(11) [Mrs. Busby] I'll tell you Sir, if you please, I did not know what I was Arrested for, it might be Murder or Treason for ought I knew, **there** was a little Boy by, Ø said Madam I know Mr Unkle. (Tryals of Haagen Swendsen, 1702)

(12) [Mrs. Rawlins] It was Saturday morning before I was releas'd, **there** was some of my Friends Ø came to the place where I was. (Tryals of Haagen Swendsen, 1702)

Finally, because of the paucity of examples, the only conclusion to be drawn considering the importance of gender is that women seem to have used fewer subject relativizers than men overall, or 7% of the total number of relativizers produced in 16% of the total number of words, leaving plenty of room for speculation.

---

4 A random sample consisting of 20% of each text was studied.

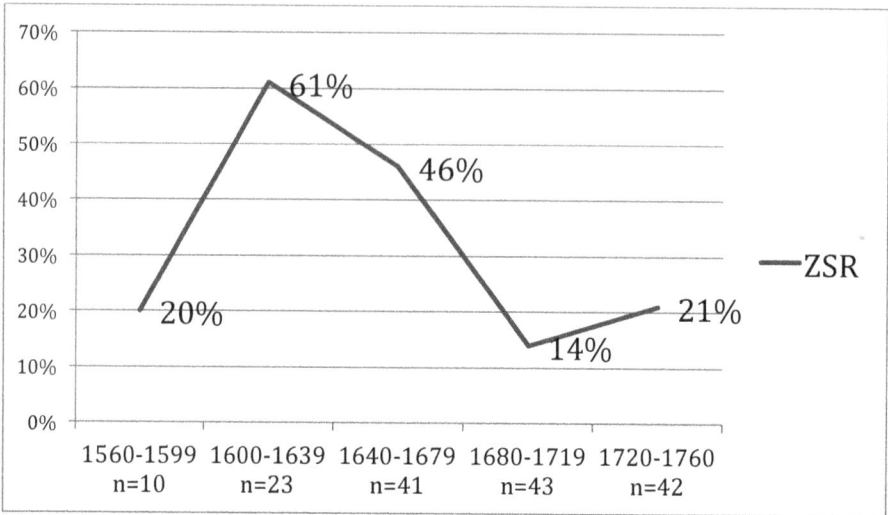

Figure 3. The distribution of ZSRs in *there*-constructions: Aggregate data for Trials and Comedy in Periods 1–5.

7.3 Change over time in Early Modern English

We have seen that ZSRs have become less frequent over time, and we therefore investigated the distribution of ZSR and surface relativizers across the time period covered by CED in Figure 3.

The data presented in Figure 3 must be analyzed with caution. Recall that the samples from the five different time periods were of very different sizes, as shown in Table 1. The low number of examples from Period 1, only 10, makes that data highly unreliable. Period 2 yields 23 examples even though the sample size is smaller, but only in Periods 3–5 do we have fairly large numbers of examples, 41, 43 and 42, respectively. Starting with period 3 (1640–1679), we see a downward trend for ZSRs; the difference between the proportions of ZSRs in Period 2 and Period 5 is significant at 0.0036 (chi-square 8.46, 1 d.f.), and between Period 3 and 5 at 0.0302 (chi-square 4.7, 1 d.f.).

7.4 Genre: Trials and Comedy

Moreover, the skewness of our sub-corpus makes it necessary to account for the distribution of ZSRs separately in Trials and Comedy. This is shown in Figure 4. For Period 2 the proportion 17% ZSR in Trials is based on a single instance out of six *there*-constructions and is thus highly uncertain. The 76% ZSR from Comedy is slightly better, but it is based on only 13 out of 17 observations. But with more data from

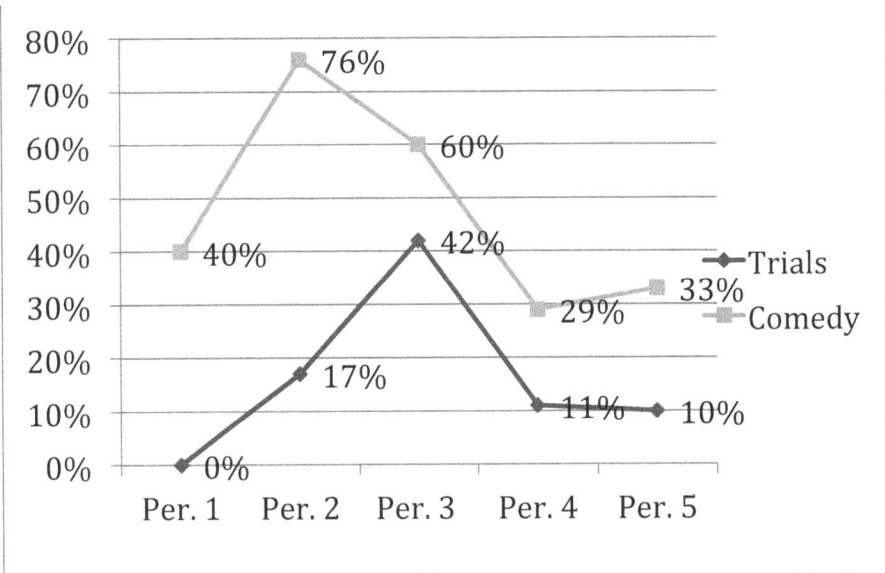

Figure 4. The distribution of ZSR over time in *(t)here*-constructions in Trials and Comedy.

periods 3–5, we see that the downward trends in Trials and Comedy parallel each other, and that the general tendency for ZSRs to decrease in frequency over time holds for both genres in Periods 3–5.

8. Intralinguistic factors

As also shown in Table 2 above, Comedy has consistently higher frequencies of ZSRs than Trials. The question must now be why there is a difference in ZSR frequency between the two genres.

8.1 *Here* and *there*

We first checked the possibility of influence of meter, as blank verse might have required either a surface or a zero realization to make lines scan. That hypothesis could quickly be discarded, as there was little blank verse (or indeed other meter) in our sample, only five instances, with two zero and three surface relatives, respectively.[5] Instead, we need a two-step explanation:

---

5 Interestingly, the vast majority of Ukaji's ZSR examples are from blank verse: only 60/303, or about 20%, are from prose. An accountable study would be necessary to find out what the proportions are in prose and poetry, respectively.

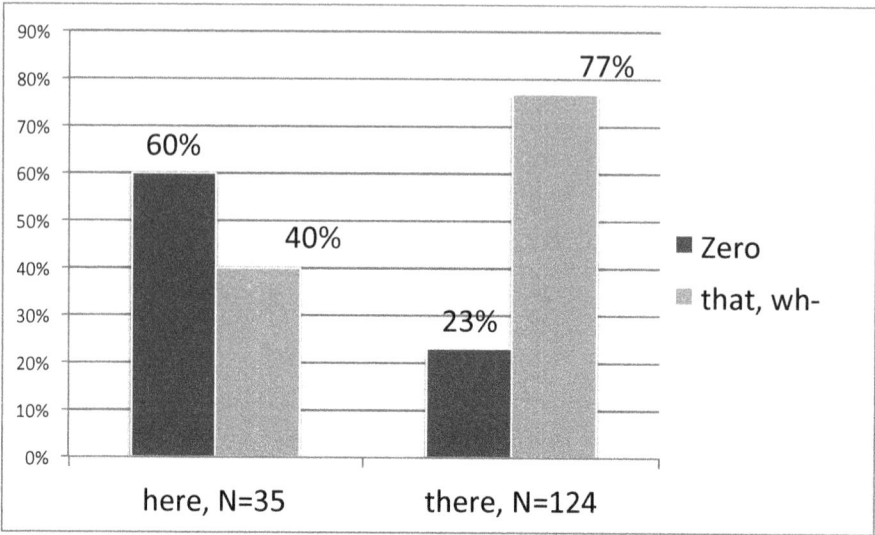

Figure 5. The use of ZSR in *here-* and *there-*constructions.

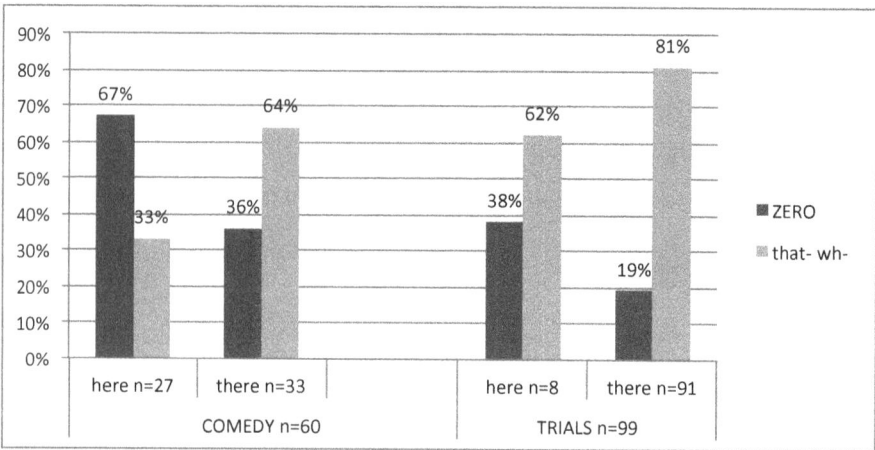

Figure 6. *Here-* and *there-*constructions in Comedy and Trials.

Firstly, *here-*constructions are more apt to take ZSR than *there-*constructions, as shown in Figure 5 and secondly, *here-*constructions are more frequent in Comedy than in Trials, as shown in Figure 6.

Figure 5 shows that *here-*constructions have 60% ZSRs, but *there-*constructions only 23%; the difference is highly significant (p<0.0001, chi-square 15.32, 1 d.f.)

Furthermore, most *here-*constructions occur in Comedy, as shown in Figure 6: *Here* accounts for 27/33 instances, or 45%, in Comedy, but only 8/99 or 8% in Trials. This difference is highly significant (p<0.0001, chi-square 27, 1 d.f.).

The fact that *here*-constructions, with their high proportion of ZSR, abound in Comedy thus goes a long way to explain why the ratio of ZSRs is higher in that text type.

The next question must be why *here*-constructions are so frequent in Comedy. The answer is supplied by the instances presented in (13) – (16):[6]

(13) [Lemot]…**here** is one Ø had hanged himselfe for loue …
(George Chapman, *An Humorous Dayes Myrth*, 1599)

(14) [Medley] Dorimant! you are luckily come to justify Your self — **here**'s Lady — [Bellinda] Ø Has a word or two to say to you from a Disconsolate person.
(George Etheredge, *The Man of Mode*, 1676)

(15) [Dash (servant)] **Here** are Gentlemen in hast Ø would speake with you.
(Lording Barrey, *Ram-Alley*, 1611)

(16) [Daffodil] My Lord Marquis, **here** is a Letter Ø has started Game for you already…
(David Garrick, *The Male-Coquette*, 1757)

Examples (13)–(16) show that *here*-constructions fulfill an important function in plays, introducing new participants or objects appearing on stage. They have mostly a locative meaning, or very occasionally, a temporal one, as in (17):

(17) [Galleypot] **Here**'s a whole Morning Ø has been thrown away…
(James Miller, *The Mother-in-Law*, 1734)

It is clear that *here* and *there*, although they have been lumped together by earlier writers, and although they are both presentatives, have different discourse functions, with *here* almost invariably having a locative meaning, and *there* an existential one. Checking the *there*-instances closely, we only found five with a locative meaning, as in (18), but (19) is typical:

(18) [Winwife] Will you see sport? looke, **there**'s a fellow Ø gathers vp to him, marke.
(Ben Jonson, *Bartholomew Fayre*, 1631)

---

[6] There were no instances in Period 4.

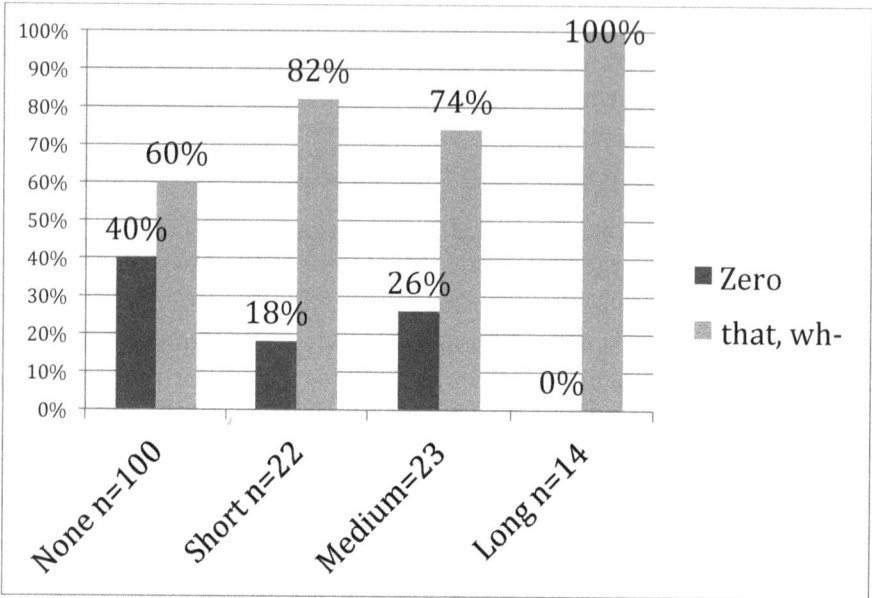

Figure 7. Distance between antecedent head and relativizer slot.

(19) [William Small-shanke] **There** be so many rascals, and tall yeomen Ø VVould hang vpon me for their maintenance…
(Lording Barrey, *Ram-Alley*, 1611)

8.2 Distance between antecedent head and relativizer

The distance between the antecedent head and the relativizer slot was also a factor influencing the choice of ZSR.[7] Compare e.g. (20), where there are no intervening words between *Day* and *goes* and (21), where there are five words between *Gentlemen* and *that*:

(20) [Scrub] There's not a **Day** Ø goes over his Head without Dinner or Supper in this House.
(George Farquar, *The Beaux Stratagem*, 1707)

(21) [Cary] …there are some **Gentlemen** at the Queens-Head at Bow **that** have sent me with a Letter to you…
(Tryals of Robert Green, 1678)

---

[7] Ukaji (2003:257f) discusses the *adjacency requirement*, i.e. the fact that a "relative pronoun is as a rule placed immediately after its antecedent NP," and he also discusses exceptions from it in his material.

We coded instances into four categories based on the number of words intervening between the antecedent head and the relativizer slot, thus:

No distance:
Short distance: 1–2 words
Medium distance: 3–4 words
Long distance: ≥ 5 words

Table 5. Proportions of ZSR according to distance antecedent head – relativizer slot.

	% ZSR
No distance (N = 100)	40%
1–4 words distance (N = 45)	22%
≥ 5 words distance (N = 14)	0%
(N = 159)	

The distribution of the categories is shown in Figure 7.

We see that no distance is by far the most frequent option, and that in those cases, the proportion of ZSR is 40%. With ≥5 words or more between the antecedent head and the relativizer slot, ZSR goes down to 0% in our material.[8] There was little difference between the results for examples with Short and Medium distance between antecedent head and the relativizer slot (4/22 or 18% ZSR vs. 6/23 or 26% ZSR); if those categories are conflated to one, we arrive at the distribution shown in Table 5. The distance between antecedent Head and relativizer slot is thus an important factor for the choice of the zero option.

9. Summary and discussion

The purpose of our paper was to describe the use of zero subject relativizers (ZSRs) in Early Modern English speech-related trials and

---

[8] ZSR is not impossible in such constructions: Cf. Shakespeare, *A Winter's Tale* (I, 2, 190):
And **many a man** there is, even at this present,
Now while I speak this, Ø holds his wife by the arm,
That little thinks she has been sluiced in's absence,
And his pond fish'd by his next neighbour...

drama (comedy) in 524,430 words taken from the Corpus of English Dialogues, CED, covering the period from 1560 to 1760. Because of the paucity of other types (*it*-clefts and a few others), we focused on present-ative constructions with *there* and *here*. We performed an accountable variationist study, i.e. we examined all contexts where subject relatives occurred, not just those showing the zero variant. We found that 50 out of a total of 159 cases – 31% – were ZSRs, thus a much higher propor-tion than those found by Lehmann (2002) for Present-Day British and American English (13% and 2.5%, respectively).

We also checked our material for factors that might favor or disfavor the choice of the zero variant. In contrast to Present-Day English, we found that socio-economic class did not influence the choice of variant as in Present-Day English, where the use of ZSRs has been described as informal or non-standard (Huddleston & Pullum 2002: 1055; Biber et al 1999: 619). In the EModE period, however, ZSRs are used as often by Upper as by Non-Upper class speakers. Influence of gender could not be determined because of the low proportion of female speakers. We had also suspected that meter would play a part in favoring ZSR, but we found only a few examples of verse in our material.[9]

We found four factors with a bearing on the choice of relativizer, viz.

Time period
Text type/genre – Trial or Comedy
Here vs. *there*-constructions
The distance between antecedent Head and relativizer

Our data substantiated earlier findings about the downward trend of ZSRs over time, from 61% in Period 2 (1600-1639) to 21% in Period 5 (1720–1760), with some fluctuations and reservations for low data in earlier periods.

Text type was another decisive factor: Comedy has consistently higher frequencies of ZSRs than Trials, 50% vs 20% overall, with some fluctuations over time. The reason for this must be that it is in this text category that most *here*-constructions are found, and they are more apt to take ZSRs than *there*-constructions. *Here*-constructions serve a particular function in plays, to introduce new characters or objects, as in *Here is an old mastiffe bitch Ø stands barking at mee.* They thus usu-ally have a locative meaning, as opposed to *there*-constructions, which

---

[9] However, as already pointed out above, among the 303 examples cited by Ukaji (2003) 253 were in verse; the factor obviously merits further study.

are almost invariably existential. This in turn makes the previous joint categorization of *here* and *there*-constructions as one type questionable.

The distance between antecedent Head and relativizer slot turned out to be an important factor. First of all, most subject relative clauses with adjacent antecedent heads and relativizer slot, i.e. no distance, is by far the most frequent type: 100/159 instances, or 63% are of this type. Moreover, among those sentences the proportion of ZSR is 40%. With a 1–4 word distance, the ZSR frequency goes down to 22%, and with ≥5 words or more between the antecedent head and the relativizer slot, ZSRs are non-existent in our data. This is in accordance with *the complexity principle* postulated by Rohdenburg (1996: 151): "In the case of more or less explicit grammatical options the more explicit one(s) will tend to be favored in cognitively more complex environments." In relative clauses, the more explicit *wh*-forms or *that* are thus preferred when elements intervene between antecedent head and relative clause.

As stated earlier, we have focused on presentative constructions with *(t)here* in our paper since this is where ZSRs are most frequent in EModE. In PDE, they occur almost exclusively in these constructions (see e.g. Quirk et al 1985: 1406–1407). According to van der Auwera (1984), ZSRs found in OE and ME began to disappear because English at later stages required explicit subjects, which had not been necessary as long as verbs were marked for person. ZSRs survived in pragmatically focused constructions, i.e. the presentative constructions, since there is less need for an explicit subject in these constructions (see van der Auwera 1984; Dekeyser 1986).

Scholars have offered different explanations why presentative *there*-constructions can occur without a subject. Lambrecht (1988) claims that they have to be without a subject in order to express the information as one grammatical unit, which is probably how they occur in discourse (*presentative amalgam constructions*, Lambrecht 1988: 336). Diessel (2004) sees ZSRs in *there*-constructions and in other contexts as precursors of relative clauses with surface relativizers in L1 acquisition, which appear with increasing frequency as children are exposed to more adult speech and become literate. Literacy also seems to have a great deal to do with the fact that ZSRs are found in Present-day English dialects without written records and in substandard varieties used by speakers with little knowledge or use of written language. In the standard language, it is possible that ZSRs and *there* are learned as one construction or chunk and that ZSRs survive in impromptu speech because of the frequency of *there*-constructions of which they are a part (cf. Bybee 2010: 156, 159).

The explanations sketched above as to why ZSRs have survived in *there*-constructions are of course not mutually exclusive; rather they support each other. We will explore these explanations and others in more detail in further work.

References

Biber, D., Johansson, S., Leech, G., Conrad, S., & Finegan, E. (1999). *Longman Grammar of Spoken and Written English*. Harlow: Longman.

Bybee, J. (2010). *Language, Usage and Cognition*. Cambridge: Cambridge University Press.

Culpeper, J., & Kytö, M. (2010). *Early Modern English Dialogues*. Cambridge: Cambridge University Press.

Dekeyser, X. (1984). Relativizers in Early Modern English. A dynamic quantitative Study. J. Fisiak (ed.), *Historical Syntax*. Berlin: Mouton, 61–87.

Dekeyser, X. (1986). English contact clauses revisited. *Folia Linguistica Historica* 7, 107–120.

Diessel, H. (2004). *The Acquisition of Complex Sentences*. Cambridge: Cambridge University Press.

Erdmann. P. (1980). On the history of subject contact-clauses in the history of English. *Folia Linguistica Historica* 1, 139–170.

Hackenberg, R.H. (1972). Appalachian English: a sociolinguistic study. Unpublished PhD thesis. Georgetown University.

Huddleston, R. & Pullum, G. K. (2002). *The Cambridge Grammar of the English Language*. Cambridge: Cambridge University Press.

Ihalainen, O. (1980). Relative clauses in the dialect of Somerset. *Neuphilologische Mitteilungen* 81, 187–196.

Jespersen, O. (1927). *A Modern English Grammar on Historical Principles*. Part 3. Copenhagen: Munksgaard.

Johansson, C. (2012). Relativization in Early Modern English: Written versus speech-related genres. L. Brinton & A. Bergs (eds) *English Historical Linguistics: An International Handbook*, Vol. I. Berlin: Mouton, 776 –790.

Kortmann, B. & Schneider, E. (eds) (2004). *A Handbook of Varieties of English*: *A Multimedia Reference Tool*. Berlin: Mouton.

Kytö, M. & Walker, T. (2006). *Guide to A Corpus of English Dialogues 1560–1760*. Acta Universitatis Upsaliensis. Studia Anglistica Upsaliensia 130.

Lambrecht, K. (1988). There was a farmer had a dog: Syntactic amalgams revisited. Paper presented at *the Berkeley Linguistics Society. Proceedings of the Fourteenth Annual Meeting*, 319–339.

Lehmann, H.-M. (2002). Zero subject relative constructions in American and British English. P. Peters (ed.), *New Frontiers of Corpus Research*. Amsterdam and New York: Rodopi, 163–177.

Nagucka, R. (1980). Grammatical pecularities of the contact-clause in EModE. *Folia Linguistica Historica* 1, 171–184.

Quirk, R., Greenbaum, S., Leech, G. & Svartvik, J. (1985). *A Comprehensive Grammar of the English Language*. London: Longman.

Rohdenburg, G. (1996). Cognitive complexity and increased grammatical explicitness in English. *Cognitive Linguistics* 7:149–182.

Romaine, S. (1981). The relative clause marker in Scots English: Diffusion, complexity and style as dimensions of syntactic change. *Language in Society* 9: 221–247.

Rydén, M. (1966). *Relative Constructions in Early Sixteenth Century English. With Special Reference to Sir Thomas Elyot*. Acta Universitatis Upsaliensis. Studia Anglistica Upsaliensia 3.

Shnukal, A. (1981). There's a lot mightn't believe this…variable subject relative pronoun absence in Australian English. D. Sankoff & H. Cedergren (eds) *Variation Omnibus*. Edmonton, Alberta: Linguistic Research, 321–328.

Tottie, G. (1997). Relatively speaking. Relative marker usage in the British National Corpus. T. Nevalainen & L. Kahlas-Tarkka (eds) *To Explain the Present: Studies in the Changing English Language in Honour of Matti Rissanen*. Helsinki: Société Néophilologique, 465–481.

Ukaji, M. (2003). Subject zero relatives in Early Modern English. M. Ike-uchi, M. Ukaji, & Y. Nishimura (eds) *Current Issues in English Linguistics* Tokyo: Kaitakusha, 248–277.

van den Eynden, N. (1993). *Syntactic Variation and Unconscious Linguistic Change. A Study of Adjectival Relative Clauses in the Dialect of Dorset*. Frankfurt a. M.: Peter Lang.

van der Auwera, J. (1984). More on the history of subject contact clauses in English. *Folia Linguistica Historica* 5, 170–183.

9 "Norfolk People Know Best": On the Written Representation of Accents as Performed and Perceived by 'Insiders' and 'Outsiders'

Gunnel Melchers
Stockholm University

1. Introduction

The quote in the title of this presentation is taken from the conclusion of Peter Trudgill's article 'Dedialectalisation and Norfolk Dialect Orthography' (Trudgill 1999b), in which he explains why

> ... the non-traditional, outsiders' spelling <bootiful> is objected to so strongly by the local community. Native dialect-speaking insiders interpret the <oo> spelling as indicating the utterly nonexistent pronunciation */buːtəfəl/ rather than the correct /bʉːtəfəl/. As usual, Norfolk people know best. (Trudgill 1999b: 329)

The concept of 'insider' vs. 'outsider' plays a significant role in the assessment and discussion throughout my paper, which – based mainly on nineteenth-century fiction – is concerned with the representation in writing of regional and social features of language in England with special reference to accents.

Writers and readers can be insiders as well as outsiders, here simply defined as members or non-members of the speech community they represent in writing or interpret in reading. From the writer's perspective, the language of a written text can be described as 'intrinsic' or 'extrinsic' to the author (cf. Hickey (2010: 9), who states that "where the language being represented is extrinsic to the author it may well be unreliable", characterized among other things by vacuous re-spellings).

A thorny issue in the analysis of dialect representation in fiction is the significance of authenticity, which is highlighted in Jane Hodson's pioneering publication *Dialect in Film and Literature* (2014), among

How to cite this book chapter:
Melchers, G. 2015. "Norfolk People Know Best": On the Written Representation of Accents as Performed and Perceived by 'Insiders' and 'Outsiders'. In: Shaw, P., Erman, B., Melchers, G. and Sundkvist, P. (eds) *From Clerks to Corpora: essays on the English language yesterday and today.* Pp. 155–176. Stockholm: Stockholm University Press. DOI:http://dx.doi.org/10.16993/bab.i License: CC-BY.

other things offering critical views on one-sided, detailed linguistic assessments but also on the generally impressionistic appraisals by literary reviewers of the accuracy of dialect representation, "approving of those representations which they felt to be authentic, and condemning those they felt to be inauthentic" (p. 220). While recognizing the importance of Hodson's subtle critique, the general view taken in this paper is that authenticity remains an important factor.

The paper is structured as follows: a brief introduction to nonstandard language in writing as a field of study is given, followed by some observations on the concepts of 'insider' and 'outsider'. Section 4 focuses on the general problem of representing accents by means of the orthographic system ('semi-phonetic spelling') and section 5 provides a more detailed account of the representation of regional accents in 19th century England. Section 6 summarizes and discusses the efforts by insiders and outsiders and presents four case studies of 19th century writers who can be said to represent both categories. The paper is concluded by an attempt to draw some general conclusions from the somewhat conflicting data and viewpoints accounted for.

2. Some notes on the study of nonstandard language in writing

Kirk (1999: 45) distinguishes two approaches to the study of nonstandard language in literary texts:

> ... the dialectological, which uses literary texts as evidence of the spoken language and considers the significance provided by the use of the dialect and the nonstandard within the literary work as evidence for the dialect, often historical .... The second approach is stylistic, which considers how effective or realistic of speech the language in a particular text is and considers the role and effectiveness of the dialect and nonstandard within the literary work as a whole.

My background may be that of a dialectologist but I recognize the importance of both the above approaches. Scholars who argue that authenticity is not a major issue in analysing dialect representation in fiction emphasize that focus should be on the function of the dialect within the text. While recognizing the importance of function, the view taken in this paper is that the importance of function does not exclude the value of authenticity. In 19th-century texts as well as their adaptations for television, for example, authenticity is generally expected with regard to physical environment, dress codes, polite behaviour etc., and language should be no exception in providing an authentic setting. Hence the paper is indeed concerned with authenticity, in comparing features found in the selected texts to authentic data, above all drawn from Wright's *English Dialect Dictionary* (EDD) and the *Survey of English Dialects* (SED). There is, admittedly, a certain amount of circularity in the case of EDD in that a great many entries are taken from literary works but these were carefully selected by its eminent editor, Joseph Wright. An important token of the value of dialect in writing as a source of information in historical linguistics is the chapter *The Dialects of England since 1776*, (Ihalainen 1994), which is based on data contained in works by Wright and other 19th century dialectologists as well as fictional writers.

Sweeping statements are often found in literary criticism such as "Her men and women have characteristic modes of speech. Sometimes they are easy to recognize, as, for instance, by their dialect, which, incidentally, she used well" (Pollard 1965: 254, writing about Elizabeth Gaskell). In my view, such observations are of no value, let alone completely misleading and faulty ad hoc views such as Q.D. Leavis' claim that in Dickens' representations of East Anglian accents the sounds are not represented ("…a matter of vocabulary and grammar only") (cf. Poussa 1999: 34). Opinions vary on this issue, however, as briefly discussed in the conclusion of this paper.

A distinction is usually made between 'dialect literature' and 'literary dialect', the former term referring to works composed wholly, or at least partly, in non-standard dialect, produced for a local readership, whereas the latter refers to the representation of non-standard speech (almost exclusively in the dialogue) in literature otherwise written in Standard English. The novels by Elizabeth Gaskell, who was "well aware of the need to balance authenticity and accuracy against accessibility" (Beal 2006: 534) are said to exemplify the latter category. This distinction is somewhat fuzzy, in that writers of dialect literature more often than not produce themselves in Standard English as well, and novelists like Gaskell may have 'insider' knowledge about the variety they represent. It is not completely true that "dialect is a variable dependent on the demands of fictional situation rather than on the probable behaviour of an actual speaker" (Page 1988: 59).

Schneider (2002: 71f), who is exclusively concerned with written texts as data for linguistic, notably variationist, studies, provides a useful and widely quoted classification of text types according to their proximity to speech, considering category (recorded, recalled, imagined, observed, invented), reality of speech event (ranging from real to hypothetical), speaker-writer relationship, and temporal distance. According to Schneider, texts should be as close to speech as possible to be of value; in addition they must fulfil certain size requirements. Literary writing is dismissed, since it normally displays 'categorical invariant usage'. Unfortunately, there has been a shortage of substantial corpora of 19th-century fiction including non-standard dialogue, in spite of the increase in dialect literature as well as literary dialect in the 19th century, related to the rise of the novel. A close reading of, for example, Gaskell's fictional texts, however, makes it obvious that they cannot be characterized as displaying categorical invariant usage. It is my opinion that her fictional representation of spoken language could be varyingly classified as any of Schneider's categories, i.e. 'recorded', 'recalled' etc.

The focus on factual knowledge above together with the plea for authenticity may have given the reader of this text the impression that authentic representation as propagated here should be characterized by minute phonetic detail. This is by no means the case. The concept of 'enregisterment', as recently developed by Joan Beal (2009) and others, whereby specific, often somewhat 'levelled', linguistic features become associated with a particular variety and 'reified', is not in opposition to authenticity as viewed in this contribution.

3. 'Insider' versus 'outsider' writers and readers

In his frustration after trying to include some phonetic symbols in rendering Cockney accents in *Pygmalion*, G.B. Shaw referred to "… this desperate attempt to represent her dialect without a phonetic alphabet" which "must be abandoned as unintelligible outside London" (*Pygmalion*, Act I). It would appear that Shaw believed only 'insider readers', i.e. Londoners, would be able to understand his Cockney representations. This may seem plausible enough, but the ability to read and interpret dialect in writing is more complicated and requires more insight than simply being a native speaker. The roles of 'outsiders' and 'insiders' can be discussed from a variety of perspectives, such as the phonological level of representation, language awareness and attitudes, and the ideology underpinning the wish to write and read dialect texts. This is illustrated in the following section by examples representing different time periods (occasionally beyond the 19th century for clarification of some particular issue), genres, and social/regional speech communities.

A number of distinguished writers have represented varieties of language of which they have insider knowledge as well as varieties of which they have acquired knowledge or limited experience. Elizabeth Gaskell, for example, wrote two novels (*Mary Barton* and *North and South*) set in Manchester, her hometown, but also a novel set in Whitby (*Sylvia's Lovers*), where she had spent only a fortnight. Another example of a writer who wrote as an insider as well as outsider is Fanny Burney, whose novel *Camilla* contains representations of a number of different regional accents. Charles Dickens, as we all know, included speakers of accents from various parts of Britain as well as abroad in his novels. He has often been accused of lacking linguistic insight and reliability and was, unlike Gaskell and Eliot, not accepted as an 'informant' by Joseph Wright for the *English Dialect Dictionary*. Such a severe assessment is somewhat unjustified, as shown by Poussa (1999) and in the sadly neglected monumental work *Sound and Symbol in the Dialogue of the Works of Charles Dickens* (Gerson 1967).

Even though writers producing non-standard spellings may be quite knowledgeable about the variety they want to represent, they often fail miserably due to the inadequacy of the orthographic system. Tennyson's elaborate use of 'outlandish' spellings in his Lincolnshire poems, for example, is known to have made them largely inaccessible to the general reader. This is an important issue and the limitations of the orthographic system are therefore discussed in some detail in the following section.

4. The problem of representing phonetics/phonology by means of the orthographic system

Whereas a near-authentic use of dialectal morphosyntax and vocabulary is – at least superficially – fairly easy, the representation of sounds, by contrast, is fraught with innumerable problems, for the writer as well as the reader. In his 1809 work on the dialect of Bedfordshire, for example, Batchelor describes "the Deficiencies of the English Alphabet, when applied in the Explanation of provincial Errors of Pronunciation" (Zettersten 1974: 157). It is an indisputable fact that the only way to truthfully represent the actual pronunciation of vowels and consonants in writing is by using a phonetic transcription (since the late 19th century preferably the International Phonetic Alphabet (IPA)), as exemplified in a simple but correct way in the title of Tony Harrison's famous poem *Them and [uz]*. Understandably, this is not a generally conceivable alternative for publishers, writers and readers (see the Shaw quotation in the previous section).

The following examples will illustrate some aspects of the problem through various employed strategies:

a) *Aj häv to tjildren* ('I have two children'; from a textbook in English for Swedish emigrants in the 1890's)
b) <foot> vs. <strut>; <arrm> vs. <ahm> ; <the rang spee-oon>; <a stee-an hoose> (Trudgill 1990)
c) laugh (*laaf*|*laf* (regional variants)); one (*wun*)‖Northern England also *won*) (Wells, *Reader's Digest Illustrated Dictionary* 1984)
d) *Ah, Apollo jars. Arcane standard, Hannah More. Armageddon pier staff.* ('I apologize. I can't stand it anymore. I'm a-gettin' pissed off') (Kingsley Amis 1968, *I want it now*)
e) To a Londoner, the strawbreez at Wimbledon ah veddy good with clotted cream ... (English Today 6, 1986)
f) Eh? good daäy! good daäy! thaw it bean't not mooch of a daäy. Nasty casselty weather! An' mea haäfe down wi' my haäy!
   (Tennyson, The Church-Warden and the Curate)

In spite of their 'outlandish' appearance, all the above examples are – with a varying degree of sophistication – exponents of some knowledge of the represented accent; yet they cannot be characterized as very successful. Whereas the 'transcriptions' no doubt make perfect sense to their creators, they are bound to be misleading, if not impenetrable, at the receiver end. Although they all are meant to represent varieties of English, some – notably a), d) and e) – clearly presuppose knowledge of the creator's variety, in the case of a) even another language. In a manner of speaking they can – with the exception of a) – be said to have been produced by 'insiders' with little or no consideration of the 'outsider' audience. More often than not, however, the transcriptions tend not to be transparent to the insider audience either.

As for d), which from a British perspective is a very amusing and adequate representation of an American accent, including rhythmical features, it "would be rather impenetrable for an American audience" (Wells 1982: 529). Conversely, e) includes apt observations of characteristic realizations and non-realizations of *r* in Received Pronunciation, which would be below awareness of the speakers of this accent.

Examples b) and c), both designed by linguists for pedagogical reasons, certainly demonstrate more insightful attempts at 'semi-phonetic spellings' (cf. Beal 2006: 531), which implies serious attempts at suggesting alternative pronunciations. Of a somewhat different nature is so-called 'eye-dialect', here used in the sense of 'respellings which reflect no phonetic facts', such as *sez* for 'says', *wimmin* for 'women', including representations of allegro speech such as *'cause*, *'bout*, showing natural phonetic processes (richly demonstrated in local glossaries, for example).

A reasonably successful system of using near-exclusively letters of the alphabet to indicate pronunciation was created by J.C. Wells for the *Reader's Digest Great Illustrated Dictionary* (1984) (cf. example c), where [ə] (for 'schwa', the most common vowel in unstressed position) is the only symbol taken from outside the alphabet. Some regional features, "considered standard in a particular region" are also catered for: *laugh*, for example, is transcribed as (laaf‖laf) and *one* is presented as (*wun*‖Northern England also *won*), in an unsuccessful attempt to indicate the 'FOOT-STRUT split' as featured in Tony Harrison's [uz], i.e. the lack of a phonemic opposition between the vowels of these words and others belonging to the same sets (Wells 1982: 350f).

Similarly, for the first edition of his introductory textbook *The Dialects of England* (1990), Trudgill designed a system consisting of alphabetic letters, exemplified in b), in which the FOOT-STRUT split is shown as (oo) vs (u), for example. In the second edition of his book, however, "at the request of many readers", he felt the need to complement these transcriptions with IPA versions, no doubt a justified step in the case of a linguistic textbook. Having taught dialect courses based on this textbook for a number of years, I can testify that students kept begging for phonetic transcriptions (not a very common experience). Trudgill's fairly detailed orthographic system is of special interest here, however, since he exemplifies most of his presentations of regional dialects by means of literary texts, as in the following extract from 'The Lincolnshire Poacher' (Mabel Peacock, 1890s):

> But I'd rather be doon wheare th'fire
> An' brimstun foriver bo'ns,
> An' just goä roond wi' a bucket
> An' give fook drink by to'ns –
> Then sit I' yon stright made heaven,
> Wheare saints an' aängels sing ...

Here the semi-phonetic spellings are the poet's own, but my general impression is that Trudgill, at least to some extent, has been inspired by genuine dialect writing in designing his own system.

Tennyson's dialect poetry, with its elaborate use of 'outlandish' spellings of the same character as 'The Lincolnshire Poacher', has been characterized as "largely inaccessible to the general reader because of an unsuccessful attempt by the poet to indicate the precise nature of the sounds of his native dialect" (Tilling 1972: 108). This is probably due to lack of phonetic insight as well as the inadequacy of the orthographic system, but above all to the poet's overenthusiastic, unrealistic attitude as a committed, 'evangelizing' insider.

Semi-phonetic spelling is also a long-standing concern of the BBC pronunciation unit (cf. http://www.phonetic-blog.blogspot.com/). In his assessment, dated 9 December, 2011, of its recommendations, Wells draws attention to some particular problems in finding satisfactory symbols in respelling systems for English, including

- the PRICE vowel, for which neither *y* nor *igh* is unambiguous, while *ī* has a diacritic
- the MOUTH vowel, for which both *ou* and *ow* are ambiguous (cf. *soul, show*)
- the GOAT vowel, for which *oh* may wrongly suggest a short vowel and *oa, ou, ow* are ambiguous (cf. *broad, loud, now*)
- schwa. If *oh* represents a long vowel, how can we make it clear that *uh* represents a short weak one?

In the following section the limitations of semi-phonetic spelling are further discussed in some detail in connection with an 'inventory' of the representation of accent in 19th century fiction, the main purpose of which is to provide a background to understanding the case studies and general discussion presented towards the end of the paper.

5. Regional accents in 19th century England – factual knowledge and fictional representation

In comparison with earlier periods, the factual knowledge of English accents and dialects as they were spoken in the nineteenth century is more than significant. The first truly ambitious as well as insightful attempt at mapping English dialect areas was that of Alexander Ellis (Ellis 1889), but of even greater importance within the context of the present paper is Joseph Wright's *English Dialect Dictionary (EDD)* (Wright 1898–1905), which contains more information, is more accessible (especially after its recent digitization), and is largely based on examples drawn from fiction, generally representing insiders. The fact that Wright, with his monumental knowledge of English dialects, has included a word form constitutes a guarantee of its real-life existence but there is, admittedly, a danger of circularity here.

An important factual source of another kind is the *Survey of English Dialects (SED)* (Orton et al. 1962–71), based on fieldwork in the mid–20th century but in its focus on old speakers reflecting regional/nonstandard usage not too distant in time from the fictional representations featuring in this paper. Indeed, according to Ihalainen (1994: 205), "no radical changes took place in English dialects in the post-1776 period until the second half of the twentieth century". The fairly recent, widely quoted mapping of 'Traditional Dialect areas' (Trudgill 1999) largely draws on SED data and is also very relevant for this presentation. His maps confirm, among other things, that the major division is a north–south one, e.g. demonstrating the FOOT–STRUT split as mentioned above. As for fictional representations of regional dialects, however, it should be pointed out that those referring to the south and middle of England are neither as easily found nor as well researched as those of the north. This may be due to a perception of general southern features as connected with the standard, whereas northern speech is 'marked'.

Trudgill's mapping based on phonological criteria defines a staggering number of dialects and subdialects, such as "Southern Eastern Central East". It is not the purpose here, nor would it be possible, to describe and exemplify all these varieties through fiction. Rather, from a selection of characteristic features, I will demonstrate how writers have – successfully as well as unsuccessfully – tried to represent different kinds of phonological features, considering the limits of semi-phonetic spellings. Interestingly, but perhaps not surprisingly, the general north–south distinctions, such as the FOOT–STRUT split, do not appear to be represented (cf. Wales 2010: 70, however). Searching for examples is not an easy task, since text corpora have, until recently, not included dialect literature and deliberately shunned literary dialect. Thanks to the launch of the Salamanca Corpus (http://salamancacorpus.usal.es/SC/index.html), searches will hopefully be more successful in the future. For the present study, most of the examples derive from the quotations found in *EDD*. Unfortunately, however, regional areas are very unevenly represented in the dictionary, as recently demonstrated by Praxmarer (2010).

In sociolinguistics and dialectology, vowels have generally attracted more attention than consonants. This also appears to be characteristic of literary representations; the reason may be that it is relatively easier to create semi-phonetic spellings by modifying vowel symbols than by drastically exchanging one consonant symbol for another. The following listing exemplifies fairly successful renderings of regional vowel features by 19th century writers in various genres (the words written in capital letters are key words, representing a category characterized by the same vowel and the words in bold exemplify a semi-phonetic spelling). By 'fairly successful' I mean that any reader (outsider as well as insider) conversant with English could be expected to perceive the intended sound quality represented by the semi-phonetic spelling. This must, unfortunately, be characterized as a qualified guess; I am not aware of any substantial study investigating the reading aloud of dialect texts.

Most of the following features are described as traditional dialect features in Trudgill 1999.

a) Realization of LAND ([land] generally in the north; [lænd] in the south; [lɒnd] in the West Midlands: *E's gotten a bwile in 'is lonk, poor bwoy* (Herefordshire 19th-century anonymous text). Other examples from the area include *mon, hond, ony* and such representations are also found in parts of the North (Wales 2010: 70). This spelling works well. Distinguishing between [land] and [lænd] is obviously more problematic; nor have any examples been found. That general north-south distinction may well be disregarded for the same reasons as the FOOT-STRUT split: it is difficult to represent and taken for granted at least if the writers are insiders.
b) Monophthongal realization of DOWN: *doon, roond* (Peacock, *Th'Lincolnsheer Poächer*), demonstrating Lincolnshire's 'northern affiliation', *coo, thoosand* (north of the Humber, cf. Wales 2010: 71).
c) Insertion of <w> before <o> (involving a semi-vowel + a vowel) (Dorset, Somerset): *primrwose, hwome* (William Barnes, *Blackmwore Maidens*).
d) Yod-dropping (East Anglia), also involving a semi-vowel: *solitoode, gratitoode* (Dickens, *Great Expectations*).
e) [y:], i.e. [i:] with lip-rounding, in GOOSE words (Devon): *güzechick, güze vlesh* (EDD, unidentified source). This will presumably work well if the reader has some knowledge of German.
f) short /a/ in the verbs *make* and *take* in the North, up to the Durham–Northumberland border: *mak/mek; tak* (Wales 2010: 70).

It is symptomatic that out of the four vowels posing particular problems in respelling according to Wells (see above) three are realised as diphthongs. This is well illustrated in Tennyson's Lincolnshire poetry, with its excess of unusual letter combinations including diacritics and diaeresis (the pronunciation of vowels in a diphthong separately) (cf. Tilling 1972). Similarly, the bulk of Gerson's (1967) inventory of Dickens' respellings relates to diphthongs.

Some examples of felicitous representations of consonants are:

- H insertion (the hypercorrect counterpart to H dropping): *hodd* 'odd', *hany* 'any' (George Eliot, *Adam Bede*), suggesting a desire to identify with the gentry on the part of one of the characters (cf. Dickens in *David Copperfield*, who characterizes Uriah Heep's speech by exaggerated H-dropping).
- voiced initial fricatives (the West Country): *vorzeaken* 'forsaken', *zot* 'sat' (William Barnes' poem *The Broken Heart*; the protagonist's name is *Fanny*, however).
- interchange of /v/ and /w/ (Eastern counties): "A man your *vorship*, may call out 'boots' and not *wiolate* any hact *vatsomdever*" (The Times, Jan. 26, 1835). Wells (1982: 333), assessing 'literary Cockney', dismisses Dickens' elaborate representation of this feature as a literary stereotype, seriously out-of-date at the time of writing. [w] for /v/, however is reported by Skeat from London in the latter half of the nineteenth century (Skeat's personal observation, cf. Gerson 1967: XIX).
- realizations of consonant /k/ clusters (Yorkshire, Cumberland): *tnit* 'knit', *tnee* 'knee'; *tlay* 'clay', *dlass* 'glass' (Wales 2010: 71).
- West Midland 'g-ful' endings: *playingk* for 'playing' in an 1886 Cheshire text (cf. Skeat 1911: 122).

A characteristic problem in the representation of consonants, i.e. rhoticity vs. non-rhoticity, was already touched upon in the previous section (cf. examples d) and e)). In 19th-century fiction, due to the relative lateness of the emergence of non-rhoticity in conjunction with the spelling convention, 'r-fulness' does not appear to be indicated. In *The Mayor of Casterbridge*, set in the West Country, Hardy occasionally marks the speech of the Scotsman Donald Farfrae, e.g. in *warrld* 'world' (presumably signalling focus), but never in the representation of his local speakers (whose speech was presumably also 'r-ful'). This may well be an 'insider effect'. The interpretation of r-fulness/r-lessness based on spelling must be made with caution, however, since the social significance of r-dropping remains unsettled even in the early twentieth century (Ihalainen 1994: 215) and it is the occasional presence of rhoticity that attracts attention (Wells 1982: 30).

With the exception of representations of allegro speech, such as *'cause*, *'bout*, usually showing natural phonetic processes but richly demonstrated in local glossaries, examples are scarce when it comes to indicating suprasegmental features such as syllabic structures or prosody. Sentence stress is occasionally indicated by capital letters, as in Mr. Podsnap's famous didactic conversation with a French gentleman: *You find it Very Large? And very Rich?* (Dickens, *Our Mutual Friend*). No examples are given here of representations of prosodic patterns such as rhythm or intonation, although 20th-century examples show that it is possible (cf. the Kingsley Amis representation of an accent from the American South ((d), above) and the trendy rising intonation in 'uptalk' as featured in Jane Smiley's *Moo* (1995): *"No, sir? You gave me an A?, See, that was the only A I've gotten here?"*. For an interesting and original analysis of significant pitch span variation expressed in fiction, including works by 19th and 18th century writers, see the chapter 'Paralinguistic features' in Gillian Brown's *Listening to Spoken English* (1977). Hodson (2014: 85) draws attention to Dickens' representation of the Artful Dodger's speech in *Oliver Twist*, in which there is

> ... some attempt to indicate his intonation through punctuation, such as the exclamation marks which indicate emphasis, the question marks which indicate a rising intonation, and the dashes in the word 'com-pan-ion' which presumably indicate that each syllable of the word is sounded out in full.

Interestingly, and clearly related to the insider/outsider thrust of this paper, Hodson continues:

> All of this can be contrasted with the way in which Oliver's speech is reported in this passage, which is given the form of indirect speech as the narrator summarizes what Oliver said, without giving any flavour of how he said it ... the dialect speech is 'other' and its peculiarities are highlighted, while the main narrative work is conducted in Standard English.

6. Insiders and outsiders in the perception, interpretation and representation of accents – a brief summary and four illustrative case studies

In studying the use of nonstandard varieties in English literature, it is important to remember that English spelling does not represent any existing dialect phonetically. By convention, therefore, when a writer uses normal English spellings in dialogue, for example, we infer that the pronunciation intended is the standard of the audience for which the work is written, while special deviant spellings indicate the pronunciation of a dialect that is not the audience's standard. This can lead to some rather unusual variations. For example, a writer representing an Irishman to a predominantly English audience might be inclined to use spelling to indicate Irish pronunciation, while the same writer might not do so when presenting an Irishman to a predominantly Irish audience.

(Traugott & Pratt 1980: 339)

In this final section of the paper the insider–outsider aspect, highlighted in the main title, takes centre stage. This aspect has already surfaced in various contexts; hence it makes sense to begin by summarizing what has emerged so far. This summary is followed by a few brief 'case studies' of certain works by 19th-century writers who have produced representations of accents both intrinsic and extrinsic to them: Fanny Burney, Elizabeth Gaskell, George Eliot, and Alfred Tennyson. By way of conclusion, various general aspects of the topic are briefly considered, such as the phonological level of representation, linguistic awareness and attitudes, and the ideology underpinning the wish to write and read dialect texts, including conscious effort-raising measures in, for example, the education system.

A brief summary

- Doubts and fears have been voiced as to the reliability of outsiders representing accents as well as being able to interpret/read representations of other accents than their own, intrinsic variety (Hickey 2010: 9; Shaw (*Pygmalion*));
- In an extended sense, the outsider/insider factor also applies to linguists as well as perceptive writers of fiction who do not envisage the problems facing the readers of their efforts (cf. examples a)–f) in section 2 above). If, for example, students exposed to the semi-phonetic spellings in Trudgill's *The Dialects of England* have a Yorkshire accent or have Swedish as their first language, they tend not to be able to read out the semi-phonetic spellings in the desired manner; hence they demand phonetic transcriptions. It has been pointed out that "any attempt at indicating accent through orthographical manipulation will only work if writer and reader share an understanding of the variety being so represented" (Hodson 2014: 92);
- Whereas the concept of 'semi-phonetic spellings' implies serious attempts at suggesting alternative pronunciations, the only purpose

of 'eye-dialect' (respellings which reflect no phonetic facts, such as *sez, wimmin, ennything*) appears to be a signal to the reader that a character uses vulgar or nonstandard language. Consider, for example, the use of nonstandard spellings in *Gone with the Wind* for the speech of blacks while using standard spelling for whites, even though the speech of both groups is phonetically very similar. In this case, writers as well as readers might well be extrinsic to the variety.

- As noted, for example, in connection with Tennyson's elaborate spellings, and also in the general analysis of regional features, representations are often inaccessible to the reader because of inability to indicate the precise sounds of an accent. This inability could be due to phonetic ignorance but above all to the sheer impossibility of representing phonetic detail in an orthographic transcription, which will suggest different realizations to outsider speakers of different accents. Representations like Tennyson's would presumably cause problems to insider readers as well, unless they were given special training.

Four case studies:

Fanny Burney:

In her widely popular novel *Camilla* (1796) Fanny Burney included a chapter containing a lively account of a performance of *Othello*, in which all the parts except Iago were played by actors speaking their own local dialect. Cassio, for example, who is presented as hailing from Norfolk, says *dewk* for 'duke' (a representation of Yod-dropping, not quite as felicitous as Dickens' <oo> exemplified in section 3 above). Othello himself is said to be 'a true Londoner', as exemplified by *wery*, *avay*, and Desdemona's father, a West Country man from Somerset, produces *zpeak, confez* (the second example not adequately exemplifying 'voicing of initial fricatives'). The actress playing Desdemona is said to come from Worcestershire, but her speech is – confusingly – represented mainly through excessive H dropping as well as H insertion.

Fanny Burney was known to have 'a good ear for dialect' which is, on the whole, apparent from her representations. She appears to be particularly successful in representing her home dialect (Norfolk), i.e. as an insider. It seems likely, however, that due to her exposure to other local accents through a wide circle of acquaintances in her London life, her awareness of the home dialect had been heightened. It is interesting to note – as pointed out by Blank (1996: 3) – that for Renaissance writers dialects appeared to have nothing to do with 'home'; Shakespeare, for example, never represented Warwickshire speech.

George Eliot:

Warwickshire speech as perceived by an insider some 300 years later, however, occasionally features in George Eliot's novels, for example *Silas Marner*. An experienced translator and editor, she had given much thought to the problem of representing local speech, as seen in the following quotation from a letter to Skeat, published in the *Transactions of the English Dialect Society*:

> It must be borne in mind that my inclination to be as close as I could to the rendering of dialect, both in words and spelling, was constantly checked by the artistic duty of being generally intelligible. But for that check I should have given a stronger colour to the dialogue in *Adam Bede*, which is modelled on the talk of North Staffordshire and the neighbouring part of Derbyshire. The spelling, being determined by my own ear alone, was necessarily a matter of anxiety, for it would be as possible to quarrel about it as about the spelling of Oriental names. The district imagined as the scene of *Silas Marner* is North Warwickshire; but here, and in all my other presentations of English life except *Adam Bede*, it has been my intention to give the general physiognomy rather than a close portraiture of the provincial speech as I have heard it in the Midland or Mercian region. It is a just demand that art should keep clear of such specialties as would make it a puzzle for the larger part of its public; still, one is not bound to respect the lazy obtuseness or snobbish ignorance of people who do not care to know more of their native tongue than the vocabulary of the drawing-room and the newspaper. (cf. Cooke 1883: 293)

George Eliot, indeed, practises as she preaches, i.e. indicating 'the general physiognomy'; hence not much of interest with regard to phonetic detail is found in her work. Instead, she provides rich and consistent details representing local syntax and morphology, including allegro features (*i'* 'in', *ha'* 'have', *wi'* 'with'). Her representations, incidentally, are strikingly in accordance with Tolkien's use of dialectal Warwickshire/Oxfordshire forms in *The Lord of the Rings*, characterized by Johannesson (1994: 55) as "selective rather than wholesale". A comparison between the dialogues in *Silas Marner* and *Adam Bede* suggests clear but subtle distinctions between the two represented regional varieties. In *Adam Bede*, especially in Lisbeth's speech, there are examples of generalized definite article reduction (*th'*) and, as stated by the author herself, there is generally a closer 'portraiture'. Hence Eliot as an outsider has produced a more detailed representation than Eliot as an insider.

Elizabeth Gaskell:

Elizabeth Gaskell was – like George Eliot – "well aware of the need to balance authenticity and accuracy against accessibility" (Beal 2006: 534). In contrast with Eliot, however, she was keen to include phonetic detail in her renderings of social and regional dialects, but an interesting shift in the character of these representations can be observed. As her writing and creative power of representing human speech and behaviour matured, she appears to have shifted from an essentially item-based approach to a more discourse-based, psychologically motivated one, yet without foregoing her linguistic intuition and knowledge.

Her linguistic reliability was recognized by Joseph Wright in that he used two of her novels (*Mary Barton* and *Sylvia's Lovers*), exemplifying two different dialect areas, as data for specimens in his dictionary. In *Mary Barton*, her first novel, which is set in Manchester, her home town for the last seventeen years, Gaskell somewhat didactically made a point of using certain tokens of Lancashire dialect vocabulary, for which she could provide explanations or etymologies in footnotes, often exemplifying the use of the same words by renowned writers such as Chaucer and Shakespeare. For the verb form *getten*, for example, a reference is made to Chaucer's *Canterbury Tales*: 'For he had *geten* him yet no benefice'. Such references seem to signal the author's explicit wish to raise the status of the dialect. As the story proceeds, she appears to have given up such elaborate references and they are not found in her later works. It has always been assumed that Elizabeth Gaskell drew a great deal of her knowledge of regional dialect from her husband, the Rev. William Gaskell, who was known to have lectured on Lancashire dialect. A close study of his lectures, however, reveals that his interest in dialect seemed to be of a more traditional character than what is signalled in the works of his wife. His articles deal exclusively with vocabulary, presented in item-based listings, including some wild etymologizing.

A close examination of the manuscript of her 'Whitby novel' *Sylvia's Lovers* reveals that she made a number of changes suggesting linguistic awareness, for example with regard to the use and form of the definite article, and for the second edition she 'corrected' the dialect, changing some Lancashire forms into East Yorkshire ones. It should be noted that she largely based her familiarity with Whitby speech on two weeks' holiday in the area and some later, more 'academic' consultations. In *Mary Barton*, published in 1848, as well as *Sylvia's Lovers* (1863) dialect is used extensively, including some detailed representation of segmental phonology, which is in accordance with SED findings (Melchers 1978: 116–18). If anything, there is more detail in the Whitby novel, i.e. the representation of the more 'extrinsic' variety.

The detailed representation in *Sylvia's Lovers*, her last novel but one, is not quite in accordance with her development as outlined above. In *North and South* (1855), set in Manchester, and – in particular – *Wives and Daughters* (1865), probably representing her most 'intrinsic' area, she develops fine nuances of social/regional differences in discourse, and the item-based features tend to be more generalized. Interestingly, the recent TV adaptations of Gaskell's novels demonstrate an awareness of 'enregisterment' in that regional and social differences are not explicit but hinted at in subtle ways and through few but recurrent linguistic features.

Alfred Tennyson:

Of the four writers featured in the case studies, Alfred, Lord Tennyson, is by far the one who has made the greatest effort to create a 'genuine' local dialect representation, resulting in a staggeringly complex array of outlandish vowel symbols. Consider, for example, the beginning of his well-known poem *Northern Farmer, Old Style*, the first of his poems written in Lincolnshire dialect:
"Wheer 'asta beän saw long and meä liggin' 'ere aloän?"

Alfred Tennyson (1809–92) was born in Somersby, Lincolnshire, but left the county for the south of England a good twenty years before he began writing poetry in dialect, paid only occasional visits to the area after that and had little contact with the speech he was trying to convey. He did, however, publish seven long poems in dialect, the last of them published posthumously. Tennyson is known to have taken great trouble in consulting experts in the field, including A.J. Ellis, who 'proofread' his poetry carefully and offered a great deal of criticism but also profited on his many discussions with the poet for the compilation of his monumental *On Early English Pronunciation* (1889). It is also worth mentioning that most of Tennyson's dialect poems were used as source material in another monumental publication, Joseph Wright's EDD (1898–1905).

In his pioneering study *Local Dialect and the Poet* (1972), Philip Tilling, editor of the SED volumes on East Midland dialects, scrutinizes and discusses Tennyson's representation of dialect in detail as collated with the findings at the Lincolnshire localities. This penetrating and knowledgeable investigation demonstrates how a substantial number of Tennyson's representations correspond to SED data from other parts of England, at best from other parts of Lincolnshire (incidentally, a most complex area which probably explains some mistaken advice from the experts consulted) but also the North and the West Country. Tilling's general conclusion is that "the poems, though they contain much that seems to be genuine, cannot really be said to give an entirely reliable impression of the Lincolnshire dialect heard by Tennyson in his youth" (p. 107).

7. Concluding remarks

In concluding this attempt to discuss some aspects of the representation of English accents in 19th-century fiction, it seems justified, if not inevitable, to ask the following question: Who does it best – the outsider or the insider? The text so far has not been conclusive: on the one hand profound knowledge of a variety is required, but it can also lead to exaggerated narrowness in the representation with a frustrated readership, including insiders, as a result. "It is to be acknowledged that even texts by native or local writers, however informal, have potential problems as accurate or reliable sources of linguistic data, particularly phonological" (Wales 2010: 68). A close study of some appreciated fictional writers, in fact, reveals that they may often be more competent in representing dialects other than their native tongue. According to Hickey (2010: 9), who talks about 'scalar insiderness', the status as complete outsider nearly always goes together with a satirical approach. This is, however, hardly borne out by the data considered here. Consider also how Dickens, who skilfully represented an amazing number of different accents, as carefully documented in Gerson 1967, reacted when accused by the *Spectator* of using dialect as a means of mockery:

> I believe that virtue shows quite as well in rags and patches as she does in purple and fine linen, … even if Gargery and Boffin did not speak like gentlemen, they *were* gentlemen.
>
> (Gerson 1967: 371–2)

From the readers' point of view, the more accurate the phonetic spelling, the more frustrating it will be to read. Most adults read word by word, not sounding words out letter by letter, so forcing adults to sound out nonstandard phonetic spellings would slow readers down, potentially irritating them, and thus distract them from the actual story. A native of Lincolnshire comments on Tennyson's elaborate use of dialect and 'semiphonetic' spelling in the following way: "ploughing through line after careful line, I found them as thick as porridge". On the same note: in his lecture *Local Speech in Writing: Surely Nobody Reads It!*, Stanley Ellis (1989: 20)) questions the value of elaborate representations of local accents even by 'insider star performers' such as Emily Brontë, wondering "whether Joseph really matters so much; if people find Emily so well worth while that they are prepared to read Wuthering Heights without even seeing the dialect bits".

In an important paper, Trudgill (1999b) shows how Norfolk Yod dropping is seen as a very salient feature by outsiders and thus represented in writing (Dickens, for example, writes *dootiful* for 'dutiful'), whereas insiders do not bother to change the spelling or, confusingly, produce spellings such as *bewtiful* (in fact, representing a traditional-dialect, closer and more centralized vowel, which is undergoing dedialectalization to [u:]) in another set of words such as *boat*, *road*, *fool*. Trudgill's conclusion is: "As usual, Norfolk people know best". This is not an unqualified truth, however, since insiders are known to have a tendency to seek to confirm their own preconceived notions and stereotypes, whereas outsiders may have 'fresh ears' (cf. Melchers 1996: 164f). Ideally, linguistic investigations of local and social dialects should be carried out by insiders and outsiders working together, as recommended, for example, by Lesley Milroy (http://www.esrc.ac.uk/my-esrc/grants/R000221074/read). The same approach would not be amiss in the representation of dialect in fiction.

References

Beal, J. (2006). Dialect representations in texts. K. Brown (ed.) *Encyclopedia of Language and Linguistics* (2nd ed.) Amsterdam; Oxford: Elsevier Ltd., 531–7.

———. (2009). Enregisterment, commodification, and historical context: "Geordie" versus "Sheffieldish". *American Speech* 84:2, 138–56.

Blank, P. (1996). *Broken English. Dialects and the Poetics of Language in Renaissance Writings*. London: Routledge.

Brown, G. (1977). *Listening to Spoken English*. London: Longman.

Burney, F. (1796). *Camilla*. E.A. & L.D. Bloom (eds) 1983. Oxford: Oxford University Press.

Cooke, G.W. (1883). *George Eliot: A Critical Study of her Life, Writings and Philosophy*. Cambridge: Cambridge Library Collection.

Ellis, A.J. (1889). *On Early English Pronunciation, Part V, the Existing Phonology of English Dialects Compared with That of West Saxon* (Early English Text Society, Extra Series 56). London: The Philological Society.

Ellis, S. (1989). Local speech in writing: Surely nobody reads it! The Hilda Hulme Memorial Lecture. University of London.

Gerson, S. (1967). *Sound and Symbol in the Dialogue of the Works of Charles Dickens. Stockholm Studies in English XIX. Acta Universitatis Stockholmiensis*. Stockholm: Almqvist & Wiksell.

Harrison, T. (1986). *Selected Poems*. Harmondsworth: Penguin.

Hickey, R. (2010). Linguistic evaluation of earlier texts. R. Hickey (ed.) *Varieties of English in Writing*. Amsterdam: Benjamins, 1–14.

Hodson, J. (2014). *Dialect in Film and Literature*. Basingstoke: Palgrave Macmillan.

Ihalainen, O. (1994). The dialects of England since 1776. R. Burchfield (ed.) *The Cambridge History of the English Language*. Vol. V. Cambridge: Cambridge University Press, 197–274.

Johannesson, N-L. (1994). Subcreating a stratified community – On J.R.R. Tolkien's use of non-standard forms in *The Lord of the Rings*. G. Melchers & N-L. Johannesson (eds) *Nonstandard Varieties of Language. Stockholm Studies in English LXXXIV. Acta Universitatis Stockholmiensis*. Stockholm: Almqvist & Wiksell International, 53–63.

Kirk, J.M. (1999). Contemporary Irish Writing and a Model of Speech Realism. I. Taavitsainen, G. Melchers & P. Pahta (eds) *Writing in Nonstandard English*. Amsterdam: Benjamins, 45–62.

G. Melchers (1978). Mrs. Gaskell and Dialect. M. Rydén & L.A. Björk (eds) *Studies in English Philology, Linguistics and Literature. Stockholm Studies in English XLVI. Acta Universitatis Stockholmiensis*. Stockholm: Almqvist & Wiksell International, 112–124.

———.(1996). On the value of the SED recordings of spontaneous speech. J. Klemola, M. Kytö & M. Rissanen (eds) *Speech Past and Present. Studies in English Dialectology in Memory of Ossi Ihalainen. Bamberger Beiträge zur Englischen Sprachwissenschaft 38*. Frankfurt am Main: Peter Lang, 152–68.

Orton, H. et al. (1962–71) *Survey of English Dialects. The Basic Material* Vols. I–IV. Leeds: E.J. Arnold.

Page, N. (1988). *Speech in the English Novel*. London: Macmillan.

Peacock, M. (c. 1890). 'Th' Lincolnsheer Poächer' in G.E. Campion, *Lincolnshire Dialects*. Boston, Lincolnshire: Richard Kay 58–59.

Pollard, A. (1965). *Mrs. Gaskell. Novelist & Biographer.* Manchester: Manchester University Press.

Poussa, P. (1999). Dickens as sociolinguist: Dialect in David Copperfield. Taavitsainen, I., G. Melchers & P. Pahta (eds) *Writing in Nonstandard English*. Amsterdam: Benjamins, 27–44.

Praxmarer, C. (2010). Joseph Wright's EDD and the geographical distribution of dialects: A visual approach. M. Markus, C. Upton & R. Heuberger (eds) *Joseph Wright's English Dialect Dictionary, and Beyond*. Frankfurt am Main: Peter Lang, 61–73.

Reader's Digest Great Illustrated Dictionary (1984). 2 vols. London: The Reader's Digest Association Ltd.

Schneider, E. (2002). Investigating variation and change in written documents. J.K. Chambers, P. Trudgill & N. Schilling-Estes (eds) *The Handbook of Language Variation and Change*. Oxford: Blackwell, 67–96.

Skeat, W. (1911). *English Dialects from the Eighth Century to the Present Day*. London: Cambridge University Press.

Tilling, P. (1972). Local dialect and the poet: A comparison of the findings in the Survey of English Dialects with dialect in Tennyson's Lincolnshire poems. M. Wakelin (ed.) *Patterns in the folk speech of the British Isles*. London: Athlone Press, 88–108.

Traugott, E.C. & M.L. Pratt (1980). *Linguistics for Students of Literature*. New York: Harcourt Brace Jovanovitch.

Trudgill, P. (1990). *The Dialects of England*. Oxford: Blackwell.

———. (1999a). *The Dialects of England*. Second edition. Oxford: Blackwell.

———. (1999b). Dedialectisation and Norfolk dialect orthography. Taavitsainen, I., G. Melchers and P. Pahta (eds) *Writing in Nonstandard English*. Amsterdam: Benjamins, 323–9.

Wales, K. (2010). Northern English in writing. R. Hickey (ed.) *Varieties of English in Writing*. Amsterdam: Benjamins, 61–80.

Wells, J.C. (1982). *Accents of English*. Vols. I-III. Cambridge: Cambridge University Press.

Wright, J. (ed.) (1898–1905). *The English Dialect Dictionary*. 6 vols. Oxford: Oxford University Press.

Zettersten, A. (ed.) (1974). *A Critical Facsimile Edition of Thomas Batchelor, An Orthoëpical Analysis of the English Language and An Orthoëpical Analysis of the Dialect of Bedfordshire (1809)*. Part I. Lund Studies in English 45. Lund: Gleerup.

10 Sublime Caledonia: Description, Narration and Evaluation in Nineteenth-century Texts on Scotland

Marina Dossena
Università degli Studi di Bergamo (I)

1. Introduction

The nineteenth century proved crucial for the establishment of a romanticized image of Scotland. Despite, or, more correctly, as a result of, the impact of the Highland Clearances, which left many areas virtually deserted, the country came to be perceived in the Lowlands, in England, and even abroad, as a picturesque wilderness, a totally appropriate setting for ballads, stories and legends. Indeed, even dramatic episodes of (often forced) emigration became the object of artistic representation, as – perhaps most famously – in the painting *The Last of the Clan* (1865, by Thomas Faed, currently at the Kelvingrove Art Gallery and Museum in Glasgow).

In this contribution I intend to highlight the main features employed in a sample of nineteenth-century texts relating to Scottish history and landscape, in an attempt to identify what linguistic choices played a key role in the construction of a romanticized environment. More specifically, I intend to discuss two case studies, Nattes's *Scotia Depicta* (1804) and Robert Louis Stevenson's *Edinburgh: Picturesque Notes* (1879), while placing them in the framework of other materials available in the *Corpus of Modern Scottish Writing*, travelogues, and other well-known publications, both literary and non-literary texts. Special attention will be paid to evaluative language and stylistic moves that enabled authors to signify their appreciation of their topics. Such strategies of description and narration clearly aimed to persuade readers of the validity of the authors' views, and were often accompanied by illustrations meant

How to cite this book chapter:
Dossena, M. 2015. Sublime Caledonia: Description, Narration and Evaluation in Nineteenth-century Texts on Scotland. In: Shaw, P., Erman, B., Melchers, G. and Sundkvist, P. (eds) *From Clerks to Corpora: essays on the English language yesterday and today*. Pp. 177–191. Stockholm: Stockholm University Press. DOI: http://dx.doi.org/10.16993/bab.j License: CC-BY.

to provide a visual counterpart of the textual statements. The role of intertextual references will thus be taken into consideration, in order to outline the textual networks that appear to be in place.

After an overview of the perception of Scotland's antiquity in Late Modern times, my analysis will focus on the two texts mentioned above (Nattes's and Stevenson's), both published with a manifestly descriptive aim, in order to assess their persuasive quality. Close readings of the texts will be supplemented with corpus-based investigations of specific lexical items. Finally, the concluding section will summarize the main strategies that appear to be at work in both texts.

2. Scotland in Late Modern times: views of language and landscape

Many eighteenth- and nineteenth-century texts discussed Scotland's unique landscape together with the specificity of its language. While Scots was stigmatized in everyday usage, its occurrence in literary texts was perceived to be both 'pithy' and appropriate. Comments on Burns's poetry were typically accompanied by remarks on the difficulty of his language (Dossena 2012a), which stressed the 'exotic' character of Scots, but praises of its antiquity were also frequent, on account of its supposedly greater proximity to 'pure Saxon'.

This attention to linguistic roots appears to have close cultural connections with the fashionable search for antiquity, the picturesque and the sublime, which persisted through the times of the Napoleonic wars and reached a turning point during the Victorian age. In particular, for the Romantics the chief attraction in Scotland was possibly the isle of Staffa, first discovered by Joseph Banks in 1772. Banks reported that "There is a cave [...] which the natives call the Cave of Fingal", and although this was probably a misunderstanding, the place inspired countless creative artists, not least J.M.W. Turner and Felix Mendelssohn-Bartholdy.[1]

It is beyond the scope of this contribution to discuss the impact of royal visits, starting from the momentous event when, in 1822, George IV visited Scotland for the first time since James VII and II's stay in 1681/82, long before the Union of Parliaments. The role played by Walter Scott in the organization of the visit is also well-known, and

---

[1] On Turner in Scotland see Grenier (2005: 56, 94, 100) and Mitchell (2013: 197–206, 219). On Mendelssohn-Bartholdy see Grenier (2005: 161).

does not need to be summarized here.[2] However, the new attitude of the monarchy after the repeal of the Act of Proscription[3] in 1782 contributed to the success of travelogues published both north and south of the border.

As for the interest in Scotland's antiquities, this had begun in the late seventeenth-early eighteenth century: Martin Martin's *A Late Voyage to St. Kilda* (1698) and *A Description of the Western Islands of Scotland* (1703) report on journeys that appear to have been made mainly at the request of an antiquary, Sir Robert Sibbald. Although earlier journeys had been made into the Highlands, it was only in the eighteenth century that their accounts became popular, as in the case of Sir Donald Monro's *Description of the Western Isles of Scotland* (1549), a few copies of which were printed in 1774. While Thomas Pennant's accounts had a more naturalistic focus (Youngson 1973 and 1974), an antiquarian focus was a common denominator in Bishop Pococke's letters of 1760 (Youngson 1973: 2).

The raging fashion for antiquity also gave rise to satire (Brown 1980: 10); nonetheless, this interest was made explicit in the 1829 reprint of Petruccio Ubaldini's *Descrittione del Regno di Scotia*, originally published in 1588. Moreover, the success of Scott's novels was a great boost to the recognition of Scotland as a tourist destination. Theodor Fontane's accounts (1860/1989: 129, 159) explicitly refer to *Rob Roy* and *The Fair Maid of Perth*; a quotation from Burns's *Drumossie Moor* introduces the section on Culloden (1860/1989: 187), while Fontane's notes on the Old Town of Edinburgh and its *Spukhäuser* (1860/1989: 22, 83) seem to anticipate Robert Louis Stevenson's *Edinburgh: Picturesque Notes* (1879). Finally, the Ossian quest had also been at the centre of Louis-Albert Necker de Saussure's *Voyage en Ecosse et aux Iles Hébrides* (1821). Towards the end of the century, an anonymous author referred to the same texts by Sir Walter Scott (Anon. 1894: 16, 37–38), but also to works by James Hogg (Anon. 1894: 63) and indeed to Robert Louis Stevenson's *Kidnapped* (Anon. 1894: 103–106, 111), outlining a trail around Rannoch Moor and 'Cluny's cage' that would then be followed by numerous readers and enthusiasts – see for instance Nimmo (2005).

---

[2] On this topic see, most recently, Kelly (2010: 187–211) and Mitchell (2013: 217–219).

[3] This is the Act of Parliament which in 1746, after the last Jacobite rebellion, forbade the use of Highland garb (19 Geo. II, ch. 39, sec. 17, 1746), thus reinforcing previous 'Disarming Acts'.

In addition to antiquity and literature, travelogues typically stressed the scenery's most romantic traits, and though they often repeated cultural stereotypes, such as the fact that "Some of the poor in Skye have scarcely a notion of any food but oatmeal" (Sinclair 1859: 181),[4] they contributed to the creation of an idealised picture of Scotland. Travelogues and geographical narratives thus appear to have had both an informative and a promotional function, not least in terms of cultural perception. In what follows I will investigate two texts currently available in electronic format, in order to assess the linguistic choices that appear to be most significant in this respect. As I mentioned above, these are case studies: other texts could be selected, so as to give greater generic depth to the study; however, space constraints suggest a more focused approach. Apart from their intrinsic interest, both Nattes's and Stevenson's texts were selected because they place themselves at significant points in the history of Late Modern English: the nineteenth century was particularly innovative both from a lexicological point of view and in relation to knowledge dissemination strategies, towards which journals and travelogues made an important contribution (Dossena 2012b and in preparation).

3. Two milestones

The value of travelogues for the dissemination of knowledge concerning specific areas and cultures is well-known: already in Elizabethan and Jacobean times the collections published by Richard Hakluyt and Samuel Purchas[5] had provided the reading public with intriguing material concerning distant, exotic places and peoples, encouraging the development of an adventurous approach to discovery, exploration, and in fact colonization (Carey & Jowitt 2012). By the beginning of the nineteenth century travel accounts were a well-established genre, in which the authors' comments and observations were not disregarded as subjective assessments, but were perceived as valuable sources of reliable information (Dossena 2013).

---

[4] This evokes one of the most notorious entries in Johnson's *Dictionary*, i.e. the one on oats – see Dossena (2014).

[5] Several collections were published in a relatively short time span: first of all, Richard Hakluyt's *Divers Voyages Touching the Discoverie of America*, of 1582, and *The Principal Navigations, Voiages, Traffiques and Discoueries of: the English Nation* of 1598–1600. These would then be followed by the works of Samuel Purchas (*Purchas, his Pilgrimage*, of 1613; *Purchas, his Pilgrim*, of 1619; and *Hakluytus Posthumus or Purchas his Pilgrimes*, of 1625).

What is particularly interesting within this framework, then, is the way in which description and evaluation appear to interact, in order to make the text both convincing and reliable. The two texts selected for this analysis, in spite of apparent similarities, place themselves at opposite ends of a chronological and generic cline. One, *Scotia Depicta*, published in London in 1804, is a prototypically illustrated narrative in which a sequence of 48 sights is presented to the reader with a clearly defined agenda; the subtitle provides a detailed list of what will be the object of representation, both in words and in pictures:

THE ANTIQUITIES, CASTLES, PUBLIC BUILDINGS, NOBLEMEN AND GENTLEMEN'S SEATS, CITIES, TOWNS, AND PICTURESQUE SCENERY, OF SCOTLAND, ILLUSTRATED IN A SERIES OF FINISHED ETCHINGS By JAMES FITTLER, A. R. A. AND ENGRAVER TO HIS MAJESTY, FROM ACCURATE DRAWINGS MADE ON THE SPOT By JOHN CLAUDE NATTES. With Descriptions, antiquarian, historical, and picturesque.

Robert Louis Stevenson's *Edinburgh: Picturesque Notes*, on the other hand, is a series of essays published in 1879, in which the author presents his own views and comments on selected traits of the Scottish capital and its suburbs. As Stevenson was born in Edinburgh, his work could not be defined as a travelogue *strictu senso*; however, the author offers his own subjective views in order to guide readers through a maze of city lamps, sights and legends with an insider's knowledge that intrigues while guaranteeing reliability. Indeed, Stevenson's own travel writings take the form of essayistic memoirs in which the journeys provide the framework for the author's thoughts and reflections.[6]

While Nattes's readers are expected to take an interest in what is majestic, antique and sublime, Stevenson highlights what is appealing in potentially familiar neighbourhoods. With more than seven decades separating them and with this different approach to narration, the two texts (*Scotia Depicta*, henceforth SD, and *Edinburgh: Picturesque Notes*, henceforth PN) may thus provide useful benchmarks for the identification of informative and persuasive strategies in their linguistic choices and textual organization.

The books are obviously quite different in many ways: SD discusses 48 images, while Stevenson never refers to the illustrations, which

---

[6] This concerns both his travels around Europe and his experiences crossing first the Atlantic and then the USA, prior to settling down permanently in Samoa. See www.robert-louis-stevenson.org/travel-writing (accessed July 2014).

are added on.[7] Text length also differs: PN includes 25,612 words, SD includes 19,628; although this difference might not seem particularly important, it becomes much more considerable when the type/token ratio is compared: PN has 20.31 vs 16.47 in SD. This finding is somewhat unsurprising in the light of the different literary skills of the authors under discussion; nonetheless, it may also be indicative of the more or less sophisticated approach taken by the two texts. In the next section a more fine-grained analysis will be offered on a few relevant features.

4. Findings

Table 1 below presents the absolute and relative frequency with which selected lexical items occur in SD, PN, and in the nineteenth-century section of the *Corpus of Modern Scottish Writing* (henceforth CMSW), employed as a reference corpus. In the case of adjectives, such items were selected on account of their evaluative quality, while nouns were selected on the basis of their relative keyness.

While percentages are too low in PN and CMSW to enable statistical generalizations, it may be interesting to compare these with the ones in

Table 1. Selected lexical items in the text under investigation and in CMSW.

	SD	PN	CMSW (19C only)
Antiquity	6 (0.03%)	2 (0.00%)	85 (0.00%)
Gothic	11 (0.06%)	3 (0.01%)	31 (0.00%)
Grand	10 (0.05%)	2 (0.00%)	337 (0.01%)
Noble	12 (0.06%)	4 (0.01%)	396 (0.01%)
Picturesque	39 (0.20%)	6 (0.02%)	97 (0.00%)
Romantic	18 (0.09%)	5 (0.02%)	108 (0.00%)
Rugged	3 (0.01%)	0	48 (0.00%)
Ruin(s)	29 (0.15%)	6 (0.02%)	82 (0.00%)
Savage	3 (0.02%)	0	92 (0.00%)
Scenery	47 (0.24%)	3 (0.01%)	166 (0.00%)
Sublime	6 (0.03%)	1 (0.00%)	120 (0.00%)
Wild(est)	14 (0.07%)	2 (0.00%)	667 (0.01%)

---

[7] In the 1879 edition there are 6 etchings and 12 vignettes, while there are 27 illustrations in the 1889 edition (see http://digital.nls.uk/99396143 and www.archive.org/stream/edinburghpictureoostev, accessed July 2014).

SD, in which *scenery* and *picturesque* emerge as recurring items, in line with the centres of interest indicated in the subtitle. Also *ruins* appear to elicit significant interest, which might have been predicted of a text published in indisputably romantic times.

In what follows a few instances are provided from both SD and PN, in which descriptive and evaluative elements are seen to co-occur; the former are italicized, while the latter are in boldface:

(1) *The top is surrounded with battlements, which project a foot beyond the walls*, and from the broad shadows formed by a declining sun, frequently produce **the most picturesque effect**. (SD, Balgonie Castle)

(2) No country is more **diversified, adorned, and benefited**, *by the different lochs*, that are scattered over its surface, than Scotland; in almost every part of which they produce great *variety of scenery*, form **a beautiful and picturesque series of views**, and afford a plentiful and cheap article of food. (SD, Taymouth)

(3) Chartered tourists, they make free with *historic localities*, and rear their young among the **most picturesque sites** with a grand human indifference (PN, ch. 1)

(4) the place is full of **theatre tricks** in the way of scenery (PN, ch. 6)

The idea of what is beautiful, picturesque and sublime is supported in both texts with intertextual references which may be literary, artistic, or historical. In the Introduction to SD the author reassures readers that 'works of authority' have been consulted for the acquisition of antiquarian details, and states that "Grose, Pennant, Cordiner, and that valuable mass of materials comprehended in the *Statistical Account of Scotland*, have been carefully examined, as well as numerous other records".[8] Such sources are intended to provide credibility and make the descriptions reliable – an important detail meant to increase the book's appeal to the reader. In addition, first-hand experience is highlighted:

---

[8] Though SD does not list these sources, apart from John Sinclair's *Statistical Account of Scotland* (1791–99), they are presumably works published in the previous three decades: Thomas Pennant's *A Tour in Scotland* (1771), Charles Cordiner's *Antiquities & Scenery of the North of Scotland, in a series of letters, to Thomas Pennant, Esqr.* (1780) and *Remarkable Ruins, and Romantic Prospects, of North Britain* (1788); and Francis Grose, *The Antiquities of Scotland* (1789 and 1791).

Nattes's drawings are said to have been made while travelling with
Dr. John Stoddart, author of *Remarks on Local Scenery and Manners
in Scotland* (1801), which is described as "a work of very considerable
merit, in which the author has united great depth of research with a
correct and enlightened taste for the picturesque, the beautiful, and the
sublime" (SD, Introduction).

Stevenson does not appeal to authority, but adds credibility with
personal anecdotes, whether referring to himself or his own family; two
examples are given below:

> (5) I look back with delight on many an escalade of garden
> walls; many a ramble among lilacs full of piping birds; many
> an exploration in obscure quarters that were neither town
> nor country; and I think that both for my companions and
> myself, there was a special interest, a point of romance, and
> a sentiment as of foreign travel, when we hit in our excur-
> sions on the butt-end of some former hamlet, and found a
> few rustic cottages embedded among streets and squares.
> (PN, ch. 6)

> (6) My father has often been told in the nursery how the devil's
> coach, drawn by six coal-black horses with fiery eyes, would
> drive at night into the West Bow, and belated people might see
> the dead Major through the glasses. (PN, ch. 4)

Another interesting difference is in the use of geographical labels: it
is tempting to perceive a unionist attitude in SD's use of 'North Britain'
as opposed to 'Scotland', choosing the term that had come into use after
the Union of Parliaments of 1707 and was sometimes abbreviated as
'N.B.'. Stevenson, on the other hand, disliked it, as seen in a letter dated
1888:[9]

> (7) Don't put 'N.B.' on your paper: put <u>Scotland</u>, and be done with
> it. Alas, that I should be thus stabbed in the home of my friends!
> The name of my native land is not <u>North Britain</u>, whatever may
> be the name of yours.
> (RLS to S. R. Crockett, c. 10 April 1888,
> in Booth & Mehew 1995: 156, original emphasis)

---

[9] I am indebted to Richard Dury, former colleague and current co-editor of the New
Edinburgh Edition of the Collected Works of Robert Louis Stevenson, for the observation of this detail, and for numerous pleasant exchanges on Stevenson's life and
works over the years.

Nevertheless, in Stevenson's text aspects of Scottish history are sometimes treated with much less rhetorical reverence than in SD. Among
these, places associated with the House of Stuart, and particularly with
Mary Queen of Scots, elicit vocabulary that leaves little doubt about
the author's stance in relation to the people and events at hand; in the
quotation below, for instance, 'mariolaters' merges 'Mary' and 'idola-
ters', suggesting the irrationality of uncritical appreciation of a controversial historical figure:

(8) On the opposite side of the loch, the ground rises to Craigmillar
     Castle, a place friendly to Stuart Mariolaters. (PN, ch. 9)

Nor is this the only instance in which Stevenson's linguistic choices
express his evaluations; the Reformation and the Covenanters are discussed in approving terms conveying the author's point of view in ways
as effective as they are unobtrusive:

(9) Down in the palace John Knox reproved his queen in the
     accents of modern democracy. [...] There, in the Grass-
     market, stiff-necked, covenanting heroes, offered up the often
     unnecessary, but not less honourable, sacrifice of their lives
     (PN, ch.1)

(10) The martyrs' monument is a wholesome, heartsome spot in
     the field of the dead; and as we look upon it, a brave influ-
     ence comes to us from the land of those who have won their
     discharge and, in another phrase of Patrick Walker's, got
     'cleanly off the stage.'

                                                        (PN, ch. 5)

On the other hand, sectarianism is condemned in equally clear terms:

(11) We are wonderful patient haters for conscience sake up here
     in the North. [...]. Indeed, there are not many uproars in
     this world more dismal than that of the Sabbath bells in
     Edinburgh: a harsh ecclesiastical tocsin; the outcry of incon-
     gruous orthodoxies, calling on every separate conventicler to
     put up a protest, each in his own synagogue, against 'right-
     hand extremes and left-hand defections.'[...]. Shakespeare
     wrote a comedy of 'Much Ado about Nothing.' The Scottish
     nation made a fantastic tragedy on the same subject.

                                                        (PN, ch. 4)

The paragraph closes with an intertextual reference to Shakespeare and, as a matter of fact, both PN and SD elicit or maintain the reader's interest with frequent literary and cultural references. These may be more or less elliptical, depending on the degree of background knowledge readers may be expected to share. References to Scottish literature, for instance, may be assumed to be fairly transparent: when Stevenson writes that Robert Burns "came [to Edinburgh] from the plough-tail, as to an academy of gilt unbelief and artificial letters" (PN, ch. 1) readers are assumed to be familiar with the sudden success story of the 'heaven-taught ploughman', as Henry Mackenzie would dub him. Similarly, Robert Fergusson's unfortunate fate is evoked in the brief statement that "Burns's master in his art, [...] died insane while yet a stripling."[10]

SD also refers to Burns assuming that readers will recognize his poem *The Brigs of Ayr*:

(12) On entering this place the most striking objects are the new and the auld bridges, which Burns has personified with so much successful humour. The former is handsome and convenient, and was built from a plan of Adams's, while the auld brig, if we may believe the poet, is so narrow and bad, that "twa wheel-barrows tremble, when they meet." (SD, The town of Ayr)

Ossian is mentioned as many as four times in SD, and Plate no. 26 is devoted to 'Fingal's cave', for which Stoddart's description is quoted in full, and where reference is made to Banks's visit of 1772 (see above), expressing appreciation for the resulting contribution to geological knowledge and 'taste'; again, descriptive and evaluative tones merge in the text:

(13) The entrance is an irregular arch fifty-three feet broad and one hundred and seventeen high; the interior is two hundred and fifty in length, and appears still longer from the diminishing perspective. The sides, which are straight, are divided into pillars; some of those on the east, having been broken off

---

[10] The paragraph then continues with Stevenson's comments on the connection between Burns and Fergusson, two poets to whom he felt very close, particularly the latter. In a letter to Charles Baxter, dated 18th May 1894, he announced he wanted to repair the gravestone that Burns had set up for Fergusson in the Canongate Kirkyard, and wrote: "I had always a great sense of kinship with poor Robert Fergusson [...]. It is very odd, it really looks like transmigration of souls" (Booth & Mehew 1995: 8/290).

near the base, form a passage along that side, by which, with some difficulty, I reached the farthest end, and seated myself in a kind of natural throne, formed in the rock. From this seat, the general effect of the cave appears truly magnificent, and well calculated to form the eye and taste of a picturesque architect. The broken, irregular, basaltic roof resembled the rich ornaments of some grand gothic building; (SD, Fingal's Cave)

From "a kind of natural throne" which the commentator has reached, the basaltic rock formations give the impression of being "the rich ornaments of some grand gothic building". The objectivity with which size and shapes are described gives way to subjective perception of something "truly magnificent".

Personal experience thus proves crucial for the presentation of striking sights and memorable venues. SD and PN, however, appear to take different approaches to personalization strategies: Table 2 below presents the absolute and relative frequency of first- and second-person subject pronouns, in order to highlight what subjects appear to take or be given responsibility for the predication.

These data show that in SD the author appears to prefer an inclusive use of *we*, allowing readers to participate in the enjoyment of what is represented on the page and, consequently, in their imagination. Stevenson, instead, like the authors in CMSW, stresses the subjectivity of his representations, using *I* twice as often as *we*, but he also appeals to the reader much more directly, *you* being the most frequently occurring pronoun in his text. See the examples below:

(14) The harbour was formerly called Slochk Ichopper, meaning the inlet, where vessels came to barter and sell their fish; and

Table 2. First- and second-person subject pronouns in SD, PN and CMSW.

1PS + 2PS Pronouns	SD	PN	CMSW (19C only)*
I	17 (0.09%)	98 (0.38%)	12241 (0.23%)
We	24 (0.12%)	49 (0.19%)	5031 (0.09%)
You	6 (0.03%)	126 (0.49%)	4008 (0.07%)

* Excluding Verse, Drama, Imaginative prose, and the works of orthoepists.

we find in the arms of the town a net with a herring and this
motto, *Semper tibi pendeat halec.* (SD, the Port of Inverary
[sic])

(15) Into no other city does the sight of the country enter so far;
if you do not meet a butterfly, you shall certainly catch a
glimpse of far-away trees upon your walk; [...]. You peep
under an arch, you descend stairs that look as if they would
land you in a cellar, you turn to the back-window of a grimy
tenement in a lane:—and behold! you are face-to-face with
distant and bright prospects. You turn a corner, and there is
the sun going down into the Highland hills. (PN, ch. 6)

As regards language, nineteenth-century travelogues did occasionally
include remarks on differences between English and Scots, but these
were typically seen as a source of puzzlement for English visitors – see
for instance Sinclair (1859: 98–99):

(16) If a Scotch person says, "will you speak a word to me," he
means, will you listen; but if he says to a servant, "I am
about to give you a good hearing," that means a severe
scold. The Highland expression for two gentlemen bowing
to each other, amused us extremely on a late occasion, when
a Scotchman said to his friend, "I saw your brother last week
exchange hats with Lord Melbourne in Bond Street!"

Stevenson's metalinguistic comments, instead, focus more on actual
usage and semantic variety. The section in which he discusses winter
weather shows how culture and environment influence lexical distinctions, to which an interesting touch of perceptual dialectology is added:
the author imagines a cold wind blowing onto his face from distant
hills even as the words are written on the page, thus emphasizing their
evocative quality:

(17) The Scotch dialect is singularly rich in terms of reproach
against the winter wind. Snell, blae, nirly, and scowthering,
are four of these significant vocables; they are all words that
carry a shiver with them; and for my part, as I see them
aligned before me on the page, I am persuaded that a big
wind comes tearing over the Firth from Burntisland and the
northern hills; I think I can hear it howl in the chimney, and
as I set my face northwards, feel its smarting kisses on my
cheek (PN, ch. 9)

Scots also occurs in snatches of conversation and the names of traditions associated with Hogmanay, i.e. the celebration of New Year's Day:

> (18) For weeks before the great morning, confectioners display stacks of Scotch bun [...] and full moons of shortbread adorned with mottoes of peel or sugar-plum, in honour of the season and the family affections. 'Frae Auld Reekie,' 'A guid New Year to ye a',' 'For the Auld Folk at Hame,' are among the most favoured of these devices. (PN, ch. 9)

Stevenson's knowledge of popular culture is also evident in his references to folk lore (Thomas the Rhymer) and ballads (*Johnnie Faa* and *Sir Patrick Spens* are mentioned explicitly). SD, instead, does not seem to go beyond the Ossian myth – whether this may be indexical of the envisaged readership's expectations can only be a matter of conjecture.

5. Concluding remarks

This overview, albeit brief and restricted to a few features, has shown a greater variety of involvement strategies in PN. While both texts examined here describe places, narrate events, and express authorial stance by means of recurrent lexical items, in Stevenson's text literary references and popular culture appear to mix more freely than in SD, which places greater emphasis on the 'romantic' and 'sublime' traits of the landscape and of the buildings represented in the tables. PN also appeals to readers more directly, using second-person pronouns more frequently and thus encouraging direct participation in the virtual journey presented in the text. In SD the constant interaction of words and images conveys meaning and maintains the readers' interest; in PN, instead, greater lexical richness, witnessed by a higher type/token ratio, stresses the value of language as a powerful communicative tool. Though both texts rely on literary and cultural references, Stevenson's linguistic skill appears to encourage readers to move from what is virtual to what is real, from a "somewhere-else of the imagination" to an experience of place and identity where they can actually 'see for themselves'.

References

Primary sources

Anon. (1894 [2002]). *Victorian Travel on the West Highland Line: By Mountain, Moor and Loch*. Colonsay: House of Lochar.

Booth, B.A. & Mehew, E. (eds) (1995). *The Letters of Robert Louis Stevenson*, vol. 6. Yale: Yale University Press.

CMSW, *Corpus of Modern Scottish Writing*. At www.scottishcorpus.ac.uk/cmsw/, accessed July 2014.

Fontane, T. (1860/1989). *Jenseit des Tweed. Bilder und Briefe aus Schottland*. Frankfurt a. M.: Insel.

Nattes, J.C. (1804). *Scotia Depicta; or, The Antiquities, Castles, [...] and Picturesque Scenery of Scotland. [...] With Descriptions, Antiquarian, Historical, and Picturesque*. London: Printed by T. Bensley and published by W. Miller et al. At http://digital.nls.uk/74465058, accessed July 2014.

Sinclair, C. (1859). *Sketches and Stories of Scotland and the Scotch, and Shetland and the Shetlanders*. London: Simpkin, Marshall, and Co.

Stevenson, R.L. (1879). *Edinburgh: Picturesque Notes*. London: Seely, Jackson & Halliday. At http://digital.nls.uk/99396143, accessed July 2014.

Secondary sources

Brown, I.G. (1980). *The Hobby-Horsical Antiquary. A Scottish Character 1640–1830*. Edinburgh: National Library of Scotland.

Carey, D. & Jowitt, C. (eds) (2012). *Richard Hakluyt and Travel Writing in Early Modern Europe*. Farnham: Ashgate.

Dossena, M. (2012a). "A highly poetical language"? Scots, Burns, Patriotism and Evaluative Language in Nineteenth-century Literary Reviews and Articles. C. Percy & M. C. Davidson (eds) *The Languages of Nation: Attitudes and Norms*. Bristol: Multilingual Matters, 99–119.

———. (2012b). Late Modern English – Semantics and Lexicon. A. Bergs & L. Brinton (eds) *HSK 34.1 – English Historical Linguistics – An International Handbook*. Berlin: De Gruyter, 887–900.

———. (2013). "John is a good Indian": Reflections on Native American Culture in Scottish Popular Writing of the Nineteenth Century. C. Sassi & T. van Heijnsbergen (eds) *Within and Without Empire: Scotland Across the (Post)colonial Borderline*. Newcastle u.T.: Cambridge Scholars, 185–199.

———. (2014). The thistle and the words: Scotland in Late Modern English Lexicography. *Scottish Language* 31–32 (2012–13), 64–85.

————. (in preparation). "I tell you this, because I come from your country." The Popularization of Science and the Linguistic Construction of Reliability in Nineteenth-century Travelogues and Ego Documents. Subplenary talk presented at the 14th ESSE Conference, Košice, 29.08-02.09.2014.

Grenier, K.H. (2005). *Tourism and Identity in Scotland, 1770–1914: Creating Caledonia*. Farnham: Ashgate.

Kelly, S. (2010). *Scott-land: The Man who Invented a Nation*. Edinburgh: Polygon.

Mitchell, S. (2013). *Visions of Britain 1730–1830: Anglo-Scottish Writing and Representation*. Basingstoke: Palgrave Macmillan.

Nimmo, I. (2005). *Walking with Murder. On the* Kidnapped *Trail*. Edinburgh: Birlinn.

Youngson, A.J. (1973). *After the Forty-five: The Economic Impact on the Scottish Highlands*. Edinburgh: Edinburgh University Press.

————. (1974). *Beyond the Highland Line – Three Journals of Travel in Eighteenth-Century Scotland: Burt, Pennant, Thornton*. London: Collins.

11 The Development of Attitudes to Foreign Languages as Shown in the English Novel

Philip Shaw
Stockholm University

It was in Sweden that his career was finally doomed. For some time past he had been noticeably silent at the dinner table when foreign languages were being spoken; now the shocking truth became apparent that he was losing his mastery even of French; many ageing diplomats, at a loss for a word, could twist the conversation and suit their opinions to their vocabulary; Sir Samson recklessly improvised or lapsed into a kind of pidgin English.

Evelyn Waugh *Black Mischief* (1932) chapter 2

1. Introduction

Societies are characterized by the patterns of language knowledge and language use which are studied in the "sociolinguistics of society" (Fasold 1984). One aspect of this is the languages people know and use at a given time and place, part of the local 'language ecology' (Haugen 1971). Haugen's term has been used of all the languages used in an environment and their mutual relations. Thus Smalley (1994) discusses all the Tai, Mon-Khmer, Malay and Chinese languages of Thailand and their status and uses in different environments in the country. In the era of globalization it can appear that what is missing from his study is the omnipresence of English (or at least the Latin alphabet) and the place of that language high up in the hierarchy. Just as alien species find a place in biological ecology, so do foreign languages play a part in language ecology.

Thus discussions of language ecology need to take account of the languages that are learned in an environment as well as those that

How to cite this book chapter:
Shaw, P. 2015. The Development of Attitudes to Foreign Languages as Shown in the English Novel. In: Shaw, P., Erman, B., Melchers, G. and Sundkvist, P. (eds) *From Clerks to Corpora: essays on the English language yesterday and today*. Pp. 193–214. Stockholm: Stockholm University Press. DOI: http://dx.doi.org/10.16993/bab.k

are spoken as first language. There is quite a large literature on the history of language teaching and learning in Britain and the rest of Europe (Hüllen 2006; McLelland 2005). Recently, for example Nicola McLelland and Richard Smith have launched a co-ordinated research project exemplified by the papers they have collected in a recent issue of *Language and History* (Glück 2014; Besse 2014; Sanchez 2014). But this type of institutional and method-oriented history tells us little about the attitudes and assumptions of English-speakers in Britain and elsewhere to the foreign languages they were taught. These attitudes and assumptions can, however be inferred from the surviving documents in a straightforward way. The twelfth-century writer Orm (e.g. Johannesson 2008) decided to write the *Ormulum* in English and this implies that he intended to address an audience for whom English was the primary language. The fact that his sources are in Latin and not Greek or Hebrew implies that he could read Latin but not the other two languages. Johannesson (personal communication) reports that when Orm noticed that he had used a Romance or Latin loanword in his writing he often replaced it with a Germanic equivalent. This tells us both that monks like him were familiar with words of this type and that ordinary lay people could not be assumed to know all of them.

Language attitudes can also be inferred from fiction, since writers can use the reader's assumed knowledge of them to characterize their creations. A well-known example is Chaucer's Prioress, who spoke French "After the scole of Stratford-atte-Bowe,/ For Frenssh of Parys was to hire unknowe" (Robinson 1957: 18). The contemporary reader had a clear idea of what was meant by Stratford French, and could infer something about the Prioress's personality from it. The modern reader has to infer the language ecology that Chaucer is referring to and might assume that her variety of French was a learner variety like modern school French or some kind of vernacular Anglo-Norman *patois*, or even an East London dialect. At any rate the reference is often taken as showing that her French was somehow inferior – if she had known Paris French she would have used it in preference. By looking at many documents and their language forms, Rothwell (1985) is able to reconstruct the place of 'insular French' in the language ecology of the time. Interestingly, it was an autonomous second-language variety like Indian English nowadays – acquired at school but needed in everyday life.

> The French used in England from the early thirteenth century to the end of the fourteenth is the only variety to be on a par with francien

in the sense of being an official language of record widely used by the dominant classes in a vigorously developing nation. (Rothwell 1985: 47)

Even so, one kind of insular French seems not have had a high status for Chaucer. Thus references in fiction can illuminate what we know from other sources and in turn are illuminated by that knowledge.

In this note I attempt to retrieve attitudes and assumptions about foreign languages from incidental observations made while reading nineteenth-century novels and then attempt a more systematic investigation of a corpus of eighteenth and nineteenth-century novels. The aim is to try to infer the wider (foreign) language ecology of these centuries in Britain as it appeared to contemporaries and to see how the changes that took place in the nineteenth century are reflected in fiction.

Language knowledge and attitudes are local and class-based. Sailors know a different set of languages from monks and prioresses – the oceans have their own language ecology. In the seventeenth century, alongside French, a poet like Milton knew the classical languages and Italian but in the repertoire of an adventurer and seaman like Edward Coxere French was accompanied by Dutch and Spanish (Meierstein 1946). Literary works from the past may be more likely to tell us about the language repertoires of writers and high-status individuals than about those languages of the majority on which language ecology studies have focused. In particular, the choice in this chapter of mainstream, predominantly English, sources means that the focus is on references to foreign-language knowledge, rather than local low-status ones. I do not consider references to Greek and Latin, although they are fairly frequent, of course, and typically gendered as male accomplishments.

As noted, a framework for the investigation is first built up by describing anecdotal observations from the work of several novelists, and then the value added by a corpus approach is assessed.

2. Pre-systematic observations

Jane Austen

References to modern language knowledge in Austen's novels seem to be confined to French and Italian, although translated German literature is mentioned (notoriously *Lovers' Vows* in *Mansfield Park*). French seems to be common knowledge. In *Emma* (1816) Mr Knightley can comment to Emma on the supposed difference in meaning between French *aimable* and English *amiable* in words that suggest both are equally familiar with the language. The impression that girls could be expected to know the language is strengthened by the rich young Miss Bertrams' contempt for their poor cousin Fanny's ignorance of French (*Mansfield Park* 1814) and Austen's assurance that Fanny learned the language once she had a governess to teach her ("Miss Lee taught her French[1].").

Italian is different. Vulgar Mrs Elton (*Emma)* irritates Emma by her references to her *caro sposo*, flaunting her knowledge of at least some of the language, while the thoughtful Anne Elliot (*Persuasion* 1818) attracts admiration for the quality of her translation of song texts despite her modest denial of proficiency. Knowledge of French seems unmarked and it is ignorance of it that is commented on in Austen, whereas knowledge of Italian is an accomplishment to be commented on and, by the vulgar, flaunted, and perhaps particularly a typically female accomplishment.

Charlotte Brontë

Thirty years on or so, it is French and German that figure in Charlotte Brontë's novels. Interestingly, there is a good deal of untranslated French (from Adèle in *Jane Eyre* (1847) and from various Belgian characters in *Villette* (1853)), which presupposes that the reader understands the language rather as Mr Knightley presupposes a knowledge in Emma. Teaching French is clearly an essential requirement for a governess. *Villette* suggests some degree of mutuality in the English-French relation, for the francophone little girls in Mme Beck's school (in a thinly disguised Brussels) are learning English from Lucy Snowe, the heroine. Furthermore, German has apparently replaced Italian as the desirable extra accomplishment. In Brussels Lucy has a colleague who teaches German, and when Jane Eyre finds her cousins they start learning this language. This is a hint of the situation around 1900 suggested in Shaw (2005) where everyone educated read all three of French, German, and English.

One other language is mentioned in *Villette,* Dutch/Flemish, but it does not share the same status. One character is so uneducated that she can only speak Dutch: ("the aboriginal tongue")

This was no more than a sort of native bonne, in a common-place bonne's cap and print-dress. She spoke neither French nor English,

---

[1] Given the variety of editions of the classic novels referred to, I do not give page numbers. All examples can be located by searching the Gutenberg Project electronic editions available at http://www.gutenberg.org/.

and I could get no intelligence from her, not understanding her phrases of dialect.

Still, it is notable that a local middle-class friend who up to now has only spoken French (and English) could in fact speak Dutch:

Addressing the aged bonne, not in French, but in the aboriginal tongue of Labassecour [Belgium], he....

Finally, in *Jane Eyre* (1847), Hindustani (what is now called Hindi/Urdu) figures as the language St John Rivers wants Jane to learn rather than German so that she can join him as a missionary.

Anthony Trollope

Writing perhaps with a wider audience in mind, Trollope never breaks into French, but the language is often called upon for characterization. In *Can you forgive her?* (1865), it is part of Burgo Fitzgerald's feckless-ness that he cannot speak the lingua franca of Baden well enough to inhibit a switch to English. Plantagenet Palliser has been established as an exemplary figure, and his French is in keeping.

Burgo, ... walked up to him, and, speaking in bad French, desired him to leave them. "Don't you see that I have a friend with me?"
"Oh! a friend," said the man, answering in bad English. "Perhaps de friend can advance moneys?"
[...]
"Misther, Misther!" said the man in a whisper.
"What do you want of me?" asked Mr Palliser, in French.
Then the man spoke in French, also. "Has he got any money? Have you given him any money?" (Trollope 1938 [1865]: 454, 457)

So a superior person like Plantagenet knows French well. Not to know French indicates social inadequacy like Burgo's or lack of education like that of Dorothy Stanbury (*He Knew He Was Right* 1869), who says 'I can't play, or talk French, or do things that men like their wives to do.[2]'

By contrast, by the 1860s and 70s knowing German indexes a kind of (male) cleverness associated with outsiderhood. Figures who are described as knowing both French and German well are often young men who have been educated at the superior German universities. These are people whose place in England is insecure like Lucius Mason,

---

[2] See below for this association of music and French.

denouncer of British legal unreason and heir of ill-gotten wealth in
Orley Farm (1862), or Ralph Newton in *Ralph the Heir* (1871) who is
illegitimate (and "spoke German and French as if they were English").
This dialogue from *The Prime Minister* (1876) between the outsider
Lopez and his crustily conventional father-in-law illustrates the point

> [Lopez] had been at a good English private school........Thence at the
> age of seventeen he had been sent to a German University,
> [Lopez:] 'I was sent to a German university with the idea that the
> languages of the continent are not generally well learned in this
> country...'
> [Father-in-law:] 'I dare say French and German are very useful. I
> have a prejudice of my own in favour of Greek and Latin'
> [Lopez :] 'But I rather fancy I picked up more Greek and Latin at
> Bonn than I should have got here....'

The alienness of outright scoundrels like Melmotte in *The Way We
Live Now* (1875) is marked by their not merely knowing French and
German but actually speaking German to people in England. Madame
Max, in several novels including *Phineas Redux* (1874), is a positive character although she has the same central European capitalist
background, and she is never shown committing this solecism, despite
having an apparently German maid.

In Trollope's later novels knowledge of German seems to have
become a normal product of education for girls. As early as 1873 the
Fawn sisters are planning to carry on conversations in French and
(with difficulty) German among themselves (*The Eustace Diamonds*).
In *Ayala's Angel* (1881) two sisters are characterized by their language
knowledge: pretty Ayala "had been once for three months in Paris
and French had come naturally to her", whereas sensible Lucy knows
"something of French and German, though as yet not very fluent with
her tongue". An intriguing detail in this connection is that we are told
in passing that Alice Vavassor in the earlier *Can you Forgive Her* (1865)
was educated in "Aix-la-Chapelle" – Aachen. She must have been sent
to this relatively fashionable stage on the grand tour to learn German.
In the 1860s this aligns her with the young outsider men and relates to
her interest in politics and resistance to conventional female roles.

Knowledge and use of Italian, on the other hand, usually indexes the
deep depravity and often the suspected bigamy of aristocratic insiders –
earls and marquises, mostly. The Stanhope family in *Barchester Towers*
(1857) are merely the least unpleasant and wealthy of this group. There

is little trace of the status of the language as an accomplishment that can be seen in Jane Austen.

Only French really worked as an international language of science. In *Orley Farm* (1862) there is a big international conference on the law in Birmingham. Lectures are given in English, French, German and Italian (and not, for example, Spanish or Dutch or Russian). The characters and the narrator comment on the ineffectiveness of German and Italian in this context, but do not mention French. Students and practitioners of the law treat French as the unmarked option for international communication, but baulk at German and Italian.

Two occluded languages are mentioned, and the attitudes expressed are similar to those of Brontë to Flemish/Dutch. Trollope's remarkable first novel *The Macdermots of Ballycloran* (1847) is set in the west of Ireland. When Macdermot, a Catholic small landowner, accidentally kills a policeman in the middle of a panic about terrorism, he makes the mistake of running away to the wild boys in the mountains. There he meets an old man who can only speak Irish – but it turns out that like Brontë's Belgian character, Macdermot himself spoke the language in his youth and can communicate effectively. In *Phineas Redux* (1874) Madame Max finds a key witness in Prague and brings him over to London. The narrator observes that he "naturally did not speak English and unfortunately did not speak German either". Not to speak English is normal for a Central European, but not to speak one of the major languages is a marker of lack of education.

George Eliot

The most famous person not to know German in nineteenth-century literature is Mr Casaubon in *Middlemarch* (1872), whose academic efforts were pointless because he did not read the cutting-edge publications in that language. We are told this by his nephew Ladislaw – an angry young outsider, like Trollope's German-speaking Englishmen of the period.

Matthew Arnold

Arnold is not of course a novelist but his comments fit into the pattern. In 1864 he observes

> How much of current English literature comes into this 'best that is known and thought in the world'? Not very much I fear, certainly less, at this moment, than of the current literature of France or Germany ("The Function of Literature at the Present Time")

As a young-ish intellectual he has access to French and German, but does not mention Italian. In 1887 he makes it clear that he reads French as easily as English, but does not make the same claim for German, and shows that no one can be expected to know Russian or Swedish.

> I take *Anna Karénine* as the novel best representing Count Tolstoi. I use the French translation.....*Anna Karénine* is perhaps .. a novel which goes better into French than into English, just as Frederika Bremer's *Home* goes into English better than into French. ("Count Leo Tolstoi")

Discussion

Mention of language knowledge or learning very often has the purpose of placing a fictional character, and is rather rarely merely a plot device. By this I mean, for example, that we are told that St John Rivers is studying Hindustani because it serves to define his dedication and thoroughness, not because later on a mysterious Indian will appear and the plot requires someone to understand him. Possible exceptions are the francophone Belgian and anglophone Irishman who happen to recall the occluded languages, and thus enable the ignorant figures to play their part.

The incidental observations give a picture of a nineteenth-century Britain in which knowledge of French was to be expected of every educated person and it was rather lack of it that was to be commented on. German became more widely known and developed into a pre-requisite for scholarship, but was never a pre-requisite for being considered educated. Nor did knowledge of the language correlate with high social status, somewhat the opposite in fact. Italian seems to have lost status, so that German rather than Italian is the extra accomplishment. Not to know one of English, French, or German is a mark of total lack of education. As in Shaw (2005), it is unclear whether or not Italian belongs to this group of required international languages.

3. Corpus investigation

Incidental observations may be influenced by priming for what one expects to notice, but corpus investigations only turn up what the search items reveal. The incidental observations showed the range of lexical items that occurred when the investigator noted references to languages by eye and knowledge of this range made it possible to create a list of items for a more extensive search. I compiled a corpus of

English novels by downloading plain-text versions from the Gutenberg Project (n.d.). 64 novels were taken from 34 novelists (mostly two each) (see Appendix 1). In addition five less fictional works were included: Borrow's autobiographical *Lavengro* (1851) and *Romany Rye* (1857), George Moore's *Confessions of a Young Man* (1888), Swift's satirical *Tale of a Tub* (1704) and Defoe's (or Nathaniel Mist's) *General History of the Pirates* (1724). The aim was to include a wide range of novels but focus on those which draw on the contemporary reader's own knowledge of the contemporary language ecology, rather than informing about the ecology of another time (historical novels) or place (novels set in exotic locations). The notion of a historical novel proved rather difficult to operationalize. Is *Vanity Fair* (1847) historical when it deals with Waterloo (1815)? And if not is *Redgauntlet* (1822) historical when it deals with a fictional uprising of the 1760s? Four novels (those by Scott and Stevenson) deal with other times and non-metropolitan spaces, and four (Haggard's *King Solomon's Mines* 1885, Kipling's *Kim* 1901, Conrad's *Nostromo* 1904, and Doyle's *The Lost World* 1912) are clearly "exotic". Many others deal at least in part with British characters travelling in Europe, but these generally focus on the cultural-insider characters rather than the non-British environment. The most recent writer examined was Virginia Woolf, represented in the Gutenberg Project by the early works *Night and Day* (1919) and *Jacob's Room* (1922). There were about 1,480,000 words in the sample.

Once the corpus was assembled the program AntConc (Anthony 2007) was used to search for instances of the words listed in Table 1, which are mainly nationality adjectives/language names. The aim was however not to observe forms but to use the corpus to find instances

Table 1. Items searched for via Antconc.

Bantu	Irish/Erse/Gaelic	Ro/umanian/
Chinese	Italian	Russian
Czech	Japanese	Saxon
Danish	language(s)s	Serbian
Dialect(s)	[Latin]	Siamese
(low) Dutch (cf. German)	Malay	Spanish
French	Norse	Swedish
German/High Dutch	Norwegian	Turkish
[Greek]	Persian	Welsh

of reference to foreign languages. The method has obvious weaknesses. Instances of actual use of French (which seemed quite frequent in Charlotte Bronte at least) or potentially German or Italian (cf. *caro sposo*) could not be captured in this way, nor was any attempt made to search, for example, for instances of the numerous Indian languages probably mentioned in *Kim*. The anecdotal survey just described suggested, however, that a high proportion of relevant text-segments could be identified in this way. To simplify the task, the numerous references to Greek (all ancient as far as I could judge), and Latin, were neglected in the analysis.

All the instances of these words found were then examined by eye and those which did not refer to language use (the majority) were excluded. Although the search was for words, the aim was to find instances of reference to languages, and it is the instances that are classified not the actual use of the word. So the example "Again, there was the little French chevalier opposite, who gave lessons in his native tongue" is classified as a reference to the teaching of French, and the example "She had a French master, who complimented her upon the purity of her language" is classified as a reference to language quality, even though the word *French* does not refer to the language in either case.

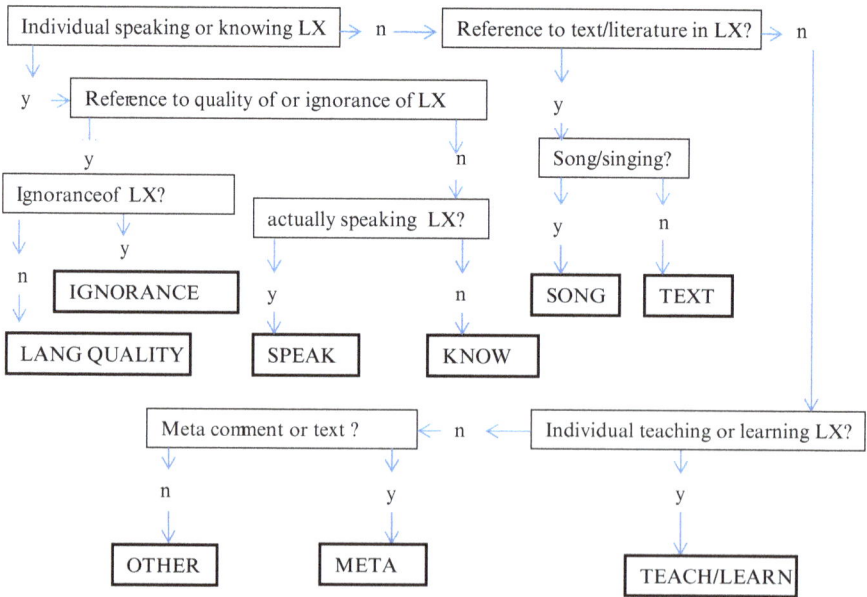

Figure 1. Flow diagram of criteria and categories for classifying instances of language reference.

The incidental survey suggested several hypotheses. First, French, German and Italian would predominate among the languages mentioned. Second, there would be rather frequent reference to the quality of the language used as a means of characterizing fictional figures, and this would be disproportionately focused on French, since knowledge of this language was an index of general education. Third, diachronically, where there was reference to knowledge of or learning a language, instances would mainly refer to French, German, and Italian, with French predominant throughout the period, and Italian gradually giving way to German. Finally, other languages would mainly be mentioned in other contexts than as being spoken or known by characters in the novels.

In order to produce some quantitative support for these hypotheses, the collected instances of reference to language were examined by eye and an attempt was made to develop categories likely to illuminate these hypotheses (Figure 1). While the categorization does indeed support the incidental observations, as I show below, its main value is to add more examples for qualitative analysis[3]. As Figure 1 shows, in some areas the categorization is rather fine, in others quite coarse, reflecting areas judged to be interesting and others judged to be less so. There is no suggestion that the categories are mutually exclusive. Thus all categories are ordered with features judged to be most interesting for the present study coming first, such that if the relevant feature is found, the instance falls into that category and potential membership of other categories is not considered. Five primary criteria were used: the first was whether or not the reference was to an individual actually knowing or speaking a foreign language. Where this was met cases were first isolated in which there was reference to someone's ignorance of the language in question and then those where there was reference to the quality of knowledge or production, and the remaining cases were subdivided into references to production and knowledge. Thus " 'X' she said in bad French" and "Her French was bad" would be in the QUALITY category while " 'X' she said in French" and "She knew French" would be respectively SPEAK and KNOW. The same procedure was followed for subsequent criteria and categories (denoted by capitalized labels in Figure 1). Examples are shown in Table 2.

---

[3] Thus it turned up the first recorded backpacker English teacher: the Vicar of Wakefield's son set off to Holland to teach English to the Dutch with only a 'satchel' as his luggage, but was frustrated when he realized that he would need to know Dutch first; the Direct Method did not occur to him.

Table 2. Examples from the analytical categories.

IGNORANCE	1	They asked me what I was, in Portuguese, and in Spanish, and in French, but I understood none of them. *Robinson Crusoe*
	2	"If Mr. Casaubon read German he would save himself a great deal of trouble." *Middlemarch*
LANGUAGE QUALITY	1	peecoly Rosiny," says James, in a fine Scotch Italian, "e la piu bella, la piu cara, ragazza ma la mawd." *The Newcombes*
	2	was genteel and extremely polite; spoke French well, and danced to a miracle; *Amelia*
	3	my bungling half-English horrid French, *Harry Richmond*
SPEAK	1	chattering to each other in the Gaelic. *Kidnapped*
	3	He promptly replied in French, "No. Not this one." *Little Dorrit*
	3	QUE VOULEZ VOUS? as the French valet said to me on the occasion. *The Absentee*
KNOW	1	And have you learnt French?" "Yes, Bessie, I can both read it and speak it." *Jane Eyre*
	2	"Of course I know French," says the other; "but what's the meaning of *this*?" *The Newcombes*
SONG	1	Percy sings a Spanish seguidilla, or a German lied, or a French romance *The Newcombes*
	2	Diana sang alone for the credit of the country, Italian and French songs, Irish also. *Diana of the Crossways*
TEXT	1	if he had to sacrifice one it would be the French literature or the Russian? *Jacob's Room*
	2	they are nothing more nor less than Chinese writing expressing something, though what I can't say *Romany Rye*
TEACH/ LEARN	1	Tibby put a marker in the leaves of his Chinese Grammar and helped them. *Howards End*
	2	kept a school in town, where he taught the Latin, French, and Italian languages; *Roderick Random*
	3	passed third in algebra, and got a French prize-book at the public Midsummer examination *Vanity Fair*
META	1	those sensations which the French call the *mauvaise honte Amelia*
	2	might be well called *den wild zee,* as the Dutch call the sea in a storm. *Robinson Crusoe*
	3	some gibberish, which by the sound seemed to be Irish *Roderick Random*
OTHER	1	"Do you think French useful in a military education, sir?" *Harry Richmond*
	2	I declare I'd as soon teach my parrot to talk Welsh *Evelina*

The example under TEACH/LEARN illustrates the principle: the reference is actually to a META text, but the higher-ranked category TEACH/LEARN is chosen because the quotation shows that Tibby is learning Chinese. The OTHER/META distinction is the least reliable. Generally, because the categories have not been intersubjectively verified, they are best regarded merely as giving a general idea of the range of uses. As noted above, the most useful data from the concordance lines are the added examples for qualitative analysis.

4. Results

Frequency of language references overall

The number of works referring to a particular language is a better measure than the number of references, since for example, the sixteen references to Danish all refer to a single item, Borrow's decision to learn Danish to study Danish folk-songs (1851). Borrow's enthusiasm also accounts for many of the references to Welsh. Similarly there are

Table 3. Overall numbers of references to languages, by occurrences and works.

	Occurrences	Works	% of all works
French	487	52	78
Italian	114	31	48
German/High Dutch	215	29	43
Spanish	34	14	21
Erse/Gaelic/Irish	92	11	16
Dutch/Low Dutch	20	11	16
Chinese	70	11	16
Arabic	24	10	15
Persian	9	7	10
Portuguese	9	6	9
Welsh	51	6	9
Hindustani etc.	21	5	7
Norse	8	2	3
Danish	16	1	1
Polish	1	1	1
Indian (Amerindian)	1	1	1

several references to Tibby's study of Chinese in *Howard's End* (1910) but what is significant is that Forster makes him study that language (and not Amharic or Hittite, for example), not how many times it is referred to.

Table 3 gives the numbers of references to languages and the number and percentage of works referring to languages. Since *Erse* may refer to Irish or Scottish Gaelic, the numbers for *Irish, Erse,* and *Gaelic* are merged. *High Dutch* and *German* are assumed to be synonyms[4].

As expected, references to French predominate. Four out of five of the works consulted mention the French language, and only half the next most frequently mentioned language, Italian. As expected, German and Italian are close to one another in frequency and the rest are far behind. The four languages that occur in as much as one-sixth of the works examined are mentioned in very different contexts. Irish/Erse/Gaelic (both in Scotland and in Ireland) occurs surprisingly frequently but this is often period colour (*Kidnapped, Redgauntlet, The Antiquary*) or expression of personal antiquarian interest (*Romany Rye, Lavengro*). Otherwise Dutch and Spanish are mentioned mainly in seafaring contexts and Arabic and Chinese in a wide variety. The Swedish, Norwegian, Serbian, Romanian, Turkish, Siamese and Japanese languages happened not to be mentioned, although there were occurrences of the words *Swedish,* etc. with other reference.

Categories of use of various languages

Table 4 shows the number of references to various languages classified by the content of the reference. It is moderately surprising that languages show relatively similar profiles across the various uses. That is, for example, the largest numbers are found in the LANGUAGE QUALITY, SPEAK, TEXT and META columns for French, and also for German, Italian, and Irish/Erse/Gaelic.

French predominates in all categories, most in references to texts (*French novel*, *French saying*), confirming, perhaps, that texts in French are regarded as accessible and valuable. It predominates greatly in judgements about quality of knowledge or performance of language, but relatively less in statements of outright ignorance. This confirms the view that some knowledge of French is conceived of as widespread, and that (as for the Prioress) a social judgement is often made on the basis of the quality of one's French.

---

4 Although by 1873 the meaning of *High Dutch* was lost and the Fawn sisters in *The Eustace Diamonds* use it to mean 'double-dutch'.

Table 4. Numbers of works containing specific types of reference to languages.

	IGNORANT	LANG/QUAL	SPEAK	KNOW	SONG	TEXT	LEARN/TEACH	META	OTHER
French	6	28	24	17	9	35	17	26	18
High Dutch/German	6	12	15	10	2	11	11	10	9
Italian	2	9	11	4	3	11	8	9	11
Irish Erse/Gaelic	2	5	5	2	3	4	2	3	4
Spanish	1	2	2	2	3	6	2	5	
Welsh		3	1	2	1	1	1	2	
Portuguese	1		3			3		2	
Arabic, Chinese, Hindustani (etc.), Persian	3	2	6	3		7	5	4	10
Danish, Dutch, Russian, Norse		2	6	4	1	5	3	5	4

This social significance of French, or the widespread extent of knowledge and therefore of ascribed ability to discriminate, is shown by the types of adjective applied to it. In the category QUALITY terms like *pure, excellent, faultless, exquisite, to perfect oneself,* are frequently applied to French but not to German or Italian. On the other hand *tolerable, bad, broken, have a smattering, clumsy* apply to all three. Not only is French more frequently referred to than other languages, knowing it well is highlighted in a different way.

A suggestive exposure of similar values appears in a few of the instances turned up by the concordance but unclassified above, where the reference is to a foreign accent in English. Thackeray refers to "the sweetest French accent," "that charming French English" (both *The Newcombes* 1855) and "Her pretty French accent" (*Vanity Fair* 1847), Gissing to "fluent French-English, anything but disagreeable" (*Born in Exile* 1892) and James to "a queer little dialect of French-English"

Table 5. Percentage of works containing reference to selected languages, by period.

Period	1 (up to 1830)	2 (after 1830)
French	85	81
German	15	60
Italian	55	47

(*Portrait of a Lady* 1881). It sounds as though a French accent can be judged positively, as further evidence of the social status of the language. Attitudes of this kind to German seem more mixed, by contrast. Although Thackeray also allows (ironically?) that one can have a good German-accented French ("said the courier in a fine German French", *Vanity Fair*), a German accent in English annoys George Eliot's characters ("suddenly speaking in an odious German fashion" (*Daniel Deronda*), "some disgust at the artist's German accent" (*Middlemarch*)). Attitudes to accent reflect the high status of French and the somewhat ambiguous position of German.

Change over time

Chaucer and Spenser read Italian, and Milton wrote in that language. But, as we have seen, by Matthew Arnold's time, German had become the literary Englishman's second foreign language. To show that this is reflected in the novels, I divided the works in the corpus into two periods – up to 1830 and after 1830. The date was chosen to put Jane Eyre (1847) learning German clearly in Period 2, and Anne Elliot (*Persuasion* 1818) using her Italian in Period 1. Table 4 shows percentages of works referring to French, Italian, and German. There was indeed a large increase in references to German, which did indeed become part of general education. From Period 1 (*Lady Susan* 1793) comes the interesting transitional observation "It is throwing time away to be mistress of French, Italian, and German, music, singing, and drawing." References to Italian in the novels did not decrease correspondingly to the rise in German, but Italian became exotic in a new way. Characters in novels visit Italy much more than in Period 1 (*Portrait of a Lady, Room with a View, Daniel Deronda*) and Italian characters are frequent (*Nostromo*). In Period 2 references to Italian arise mainly in references to this travel, while those to German make it part of a general education.

5. Further Observations

In this section I note, qualitatively, two usages where the special position of French is very noticeable, both of which seem to be commonplaces in earlier novels but less frequent in later ones, and one that might show the Celtic languages becoming even more occluded.

From "French and dancing" to "French and German"

In texts from Period 1 it is common for French to be mentioned along with dancing and music as a polite accomplishment, but such references are much less frequent in Period 2.

Moll Flanders (1722) is made to say "in short, I learned to dance and speak French as well as any of them, and to sing much better". In *Amelia* (1751) we can read "the gentleman was genteel and extremely polite; spoke French well, and danced to a miracle; ......". In *Humphrey Clinker* (1771) we read: "the girl's parts are not despicable, and her education has not been neglected; that is to say, she can write and spell, and speak French, and play upon the harpsichord; then she dances finely, ..." In *Evelina* (1778) the ill-bred Captain Mirvan rejects both dancing and French as possibilities for himself: "What, I suppose you'd have me to learn to cut capers? and dress like a monkey? and palaver in French gibberish? hey, would you?" French and dancing are part of a non-academic training for polite life suitable perhaps especially, though not exclusively, for women. Italian does not occur in these contexts; it is not basic in the same way.

Similar quotations, again not always referring to female education, can be found from the later nineteenth century. Thackeray writes: "She could not play on the piano; she could not speak French well; she could not tell you when gunpowder was invented:..." (*The Newcombes* 1855), and also "Tom was absent taking his French and drawing lesson of M. de Blois." Quite a bit later George Eliot gives Gwendolen Harleth's qualifications to be a governess: "your French, and music, and dancing – and then your manners and habits as a lady, are exactly what is wanted" (*Daniel Deronda* 1876). But in the course of the nineteenth century modern languages became part of an academic syllabus (Archer 1921) and examples like those above become less frequent. Two things happen. First, knowledge of German appears as an accomplishment. Ann Brontë describes an unsatisfactory pupil: "everything was neglected but French, German, music, singing, dancing, fancy-work, and a little drawing", ...(*Agnes Grey* 1847). And Charlotte lets a similar character describe herself: "I know nothing--nothing in the world – I assure you; except that I play and dance beautifully, – and French and German of course I know, to speak; but I can't read or write them very well." (*Villette* 1853). Second, mention of learning French in connection with artistic and aesthetic skills seems to become less frequent, and the associations of French seem to be more those suggested by Moore's "Neither Latin, nor Greek, nor French, nor History, nor English composition could I learn" (*Confessions of a Young Man* 1886) – a school subject like others. It is possible that when Trollope makes Dorothy Stanbury say "I can't play, or talk French, or do things that men like their wives to do." (*He Knew He Was Right* 1869) he is characterizing her as someone whose idea of a sophisticated education itself is a bit old-fashioned.

In general, references to learning French decrease and those to the quality of French knowledge certainly do not increase[5]. *Portrait of a Lady* (1881) has a reference to perfecting one's French and one to a character's imperfect French while the otherwise rather similar *The Good Soldier* (1915), also set mainly in continental Europe and very concerned with social distinction, never refers to the French language.

"As the French have it"

In the corpus it is not uncommon to show knowledge of a language by citing a word or phrase and naming the source language as in "T, on the left arm of the dead man, signified the Italian word 'Traditore,'" (*The Woman in White* 1860) or " ... must be my amende honorable, as the French have it" (*Clarissa* 1748). Borrow uses phrases or literal translations from Welsh, Irish, and Chinese like this; otherwise Dutch occurs in *Robinson Crusoe* (1719) and *Humphrey Clinker* (1771), Italian in *The Woman in White* (1860) and *A Room with a View* (1908), and German in *Confessions of a Young Man* (1886) and *The Adventures of Sherlock Holmes* (1892). French is much more common: no less than fourteen of the works examined use it in this way, from "those sensations which the French call the *mauvaise honte*" in *Amelia* (1751) to "Bon voyage, my dear sir – bon voyage, as the French say." in *The Woman in White* (1860). Again the references seem clustered in the earlier works, and to be less frequent later in the nineteenth century.

---

[5] The social and geographical range covered by the novel as a form also changed, so that we are not always comparing like with like.

"All Greek to me"

Some languages are marked as incomprehensible, in occasional usages like "Most of the matter might have been written in Chinese for any definite meaning that it conveyed" (*The Lost World* 1912) or "as intelligible to me as if he had spoken in Arabic or Irish" (*Roderick Random* 1748) or "I declare I'd as soon teach my parrot to talk Welsh." (*Evelina* 1778). These few examples suggest a greater presence of the Celtic languages in Period 1, but also their status as strange and difficult. No one says "It could have been French/ German/ Italian/ Spanish for all I understood."

6. Conclusion

Use of a corpus does indeed confirm the special status of French and the rise of German. It also confirms that Italian was the only other language that was widely known or referred to. It confirms that some knowledge of French was presupposed, perhaps especially later in the period, and that the quality of one's spoken French was a significant index of one's status as a cultured person, for both sexes, perhaps especially earlier. We can probably see a shift in the status of modern languages from polite accomplishments along with dancing and music to school subjects along with History and Geography, and this may be associated with increasing identification of all education (and not just the classics) with the institution of the school.

Use of a corpus implies quantification and led me to attempt to classify references to languages in terms of their content. This proved difficult to do reliably, but nonetheless produced the unexpected finding that similar proportions of references to most languages fell into each category. Apart from particular usages (such as the identification of Chinese, Arabic, Welsh and Irish as incomprehensible, or the co-occurrence of French with dancing) similar sorts of thing seem to be said about all the languages mentioned; it is frequency of reference that differs dramatically, not content. The "linguicist" attitudes towards minor European languages noted from Brontë and Trollope, the condemnation of those who cannot manage English, French German, or Italian, are not prominent in the corpus, but on the other hand the minor languages are not mentioned much at all.

Though knowledge of German is represented as having spread quite rapidly after, say, 1830, the language never acquired the position of French, and speaking German could be used for negative categorization in a way that speaking French could not. While French was clearly the main lingua franca in Europe in the nineteenth century, the corpus data perhaps suggest a weakening in its position as a status symbol from the second half of the nineteenth century. Nonetheless the fate of Sir Samson in the passage used as an epigraph to this chapter is worth noting: humiliated by his inability to speak French in Stockholm, he was exiled to the remotest of outposts. From Chaucer to Evelyn Waugh, characters' French defines their status.

Appendix

Period 1	21 works
Daniel Defoe	*General History of the Pirates* 1724, *Moll Flanders* 1722, *Robinson Crusoe* 1719
Jonathan Swift	*Gulliver's Travels* 1726, *Tale of a Tub* 1704
Henry Fielding	*Tom Jones* 1749, *Amelia* 1751

Period 1	21 works
Oliver Goldsmith	*The Vicar of Wakefield* 1766
Samuel Richardson	*Clarissa* 1748
Tobias Smollett	*Peregrine Pickle* 1751, *Humphrey Clinker* 1771, *Roderick Random* 1748
Fanny Burney	*Camilla* 1796, *Evelina* 1778
Jane Austen	*Lady Susan* 1793, *Mansfield Park* 1814, *Persuasion* 1818
Maria Edgworth	*Castle Rackrent* 1800, *The Absentee* 1812
Walter Scott	*Redgauntlet* 1824, *The Antiquary* 1816

Period 2	48 works
Ann Brontë	*Agnes Grey* 1847
Charlotte Brontë	*Jane Eyre* 1847, *Villette* 1853
Emily Brontë	*Wuthering Heights* 1847
WilliamThackeray	*The Newcombes* 1855, *Vanity Fair* 1847
George Borrow	*Lavengro* 1851, *Romany Rye* 1857
Anthony Trollope	*Framley Parsonage* 1861, *The Way We Live Now* 1875
Benjamin Disraeli	*Sybil* 1845, *Tancred* 1847
Charles Dickens	*Little Dorrit* 1857, *Our Mutual Friend* 1865
Elizabeth Gaskell	*Cranford* 1851, *North and South* 1855

George Eliot	*Middlemarch* 1872, *Daniel Deronda* 1876
George Gissing	*Born in Exile* 1892, *Henry Ryecroft* 1903
George Meredith	*Diana of the Crossways* 1885, *Harry Richmond* 1871
George Moore	*Esther Waters* 1894, *Confessions of a Young Man* 1886
Henry James	*Portrait of a Lady* 1881, *What Maisie Knew* 1897
Oscar Wilde	*The Portrait of Dorian Gray* 1890
Rider Haggard	*King Solomon's Mines* 1885
Rudyard Kipling	*Kim* 1901, *The Light that Failed* 1890
Thomas Hardy	*Jude the Obscure* 1895, *Tess of the Durbervilles* 1891
Wilkie Collins	*The Moonstone* 1868, *The Woman in White* 1860
Robert Louis Stevenson	*Kidnapped* 1886, *Treasure Island* 1881
Conan Doyle	*Adventures of Sherlock Holmes* 1892, *The Lost World* 1912
Period 2	**continued**
E.M. Forster	*A Room with a View* 1908, *Howards End* 1910
Ford Madox Ford	*The Good Soldier* 1915
H.G. Wells	*Ann Veronica* 1909, *Tono Bungay* 1909
Joseph Conrad	*Nostromo* 1904, *The Secret Agent* 1902, *Under Western Eyes* 1911
Virginia Woolf	*Jacob's Room* 1922, *Night and Day* 1919

References

Anthony, L. (2007). *AntConc 3.2.1w* (Windows) [Computer Software]. Tokyo, Japan: Waseda University. Available from http://www.antlab.sci.waseda. ac.jp/.

Archer, R.L. (1921). *Secondary Education in the Nineteenth Century*. London: Cassel.

Besse, H. (2014). La SIHFLES, ou vingt-cinq ans d'investigations historiographiques sur l'enseignement/apprentissage du français langue étrangère ou seconde. *Language & History* 57:1, 26–43.

Fasold, R. (1984). *The Sociolinguistics of Society* (Vol. 1). Oxford: Basil Blackwell.

Glück, H. (2014). The history of teaching German as a foreign language in Europe. *Language & History* 57:1, 44–58.

Haugen, E. (1971). The ecology of language. *Linguistic Reporter. Supplement* 25, 19–26.

Hüllen, W. (2006). Foreign language teaching – a modern building on historical foundations. *International Journal of Applied Linguistics* 16:1, 2–15.

Johannesson, N.-L. (2008). *Icc hafe don swa summ þu badd*: An Anatomy of the Preface to the *Ormulum*. *SELIM: Journal of the Spanish Society for Medieval English Language and Literature* 14, 107–140.

Mclelland, N. (2005). Dialogue and German language learning in the Renaissance. D.B. Heitsch & J.-F. Vallée (eds) *Printed Voices: The Renaissance Culture of Dialogue*. Toronto: University of Toronto Press, 206–226.

———. (2012). Walter Rippmann and Otto Siepmann as Reform Movement textbook authors: a contribution to the history of teaching and learning German in the United Kingdom. *Language & History* 55:2, 123–143.

Meyerstein, E. (ed.) (1946). *Adventures by Sea of Edward Coxere*. Oxford: The Clarendon Press.

Project Gutenberg. (no date) http://www.gutenberg.org/.

Robinson, F.N. (ed.) (1957). *The Works of Geoffrey Chaucer*. Oxford: The Clarendon Press.

Rothwell, W. (1985). Stratford atte Bowe and Paris. *The Modern Language Review* 80, 39–54.

Sanchez, A. (2014). The teaching of Spanish as a foreign language in Europe. *Language & History* 57:1, 59–74.

Shaw, P. (2005). The languages of international publication in economics in 1900. U. Melander-Marttala, H. Näslund, I. Bäcklund, & U. Brestam (eds) *Text i Arbete/Text At Work*. Uppsala: Institutionen för Nordiska Språk, 340–348.

Smalley, W.A. (1994). *Linguistic Diversity and National Unity: Language Ecology in Thailand*. Chicago: University of Chicago Press.

12 "Mythonomer": Tolkien on Myth in His Scholarly Work

Maria Kuteeva
Stockholm University

By the bye, we now need a new word for the 'science of the nature of myths' since 'mythology' has been appropriated to the myths themselves. Would 'mythonomy' do? I am quite serious. If your views are not a complete error this subject will become more important and it's worth while trying to get a good word before they invent a beastly one.

(C. S. Lewis to J.R.R. Tolkien, in Lewis 1988: 255)

1. Introduction

This article is dedicated to Nils-Lennart Johannesson's life-long interest in Tolkien. Nils-Lennart shares Tolkien's scholarly interests in Anglo-Saxon and Middle English and continues the tradition of the philological school that developed at Oxford in the late nineteenth century (e.g. Palmer 1965, Shippey 1982). This approach to the study of language in connection to literary and historical texts made a paramount contribution to the study of historical development of English and the compilation of what is known today as the *Oxford English Dictionary*. For example, Tolkien's essay on '*Beowulf*: the Monsters and the Critics' marked a new epoch in the study and appreciation of the poem. For Nils-Lennart, the study and publication of the *Ormulum* manuscript has been the major project of his academic career.

In this article I examine the ideas of myth as expressed in Tolkien's scholarly work. What is 'myth'? The meaning of this word has changed throughout human history, causing a certain degree of semantic confusion. As a result, today myth is thought of as 'fiction' or 'illusion'. People generally distinguish between myth as a story about ancient

How to cite this book chapter:
Kuteeva, M. 2015. "Mythonomer": Tolkien on Myth in His Scholarly Work. In: Shaw, P., Erman, B., Melchers, G. and Sundkvist, P. (eds) *From Clerks to Corpora: essays on the English language yesterday and today*. Pp. 215–228. Stockholm: Stockholm University Press. DOI: http://dx.doi.org/10.16993/bab.l License: CC-BY.

gods and myth as any fictitious narrative. However there is more to find in 'myth'. In the OED the word is given the following definitions: "A purely fictitious narrative usually involving supernatural persons, actions or events, and embodying some popular idea concerning natural or historical phenomena. Properly distinguished from *allegory* and from *legend*."; and in generalized use: "an untrue or popular tale, a rumour". The second meaning is identified as concerned with "a fictitious or imaginary person or object." Whether regarding a tale or an object, one quality seems to be particularly underlined in the above definitions of 'myth', that of falsehood.

It is not only in English but in all European languages that the word 'myth' denotes a 'fiction', and this connotation goes back some twenty-five centuries. It was in ancient Greece that myth became crucial for the development of epic poetry, tragedy, comedy and the plastic arts. But, on the other hand, due to the highly advanced philosophy, 'myth' was subjected to a subtle and critical analysis, which contributed to the process of its demystification. The Sophists interpreted myths as allegories revealing naturalistic and moral truths. Socrates, along with his disciple, Plato, was rather sceptical about such attempts at explaining mythical narratives (*Phaedrus, Republic* E378). Nevertheless, they both also pointed to the existence of "the under-meaning of ancient mythology" (Müller 1881: 580). For Plato, 'myth' was a form of knowledge itself, one of the human ways of knowing the world. Even earlier Ionian rationalism intensely criticised the classic mythology expounded by Homer and Hesiod. Xenophanes of Colophon (*circa* 565–470) was the first to reject mythological concepts of divinity employed by the two poets as "the fables of men of old" (Spence 1921: 41). From that point, the Greeks continued to empty *muthos* of its religious and metaphysical value. In short, the debate about the origins and validity of myths began in ancient Greece, the country with which today many people associate the word *mythology*. The following sections will focus on Tolkien's views on myth.

2. J.R.R. Tolkien on Myth

The study of myth was not Tolkien's chief occupation as a scholar, and in his writings he largely expresses his personal views and beliefs. Two main concerns for him are myth as story and the relationship between myth and history. He touches upon the matter of myth in his famous essay on '*Beowulf*: the Monsters and the Critics' (1936) and chooses to speak on a related subject in his Andrew Lang lecture 'On Fairy-Stories' (1939).

In '*Beowulf*: The Monsters and the Critics' Tolkien argues against definitions of the poem as "a wild folk-tale" or "mythical allegory". He asserts that the account of myth as mythical allegory of nature – the sun, the season, and so forth – is to be discredited. He also sees the term 'folk-tale' as misleading. In Tolkien's opinion, there should not be any special distinction between myth and folk-tale:

> Folk-tales in being, as told – for the 'typical folk-tale', of course, is merely an abstract conception of research nowhere existing – do often contain elements that are thin and cheap, with little even poten-tial virtue; but they also contain much that is far more powerful, and that cannot be sharply separated from myth, being derived from it, or capable in poetic hands of turning into it: that is of becoming largely significant – as a whole, accepted unanalysed. The significance of myth is not easily to be pinned on paper by analytical reasoning. It is at its best when it is presented by a poet who feels rather than makes explicit what his theme portends; ... myth is alive at once and in all its parts, and dies before it can be dissected. (Tolkien 1983: 15)

Another interesting point is made by Tolkien with regard to the features of northern and southern mythologies. Tolkien deeply regrets that prac-tically nothing has survived from pre-Christian English mythology. His general assumption is that it was essentially similar to Norse mythol-ogy. In connection with *Beowulf*, he suggests similarities between pagan English and Norse mythic imagination in their "vision of the final defeat of the humane (and of the divine made in its image), and in the essential hostility of the gods and heroes on the one hand and the monsters on the other" (Tolkien 1983: 21). Since the status and significance of monsters are of particular importance in his essay, the differences between southern and northern mythologies are discussed in connection with this theme:

> We may with some truth contrast the 'inhumanness' of the Greek gods, however anthropomorphic, with the 'humanness' of the Northern, however titanic. In the southern myths there is also rumour of wars with giants and great powers not Olympian ... But this war is differently conceived. It lies in a chaotic past. The ruling gods are not besieged, not in ever-present peril or under future doom ... The gods are not allies of men in their war against these or other monsters ... In Norse, at any rate, the gods are within Time, doomed with their allies to death. Their battle is with the monsters and the outer darkness. (Tolkien 1983: 25)

Thus the northern gods degenerated in mythic imagination into the mighty ancestors of northern kings: "When Baldr is slain and goes to Hel he cannot escape thence any more than mortal man" (ibid.).

Tolkien admits that, in the case of southern mythology, gods appear to be more godlike. They are timeless and have no fear of death. Such a mythology is more likely to contain profound thought behind it. Yet one of the characteristics of classical mythology was its continuous development and change. Thus, he claims, it gradually evolved into philosophy (Greece) or regressed into anarchy (Rome). According to Tolkien, the northern mythology escaped this destiny by putting monsters in the centre:

> It is the strength of the northern mythological imagination that it faced this problem, put the monsters in the centre, gave them victory but no honour, and found a potent but terrible solution in naked will and courage ... So potent is it, that while the older southern imagination has faded for ever into literary ornament, the northern has power, as it were, to revive its spirit even in our own times. (Tolkien 1983: 25–6)

The power ascribed by Tolkien to northern mythology is also significant for his own mythopoeic work.

'On Fairy-Stories' was an Andrew Lang lecture delivered at the University of St Andrews on 8 March 1939. Lang's twelve-volume collection of fairy-stories is referred to as having no rivals in "the popularity, or the inclusiveness, or the general merits" in English (Tolkien 1983: 114).[1] However, Tolkien entirely disagrees with Lang's presentation of the material as intended specifically for children.

'On Fairy-Stories' is Tolkien's most well-known piece of academic writing. As Richard Purtill remarks it is even "too well known", although "the more obvious points Tolkien makes in this essay have been repeated over and over again, and the subtler points have often been neglected" (Purtill 1984: 13). One of the latter points is the relationship between fairy stories and myth. As Tolkien argued in his lecture on *Beowulf*, folk-tales are nothing else but derivatives of myth. Folk-tales, in turn, belong to what he generally defines as *fairy-stories* which he considers to be 'lower mythology,' the humbler part of mythology. Therefore a great deal of what Tolkien says about fairy-stories can be applicable to myth.

---

[1] Tolkien is referring to the twelve volumes of different colours published between 1889 and 1910 by Longmans and Green.

Myth in Tolkien's understanding is, above all, a *story*. Discussing the question of its origins, he emphasises that when enquiring into the origins of 'fairy-stories', one should enquire into the origins of the fairy elements: "To ask what is the origin of stories (however qualified) is to ask what is the origin of language and of the mind" (Tolkien 1983: 119). The parallel he draws between story (or myth), language, and the mind gives us clues for understanding Tolkien's own account of myth.

Before considering the question of origins, Tolkien argues against the application of certain approaches to the study of fairy-stories. In fact the fundamental question of the origin of "the fairy *element*" ultimately leads the enquirer to the same mystery of the origin of story, language and the mind. There are many *elements* in fairy-stories that can be studied regardless of this main question. These kinds of studies, Tolkien asserts, are usually scientific by intention: "they are the pursuit of folklorists or anthropologists: that is of people using the stories not as they were meant to be used, but as a quarry from which to dig evidence, or information, about matters in which they are interested" (Tolkien 1983: 119). Tolkien expresses particular distaste with scholarly interest in recurring similarities, typical of certain schools: "We read that *Beowulf* "is only a version of *Dat Erdmänneken*"; then "*The Black Bull of Norroway* is *Beauty and the Beast*", or "is the same story as *Eros and Psyche*", and the Norse *Mastermaid* . . . is "the same story as the Greek tale of Jason and Medea"" (ibid.). For him, such comparisons appear to be pointless whether in art or literature. As he remarks in his essay on *Beowulf*: "myth is alive at once and in all its parts, and dies before it can be dissected" (Tolkien 1983: 15).

Tolkien admits that the fascination of the desire to explain the history of the evolution of stories is very strong in himself. He expresses certain reservations regarding this kind of investigation of the Tree of Tales:

> It is closely connected with the philologists' study of the tangled skein of Language, of which I know some small pieces. But even with regard to language it seems to me that the essential quality and aptitudes of a given language in a living moment is both more important to seize and far more difficult to make explicit than its linear history. I feel that it is more interesting, and also in its way more difficult, to consider what they are, what they have become for us, and what values the long alchemic processes of time have produced in them. In Dasent's words I would say: "We must be satisfied with the soup

that is set before us, and not desire to see the bones of the ox out of which it has been boiled."[2] (Tolkien 1983: 120)

Tolkien believes that to find out how the whole *picture* is formed is often too challenging a task. What can usually be done is to explain one particular element or detail (like a word in language).

Thus Tolkien believes it unworthy to go into inquiries concerning the history of stories. Fairy-stories are ancient indeed, and are found wherever there is a language. As in archaeology or comparative philology, the debate arises "between *independent evolution* (or rather *invention*) of the similar; *inheritance* from a common ancestry; and *diffusion* at various times from one or more centres" (Tolkien 1983: 121). *Invention* is considered by Tolkien to be the most important and fundamental, and, at the same time, the most mysterious factor of these three: "To an inventor, that is to a storymaker, the other two must in the end lead back" (ibid.). Thus Tolkien shows that both *diffusion* (borrowing in space) and *inheritance* (borrowing in time) are ultimately dependent on *invention*.[3]

Tolkien dismisses Max Müller's account of mythology as a "disease of language",[4] although, he admits, language "may like all human things become diseased" (Tolkien 1983: 121). He emphasises how intimately linked the origin of language, the mind, and mythology are:

> You might as well say that thinking is a disease of the human mind. It would be more near the truth to say that languages, especially modern European languages, are a disease of mythology. But Language cannot, all the same, be dismissed. The incarnate mind, the tongue, and the tale are in our world coeval. (Tolkien 1983: 122)

What creates the fairy element, typical of fairy-story and myth, is the human art of 'Sub-creation'. The latter, in turn, is based upon a unique admixture of human capacity for abstract thought and generalisation, for distinguishing objects from their qualities (e.g. *green-grass*). Indeed,

---

[2] Tolkien refers to Sir George Dasent's translation of *Popular Tales from the Norse*, collected by P. C. Asbjörsen and J. I. Moe (Edinburgh, 1859), p. xviii.

[3] On Tolkien's understanding of *invention* as 'discovery' see Shippey, *The Road to Middle-Earth*, p. 22.

[4] In the second series of his *Lectures on the Science of Language* (1864) Müller dedicates five chapters to the discussion of myth. *Here he states: "Mythology, which was the bane of the ancient world, is in truth a disease of language. A mythe means a word, but a word which, from being a name or an attribute, has been allowed to assume a more substantial existence"(p. 12, emphasis added).*

the invention of the adjective is seen by Tolkien as a great step in the evolution of mythical grammar: "When we can take green from grass, blue from heaven, and red from blood, we have already an enchanter's power - upon one plane; and the desire to wield that power in the world external to our minds awakes" (Tolkien 1983: 122). Tolkien believes that this is how by 'fantasy' a new form is made, and a human being becomes a sub-creator.

Tolkien points out that, as an aspect of mythology, sub-creation has been given too little consideration.[5] Rather, a good deal of attention has been spent on examining representation or symbolic interpretation of various phenomena of the real world. Thus certain opinions divide mythology into 'lower' and 'higher', distinguishing 'Faërie', "the realm or state in which fairies have their being" (Tolkien 1983: 113) from Olympus.

Tolkien rejects the allegorical explanation of myths which claims that 'nature-myths' are based upon personification of natural phenomena (the sun, the dawn, and so forth) and that fairy tales are simply a sort of debased mythology. This seems to Tolkien "the truth almost upside down" (Tolkien 1983: 123). Indeed, the closer the so-called 'nature-myth' is to its prototype, the less interesting it is as a myth offering an explanation of the real world. Any 'personality' can only be obtained from a person. Thus Tolkien concludes:

> The gods may derive their colour and beauty from the high splendours of nature, but it was Man who obtained these for them, abstracted them from sun and moon and cloud; their personality they get direct from him; the shadow or flicker of divinity that is upon them they receive through him from the invisible world, the Supernatural. There is no fundamental distinction between the higher and lower mythologies. Their peoples live, if they live at all, by the same life, just as in the mortal world do kings and peasants. (ibid.)

Tolkien illustrates this point by the example of the Norse god Thórr. His name means 'thunder', but his character and appearance cannot originate in thunder or lightening. He looks more like a not particularly clever, red-bearded, and remarkably strong Northern farmer, the kind by whom Thórr was beloved. So, what came first, Tolkien asks, the thunder or the farmer? It seems to him that "the farmer popped up in

---

[5] Zettersten (2011) devotes an entire chapter "Tolkien's double worlds" to the subject of sub-creation.

the very moment when Thunder got a voice and face; there was a distant growl of thunder in the hills every time a story teller heard a farmer in a rage" (Tolkien 1983: 124).

Another important point in Tolkien's discussion of mythology is its relation to religion. This is where its 'higher' element comes from. Tolkien refers to the view, previously expressed by Andrew Lang, that mythology and religion are two different things. Although they have become confused, mythology as such does not have any religious significance. Tolkien largely agrees with this distinction, although he admits that in fact religion and mythology have become entangled. He does not deny a possibility that they could be separated long ago, but since then, through error and confusion, came back to re-fusion.

In Tolkien's view, confusion itself appears to be a significant factor in the process of making mythical or fairy-story characters. Using Dasent's image of the 'Soup', he talks about the continuously boiling 'Cauldron of Story' (Tolkien 1983: 125). Thus many famous historical characters find themselves "thrown" into the Cauldron, from which they re-appear changed into mythical characters. The most obvious example of this kind is king Arthur, but Tolkien also mentions Charlemagne's mother, the Archbishop of Canterbury, Froda, King of the Heathobards, and others. His conclusion is this: "History often resembles 'Myth', because they are both ultimately of the same stuff" (Tolkien 1983: 127). This notion is anticipated in 'The Monsters and the Critics'.

Above all, Tolkien is concerned with the question: What effect is produced by fairy-stories **now**? Myths and fairy-stories are old and therefore appealing but there is more to them:

> Such stories have now a mythical or total (unanalysable) effect, an effect quite independent of the findings of Comparative Folk-lore, and one which it cannot spoil or explain; they open a door on Other Time, and if we pass through, though only for a moment, we stand outside our own time, outside Time itself, maybe. (Tolkien 1983: 128–9)

It is because of this 'timeless' effect that old elements in myths and fairy-stories have been preserved. Even though some ancient elements in such stories are often dropped out, replaced, or changed by their oral narrators, the essential mythical elements survive because of their felt literary significance. For example, when a myth has an explanation of some ritual or taboo which no longer means anything, the value of the story itself still depends upon this ritual or taboo.

To sum up Tolkien's argument, "There is no fundamental distinction between higher and lower mythologies" (Tolkien 1983: 123), regardless of whether myth and folk-tale speak of real persons and things, or whether they are merely a product of human imagination. Since he speaks of fairy-stories and myths as *stories* enjoyed by people today, the main criterion for defining a good story is how well it temporarily convinces the reader of the imaginary world of the story, with its own standards of truth. Thus the secondary worlds of fairy-stories, as products of sub-creation, require from the reader a special kind of Secondary Belief. The 'primal desire' for Faërie is often constrained in the modern reader by religion (or lack of it) and science. This was not the case for pre-Christian pagans who lived under the 'spell' cast by myths which led them to a more or less permanent state of secondary belief.

As a philologist, Tolkien was aware of the historical relationship between *spell* and *evangelium*. As Shippey notes:

> ... for the Old English translation of Greek *evangelion*, 'good news', was *gód spell*, 'the good story', now 'Gospel'. *Spell* continued to mean, however, 'a story, something said in formal style', eventually 'a formula of power', a magic spell. The word embodies much of what Tolkien meant by 'fantasy', i.e. something unnaturally powerful (magic spell), something literary (a story), something in essence true (Gospel). At the very end of his essay he asserts that the Gospels have the 'supremely convincing tone' of Primary Art, of truth - a quality he would also like to assert, but could never hope to prove of elves and dragons. (Shippey 1982: 47)

Tolkien finishes 'On Fairy-Stories' with a discussion of the fairy-story element in the Gospels. They contain "a story of a large kind which embraces all the essence of fairy-stories" (Tolkien 1983: 155).

3. Pretence or Belief?

'On Fairy-Stories' was written for a non-specialised audience, and is therefore the least 'philological' of Tolkien's scholarly works. This lack of philological core, as well as the comparatively popular style of the essay, has caused Shippey to remark that there is a sign that Tolkien tried to "talk down" to his audience, "pretending that fairies are real" (Shippey 1982: 45). On the other hand, if there had been an element of 'pretending', it could have also been intended to keep a form of seriousness about the works of sub-creation. As noted earlier, Tolkien believed that in order to create secondary belief in the modern reader, there must be no laughing at the magic: "That must in that story be taken seriously, neither laughed at nor explained away" (*Tolkien 1983: 114*).

It seems that the merits of 'On Fairy-Stories', and its consequent popularity, are rooted in Tolkien's less formally academic and more personal approach to the subject. The essay is invaluable for shedding light upon his views on myth and language. After all, philology was not the only, although surely the major, source of Tolkien's inspiration. 'On Fairy-Stories' seems to be written more by Tolkien-the artist and Tolkien-the believer, rather than Tolkien-the philologist or Tolkien-the scholar. As he remarked in 1951 to Milton Waldman:

> I am not 'learned'* in the matters of myth and fairy-story ... for in such things (as far as known to me) I have always been seeking material, things of a certain tone and air, and not simple knowledge ... Myth and fairy-story must, as all art, reflect and contain in solution elements of moral and religious truth (or error) but not explicit, not in the known form of the primary 'real' world. (I am speaking, of course, of our present situation, not of ancient pagan, pre-Christian days). (Carpenter & Tolkien: 144)
> * Though I have thought *about* them a good deal.

Later in the same letter he again recalls the theme of the Fall which he touches upon in 'On Fairy-Stories':

> After all, I believe that legends and myths are largely made of 'truth', and indeed present aspects of it that can only be received in this mode; and long ago certain truths and modes of this kind were discovered and must always reappear. There cannot be any 'story' without a fall – all stories are ultimately about the fall – at least not for human minds as we know them and have them. (Carpenter & Tolkien: 147)

For Tolkien, myth is a form of art which inexplicitly transmits elements of truth. He strongly disagrees with the confusion of myth with allegory and the explanation of pagan gods as 'personifications' of natural phenomena. On the other hand, he also does not draw any clear distinction between mythology and folklore. Myth is interesting to Tolkien as a story with literary merits. In his opinion, the Tree of Tales should be left to be enjoyed rather than examined.

4. Myth: thought, language, and story

As mentioned in Section 1, Tolkien disagrees with the account of myth as an allegory of nature. The debate concerning this problem started in ancient Greece when Socrates and Plato argued against the Sophists' explanation of myths as revealing naturalistic and moral truths (Spence 1921: 40–43). During the period of the Enlightenment, myth was interpreted as a lack of rationality, as a "defective understanding of scientific causes".[6] One of the results of this "defective understanding" is the account of myth based on the personification of natural forces.

In the nineteenth century, Schelling (e.g. 1856) rejects the principle of allegory and turns to the problem of symbolic expression in myths. However, later Müller (e.g. 1881) returned to explaining myths by natural phenomena, although this time his conclusions were supported with reference to philological studies. Müller's explanation was attacked by Andrew Lang and by the time of Tolkien's scholarly activities was virtually discredited. Tolkien also rejects Müller's account of myth (see Section 1).

Let us briefly consider the link between myth, language and thought, as understood by nineteenth-century scholarship. Max Müller, for example, claims that mythology is "the dark shadow which language throws on thought, and which can never disappear till language becomes altogether commensurate with thought, which it never will" (Müller 1881: 590). Tolkien, however, does not derive one phenomenon from another. Objecting to the account of myth as a "disease of language", he asserts: "It would be more near the truth to say that languages, especially modern European languages, are a disease of mythology" (Tolkien 1983: 122). It is clear that Tolkien is being ironic here but his claim echoes Schelling's definition of language as 'verblichene Mythologie' ('faded mythology') (Schelling 1856: 52).

In spite of his scepticism regarding attempts to discover the origins of myth, Tolkien points out three significant factors: *invention*, *inheritance* and *diffusion*, of which the first is considered as the most fundamental. The fairy element, typical of myth, is the product of the human art of sub-creation, or *fantasy*. Tolkien's theory of sub-creation and the parallels found in the ideas of Coleridge, Grundtvig, and other Romantics, have been discussed by a number of scholars (e.g. Agøy 1995, Seeman 1995).

When Tolkien discusses myth as story in its present form, he equates it with what is often defined as 'folk-tale'. He refers to these two kinds of narrative as 'higher' and 'lower' mythologies. It is noteworthy that instead of looking for certain criteria to distinguish myth from other kinds of stories, Tolkien rather draws a link between mythology and

---

[6] J. W. Rogerson, 'Slippery Words: V. Myth', *The Expository Time* 90 (October 1978), 11.

what is usually regarded as folklore. This type of approach has a few analogies in both nineteenth and twentieth centuries, the most obvious of which lie in the ideas of Jacob Grimm.

Grimm's treatment of myth and mythology implies a very close connection with folklore, in particular with the tales and legends of Germany, and surely with the comparative study of languages. Since much of Germanic mythology is irrecoverably lost, in order to dig out Germanic divinities and beliefs, Grimm turns to the study of written and oral testimonials, especially legends, fairy tales, and superstitious beliefs, to runes and early language. As a result, Grimm is held "responsible for the development by which mythologic study has become the study mainly of folklore" (Feldman & Richardson 1972: 410). In his Preface to *Teutonic Mythology* he asserts:

> ... these numerous written memorials have only left us sundry bones and joints, as it were, of our mythology, its living breath still falls upon us from a vast number of Stories and Customs, handed down through lengthened periods from father to son ... Oral legend is to written records as the folk-song is to poetic art, or the ruling recited by schöffen (scabini) to written codes. But folk-tale wants to be gleaned and plucked with a delicate hand. (Grimm 1883, volume III: xiii)

In this Preface Grimm analyses fairy-tales as different from folk-tales (pp. xiv–xv), as Tolkien does in 'On Fairy-Stories'. He finally comes to the definition of the fairy-tale in relationship to other forms of common lore. Although Grimm does not point out the existence of 'higher' and 'lower' mythologies, he intimately links myths with folk tales and legendarium. Tolkien is careful in his use of the words 'myth' and 'mythology', often preferring the word 'legend' and 'legendarium', particularly when referring to his own work (Stenström 1995: 310). Both Grimm and Tolkien are especially enthusiastic about the vivid tales of the North as opposed to the ones of the South. Whereas Grimm is concerned with the reconstruction of Germanic heritage, Tolkien in particular regrets the loss of Anglo-Saxon myths (for further details see Kuteeva 1999, chapters 3–5).

Tolkien's understanding of myth demonstrates strong adherence to the symbolic interpretations of this phenomenon, which allies him with the Romantic movement. In other words, Tolkien can be seen as a 're-mythologiser' of the ideas 'de-mythologised' in the second half of the nineteenth century (e.g. Müller), and his views also appear to be strongly anti-modernist. This is particularly obvious in Tolkien's creative writings, in which he weaves together language and myth in order to construct his own mythology dedicated to England.

References

Agøy, N. I. (1995). Quid Hinieldus cum Christo? - New Perspectives on Tolkien's Theological Dilemma and his Sub-creation Theory. P. Reynolds & G. GoodKnight (eds) *The Proceedings of the J. R. R. Tolkien Centenary Conference*. Milton Keynes and Altadena: Tolkien Society, 31–38.

Asbörsen, P. C. & Moe, J. I. (1859). *Popular Tales from the Norse*, trans. Sir George Dasent. Edinburgh: n/p.

Carpenter, H. & Tolkien, C. (eds) (1981). *The Letters of J.R.R. Tolkien*. London: George Allen & Unwin.

Feldman, B. & Richardson, R. D. (eds) (1972). *The Rise of Modern Mythology, 1680–1860*. Bloomington, London: Indiana University Press.

Grimm, J. (1882–1883). *Teutonic Mythology*, trans. from the fourth edition, notes and appendix by James Steven Stallybrass, 4 Vols. London: George Bell & Sons.

Herder, J. G. (1833). *The Spirit of Hebrew Poetry*, trans. J. Marsh, 2 vols. Burlington: n/p.

Kuteeva, M. (1999). Scholarship and Mythopoeia: The Ideas of Language and Myth in the Works of Owen Barfield, C.S. Lewis and J.R.R Tolkien. Unpublished PhD thesis. University of Manchester.

Lewis, W. H. (ed.). (1988). *Letters of C. S. Lewis* (2nd ed.) revised and enlarged by Walter Hooper. London: Fount Paperbacks.

Mitchell, B. (1995). J. R. R. Tolkien and Old English Studies: An Appreciation. P. Reynolds & G. GoodKnight (eds) *The Proceedings of the J. R. R. Tolkien Centenary Conference*. Milton Keynes and Altadena: Tolkien Society, 206–213.

Müller, F. M. (1861). *Lectures on the Science of Language: First Series*. London: Longman, Green, Longman, and Roberts.

———. (1864). *Lectures on the Science of Language: Second Series* (London: Longman, Green, Longman, Roberts, & Green.

———. (1881). *Selected Essays on Language, Mythology and Religion*. London: Longmans, Green and Co.

Palmer, D. J. (1965). *The Rise of English Studies: An Account of the Study of English Language and Literature from its Origins to the Making of the Oxford English School*. Oxford: Hull University Press.

Purtill, R. (1984). *J.R.R. Tolkien: Myth, Morality, and Religion.* San Francisco: Harper and Row Publishers.

Rogerson, J. W. (1978). Slippery Words: V. Myth, *The Expository Time* 90 (October 1978), 10–14.

Schelling, F. W. (1856). *Einleitung in die Philosophy der Mythology*, in *Sämmliche Werke*, I. Stuttgart and Augsburg: J. Verlag.

Seeman, C. (1995). Tolkien's Revision of the Romantic Tradition. P. Reynolds & G. GoodKnight (eds) *The Proceedings of the J. R. R. Tolkien Centenary Conference.* Milton Keynes and Altadena: Tolkien Society, 73–83.

Shippey, T. A. (1992). *The Road to Middle-earth*, 2nd enlarged edition. London: HarperCollins.

Spence, L. (1921). *An Introduction to Mythology.* London: G. Harrap.

Stenström, A. (1995). A Mythology? For England. P. Reynolds & G. Good-Knight (eds) *The Proceedings of the J. R. R. Tolkien Centenary Conference.* Milton Keynes and Altadena: Tolkien Society, 310–314.

Tolkien, J.R.R. (1983). *The Monsters and the Critics and Other Essays.* London: Allen & Unwin.

Zettersten, A. (2011). *J.R.R. Tolkien's Double Worlds and Creative Processes: Language and Life.* New York: Palgrave Macmillan.

13 Reflections on Tolkien's Use of *Beowulf*

Arne Zettersten
University of Copenhagen

Beowulf, the famous Anglo-Saxon heroic poem, and *The Lord of the Rings* by J.R.R. Tolkien, "The Author of the Century",[1] have been thoroughly analysed and compared by a variety of scholars.[2] It seems most appropriate to discuss similar aspects of *The Lord of the Rings* in a Festschrift presented to Nils-Lennart Johannesson with a view to his own commentaries on the language of Tolkien's fiction. The immediate purpose of this article is not to present a problem-solving essay but instead to explain how close I was to Tolkien's own research and his activities in Oxford during the last thirteen years of his life. As the article unfolds, we realise more and more that *Beowulf* meant a great deal to Tolkien, culminating in Christopher Tolkien's unexpected edition of the translation of *Beowulf*, completed by J.R.R. Tolkien as early as 1926.

Beowulf has always been respected in its position as the oldest Germanic heroic poem.[3] I myself accept the conclusion that the poem came into existence around 720–730 A.D. in spite of the fact that there is still considerable debate over the dating. The only preserved copy (British Library MS. Cotton Vitellius A.15) was most probably completed at the beginning of the eleventh century.

---

[1] See Shippey, *J.R.R. Tolkien: Author of the Century*, 2000.
[2] See Shippey, T.A., *The Road to Middle-earth*, 1982, Pearce, Joseph, *Tolkien. Man and Myth: A Literary Life*, 1998, Drout, Michael D.C., *Beowulf and the Critics*, 2002.
[3] See, for example, Alexander, Michael, *Beowulf: A Glossed Text*, 1995, and McNamara (ed.), *Beowulf*, 2005.

How to cite this book chapter:
Zettersten, A. 2015. Reflections on Tolkien's Use of *Beowulf*. In: Shaw, P., Erman, B., Melchers, G. and Sundkvist, P. (eds) *From Clerks to Corpora: essays on the English language yesterday and today*. Pp. 229–238. Stockholm: Stockholm University Press. DOI:http://dx.doi.org/10.16993/bab.m License: CC-BY.

1. Personal memories of Tolkien and biographical background

I met and was in close contact with Professor Tolkien during the last 13 years of his life. I worked and published *Ancrene Wisse* texts for the Early English Text Society, Oxford University Press, together with an international group of Tolkien-inspired scholars. Tolkien had edited the most important of the *Ancrene Wisse* texts (MS. Corpus Christi College Cambridge 402) in 1962, and I later edited three of the other MSS. In that period I sometimes got first-hand evidence of his views on both the anonymous *Beowulf* and his own *The Lord of the Rings*. I often wondered why Tolkien was so keenly interested in discussing scholarly matters with me as a much younger person. I soon realized that the fact that I represented the Nordic countries and was able to pronounce the languages and also some of the dialectal variants made a great impression on him. Once I selected a text from the Gospel according to St. Mark and read it in Danish, Norwegian and Swedish, as well as in Gothic. The Gothic text was taken from Wulfila's translation of the new Testament into Gothic, probably produced at Ravenna but now kept as the magnificent Silver Bible from c. 550 in Uppsala, written with silver and gold ink on purple-coloured parchment. I could understand Gothic fairly well but Tolkien could speak the language, and amazingly enough, he was able to construct words in Gothic that would have been regarded as real, if the corresponding texts and contexts could have been expected in written form. I should like to regard this as a kind of oral emendation. It may be seen as one of Tolkien's most remarkable gifts as a linguistic scholar.

Tolkien was extremely fond of telling stories, remembrances and comparisons between different types of medieval literature. His interest in all literature after Shakespeare was said to be next to negligible. The meetings I had with Tolkien in his homes, first in Sandfield Road outside Oxford and later in his flat in Merton Street, close to Merton College, were structured according to one and the same pattern. Tolkien did most of the talking and I was the attentive listener, with the option of asking questions at irregular intervals. His eloquent talks were similar to well-structured animated oral essays.

An interesting point about Tolkien's time as a new professor at Oxford is the fact that it coincides rather well with C.S. Lewis becoming a tutor in English and at the same time a fellow of Magdalen College. The two of them were to mean enormously much to each other as colleagues and friends but also as critics and competitors. They each became a springboard for the other in questions that extended from a dry syllabus to Nordic mythology, from marriage to the existence of a God, from Tolkien's *The Lord of the Rings* to Lewis's *Narnia*.

Lewis's note in his diary from 13 May 1926 concerning Tolkien (pp. 392–93), before they had become good friends, is a good example of Lewis's combination of mental agility and wit:

> Tolkien managed to get the discussion round to the proposed English Prelim. I had a talk with him afterwards. He is a smooth, pale, fluent little chap—can't read Spenser because of the forms—thinks the language is the real thing in the school—thinks all literature is written for the amusement of men between thirty and forty—we ought to vote ourselves out of existence if we were honest—still the sound-changes and the gobbets are great fun for the dons. No harm in him: only needs a smack or so. His pet abomination is the idea of 'liberal' studies. Technical hobbies are more in his line.

When Tolkien had been established as professor and scholar at Oxford after 1925, he started on a new phase of his career, devoting much time to the critical essay. He incorporated this type of essay as a genre in English philological contexts. Several of his essays from the end of the 1920s to the end of the 1950s, through all his active life as professor, point back to important lectures that he was invited to give both in and outside Oxford. This genre in Tolkien's writing is the very core of his scholarly achievement. His philological activity with his editions of *Sir Gawain* and the *Ancrene Wisse*, his word studies and his translation of Middle English poetry into Modern English are examples of his solid learning, but it is within the art of essay-writing that he can introduce innovative ideas and new results.

> Tolkien managed to develop this part of his activities into a kind of mastership. An example is the essay from 1929, which describes how he identifies the new literary language from 13th-century England, the so-called AB-language. There are also, besides "Beowulf: The Monsters and the Critics", important essays such as "A Secret Vice" (1931), "On Fairy-Stories" (1939), "On Translating Beowulf" (1940), "Sir Gawain and the Green Knight" (1953) and "English and Wales" (1955).

I realized that I had found the origin of this art of essay-writing when I first set eyes on the series of essays and summarizing notes kept in the note-books in the Tolkien Collection from 1913 at the Bodleian Library. Naturally, these mature essays are the result of the tradition of essay-writing characterizing the whole of the English school system. On top of that, the tradition at the universities was that the students wrote essays for a tutor every week, which were read, analyzed and criticized in every detail.

The Tolkien material kept at the Bodleian Library is considerably larger than what one can imagine here from a brief summary. If we add the collection at Marquette University, Milwaukee, Wisconsin, we end up with a great number of texts, which may be used for analyzing the whole background of Tolkien's interest in medieval literature and his ability to write analytical essays within Old and Middle English philology.

Tolkien always felt an irresistible eagerness to throw himself into new research projects, new languages and new problems. One way of learning about his intellectual curiosity is to read through his own preserved letters and notes. In the Tolkien Collection at the Bodleian Library, under item A 21/1-12, there are among other things a series of essays or philological annotations from the period May–June, 1913, and later. Nr A 21/1 contains essays within the following varied areas:

1. Gradation [vowel-changes, for example from 'i' or 'e' to 'a'].
2. The origin of the English people.
3. Some sound changes.
4. Chaucer's language.
5. *Deor's Lament* (an Old English poem).
6. Anglo-Norman.
7. Scandinavian influence on English.
8. The Old English poem *Waldere*.
9. Dialect problems.
10. Lengthening of short vowels in Middle English (1100–1500).
11. Classifying consonants in Old English (700–1100).

The first impression one gets from this fascinating material is that Tolkien is capable as a student only after a year's study to draw advanced conclusions about etymology and philology, which normally fit the work of an accomplished scholar. At the same time he is ambitious enough to make careful notes about sound-changes and etymologies described in the best known handbooks in Old English. It is also fascinating to study the attention he pays to the use of a clear handwriting and an unusually elegant calligraphy.

In the part of the manuscript collection from 1913, No A 21/2, there are notes about lectures that Tolkien attended on historical grammar with references to well-known philologists, such as Sisam, Emerson, Napier and Morsbach. Nr 21/5 is particularly interesting with all its comments on *Beowulf*, both its contents and language. Tolkien refers to passages in *Beowulf*, dealing with legendary persons as well as geographical names related to Denmark. The Danish king Rolf Krake (=Hrothulf in *Beowulf*) and place-names such as the old village of Lejre (=Hleidr; Lat. Lethra) outside Roskilde could be mentioned here. In the historical little village of Lejre, archaeologists have recently excavated the rest of an impressive hall similar to the great hall Heorot, where Beowulf fought against the monster Grendel in the poem. This excavated hall at Lejre corresponds closely to the one depicted in the poem.

2. Tolkien and *Beowulf*

The view of the American scholar Michael D.C. Drout is that Tolkien was greatly inspired by the poem *Beowulf* and that Tolkien's "Beowulf: The Monsters and the Critics" (edited by Drout in 2002) is a point of origin of modern *Beowulf* study. Tolkien may not have been the only scholar to have helped to change the direction of *Beowulf* studies and the attitude to the poem, but he was the driving force with very sound arguments, which led Michael Drout to call the essay "the single most important critical essay ever written about *Beowulf*" (Drout, *Beowulf and the Critics,* 1).

The critics had earlier regarded *Beowulf* as an important historical or philological work with uncertain literary qualities. Tolkien´s essay became a distinct turning-point, even a revolution in the discussion of the poetic value of the poem. Tolkien could indicate that *Beowulf* as poetry is more beautiful and every line more significant than those of other Old English poetry.

Previously scholars had regarded *Beowulf* as an epic poem consisting of two separate parts which did not hang together very successfully. Tolkien proves very clearly that the poem forms a unity of two connected parts, which help to create a poetic wholeness. In contrast to previous critics Tolkien makes clear that the structure is remarkably strong. He calls the structure inevitable and the design of the poem admirable. Tolkien also argues convincingly that Beowulf's various adversaries, i.e. Grendel, Grendel's mother and the dragon are the central entities in the poem.

Tolkien was greatly engaged in all aspects of the extensive lost literature within the whole Indo-European language area. At some of our meetings we discussed that topic most vividly in relation to the Old English poetic fragments. We also discussed the fascinating book, *The Lost Literature of Medieval England*, originally published in 1952 by R.M. Wilson, but which had appeared in a new and revised edition in 1970. The whole of the great lost treasure of ancient literature is a most relevant key area for the understanding of Tolkien's thinking in building up a whole fictional world in an age different from his own.

Already at school, Ronald began to read *Beowulf* in Old English, *Sir Gawain and the Green Knight* in Middle English and several Icelandic tales in Old Icelandic. Through his deep knowledge of many languages he became a precocious philologist, who could combine language and literature research at an advanced level even at the age of 15–16.

A working philologist needs not only to read, analyze and compare a large number of literary texts. A medieval philologist must also study palaeography, meaning the knowledge of manuscripts, characters and styles, the relations between the manuscripts, and much else regarding the cultures where the manuscripts belong, and also be well acquainted with the medieval manuscript collections in England.

It is of course a great advantage for a scholar to have easy access to the great manuscript collections in, for example, Oxford, Cambridge and London. For Tolkien it was important to have his favourite texts *Beowulf* and *Sir Gawain* in London and *Ancrene Wisse* (MS. Corpus Christi College) in Cambridge. The various college libraries in Oxford and Cambridge are often well equipped as regards medieval manuscripts. The unique medieval library at Tolkien's own college, Merton, owns, for example, a copy of the Latin version of *Ancrene Wisse*, published by the Early English Text Society in 1944. This library at Merton creates a most remarkable atmosphere. Once I was guided by Tolkien himself through the library, where some of the medieval manuscripts were so valuable that they were chained to the shelves.

The poem *Beowulf* appeared in a new translation into Modern English in 1999 by the Irish poet and Nobel Prize winner Seamus Heaney. In the same year Seamus Heaney was invited by the University of Copenhagen to Lejre near Roskilde in order to read from his English translation in the excavated great hall mentioned above. He read with special focus on the passage in the heroic poem where the huge monster Grendel enters the great hall Heorot and walks towards the sleeping Danes. Since I had taken the initiative to invite Heaney to read and myself read the original Anglo-Saxon text passage before Heaney in this reconstruction of the special Beowulf atmosphere of the sixth century, it was a pleasure for me to link all this to Tolkien, who had meant so much to *Beowulf* research in the 1930s.

A great part of the Germanic treasure of heroic legends has disappeared in the course of time and in the relevant countries only a small part is still extant. The only fully preserved long heroic poem in England is *Beowulf*, and furthermore there are only two short poems, *Widsith* and *Deor*, and the two fragments, *Waldere* and *Finnsburg*. Tolkien rewrote and commented on all these texts in various ways. Both *Deor* and *Waldere* belong to the areas he wrote essays about in his notebooks.

The heroic poetry from Anglo-Saxon times seems after this brief presentation to be rather modest in size, but important considering that a great deal of what once existed is no longer there. The fact that *Beowulf* in the first place, but also the other, shorter poems caught Tolkien's interest was not only due to their literary qualities but also to their fates as manuscripts and their connections with other literary traditions within the Germanic mythological field. All names of heroes in the Germanic traditions and legends circulating through references to Gothic, Burgundian, Icelandic, and to other myths indicate that they were current in oral traditions in Anglo-Saxon England. The absence of written tales of these legends may possibly indicate that the literary traditions survived in oral form.

As Tolkien mentioned himself in his letters,[4] he had been influenced by *Beowulf* during his work on *The Hobbit* and *The Lord of the Rings*. For example, some names from *Beowulf*, such as Eomer, Hama and Wealhtheow appear in *The Lord of the Rings*.

It has been known for a long time that Tolkien made a translation of *Beowulf* in the 1920s. He finished it in 1926 and put it aside perhaps without actually wanting to publish it. It could very well have served as a kind of working copy to be used in connection with lectures or citations or commentaries for a text edition. Now suddenly, in 2014, Christopher Tolkien has published an edition of *Beowulf, a translation and commentary, together with Sellic Spell* (HarperCollins Publishers). Christopher Tolkien's edition is a complete prose translation of *Beowulf* made by his father.

It is fairly well known that Michael D.C. Drout was involved in editing Tolkien's translation of *Beowulf* at the beginning of the 21st century. It may therefore be of interest to know that Drout's edition was discontinued before it was ready for publication. Drout had received the permission of The Tolkien Estate to publish a two-volume edition including some of the comments on textual problems written by Tolkien. Drout had planned to edit the partial verse translation and a complete prose translation. The companion volume was supposed to include commentaries made by Tolkien. Before Drout had finished the project, the permission to publish his edition was withdrawn by The Tolkien Estate.

As a great surprise to many, the translation of *Beowulf* by J.R.R. Tolkien was suddenly published by HarperCollins in 2014 with Christopher Tolkien as editor. Christopher has also included his father's

---

[4] See a letter to *The Observer*: "*Beowulf* is among my most valued sources"; *The Letters of J.R.R. Tolkien*. 31.

Sellic Spell, a 'marvellous tale', which, as Christopher suggests, is in the form and style of an Old English folk-tale of Beowulf with no connection with the 'historical legends' of the Northern kingdoms.

Furthermore, Christopher included two versions of his father's *Lay of Beowulf*, which is a rendering of the story in the form of a ballad supposed to be sung, now a clear memory after more than eighty years of Christopher's first acquaintance with Beowulf and the golden hall of Heorot. With very little imagination needed, one may quite easily hear J.R.R. Tolkien's voice singing the first stanza of the later of the two poems *The Lay of Beowulf*, called 'Beowulf and the Monsters':

> Grendel came forth at dead of night;
> the moon in his eyes shone glassy bright,
> as over the moors he strode in might
>   until he came to Heorot.
> Dark lay the dale, the window shone;
> by the wall he lurked and listened long,
> and he cursed their laughter and cursed their song
>   and the twanging harps of Heorot.

Tolkien's translation of *Beowulf*, as presented by Christopher, is all in prose, as mentioned above, starting in the following way:

> Lo! The glory of the kings of the Spear-Danes in days of old we have heard tell, how these princes did deeds of valour. Oft Scyld Scefing robbed the hosts of foemen, many peoples, of the seats where they drank their mead, laid fear upon men, he who first was found forlorn; comfort for that he lived to know, mighty grew under heaven, throve in honour, until all that dwelt nigh about, over the sea where the whale rides, must hearken to him and yield tribute – a good king was he!

The Anglo-Saxon original looks as follows:

> /Hwæt we Gar-Dena   in geardagum,
> þeodcyninga   þrym gefrunon,
> hu ða æþelingas   ellen fremedon.
>   Oft Scyld Scefing   sceaþena þreatum,
> monegum mægþum   meodosetla ofteah,
> egsode eorl[as],   syððan ærest wearð
> feasceaft funden¸   he þæs frofre gebad,
> weox under wolcnum,   weorðmyndum þah,
> oðþæt him æghwylc þ[ær]   ymbsittendra
> ofer hronrade   hyran scolde
> gomban gyldan,   þæt wæs god cyning!/

In order to make the contents of the beginning of the poem even more clear, I conclude by presenting Seamus Heaney's translation of the same lines into modern English:

/So. The Spear-Danes in days gone by
and the kings who ruled them had courage and greatness.
We have heard of those princes' heroic campaigns.
    There was Shield Sheafson, scourge of many tribes,
a wrecker of mead-benches, rampaging among foes.
This terror of the hall-troops had come far.
A foundling to start with, he would flourish later on
as his powers waxed and his worth was proved.
In the end each clan on the outlying coasts
beyond the whale-road had to yield to him
and begin to pay tribute. That was one good king./

While Christopher Tolkien presented his father's translation of the text into modern English prose, Drout, on the other hand, had announced that he had planned to use both prose and part poetry.

Whether the text of Christopher Tolkien's edition could have been expressed more clearly, if his edition had included both prose and part poetry, is not easy to say. The fact that this edition is now out is, however, an astounding event in itself. In whatever case, the special relations between Tolkien and *Beowulf* are clearly made public and are often well illustrated through Christopher Tolkien's publication.

References

Published works by J.R.R. Tolkien or Christopher Tolkien

The Hobbit: Or There and Back Again. (1937). London: George Allen & Unwin.

The Fellowship of the Ring: Being the First Part of The Lord of the Rings. (1954). London: George Allen & Unwin.

The Two Towers: Being the Second Part of The Lord of the Rings. (1954). London: George Allen & Unwin.

The Return of the King: Being the Third Part of The Lord of the Rings. (1955). London: George Allen & Unwin.

Ancrene Wisse: The English Text of the Ancrene Riwle. (1962). Edited by J.R.R. Tolkien from MS. Corpus Christi College Cambridge 402. Early English Text Society O.S.249. London: Oxford University Press.

The Silmarillion. (1977). Edited by Christopher Tolkien. London: George Allen & Unwin.

The Letters of J.R.R. Tolkien. Edited by Humphrey Carpenter with the Assistance of Christopher Tolkien. (1995). London: HarperCollins Publishers.

The Monsters and the Critics and Other Essays. (1983). Edited by Christopher Tolkien. London: George Allen & Unwin.

Books related to J.R.R. Tolkien

Alexander, M. (ed.) (1995). *Beowulf: A Glossed Text.* London: Penguin Books.

Carpenter, H. (1977). *J.R.R. Tolkien: A Biography.* London: George Allen and Unwin.

———. (1978). *The Inklings: C.S. Lewis, J.R.R. Tolkien, Charles Williams and their Friends.* London: George Allen and Unwin.

Drout, M.D.C. (2002). *Beowulf and the Critics.* Tempe, Arizona Center for Medieval and Renaissance Studies.

McNamara, J. (ed.) (2005). *Beowulf.* New York: Barnes & Noble Classics.

Pearce, J. (1998). *Tolkien. Man and Myth: A Literary Life.* London: HarperCollins.

Shippey, T.A. (1982). *The Road to Middle-earth.* London: George Allen and Unwin.

———. (2000). *J.R.R. Tolkien: Author of the Century.* London: HarperCollins.

Zettersten, A. (2008). *Tolkien—min vän Ronald och hans världar.* Stockholm: Atlantis.

———. (2011). *J.R.R. Tolkien's Double Worlds and Creative Process— Language and Life.* New York: Palgrave Macmillan.

14 Commentators and Corpora: Evidence about Markers of Formality

David Minugh
Stockholm University

1. Introduction

Dictionary-makers and stylists have long singled out various terms for special notice, and at times had strong opinions about their use and abuse. These comments were in many cases essentially a matter of taste (often masquerading as logic), but until corpus linguistics and powerful computers arrived on the scene, no tools existed to demonstrate actual usage, beyond collections of (laudable and reprehensible) examples. Logical and sentential connectors have not escaped such scrutiny, and here we shall focus on three fairly formal such terms, all of which have interesting characteristics from a learner perspective: *albeit, notwithstanding* and *thus*. After briefly considering their origins, we will examine some of the comments about them, particularly by grammarians and style police, and then bring in data from recent corpora to examine their actual use, which will not always prove to be in formal settings.

2. Origins

The lexical items *albeit, notwithstanding* and *thus* are not particularly obscure in their development, although they do have a reasonably venerable pedigree. The *OED Online* considers the etymology of **albeit** as straightforwardly deriving from *all* as a conjunction and the present subjunctive of *be*, with the first instances surfacing with clauses in the late 14th century:

> [1] "But syn my name is lost thurgh you," quod she,
> "I may wel lese a word on yow or letter,

How to cite this book chapter:
Minugh, D. 2015. Commentators and Corpora: Evidence about markers of formality. In: Shaw, P., Erman, B., Melchers, G. and Sundkvist, P. (eds) *From Clerks to Corpora: essays on the English language yesterday and today.* Pp. 239–265. Stockholm: Stockholm University Press. DOI: http://dx.doi.org/10.16993/bab.n License: CC-BY.

Al be it that I shal be neuer the better"
[Chaucer, *Legend of Good Women*, 1361–63][1]

Further instances soon show it introducing other constructions, such as PPs:

[2]   We dyd graunte (albeit not for this argumentacyon) that...
[Marshall, 1535]

or as an adverb, as in the OED's quite recent final citation:

[3]   Young skunks begin to spray, albeit inaccurately, at about one month of age.
[1995, *Animals' Voice* Spring 13/1]

Notwithstanding is also a compound form, straightforwardly derived, as Johnson noted,[2] from *not* + *withstand*, on the pattern of Anglo-Norman and Old French *non obstant* and post-classical Latin *nōn obstante*, with the same sense, appearing shortly after *albeit*:

[4]   Natwith-stondinge his grene mortal wounde, He ros ageyn.
[c1425, Lydgate *Troyyes Bk.*]

Its most striking grammatical feature, the ability to function as a postposition (or adverb, depending on your analysis),[3] is also documented from within less than a century later, as in Caxton:

[5]   This notwystondyng, alwaye they be in awayte.
[*Eneydos*, 1490]

a variation which remains its hallmark until the present day.

Our final (and oldest) item, ***thus***, apparently has its roots in the demonstratives (the OED suggests derivation via either *that* or *this*). Some early examples from the OED:

[6]   *Sicini* [*siccine*], ac ðus
[*c725 Corpus Gloss.* 26]

---

[1] Much of the detailed *OED* information has been removed from these citations; the Chaucer quote follows the text in Fisher 1977:643. The *OED* also mentions variants such as *al were it, albe* (both with further citations from Chaucer), but the clearest view of the range of this type of construction actually emerges from the examples cited in Jespersen 1940.

[2] "*[Notwithstanding]* is properly a participial adjective, as it is compounded of *not* and *withstanding*, and answers exactly to the Latin *non obstante*" (1783, Vol. II).

[3] Cf. Rissanen 2002 and Weber (2010:181–86) for Middle English developments, Minugh 2002 for modern English use.

[7]   & tuss ʒho seʒʒde inn hire þohht..Þuss hafeþþ drihhtin don
      wiþþ me.
                    [?*c*1200 *Ormulum* (Burchfield transcript) l. 235–7]

[8]   Here vn-to you þus am I sente.
                                        [*c*1440 *York Myst.* vii. 6]

3. Learners' perspectives

Albeit. From the start, the term *albeit* stands out for phonetic reasons.
For foreign learners and young native speakers alike, the word is normally first encountered in written form, so that the trisyllabic pronunciation /ɔːlˈbiːɪt/, with a clear *be*, often comes as a distinct surprise,
particularly if they have previously paid attention to items with reduced
stress, such as the RP pronunciation of *secretary*. To most speakers of
English, the etymological links to *al-* (as in *although*) and subjunctive *be*
are not at all obvious, particularly since the latter's primary current use,
the mandative subjunctive (e.g. *I move that the meeting be adjourned*),
is not frequent (Hundt 1998); in addition, the pronunciation of the
final *-it* as a distinct final syllable is unexpected. Placing the stress
on the first syllable (as in *alien, alias*) would lead to something like
*/ˈeɪlbɪt/, which has apparently never been current. John Wells (2008:
19) records the frequent but "non-RP" pronunciation /ælˈbiːɪt/ (he also
notes it for AmE, a form that e.g. Elster [1999:13] takes violent exception to). Once learned, its pronunciation is easy enough (in parallel to
although), and as regards usage, it presents no particular difficulties,
functioning as a synonym of *even though* or *although*.

   Notwithstanding. For learners, the pronunciation of ***notwithstanding*** ought to be straightforward (once they grasp that it is a single unit),
and as for usage, its preposed placement predominates in BrE, and
causes no problem. This position allows it to control fairly long (and
relatively complicated) constructions, whereas its postposed use tends
to be limited to controlling short NPs. The postposed use is above all
found in more formal AmE (cf. Minugh 2002 for statistics).

   Thus. The voiced initial consonant of ***thus*** follows the normal deictic
patterns seen in *the, this, those, thy* and so on. It has no direct cognates
in Romance or Germanic languages (the sole exception is Dutch *dus*).[4]

---

[4]   *Dus* is considerably more frequent than its English counterpart: the *Dutch Web
Corpus* (via the commercial program called *SketchEngine*) reports it as having an
occurrence of 1,299 per M words; by comparison, the *Oxford English Corpus*
(again via *SketchEngine*) reports *thus* as having an occurrence of 153 per M words.

Its simple monosyllabic form and its use parallel those of other logical connectors such as *so*. But like *therefore* and *as a result*, *thus* has a distribution heavily slanted towards formal written English; this (and the lack of cognates) appears to delay its acquisition, at least in Sweden, where informal English is given priority in the school system.

Of these three items, only *thus* (which has the widest functional range) was regarded as sufficiently important to be included in the classical General Service List (West 1953), the first reasonably modern word list for learners. When the *Academic Word List* was developed (Coxhead 2000), all GSL words were excluded, as already covered, so that *thus* was not included in the AWL; the latter does, however, include both *albeit* and *notwithstanding*.[5]

4. Stylistic comments by dictionaries, grammars and style manuals

In this section, we will briefly survey what various reference works have had to say about our three terms, and what claims, if any, they make about the validity of their comments about the use of *albeit, notwithstanding* and *thus*. It should be noted at the outset that there is no significant disagreement about the semantics of these terms; what is at issue are matters of register and style.

4.1 Major dictionaries

Johnson's epoch-making *Dictionary* (1755) records all three items without further ado, notably without any comments on their stylistic level. The reader is reminded that he was by no means above pronouncing judgments about usage: while *thus* is merely recorded, compare his comment on the very next word, *thwack*: "A ludicrous word" (1799, Vol. II).

The first edition of the *OED* (1933) passes over the stylistic value of *albeit* and *notwithstanding* in silence, but begins the article for *thus* with the note "now chiefly literary and formal" (1933:XI, 397); more interestingly, no changes in this judgment are to be noted even in the contemporary *OED Online*. In addition, the one-volume *New*

---

[5] The increasing impact of the *AWL* is seen not least at the English Department of Stockholm University, where an "AWL Vocabulary" test is administered to entering students early in their first semester. Not until 2013 did its first serious competitor appear (http://www.academicvocabulary.info/); cf. Gardner & Davies 2013. Note also section 4.4, below.

Oxford Dictionary of English (1998) similarly has a note only for *thus*: "poetic/literary or formal". *Webster's New International Dictionary of the English Language* (1941) records all three without further comment, as do *Webster's Collegiate Dictionary* (1988, 1993) the *American Heritage Dictionary of the English Language* (1970) and Australia's *Macquarie Dictionary*.[6]

4.2 Grammars

Turning now to earlier 20th-century grammars, we find that Poutsma comments "[i]n Present-day English *[albeit]* is used only in the higher literary style, mostly without *that*" (1929:I, ii, 712), with a similar comment on *notwithstanding* (711). Curme notes that conjunctions used in concessive clauses include *notwithstanding* and "[i]n older or archaic English: *albeit* (i.e., *all be it = be it entirely*) *that* or simple *albeit, albe*" (1931:II, 333). Jespersen (1940:51) remarks on the alternate pre-/post-position of *notwithstanding* and provides numerous examples of *albeit* and related subjunctive constructions (1940:364). Interestingly enough, his volume on pronunciation (1949) does not mention *albeit*.

For our triad of terms, Swedish-based university grammars of English have a long tradition of silence as regards form and use, although register is occasionally touched on. Elfstrand & Gabrielsson (1960) only mention *notwithstanding that* as a concessive conjunction. Svartvik & Sager (1977, 1996) mention *albeit* functioning to link adjectives (§353D) in "formal language" and *thus* as a linking adverbial (§439E) "in formal style". More recently, Estling Vannestål merely mentions *thus* as one of the linking adverbials (2008:269), omitting *albeit* and *notwithstanding*.

In Quirk et al., the first major grammar with a dawning awareness of corpus data, *albeit* is dismissed in a footnote: "the following archaic subordinators still have a limited currency: *albeit, whence, whereat, wherefore, whither*" (1985:998, note [b]). *Notwithstanding* is mentioned several times, usually with the label "formal"; note particularly: "*Notwithstanding* ['in spite of'] is formal and rather legalistic in style, particularly when postposed" (1985:706). Together with other prepositional phrases (*despite, in spite of, irrespective of, regardless of*),

---

[6] The *New Oxford Dictionary* also includes an entry on *thusly*, which is labeled "informal" (1998:1935b), while the *American Heritage* goes further, labelling it "nonstandard," noting that it "is termed unacceptable by 97 per cent of the Usage Panel" (1970:1342); cf. Menken's comments, in section 4.3, below.

notwithstanding is "considered stylistically clumsy" (1985:1098). *Thus* is consistently labeled "formal", e.g. "The form *thus* is largely formal" (e.g. 1985:557, note [b]).

In their brief discussion of register, Celce-Murcia & Freeman remark: "In any kind of informal situation, a native speaker of English would be surprised to hear somebody say *notwithstanding the fact that* to express the notion of concession. A connector such as *even though* would be much more likely" (1983:323). They nevertheless list *albeit* and *notwithstanding* under "Concession," without any comments on register (326).

Turning to modern general learner grammars, we find that *A Communicative Grammar of English* (2002) does not include *albeit*, but does mention *notwithstanding* ("very formal" [2002:113]) and *thus* ("formal" [2002:110]). The *Longman Student Grammar of Spoken and Written English* (Biber, Conrad & Leech 2002) appears to contain no information on our three terms.[7] The *Cambridge Grammar of English* (Carter & McCarthy 2006) is silent on *albeit* and *notwithstanding*. They list *thus* as an option among many, but the only concrete information given is that initial *thus* can allow inversion:

> [9]   Thus does Mr Major find himself ever more closely closeted with Mr Campbell. (2006:782)

4.3 Prescriptive stylists and manuals of style

Like most of the grammars cited above, nearly all of the works cited below were written in the pre-corpus era. With a single exception to be discussed below, however, they rarely cite extensive examples to bolster their claims. Fowler & Fowler (1930:29), for example, using guilt by association, dismiss *albeit* as an archaism, listing it with the likes of *bashaw, certes, damsel* and *quoth(a)*, terms few would wish to champion as shining examples of modern English. They are silent on *notwithstanding*, but object strongly to *thus* in one case:

> In this use *thus* is placed before a present participle (*thus enabling* &c.), & its function, when it is not purely otiose, seems to be that of apologizing for the writer's not being quite sure what noun the participle belongs to, or whether there is any noun to which it can properly be attached (cf. UNATTACHED PARTICIPLES); (1929:652)

---

[7] A caveat: since lexical items are not included in the index, the search by subject area may have missed a minor comment on these words.

This actually sounds rather like the discourse markers sometimes referred to as *shell nouns*, i.e. a way of summing up a form of logical relationship previously presented in detail in the text (Schmid 2000), a use which they find to be too vague. In all other respects, *thus* is passed over in silence.

The Americanist H.L. Mencken found nothing to comment about on *albeit* and *nevertheless*, but was interested enough in the American use of *ly*-less adverbs to comment that: "the use of *illy* and *thusly* is confined to the half educated" (1936:467).[8] Copperud (1964) only warns against the use of *for* or *thus* at the beginning of sentences: "…an affectation by some writers, particularly columnists. This is warranted only when the sentence draws a conclusion based on what has gone before" (1964: 165). The *Longman Guide to English Usage* (Greenbaum & Whitcut 1988), silent on *notwithstanding*, does warn against "the FACETIOUS variant *thusly*", and waxes truly eloquent on *albeit*:

> This is often regarded as pretentious when used, unless for humorous effect, as an alternative to *(even) though*. It is perhaps justified as a convenient way of linking pairs of adjectives (*a small albeit crucial mistake*), although *but, yet,* and *though* will also do in this case (1988: 27).[9]

Oxford's *Authors' and Printers' Dictionary* (1956), the Chicago University Press *Manual of Style* (1969), Michael Swan's *Practical English Usage* (2005) and Collins COBUILD *English Usage* (1992) are among the numerous works silent on these three words. As for student writing manuals, an examination of the popular *Writing Academic English* revealed only that *thus* appears in several lists of "connecting words and transition signals" (Oshima & Hogue, 2006, Appendix C), while *albeit* and *notwithstanding* are passed over in silence.

However, one work stands out in its detailed comments on *albeit*, as well as its extensive use of 20th century citations (almost unique among style manuals): the *Merriam-Webster's Dictionary of English Usage* (1994). Their opening shot deserves quotation *in extenso*:

> Copperud 1970, 1980 observes that "a generation ago" *albeit* was considered archaic but is "now being revived." The source of the

---

[8] In Supplement Two, he records a congressman using *thusly*, but adds, "However, it is often difficult to tell whether a congressman is serious or spoofing" (1948: 390, n. 3).

[9] Also noted by Svartvik & Sager 1977 (see section 4.2, above).

notice of revival is Gowers (in Fowler 1965). This is a most curious business, since *albeit* seems never to have gone out of use, though it may have faded somewhat in the later 19th century. If it did, the revival began decades before the commentators noticed. (1994:65)[10]

They go on to trace a lineage of *albeit* quotes from 1907 to Krapp's grammar in the late 1920s, with a last example from the 1980s. As noted in section 4.2, above, as late as 1985 Quirk et al. labelled *albeit* as archaic, despite such evidence.

What we seem to find, then, is a series of fairly random objections to specific uses or forms (such as *thusly*), while "allowing" others. This is hardly surprising, given that these writers were unable to systematically trawl through large amounts of text from many different domains for matters of interest. To do so, we must turn to recently-compiled corpora for documentation. In doing so, we will concentrate on these three terms and their frequencies over the last two centuries. The first indications of what this can result in may be seen in modern learner dictionaries, to which we now turn.

4.4 Learner dictionaries

Starting with the first edition of the Collins COBUILD dictionary (1987), but increasingly in the period after 2005, learner dictionaries have based their labelling on data drawn from (usually in-house) large corpora, i.e. corpora now normally in excess of 100 M words. It is nevertheless worth noting the comments from the editors of the Oxford *Advanced Learner's Dictionary (ALD)*: when it comes to deciding on the recently-introduced "Oxford 3000" keywords ("the words which should receive priority in vocabulary study because of their importance and usefulness"), they based their decision on corpus frequency and range of text types—but also as being "very familiar to most users of English", as judged by "language experts and experienced teachers" (2005:R99). In other words, for Oxford, the corpus is definitely not considered the sole arbiter in adjudicating on such matters.

What, then, do learner dictionaries say about our three terms? A pre-corpus edition of the Oxford *ALD* (2nd ed., 1963) labels *albeit*

---

[10] Gowers states that "*[albeit]* has since been picked up and dusted and, though not to everyone's taste, is now freely used, e.g. *It is undeniable that Hitler was a genius, a. the most evil one the modern world has known*" (1965:16). Note also that Copperud 1964 was silent on *albeit*; in later editions he is clearly aware of the changing perception of *albeit*'s status.

as "not colloq[uial]", but is otherwise silent on this issue. By the 7th (corpus-aware) edition of 2005, it labels all three as "formal", while including *thus* as one of its "Oxford 3000" keywords. In the 8th edition (2010), *albeit* and *notwithstanding* are additionally labeled as AW (i.e., part of the Academic Word List, which has now made its entry into the *OALD*).

COBUILD editions (1987, 1995) are relatively consistent, labelling *albeit* and *notwithstanding* as "a formal word", but *thus* as "a fairly formal word".

By its 4th edition, the Longman *Dictionary of Contemporary English* labels all three as "formal". *Thus* is noted as W1, i.e. among the 1000 most common words of written English, but with a warning triangle indicating that when it is used as a sentence adverb, "in spoken English it is more usual to use *so*". In the 5th edition (2009), *albeit* and *notwithstanding* receive the additional label AC (i.e., part of the Academic Word List, which has now made its entry into *LDOCE*, as well).

The *Cambridge Advanced Learner's Dictionary* (3rd ed., 2008) labels all three as "formal". *Thus* is additionally noted as I, for "improver", the middle category in its high-frequency words.[11]

Table 1. Learner dictionary labels for albeit, notwithstanding and thus.

	albeit	*notwithstanding*	*thus*
ALD (1963)	not colloq.	(no label)	(no label)
ALD (2005)	formal	formal	formal **Oxford** 3000
ALD (2010)	formal **aw**	formal **aw**	formal **Oxford** 3000
COBUILD (1987)	formal	formal	fairly formal
COBUILD (1995)	formal	formal	fairly formal
LDOCE (2005)	formal	formal	formal
LDOCE (2009)	formal **ac**	formal **ac**	formal **W1**
CALD (2008)	formal	formal **I**	formal
MEDAL (2007)	formal ★	formal	formal ★★★
CDAE (2000)	(omitted)	(no label)	formal
OADCE (1999)	(no label)	(no label)	formal

---

[11] More specifically, this applies to *thus* in the senses 'in this way' and 'with this result', with a frequency typically of 200–400 per 10 million words (2008:VIII).

The *Macmillan English Dictionary for Advanced Learners* (2nd ed., 2007) also labels all three as "formal", but includes *albeit* among the 7000 most common words of English (one star) and *thus* among the 2500 most common words (three stars, its highest frequency rating).[12]

As for these dictionary-makers' American offshoots (which are invariably smaller, presumably in order to sell better in America), the *Oxford American Dictionary of Current English* (1999) notes that *thus* is formal, but has no labels for *albeit* or *notwithstanding*. The *Cambridge Dictionary of American English* (2000) omits *albeit* altogether, but includes *notwithstanding* (with only one example—a postposed one!) and *thus* (considered "formal").

Summarizing, we obtain the table below, from which it appears clear that the dictionary-makers are in agreement on both register and frequency. This should not lead to conspiracy theories about borrowing from one another, but rather is a consequence of their now having access to large, proprietary corpora yielding similar results. However, it has recently become possible for scholars independently to check on these results, thanks to large-scale publicly-available corpora, to which we now turn.

Table 2. Frequencies from the BNC (Lancaster interface), including comparative data for *therefore*.

Term	Written	%	Per M wds	Spoken	%	Per M wds
albeit	1330	96.6%	15.13	47	3.4%	4.51
notwithstanding	701	97.4%	7.97	19	2.6%	1.83
thus	20,127	99.6%	228.97	84	0.4%	8.07
therefore	21,406	93.2%	243.52	1567	6.8%	150.53

---

[12] This is the BrE version; the AmE edition is *Macmillan English Dictionary for Advanced Learners of American English*, which had no second edition, their subscription website having instead taken over all updating.

5. Corpus data for *albeit, notwithstanding* and *thus*

5.1 Contemporary corpora[13]

The earliest "large" (= 1M word) corpora of contemporary written English are the *BROWN* series: *BROWN* and *LOB* have matched AmE/BrEtexts from 1961, and *FROWN* and *FLOB* similarly matching texts from 1991: They produce quite small numbers (only *thus* yields results larger than 20 examples per corpus), but they will turn out to be quite close to the results from the much larger corpora now available.[14]

The major 90s corpus, the *British National Corpus (BNC)*, at 100M words (British English only) yields our first solid data on how these words are distributed along the written/spoken dimension:[15]

This clear preponderance of written instances suggests that we are dealing with what is tantamount to words found in written English only, particularly if one considers that some of the "spoken" data consists of prepared transcripts for radio and TV. In absolute numbers, *thus* is once again more common than the other two by more than an order of magnitude. Using a further analysis from the Brigham Young (BYU) interface, we can break down the results into different domains (Figure 1):[16]

---

[13] The corpora in this section all seek to portray modern English from the 1990s onward. The most purely synchronic of these corpora are of course the BROWN group, each of which samples only one year. The diachronic corpora in section 5.2, on the other hand, cover a much larger temporal range, precisely in order to track changes over time.

[14] For descriptions of these earlier corpora, see any standard undergraduate textbook on corpus linguistics, e.g. McEnery, Xiao & Tono 2006.

[15] The now much larger Collins COBUILD *Bank of English* was the first modern corpus of English, but the open-access policy of the *BNC* continues to be crucial to scholarship; meanwhile, the publicly available component of the *BOE* has evolved into the 57M Collins *Wordbanks Online*, currently openly available at http://www.collinslanguage.com/content-solutions/wordbanks.

[16] A technical note: by comparing instances per 1M words, and selecting for each word the domain with the largest number of instances as 100%, we can graphically compare all domains for each word individually.

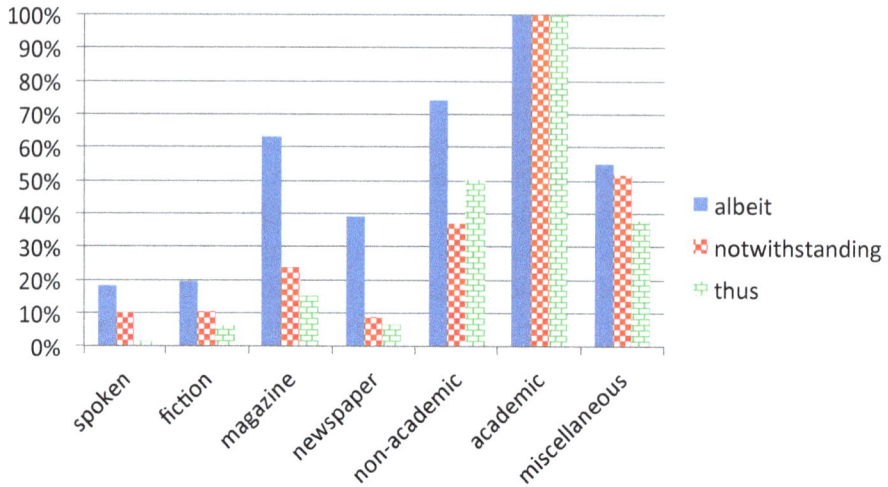

Figure 1. *BNC* distribution frequencies (BYU interface).

As expected, all three connectives occur most frequently in the academic domain. However, the most striking aspect of this comparison is that *albeit* is considerably more evenly distributed than the other two; the discrepancy is so large that it is difficult to ascribe it merely to being an artefact of the domain definitions.[17] The chi-square test returns a significance of well below p< .001.

Since the *BNC* is specifically limited to BrE, let us next turn to the *Corpus of Contemporary American English (COCA)*, which now covers a little over two decades, from 1990 on.[18] Containing 450 M words, including a "spoken" section (largely derived from radio/TV transcripts), it is the largest broadly-based contemporary corpus with free access, although also limited geographically. Not surprisingly, in raw numbers, *thus* again dominates by more than an order of magnitude, with 62,764, compared to *albeit* and *notwithstanding*, with 4,061 and 2,683, respectively. We therefore again choose to display the data as percentage comparisons to the largest category for each item, again based on frequency per 1M words (Figure 2):

---

[17] The values for the category "miscellaneous", on the other hand, clearly indicate that something is escaping this categorization.

[18] It has been expanding as time passes, now including up to 2012, so that this is an evolving synchronic record of "contemporary" American English. Like several other contemporary corpora, it thus will not yield replicable results over time, since the corpus itself is growing; cf. the "monitor corpus" solution adopted by John Sinclair and the COBUILD team (for an early description, see e.g. Clear 1998).

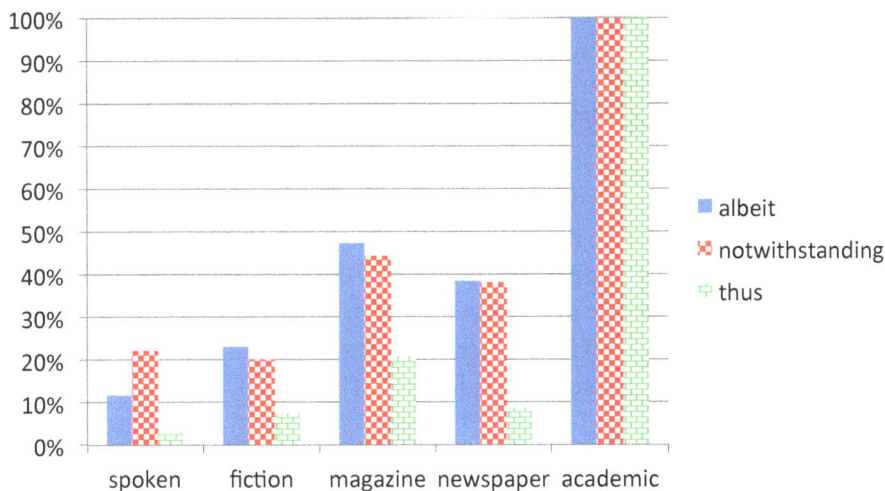

Figure 2. *COCA* distribution frequencies.

From Figure 2 it is clear that for all three items, the academic domain dominates, having more than twice the frequency found in the other domains. For *thus*, the dominance of the academic domain is overwhelming, while both *albeit* and *notwithstanding* have a certain currency in magazines and newspapers, perhaps due to their feature

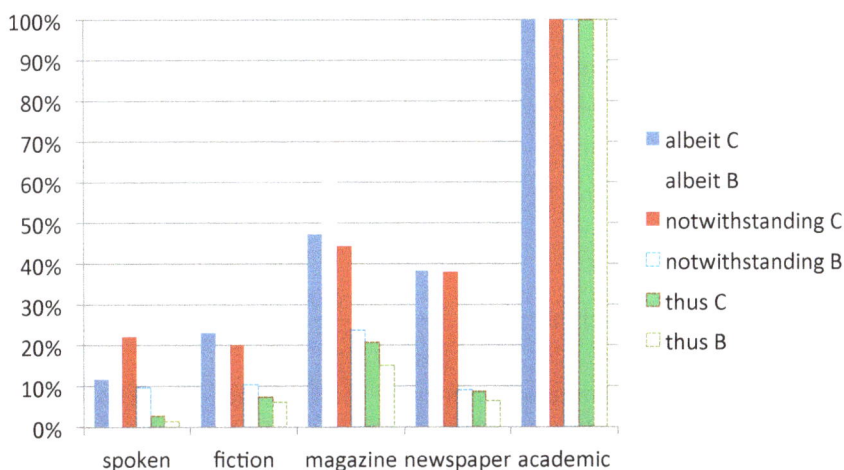

Figure 3. *COCA* (C) and *BNC* (B) distribution frequencies (comparable domains).

articles. With the possible exception of spoken *notwithstanding*, the three items show similar distribution patterns, with *thus* having the widest gap between the other domains and academic English. Via the chi-square test, both *albeit* and *thus* distributions are significant at p < .001, while *notwithstanding* has p < .0157.

Naturally, it is interesting to compare the British and American data. Since both corpora are available with the same (BYU) interface, this would appear to be simple, but the *BNC* data has the two extra categories of **non-academic** and **miscellaneous**, which in unknown fashion are redistributed in *COCA*'s fewer domains. Omitting those two *BNC* categories, our comparison looks like this (Figure 3).

The fit between these two geographical domains is quite good for both *albeit* and *thus*, which is not surprising, given that four of the five are written, the domains where BrE and AmE are traditionally considered to have the smallest differences. The odd man out is

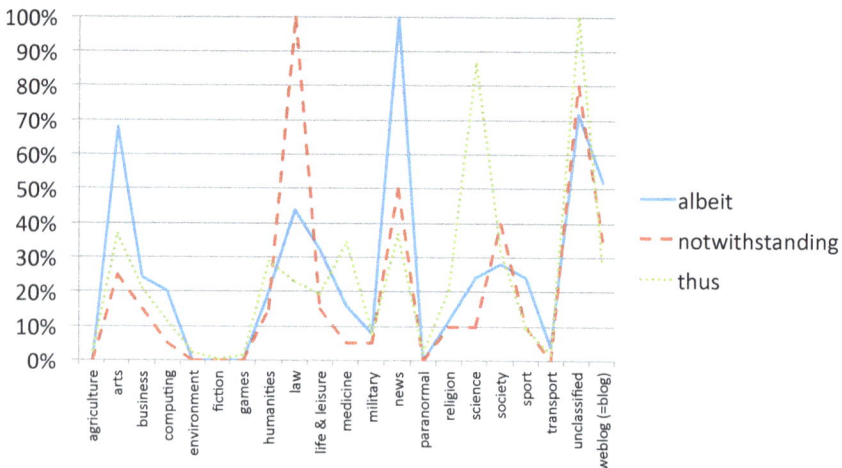

Figure 4. *OCE* distribution frequencies (SketchEngine interface).

notwithstanding, which seems to be more favored in AmE, again with the reservation for the *BNC* data loss.

Stepping up to an even larger corpus, the Oxford Corpus of English, a corpus from the early 2000s based on material from the Web, now supplemented to reach 1736 M, and including significant input from English in other parts of the world, we again find that *thus* is more frequent by an order of magnitude: 152.4 words per million, versus *albeit*

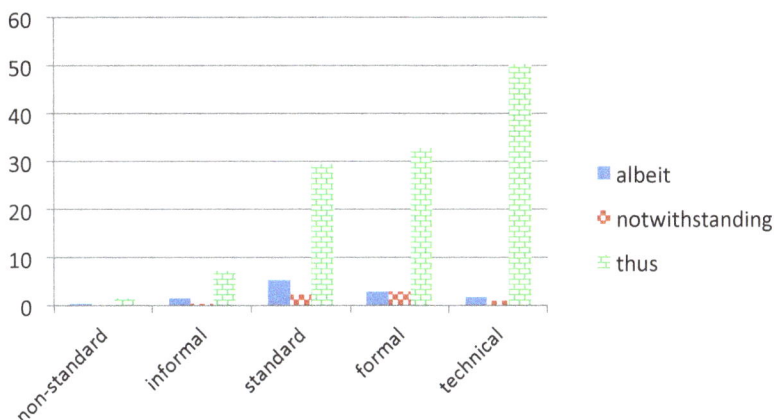

Figure 5. *OCE* frequencies vis-à-vis formality, per 1M words (SketchEngine interface).

and *notwithstanding* at 13.7 and 8.4, respectively. Comparing their frequency relative to the largest domain (SketchEngine provides 21 different domains), we see a largely parallel pattern for the three, including great differences between domain frequencies (Figure 4).[19] *Albeit* weighs in heavily in the arts, and above all, in news—perhaps an attempt to give news greater weight? Not surprisingly, *notwithstanding*'s single largest component is legal texts. *Thus*, however, turns out to be relatively evenly distributed, with the single spectacular exception of science texts, where it occurs three times more frequently than in any other domain (except the dubious "unclassified"). All three terms are relatively well represented in "weblogs", perhaps because these are relatively early blogs, when they had not yet reached the demotic level of today's twittering. Also of interest is that for all three terms, only a few domains reach levels more than 33% of the most frequent domain, again indicating that the distribution of these words is quite domain-sensitive.[20]

The SketchEngine software for the *OCE* also allows us to look at this data via degrees of formality, ranging from *non-standard* to *formal* and

---

[19] The values for the category "unclassified" are uniformly high, again suggesting that something fairly formal about them is escaping the categorization.
   A technical note: to keep the diagram legible, the type of graph has been changed, but the domains are of course independent of one another.

[20] In terms of raw numbers, these are quite robust samples, with 16,293 instances of *albeit*, 9,024 of *notwithstanding*, and 189,969 of *thus*, so that even one of the smallest, the fiction examples of *thus*, weighing in at 0.1 per million, still totals 109 separate tokens.

technical.²¹ Here, the most striking distribution is that of *thus*, whose use peaks in the *technical* texts (suggesting that this group, rather than *formal*, includes most scientific texts), but which is still a clear presence from the *standard* level on upward. The other, somewhat surprising factor is that *albeit* seems above all to be a marker of *standard* texts, as seen in the peaks in the arts and news domains; domains such as science and law are less entranced with its quasi-literary flavor, it seems.

5.2 Diachronic corpora

Here, we shall consider three very recent diachronic corpora: the *TIME* corpus (100 M words, 1923–1996), the *Corpus of Historical American English* (COCA; 406 M words, 1810–2009), and the *GOOGLE US/ UK* corpus (in two parallel parts: AmE 155 B words, BrE 34 B words, 1810–2000), all of them created at Brigham Young University, and with the same interface.

The *TIME* corpus is one of the few corpora that chart a single source over a long period.²² *Time Magazine* began publication in 1923, and this corpus includes all the texts in *Time* (excluding ads, picture captions, etc.) from its inception until 1996. Two factors are of particular importance when using this corpus: first, nearly all of its articles

---

²¹ Their category *technical* is clearly not automatically "more formal" than, say, *formal*, but presumably much narrower in domain. Since SketchEngine makes this division of the entire corpus, *technical* is included in the present discussion.
²² There is a small, but clear overlap between this corpus and both *COCA* and *COHA*, as the latter two corpora could hardly ignore *Time* when dealing with contemporary and historical American magazine writing.

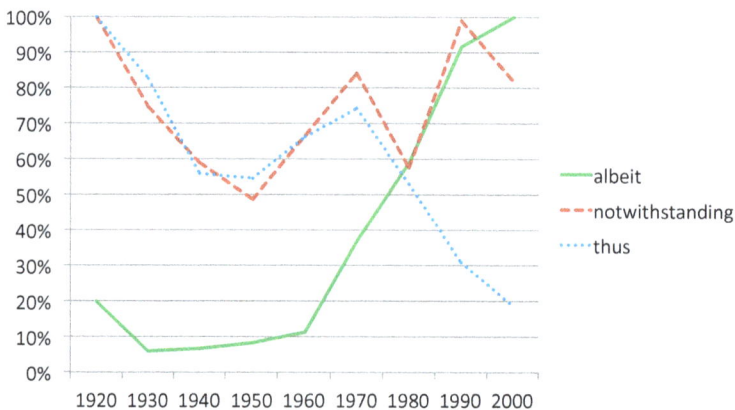

Figure 6. *TIME* distribution frequencies.

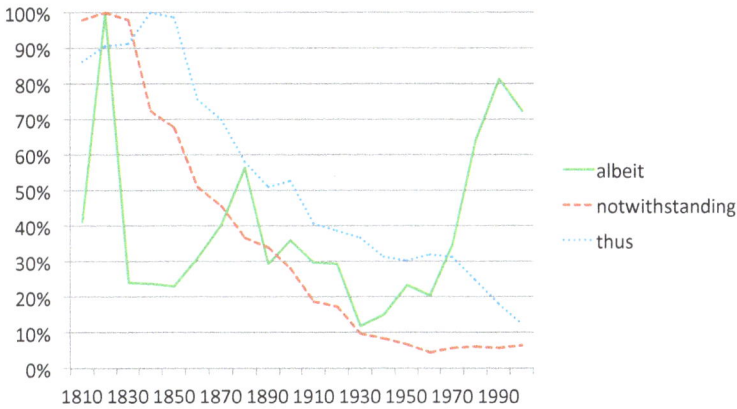

Figure 7. *COHA* distribution frequencies.

are collectively written, with a small staff of writers and editors interacting on many articles; second, it has been read in a large number of middle-class American homes for generations. As such, it is hardly representative of all American writing, but is disproportionately influential (although with a penchant for word play and *bons mots*). Again, the most revealing way to look at its statistics is to compare changes in relative frequencies per decade (Figure 6).

There are two striking changes for our word trio: first, *thus* has undergone a steep decline, broken only by a resurgence during the 60s and 70s, and ending up at less than 20% of its frequency in the 20s, from 347 per M words to 65 per M words after 2000. This is clearly in line with the specialization (tantamount to domain loss) we see in the contemporary corpora, where the vast majority of the modern instances are in science articles, a domain that does not feature prominently in *Time*. The second is the rise of *albeit*, which, at 0.6 per M words in the 1930s (i.e. less than the frequency of recondite words such as *germane*, which in turn is almost 40 times less frequent than *relevant*), rises uninterruptedly to 10.4 per M words in the 2000s. This is almost double the peak frequency of *notwithstanding*, which fluctuates from 3.2 to 5.5 per M words throughout this time period. The fluctuations of *notwithstanding* suggest that we may not be seeing change that is a trend, but rather a fairly stable term with a variation of ± 1 per M.

Turning to the *COHA* corpus, we shift to a more traditional type of linguist's corpus, i.e. a sample selected for linguistic purposes. It covers two centuries, and again our comparison is of relative frequencies (Figure 7). From the perspective of this longer time scale, we see that

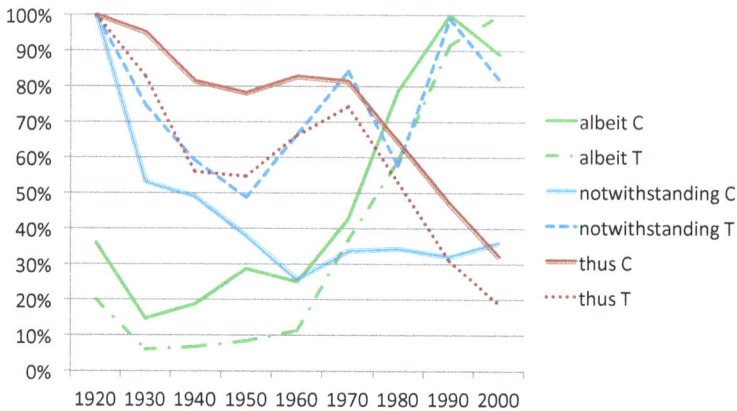

Figure 8. COHA and Time distribution frequencies, 1920s–2000s.

both *thus* and *notwithstanding* have declined drastically from the early 19th century to the present, and furthermore, rather consistently. The odd man out is *albeit*, which has an extraordinary peak in the 1820s (probably a result of its sampling,[23] and a more genuine higher level in the late 19th century, but which rises steadily from its low point of 1.22 per 1 M words in the 1930s to 7.41 in the 2000s. The shifts in *notwithstanding* and *thus* are both statistically significant (both with p < .001), but not the variation in *albeit*.

   If we compare these two corpora during the time period 1920–2010 (ignoring for the moment the obvious distortion effects of comparing an entire range of written language with the language of a small group of editors and writers working at one publishing house), we find the following (Figure 8). Both *Time* and *COHA* begin with a high level of *thus* and *notwithstanding*, but quite a low level of *albeit*. They match quite well for both *albeit* and *thus*, the former dipping, then rising sharply, and the latter dipping, then dropping off sharply (probably a reflection of the domain loss suffered by *thus*). *Time*'s retention of

---

[23] These early decades have far fewer works to draw upon than the rest of the corpus, and are thus more vulnerable to sampling peculiarities. In particular, of the 71 instances of *albeit* in the 1820s, 55 are from a single work, *The Buccaneers: A Romance of Our Own Count[r]y in Its Ancient Day* . . . [by] Yclept Terentius Phlogobombos [pseud, actually Samuel Judah].

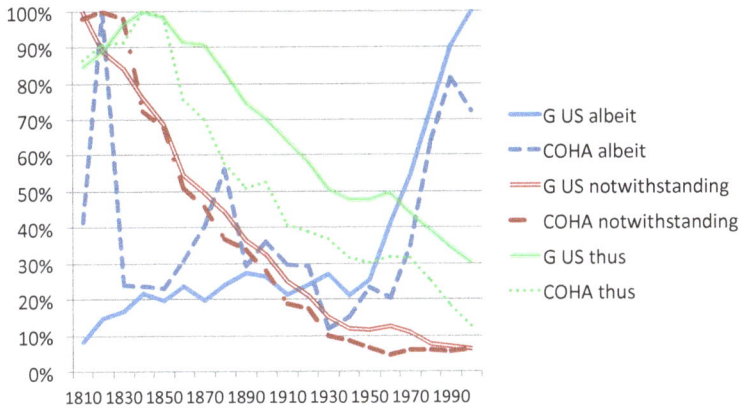

Figure 9. *Google US* and *COHA* distribution frequencies.

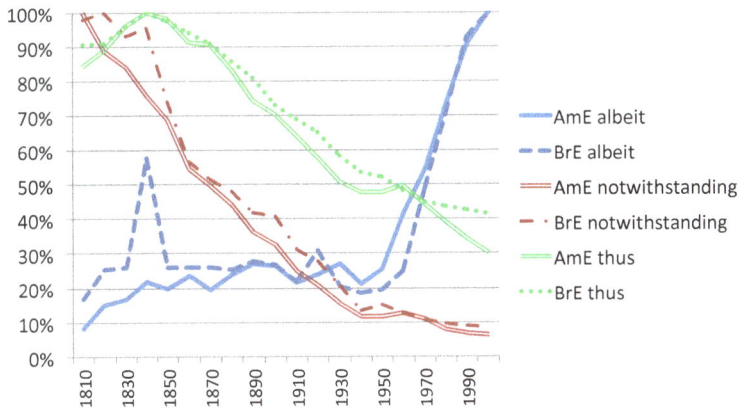

Figure 10. *Google* frequency distributions, 1810–2000.

notwithstanding, however, appears to be out of step with its reduced role in written language in general.[24]

Further comparison may now be made with material from the newly-released Google corpus from 1810 to 2000 (actually two parallel corpora of AmE and BrE, respectively). The vast amount of material available, with text masses in the billions of words, would seem to imply

---

[24] A word of caution about the 1920s issues of *Time*: a number of other searches indicate that the 20s was a period when the magazine was finding its level of readership, and is an atypical decade; e.g its use of *shall* dropped by 50% from the 20s to the 30s; no other decade-to-decade comparison indicates such a major shift for *shall*.

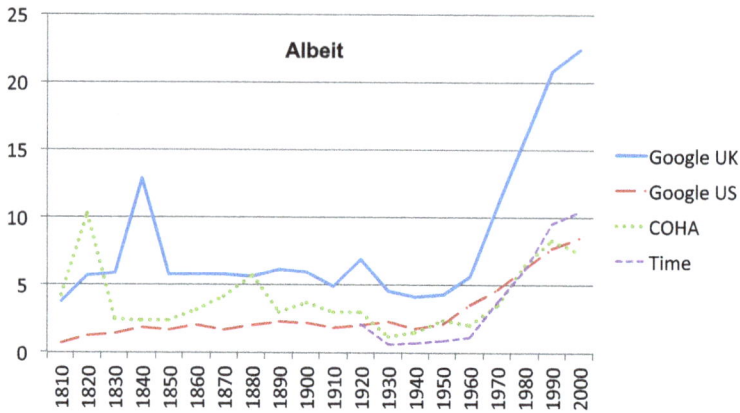

Figure 11. Comparison 1810–2000 for the three major diachronic corpora, plus *Time* (from 1923 to 1996).

a major improvement in quality of data, but in his comparison website, its creator Mark Davies remarks, "All three resources—Google Books (both versions) and COHA—give nearly the same results for [word and frequency] searches. The 400 million words in COHA is probably sufficient for nearly all searches of individual words and phrases."[25] It is consequently interesting to compare the *COHA* and *Google US* material for this period, as seen in Figure 9.

For *thus*, and even more so for *notwithstanding*, the fit appears to be quite good, but much less so for *albeit*, at least during several periods of the 19th century, whereas the 20th century appears to be a good fit. The explanation lies in the data mentioned in note 23, above: a single book in the 1820s accounts for 77% of the instances in the 1820s COHA data. This is a useful reminder when there are startling shifts in the data between adjacent periods.

Within Google, one can compare the relatively massive AmE corpus with the five times smaller BrE corpus for our three items (Figure 10). As the graph shows, the fit over two centuries is astonishingly good, with only a minor blip in the figure for *albeit* in BrE in the 1840s to disturb the picture.[26] The fit is also relatively good with the *COHA* data, and bears out Davies' prediction for both *thus* and *notwithstanding*.

[25] http://googlebooks.byu.edu/compare-googleBooks.asp, accessed March 10, 2014.
[26] The possibility that *albeit* was an OCR error for *(Prince Consort) Albert* was explored, but the readings are accurate; the Google image was quite clear in all instances checked—the BrE 1840s texts had a penchant for *albeit*.

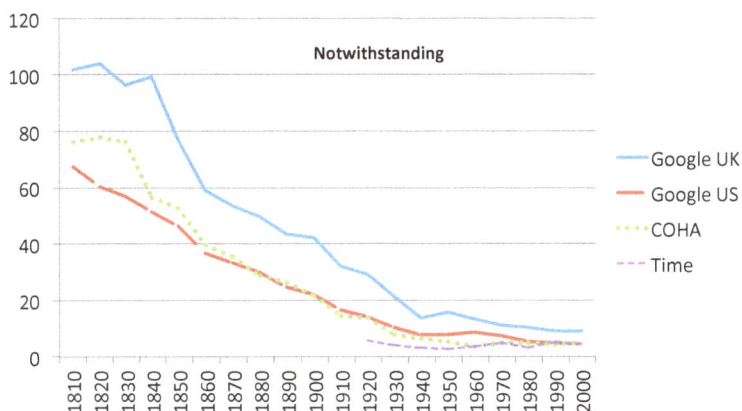

Figure 12. Comparison 1810–2000 for the three major diachronic corpora, plus *Time* (from 1923 to 1996).

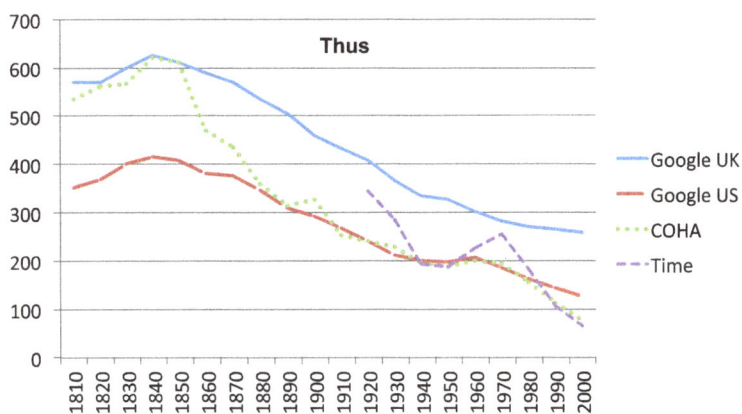

Figure 13. Comparison 1810–2000 for the three major diachronic corpora, plus *Time* (from 1923 to 1996).

The larger-sized Google data on *albeit* shows far less variation per decade, but from the 1950s onward shows the same sharp, consistent rise in its use.

Finally, combining these large corpora and looking at the four-corpora data for each word, i.e. the words in *Google US/GB, COHA* and *Time*, converted to frequencies per 1 M words, we see the same patterns in even stronger relief. The numbers are not fully consistent, particularly in the earlier decades, but what clearly emerges is that the

British frequencies are consistently a bit higher. This can of course indicate either that these three items are more markedly formal in AmE (and thus less used), or merely that the distribution of domains (and hence of formality) differs between BrE and AmE data in the corpora. Given that all three AmE corpora are in striking agreement for the 20th century, it seems probable that there is a difference between BrE and AmE invoved. Furthermore, whether BrE or AmE, it is clear that *notwithstanding* and *thus* are dropping in use (except for *thus* in scientific texts). As for *albeit*, the frequency per million is much lower than for most logical and attitudinal connectors, but rumors of its demise are clearly exaggerated (it is currently actually more frequent in AmE than *notwithstanding*). The key to its revival is to be found in the distributional data from the *OCE* corpus: the arts and news are the major domains for its use.

It seems reasonable to argue that earlier style mavens such as Fowler and Gowers (1965) were particularly aware of domains such as the arts, and less interested in stylistic uses in e.g. the sciences, so that it would not be surprising that Gowers should become aware of the revival of *albeit*—but the chronology is slightly wrong: the nadir in its use appears to have been the period 1930–1960, with the real rise taking place after 1965, the publication date of his revision of Fowler; moreover, it had always been more in use in BrE (his dialect) than in AmE, something that is even more clear today.[27]

6. Some final words

Since this paper has been written with a specific Stockholm Metaphor Festival scholar in mind, it may be worth mentioning that a review of the 2006 to 2010 articles from the Festival produced about 170,000 words in English (other languages discounted), and per million statistics of 22/M for *albeit*, 6/M for *notwithstanding* and 750/M for *thus*, figures which are quite close to the 2000 data for *albeit* and *notwithstanding*, but just about double the BrE figure for *thus*, which is not surprising, given that the majority of these papers were linguistically oriented, and follow the scientific pattern seen in e.g. Figure 4.

---

[27] Yet another recently-released web corpus, the *Corpus of Global Web-Based English* (also from BYU), reports post-2000 frequencies of 20.24 per M for BrE and 12.61 per M for AmE, which is in agreement with the other corpus data. Released in 2013, *GloWbE* contains 1.9 B words from the entire English-speaking world. See http://corpus2.byu.edu/glowbe.

It turns out that by and large, our corpus data from multiple corpora tends to be in agreement, although since these corpora are constructed with different metainformation, they will provide us with different types of information about matters such as style and domain. Even so, they are clearly of great help in enriching our picture of English, not to mention their forming the basis for the information found in our modern learner dictionaries. If there is one specific matter which the present corpus data suggests, it is that the Academic Word List needs to be re-examined, based on more extensive corpus data (as Gardner & Davies 2013 does).

Corpus data can of course only produce (massive) descriptive evidence of what people are doing with English at any given time, so that there will always be room for stylists and language police who wish to impose prescription upon us—even if they would do well to be far more heedful of the complexity of language, in particular the different domains within which language operates. All our data seems to indicate that while *notwithstanding* has indeed become relatively infrequent, *thus* has found a niche in scientific writing, where it seems to be flourishing. But the most astonishing of our triad is clearly *albeit*, which has returned from the moribund, to the joy of those who rejoice at seeing quirks of syntax live on, albeit in frozen form.

References

American Heritage Dictionary of the English Language. (1970). New York: American Heritage Publishing & Houghton Mifflin.

Biber, D., Conrad, S. & Leech, G. (2002). *Longman Student Grammar of Spoken and Written English.* Harlow, UK: Pearson Education.

Cambridge Advanced Learner's Dictionary. (2008). (3rd ed). Cambridge: Cambridge University Press.

Cambridge Dictionary of American English. (2000). Cambridge: Cambridge University Press.

Carter, R. & McCarthy, M. (eds) (2006). *Cambridge Grammar of English.* Cambridge: Cambridge University Press.

Celce-Murcia, M. & Larsen-Freeman, D. (1983). *The Grammar Book: An ESL/EFL Teacher's Course.* Rowley, Mass: Newbury House.

Clark, S. & Pointon, G. (2009). *Words: A User's Guide.* Harlow, UK: Pearson Education.

Clear, J. (1988). Trawling the Language: Monitor Corpora. M. Snell-Hornby (ed.), *ZuriLEX '86 Proceedings.* Tübingen: Francke.

Collins COBUILD English Language Dictionary. (1987). (1st ed.) London: Collins.

Collins COBUILD English Usage. (1992). Glasgow: HarperCollins.

Collins, F.H. (1956). *Authors' and Printers' Dictionary*. (10th ed.) London: Oxford University Press.

Copperud, R. (1964). *A Dictionary of Usage and Style*. New York: Hawthorn Books.

Corpus Of Contemporary American English (COCA), http://www.american corpus.org/.

Corpus Of Historical American English (COHA), http://corpus.byu.edu/coha.

Coxhead, A. (2000). A New Academic Wordlist. *TESOL Quarterly*, 34(2), 213–238.

Curme, G.O. (1983 [1931]). *A Grammar of the English Language*, Vol. II: *Syntax*. Essex, Conn: Verbatim.

Davies, M. http://googlebooks.byu.edu/compare-googleBooks.asp, accessed Mar. 10, 2014.

Elfstrand, D. & Gabrielsson, A. (1960). *Engelsk Grammatik för universitet och högskolor*. (4th ed.) Stockholm: Läromedelsförlagen.

Elster, C.H. (1999). *The Big Book of Beastly Mispronunciations*. New York: Houghton Mifflin.

Estling Vannestål, M. (2008). *A University Grammar of English with a Swedish Perspective*. Lund: Studentlitteratur.

Fisher, J.H. (ed.). (1977). *The Complete Poetry and Prose of Geoffrey Chaucer*. New York: Holt, Rinehart and Winston.

Fowler, H. (1926). *A Dictionary of Modern English Usage*. Oxford: Oxford University Press. See also Gowers (1965).

Fowler, H. & Fowler, F. (1930). *The King's English*. (3rd ed.) Oxford: Oxford University Press.

Gardner, D. & Davies, M. (2013). A New Academic Vocabulary List. *Applied Linguistics*, *doi: 10.1093/applin/amt015*, published Aug. 2, 2013.

Gowers, E. (1965). *Fowler's Modern English Usage*. (2nd ed.) Oxford: Oxford University Press. See also Fowler (1926).

Greenbaum, S. & Whitcut, J. (1988). *Longman Guide to English Usage*. Harlow: Longman.

Hundt, M. (1998). It is Important that This Study (Should) Be Based on the

Analysis of Parallel Corpora: On the use of mandative subjunctive in four major varieties of English. H. Lindquist et al. (eds) *The Major Varieties of English*, Papers from MAVEN 97, Växjö: Växjö University,159–175.

Jespersen, O. (1940). *A Modern English Grammar on Historical Principles, V: Syntax* (Fourth Volume). Copenhagen: Ejnar Munksgaard.

———. (1949). *A Modern English Grammar on Historical Principles, I: Sounds and spellings*. Copenhagen: Ejnar Munksgaard.

Johnson, S. (1783). *A Dictionary of the English Language...Abstracted from the Folio Edition*. London.

———. (1799). *A Dictionary of the English Language*. (8th ed.) London.

Leech, G. & Svartvik, J. (2002). *A Communicative Grammar of English*, 3rd ed. Harlow, UK: Pearson Education.

Longman Dictionary of Contemporary English. (2005). (4th ed.) Harlow, UK: Pearson Education.

Longman Dictionary of Contemporary English. (2009). (5th ed.) Harlow, UK: Pearson Education.

McEnery, T., Xiao, R & Tono, Y. (2006). *Corpus-based Language Studies: An advanced resource book*. London: Routledge.

Macmillan English Dictionary for Advanced Learners. (2007). (2nd ed.) Macmillan Education: Oxford.

Macmillan English Dictionary for Advanced Learners of American English. (2004). Macmillan Education: Oxford.

Macquarie Dictionary. (1997). (3rd ed.). Sydney: The Macquarie Library.

Manual of Style, A. (1969). (12th ed.) Chicago: University of Chicago Press.

Mencken, H.L. (1936). *The American Language*. (4th ed.) New York: Alfred A. Knopf.

———. (1948). *The American Language, Supplement Two*. New York: Alfred A. Knopf.

Merriam-Webster's Collegiate Dictionary. (2003). (11th ed.) Springfield, Mass: Merriam-Webster.

Merriam-Webster's Dictionary of English Usage. (1994). Springfield, Mass: Merriam-Webster.

Minugh, D. (2002). "Her COLTISH Energy Notwithstanding": An examination of the adposition *notwithstanding*. L. E. Breivik & A. Hasselgren (eds) *Language and Computers: From the COLT's Mouth... and others'*. Amsterdam: Rodopi, 213–29.

New Oxford Dictionary of English. (1998). Oxford: Oxford University Press.

Oshima, A. & Hogue, A. (2006). *Writing Academic English*. (4th ed.) Harlow, UK: Pearson Education.

Oxford Advanced Learner's Dictionary (ALD). (1963). (2nd ed.) Oxford: Oxford University Press.

Oxford Advanced Learner's Dictionary (ALD). (2005). (7th ed.) Oxford: Oxford University Press.

Oxford Advanced Learner's Dictionary (ALD). (2010). (8th ed.) Oxford: Oxford University Press.

Oxford American Dictionary of Current English. (1999). New York: Oxford University Press.

Oxford English Dictionary. (1933 [1928]). (1st ed.) Oxford: Oxford University Press.

OED Online. Accessed Feb. 25, 2014, at www.oed.com.

Poutsma, H. (1929). *A Grammar of Late Modern English. Part I: The sentence*, 2nd ed. Groningen: P. Noordhoff.

Quirk, R., Greenbaum, S, Leech, G. & Svartvik, J. (1985). *A Comprehensive Grammar of the English Language*. London: Longman.

Rissanen, M. (2002). On the Development of Concessive Prepositions in English. A. G. Fischer, G. Tottie, & H. M. Lehman (eds)*Text Types and Corpora : Studies in honour of Udo Fries*. Tübingen: Gunter Narr, 191–203.

Schmid, H.-J. (2000). *English Abstract Nouns as Conceptual Shells: From corpus to cognition*. Berlin: Mouton de Gruyter.

Svartvik, J. & Sager, O. (1996). *Engelsk universitetsgrammatik*. (2nd ed.) Stockholm: Almqvist & Wiksell.

———. (1977). *Engelsk universitetsgrammatik*. Stockholm: Esselte Studium.

Swan, M. (2005). *Practical English Usage*. (3rd ed.) Oxford: OUP.

Weber, B. (2010). *Sprachlicher Ausbau: konzeptionelle Studien zur spätmittelenglischen Schriftsprache*. Frankfurt am Main: Peter Lang.

Webster's New Collegiate Dictionary. (1993). (10th ed.) Springfield, Mass: Merriam-Webster.

Webster's New International Dictionary of the English Language. (1941). (2nd ed.) Springfield, Mass: Merriam.

Webster's Ninth New Collegiate Dictionary. (1988). Springfield, Mass: Merriam-Webster.

Wells, J. (ed.). (2008). *Longman Dictionary of English Pronunciation*. (3rd ed.) Harlow, UK: Pearson Education.

West, M. (1953). *A General Service List of English Words*. London: Longman, Green.

Corpora

British National Corpus, http://corpus2.byu.edu/bnc/.

British National Corpus, http://bncweb.lancs.ac.uk/bncwebSignup/user/login.php.

Brown Corpus (Brown University Standard Corpus of Present-Day American English), available via ICAME: http://icame.uib.no/newcd.htm.

Corpus of Global Web-Based English. http://corpus2.byu.edu/glowbe.

Dutch Web Corpus. 111 M words, accessed via SketchEngine, https://www.sketchengine.co.uk/.

Frown Corpus (Freiberg-Brown Corpus of American English), available via ICAME: http://icame.uib.no/newcd.htm.

FLOB Corpus (Freiburg-LOB Corpus of British English), available via ICAME: http://icame.uib.no/newcd.htm.

LOB Corpus (Lancaster-Oslo-Bergen Corpus of British English), available via ICAME: http://icame.uib.no/newcd.htm.

Oxford English Corpus (with BiWeC), 1736M words, accessed via SketchEngine, https://www.sketchengine.co.uk/.

Time Corpus. http://corpus.byu.edu/time/.

Wordbanks Online, http://www.collinslanguage.com/content-solutions/wordbanks.

15 Recent Changes in the Modal Area of Necessity and Obligation – A Contrastive Perspective[1]

Karin Aijmer
University of Gothenburg

Introduction

Recently we have witnessed a lively discussion about modal changes in contemporary English. Leech et al. (2009) have for instance shown, on the basis of corpora from different periods, that the modal auxiliaries in general and *must* in particular have declined in frequency over the relatively short period between 1960 and 1990. The changes affect both the epistemic and deontic meaning but have been particularly drastic for deontic *must*.

There are still many questions in the air; for example what do speakers use to compensate for the loss of the modal auxiliary (if anything). This question has given rise to the hypothesis that the disappearance of *must* is counterbalanced by the emergence and growth in the frequency of other modal elements in particular semi-modals. However the range of alternatives which have been studied has been fairly restricted.

The aim of my paper is to contribute to the discussion of the decline of the modal auxiliary *must* by a comparison with its Swedish cognate *måste* which has not undergone the same semantic developments. We can study both when *must* is chosen as a translation and when a different lexical item or construction is preferred. This approach can provide a rich panorama of expressions of obligation and necessity. Translations can also confirm hypotheses which have been suggested on the basis of monolingual corpora.

The structure of my paper is as follows. I will first discuss my methodology and the use of a parallel or translation corpus. I will then

[1] With many thanks to Bengt Altenberg for excellent comments on an earlier version of the article

How to cite this book chapter:
Aijmer, K. 2015. Recent Changes in the Modal Area of Necessity and Obligation – A Contrastive Perspective. In: Shaw, P., Erman, B., Melchers, G. and Sundkvist, P. (eds) *From Clerks to Corpora: essays on the English language yesterday and today.* Pp. 267–284. Stockholm: Stockholm University Press. DOI: http://dx.doi.org/10.16993/bab.o License: CC-BY.

analyse the translation paradigms with *must* and alternative realisations of obligation or necessity. The translations will also provide the raw material for a qualitative analysis contrasting the functions of *must* and its most frequent competitors. I will then compare the translation paradigms in fiction and non-fiction texts in order to look for text-type specific differences. My paper will end with a summary and a discussion of the advantages of using data from a parallel corpus.

2. Methodology

The data for the present study are taken from the English-Swedish Parallel Corpus (ESPC) (see Altenberg and Aijmer 2001). The corpus contains roughly comparable original texts in English and Swedish with their translations, altogether 2.8 million words. The Swedish and English texts have the same size and represent the same genres namely fiction and non-fiction texts. (see Table 1).

The relationship between *måste* or *must* in the original texts and their correspondences in the target texts can be exhibited as a translation paradigm showing how often *must* and *måste* correspond to each other in translation. The translations also show what the alternatives are when *must* and *måste* are not translated into each other.

3. The frequency of *must* and of *måste*

I became interested in the on-going restructuring of the English modality system through the observation that English *must* seemed to be much less frequent in English than its cognate *måste* in Swedish. There were 544 examples of *must* in the English originals in the corpus. There were more than twice as many examples of *måste* in the Swedish original texts (1104 examples). The difference in frequency is found both in fiction and non-fiction (See Table 2).

The smaller number of examples of *must* in the English original texts compared with Swedish *måste* is interesting against the background of

Table 1. Size of the English-Swedish Parallel Corpus.

	Number of words
Fiction	1,328,929
Non-fiction	1,475,582
Total	2,804,511

Table 2. *Must* and *måste* in the English and Swedish original texts. Normalized figures to 10,000 words in parentheses.

	English originals ('*must*')	Swedish originals ('*måste*')
Fiction	210 (1.58)	454 (3.42)
Non-fiction	334 (2.26)	650 (4.41)
Total	544 (1.94)	1104 (3.4)

what has been claimed about the decline of *must* in English and the emergence of competing variants.

The English-Swedish Parallel Corpus is designed as a bidirectional corpus which can be used to study translations between languages in two translation directions:

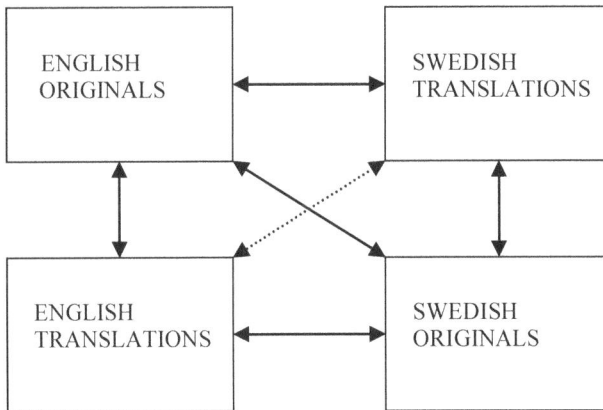

Figure 1. The structure of the English-Swedish Parallel Corpus.

We can therefore use the corpus to test the hypothesis that *must* is disappearing in the translation. *Must* and *måste* are cognates and 'favoured' correspondences in a translation perspective. According to Gutknecht and Rölle (1996: 237), 'modals should preferably be rendered by modals, because they correspond to each other in terms of various kinds of non-specificity.' If *must* is avoided in the translation this may therefore suggest that it is losing out in the competition with other grammaticalizing elements.

Correspondences between languages can be established by studying translations and sources. If *must* is in the process of disappearing we would also expect it to be less frequent in English sources of *måste* (going from Swedish translations to English originals).

4. Epistemic and deontic *must*

At the outset, a distinction needs to be made between deontic and epistemic meanings of *must*. Epistemic meaning has been defined in terms of a judgment by the speaker: 'a proposition is judged to be uncertain or probable in relation to some judgment' (van der Auwera and Plungian 1998: 81).

With *must* the speaker represents a situation as relatively certain:

1. "That's Davina Flory." I guessed it <u>must</u> be," Burden said quietly. (RR1)

Must can also be deontic. Deontic modality "identifies the enabling or competing circumstances external to the participant as some person(s), often the speaker, and/or some social or ethical norm(s) permitting or obliging the participant to engage in the state of affairs" (van der Auwera and Plungian 1998: 81).

2. I put a finger to his mouth: "Don't bring it up again. You must allow me this chance in Provence to make up my mind." (BR1)

4.1 Epistemic meaning

The epistemic meanings of *must* are generally infrequent. Only 109 examples (25%) of the examples of *måste* (454 examples) were epistemic and 328 (75%) deontic. Moreover when we compare Swedish *måste* in the epistemic meaning and English *must* we find a fairly high correspondence (Table 3).

Must dominated in the translations of Swedish epistemic *måste* (78.9%) and in the sources (83.5 %). The mutual correspondence between *måste* and *must* (based on the translations in both directions) is 81.2%.[2] Epistemic *must* seems to be stable. In diachronic terms it is not threatened by semi-modals which belong to the area of deontic modality (*have got to* was only found three times). (See further below.) In non-fiction texts (not shown in the table) epistemic *must* was even more infrequent than in fiction (24 examples) and the translations did not contain any alternatives.

The translations consist of modal auxiliaries (besides *must*) such as *could, might, will, would*. Other alternatives are adverbs (*obviously,*

---

[2]   Mutual correspondence refers to 'the frequency with which different (grammatical, semantic and lexical) expressions are translated into each other (Altenberg 1999: 254).

Table 3. The English Translations (SO->ET) and sources of Swedish *måste* (ST <-EO). Epistemic meanings. Fiction only.

Translation	Correspondence	Sources	Total
must	86 (78.9%)	91 (83.5%)	177 (81.2%)
surely	0	5	5
would (maybe)	1	3	4
have got to	2	1	3
(you) can be sure	2	0	2
could (perhaps)	2	0	2
will	0	2	2
I suppose	1	0	1
maybe	1	0	1
presumably	1	0	1
obviously	1	0	1
perhaps would	1	0	1
doubtless	1	0	1
sounds like	1	0	1
might	1	0	1
must surely	1	0	1
may	0	1	1
of course	0	1	1
I suppose	0	1	1
it is certain to	0	1	1
omission	6	0	6
other	1	2	3
Total	109	109	211

presumably, doubtless, maybe, perhaps) or verbs and adjectives (*you can be sure, I suppose, sounds like*).

4.2 Deontic modality

Deontic modality (obligation/necessity) is a more complex semantic field than epistemic modality. As shown by its translations deontic *must* has many competitors or what Leech et al. (2009) describe in diachronic terms as the present-day beneficiaries of *must*'s decline. For this reason I will focus on the deontic *must* and its competitors in the domain of obligation and necessity (Table 4).

Table 4. The English translations and sources of Swedish *måste* (SO ->ET and ST<-EO). Deontic meanings. Fiction only.

Correspondence	Translations	Sources	Total
have to	91 (27.7%)	91 (30.5%)	182 (29.1%)
had to	91 (27.7%)	81 (27.2%)	172 (27.5%)
must	78 (23.8%)	38 (12.6%)	116 (18.5%)
(have) got to	14 (4.3%)	19 (6.4%)	33 (5.3%)
need to	8	9	17
should	5	3	8
need (main verb)	2	4	6
will/would	2	4	6
is to/was to	4	1	5
ought to	4	0	4
imperative	1	3	4
be going to	1	2	3
had better	2	1	3
make sb do sth	3	0	3
it meant -ing	0	3	3
be due to	1	1	2
NP modification	0	2	2
formulaic	0	2	2
can't wait to	0	2	2
be in need of	1	0	1
be expected to	1	0	1
it was natural for X to	1	0	1
couldn't possibly	1	0	1
necessarily	1	0	1
past tense	1	0	1
could not help	1	0	1
it does not necessarily follow that	1	0	1
emphatic do	1	0	1
it's time	1	0	1
be required	0	1	1
want	0	1	1
be forced to	0	1	1

Table 4. Continued

Correspondence	Translations	Sources	Total	
inevitably	0	1	1	
know to do something	0	1	1	
be obliged to	0	1	1	
I don't mind	0	1	1	
could only	0	1	1	
omission	4	1	5	
other	7	23	30	
Total	328	298	626	

The percentages are based on 328 examples in the translations and 298 examples in the sources. In all there were 39 different translation alternatives. There is a low degree of mutual correspondence between *måste* and *must*. The mutual correspondence of *must* was 18.5% to be compared with *have to* which had a mutual correspondence of 29.1%. The higher frequency of *must* in the English translations than in sources may be induced by the high frequency of 'måste' in the Swedish original; cf Johansson (2007: 32–33) a 'translation effect'. The translator uses a cognate even when a more 'idiomatic' translation is available. *Have to* was used in translations (27.7%) and in sources (30.5%). The frequency of *have to* would have been even higher if I had included *had to*. However *had to* has been used as an alternative of *must* for syntactic reasons. It was used in roughly 23% of the examples (both in translations and sources) as a past tense form mainly in narrative contexts. *Had better* is associated with weaker obligation than *have to* and it only occurred three times as a correspondence. *Need to* was more frequent than *should* but not as frequent as *have got to*.

The translations draw attention to the fact that *must* has a large number of co-players in the domain of obligation/necessity. Many different grammatical categories are represented in the translations (see Table 5).

Other modal auxiliaries than *must* are *should, ought to, will/would*. A difference between English and Swedish is that English can express deontic modality by means of semi-modals. ' " Semi-modals" are not full modals but are verb constructions (...) which have been moving along the path of grammaticalization and have gradually acquired an

Table 5. Grammatical categories of deontic modality.

modal auxiliaries	must, should, ought to, will/would
semi-modals	have to, need to, have got to, be to, be due to, had better
modal adverbs	necessarily, inevitably
modal adjectives	it was natural for X to
modal nouns	be in need of
lexical verbs	be required, be forced to, be obliged to
idioms	I cannot wait to do, I don't mind doing
imperative	let us VP
NP modification	three points to consider
emphasis	emphatic do, prosodic stress

auxiliary-like function' (Leech et al. 2009: 91). The semi-modals with the meaning of obligation/ necessity mostly contain *have. Have to, have got to, had better* are all semi-modals. Less frequent semi-modals are *be to, be due to.* In addition we find modal adjectives and adverbs (*it was natural for X to, necessarily, inevitably*), verbo-nominal expressions of modality (*be in need of*), lexical verbs (*be obliged, forced, compelled*). More idiomatic translations are for example *I cannot wait to do.* The deontic *must* also shares directional force with the imperative as shown by the translations. *Three points to consider* can be paraphrased 'three points which need to or must be considered'. The translation is an example of NP modification. There is also a close association between deontic modality and emphasis.

4.3 Summing up deontic modality in fiction

Grammaticalization and change are lurking in the background when we interpret the translation correspondences. The frequency of a certain translation can reflect its status as a 'substitute' of the declining *must.* In view of the diachronic findings about the decline of *must* it is not surprising that *have to* is more frequent than *must* in translation. The increase of *have to* in fiction is remarkable compared to other studies. Biber et al. (1999: 489) have compared the frequencies of modals and semi-modals in different registers. *Must* and *have to* had the same frequency in fiction but *have to* was more frequent in the conversational data.

4.4 Competition between *must* and *have to*

The translation paradigms only provide the raw material for the semantic analysis. The meanings range from strong obligation or necessity (represented by *must* and *have to)* to weaker elements such as *should* or *need to. Have to* and *must* differ semantically. *Have to* (unlike *must*) refers to what van der Auwera and Plungian (1998:81) have described as participant-external necessity. Participant-external necessity makes reference to the circumstances that are external to the participants and make a state of affairs necessary.

> 3. För att hålla mig igång krävs inte mer än ett par 1,5 volts fickbatterier. Jag omsätter samma <u>mängd</u> energi som en 20-wattslampa. Vattenlösningen, som jag vilar i, måste vara helt steril. (PCJ1)
> To keep me going requires nothing but a couple of 1.5-volt batteries. I consume no more energy than a 20-watt bulb. The aqueous solution in which I rest <u>has to</u> be absolutely sterile. (PCJ1T)

In this example the source is clearly not the speaker but the properties of the aqueous solution.

If *must* is declining and *have to* is increasing in frequency we would expect the boundaries between them to be drawn up differently. The translations can be the basis for a deeper and more detailed analysis of the variation between *have to* and *must*. A factor such as the person of the subject has the advantage that it can be compared in the translations.

In the English Swedish Parallel Corpus *have to* was more frequent than *must* with an impersonal subject (e.g. generic *you*) than with the 'direct' *you*. It was also frequent with *we* as the subject (collective *we*)

Table 6. Variation between *have to* and *must* with different subjects.

Type of subject	must	have to
I	44	28
you generic	4	37
you direct	19	11
animate subject	32	44
we collective	8	17
non-animate subject	4	13
passive	2	15

or with the passive. *Must* on the other hand was more frequent with a first person subject and with the 'direct' *you* (Table 6).

The use of *have to* with a generic subject is illustrated in the following example:

4. Man <u>måste</u> lära sig ta skydd. (JMY1)
You <u>have to</u> learn how to take cover. (JM1T)

We can also be used impersonally:

5. Nu när det är krig <u>måste</u> man hjälpa varandra. (JMY1)
"Now that the war is on we <u>have to</u> help each other." (JMY1T)

Have to is used in an abstract way to make a recommendation (if something is favourable) or an instruction formulated in general terms.

The following example illustrates that *must* can have a strong emotional meaning urging the hearer to do something. According to Smith (2003: 259) such insistence can however sound odd in present-day English: 'Even where MUST is used with no obvious hint of speaker-imposed deontic meaning. …, in Present Day English it is liable to be perceived as off, perhaps because it sounds unduly insistent'.

6. Ja, faster <u>måste</u> förstå mej: det är en ära att få arbeta ihop med ett sånt snille. (ARP1)
"Yes. You <u>must</u> understand me, Auntie. It's an honour to be allowed to work with such a genius." (ARP1T)

Moreover *have to* unlike *must* can be softened and is therefore used when more politeness is required:

7. Då <u>måste</u> du stanna hemma från skolan och passa henne. (GT1)
"Then you <u>ll have to</u> stay home from school and take care of her." (GT1T)

8. Då <u>måste</u> jag sätta mig hos ålen. (KE1)
Then <u>I 'll have</u> to sit with the eel. (KE1T)

Other examples of softening are illustrated by *would have to* and *might have to* (mitigating an inconvenience): The speaker's staying for a month may involve an inconvenience for the hearer:

9. Kanske <u>måste</u> jag stanna hos er en hel månad. (KOB1)
"<u>I might have to</u> stay with you for a whole month." (KOB1T)

Checking in with the concierge involves some extra effort for the visitor:

10. A visitor <u>would have</u> to check in with the concierge. (FF1)
En besökare <u>måste</u> anmäla sig hos portvakten. (FF1T)

5. Non-fiction translations

By including non-fiction in the study of *must* and its competitors we can get a more detailed and richer picture of the expressions of obligation and necessity. The number of examples is higher in non-fiction than in fiction texts. There were 526 examples in translation of *måste* and 412 examples in sources (deontic examples only). There were 41 different competing forms (most of them occurring only once or twice). See Table 7:

Table 7. English translations and sources of Swedish 'måste'.

Correspondence	Translations	Sources	Total
must	295 (56%)	177 (43%)	472 (50.3%)
have to	63 (12%)	100 (24.3%)	163 (17.4%)
need to	27 (5.1%)	47 (11.4%)	74 (7.9%)
should	48 (9.1%)	16 (3.9%)	64 (6.8%)
had to	17 (3.2%)	44 (10.7%)	61 (6.5%)
need main verb	7	5	12
mean V-ing	1	5	6
ought to	4	1	5
to be -ed	4	0	4
require	3	0	3
it is necessary	2	1	3
to-modification	1	2	3
would	2	1	3
oblige to	1	2	3
have got to	1	2	3
was made to	2	0	2
will inevitably	2	0	2
(what may happen is) for X to V	2	0	2
it is essential	2	0	2

Table 7. Continued

Correspondence	Translations	Sources	Total
will be to	1	1	2
should like to	2	0	2
be bound to	0	2	2
was compelled to	1	0	1
I have no choice but	1	0	1
I cannot help but	1	0	1
agree on the need to	1	0	1
appreciate the need to	1	0	1
be of the need to	1	0	1
to be compelled to	1	0	1
I would note	0	1	1
subject to	0	1	1
was to	0	1	1
entail the need	0	1	1
I regret to say	0	1	1
I'm sorry to tell you	0	1	1
embarrassed to speak to me	0	1	1
forced to	0	1	1
recognize the necessity of	0	1	1
necessarily	0	1	1
other	16	25	41
ø	11	2	13
total	526	412	938

Måste was translated into 'must' in 56% of the examples and in the examples with English sources it was found in 50.3% of the examples. *Have to* was chosen less often. *Need to* and *should* are also among the most frequent correspondences. It is interesting to make comparisons with fiction where the percentages of the most frequent variants are quite different. The ranking of the most frequent variants in fiction and non-fiction is shown in Table 8 (percentages only).

Must was more frequent both in translations and in sources in non-fiction reflecting the fact that *must* has not declined in frequency to the same extent as in fiction. *Have to*, on the other hand is less frequent in non-fiction where it is ranked below *must*. *Had to* is more frequent

Table 8. Ranking of the most frequent variants in fiction and non-fiction texts.

	Non-fiction	Fiction
must	50.3%	18.5%
have to	17.4%	29.1%
need to	7.9%	17 (2.7%)
should	6.8%	8 (1.3%)
had to	6.5%	27.5%
(have) got to	0.32	5.3%

in fiction reflecting the fact that it is associated with narrative contexts. *Have got to (gotta)* was rare in non-fiction. On the other hand. *need to, should (*and *ought to)* were strikingly more frequent in non-fiction than in fiction.

5.1 Text-type specific correspondences

Certain correspondences are text-type specific. *Have to, need to* and *should* function as rhetorical devices in non-fiction texts (for example EU regulations) imposing an obligation also when no specific individual is mentioned. The following example uses *have to* (and *must*).

> 11. Den andra faktorn är att <u>vi måste</u> se till att skaffa en utbildning som går att använda under lång tid när vi skaffar **oss** en utbildning. <u>Det måste</u> vara en bred grundutbildning, eftersom samhället förändras i allt snabbare takt. Det går inte att ha snabba utbildningar. Vidare <u>måste det</u> också vara ett livslångt lärande. (EAND1)

> The other factor is that <u>we must ensure</u> that when we obtain an education we obtain one which can be used for a long time. <u>There has to be</u> a broad basic education, because society is changing ever more rapidly. It is not possible to have a quick education. Furthermore, <u>there has to also be</u> life-long learning. (EAND1T)

The reference is to a situation in the future when *have to* is used. The speaker envisages a broad basic education for everyone. The obligation is only weak since no individual is under the obligation to do something. *Must* in the same sentence implies greater imposition (we must ensure that we obtain a broad discussion even in the face of resistance).

Should is weaker than *have to* or *must*. It merely expresses that the situation referred to is favourable to the speaker, the hearer or to people in general:

12. Det viktigaste <u>måste</u> väl ändå vara Sveriges ekonomi och dess förmåga att kunna 'platsa' i sällskapet när det gäller inflation, ränte-villkor osv. (EAND1)

The most important aspects <u>should</u> still be Sweden's economy and its eligibility for a place in the club in terms of inflation, interest rates and so on. (EAND1T)

When *should* and stronger deontic forms are used in the same con-text they overlap semantically. The ordering between *must* and *should* could be changed without any difference in meaning:

13. Särskild vikt <u>måste</u> läggas vid tidig förvarning och tidigt ager-ande i konfliktlösning. Förebyggande diplomati måste ytterligare stärkas. (LHW1)
There <u>must</u> be a particular focus on early warning and early action in conflict resolution. Preventive diplomacy <u>should be</u> further strength-ened. (LHW1T)

Need to is particularly frequent in non-fiction texts. However it is not used with its basic meaning of internal necessity or compulsion but in a more abstract sense imposing an obligation on a non-specific individual. Because of its basic meaning *need to* ('having a need') is especially appropriate to express that something is a desirable goal or in the hearer's best interest. Like *should* and *have to* it was frequent with the collective *we* or with a following passive. The combination *we need to* was used as a correspondence (as a translation and as a source) in 34 examples or almost half of the examples of *need to* (also when the Swedish original did not contain 'we') and *need* with a fol-lowing passive verb in 25 examples. When the subject was not *we* it was for instance 'Countries of the European Union' or 'Swedes living and working abroad'. Leech et al. (2009: 111) emphasise the strate-gic or manipulative function of *need to:* 'Here a double mitigation of imperative force occurs: not only is obligation represented as in the best interests of 'us', but by referring to 'we' rather than 'you' as the people with the need, the writer imposes a collective obligation on an often rather vague community of people including the addresser and the addressees'. [3]

---

[3] Nokkonen (2006: 48) also points out cases where 'we need' is used in an imper-sonal, 'strong' way. She finds examples of this use in informative genres in the FLOB corpus.

14. Det <u>måste</u> bli en omprövning av de traditionella attityderna gentemot äldre och de roller som man vill ge dem. Speciellt gäller detta på arbetsmarknadsområdet. (EISC1)
We <u>need to</u> review our traditional attitudes towards senior citizens and rethink the roles we expect them to play in society. This applies particularly to the world of work. (EISC1T)

Rather than saying 'you must' (which is strongly impositive), the more polite *we need to* is used strategically as a way of urging an individual or the community in general to do something.

With a passive following *need* and a third person subject no direct reference is made to the speaker and hearer:

15. Flexibiliteten för medlemsstaterna <u>måste</u> matchas av en grupp indikatorer som skall identifiera behovet. (EMCC1T)
The flexibility for Member States <u>needs to</u> be matched by a range of indicators to identify need. (EMCC1)

The use of *need* conveys that the action (matching the flexibility of EU member states by certain criteria) is judged to be favourable (needs to be done). The imposition is only expressed weakly since it is not directed to a special individual.

There is a great deal of overlap between *need to* and other markers as indicated by examples where they are used in the same neighbourhood:

16. Alla bidrag för att nå Kyotomålen <u>måste</u> användas, men man <u>måste</u> också ha deras inbördes relationer klara för sig;. (EVIR1)
<u>Maximum efforts should be made</u> to meet the Kyoto targets, but <u>we still need</u> to keep a sense of proportion.

Should and *need* are used in a similar way. Their ordering can therefore be exchanged without a difference in meaning.

6. Conclusion

The present study can be seen as a complement to comparative historical corpus studies of *must* and its changes over time. The developments and changes in the area of modality which have taken place between 1960 and 1990 are at least to some extent visible in translations. Translations can therefore confirm observations which have been made on the basis of monolingual corpora about the decline of *must* and the emergence of semi-modals and other variants.

- The translations confirm the observation that *must* has declined above all in the area of deontic modality

- The translations also confirm the hypothesis that semi-modals are becoming more frequent to fill the gap left by *must*
- The translations also confirm the proposal that other modal auxiliaries such as *need to* and *should* compete with *must* and *have to*

The translations also showed that:
- *must* was more frequent than *have to* in non-fiction suggesting that the decline of *must* has made less progress there
- *should/ought to* and *need* were more frequent in non-fiction than in fiction
- *have got to* was infrequent in non-fiction

Translations also have certain advantages over monolingual corpora. In a monolingual corpus the range of forms with obligation/necessity meanings competing with *must* is not apparent. Monolingual studies have mainly discussed the rivalry between *must* and a few selected semi-modals.

Translations on the other hand provide a large number of variants of *must*. They may therefore add something to the picture of who the players are in the semantic domain of obligation and necessity. As an extra bonus they can also contribute to the discussion of the factors motivating the choice of a particular form. Leech et al. (2009: 114) used the term 'ecology' to capture the idea that each form [in the same field of meaning] 'evolves its own niche in the expression of modality, expanding, contracting or maintaining its "habitat" in relation to other, partially competing, forms'. The translations show that obligation and necessity can be expressed in many different ways and that there are conventions for how the different forms are used. In fiction *have to* (unlike *must*) was generally used with generic or impersonal subjects to make recommendations or to give instructions. The area of semantic overlap between *must* and *have to* is therefore restricted to certain contexts. *Have to* was used as a mitigator unlike *must* which was insistent and emotional.

In non-fiction texts *have to, should* and *need to* were typically used as rhetorical strategies when the speaker addresses a vague community of individuals. They were for instance used with a similar function in contexts with the passive or *we* as the subject. However the high frequency of *need to* and *should* may also have to do with their basic meaning to refer to what is beneficial or the right thing to do.

References
Primary sources:

Fiction –Swedish originals

ARP1   Pettersson, Allan Rune, Frankenstein's faster-igen. Stockholm 1989.
GT1   Tunström, Göran, Juloratoriet. Stockholm 1983.
HM2   Mankell, Henning, Den vita lejoninnan. Stockholm 1993.
KE1   Ekman, Kerstin, Händelser vid vatten. Stockholm 1993.
KOB1   Bornemark, Kjell-Olof, Handgången man. Stockholm 1986.
MS1   Scherer, Maria, Kejsarvalsen. Stockholm 1983.

Fiction –English originals

BR1   Brink, André, The wall of the plague. London 1984.
FF1   Forsyth, Frederick, The fourth protocol. London 1984
RR1   Rendell, Ruth, Kissing the gunner's daughter. London 1992.

Non-fiction-Swedish translator/author

EAND1 Europaparlamentets överläggningar.
EISC1 Europaparlamentets överläggningar.

Secondary sources:

Altenberg. B. (1999). Adverbial connectors in English and Swedish: Semantic and lexical correspondences. In Hasselgård, H. & S. Oksefjell (eds) *Out of Corpora. Studies in Honour of Stig Johansson*. Amsterdam and Atlanta, GA: Rodopi, 249–268.

Altenberg, B. & K. Aijmer. (2001). The English-Swedish Parallel Corpus: A resource for contrastive research and translation studies. Mair, C. & M. Hundt (eds) *Corpus Linguistics and Linguistic Theory. Papers from the 20th International Conference on English Language Research on Computerized Corpora (ICAME 20), Freiburg im Breisgau 1999*. Amsterdam and Atlanta, GA: Rodopi, 15–33.

Biber, D., S. Johansson & G. Leech. (1999). *Longman Grammar of Spoken and Written English*. London: Longman.

Gutknecht, C. & L.J. Rölle. (1996). *Translating by Factors*. New York: State University of New York Press.

Johansson, S. (2007). *Seeing Through Multilingual Corpora. On the Use of Corpora in Contrastive Studies*. Amsterdam/Philadelphia: John Benjamins.

Leech, G., M. Hundt, C. Mair,. & N. Smith. (2009). *Change in Contemporary English: a Grammatical Study*. Cambridge: Cambridge University Press.

Nokkonen, S. (2006).The semantic variation of NEED TO in four recent British English corpora. *International Journal of Corpus Linguistics* 11:1, 29–71.

Smith, N. (2003). Changes in the modals and semi-modals of strong obligation and epistemic necessity in recent British English. In Facchinetti, R., M. Krug & F. Palmer (eds) *Modality in Contemporary English*. Berlin and New York: Mouton de Gruyter, 240–266.

van der Auwera, J. & V. Plungian. (1998). Modality's semantic map. *Linguistic Typology* 2: 79–124.

16 Motion to and Motion through: Evidence from a Multilingual Corpus [1]

Thomas Egan
Hedmark University College

1. Introduction

Over the course of the last twenty years, there has been a considerable amount of comparative research into the coding of motion events in various languages (see, for instance, Filipović & Jaszczolt 2012, Hickmann & Robert 2006, Viberg 1998, 2003, 2013). This research has led to a reassessment and subsequent refinement of Talmy's typology (1991, 2000), according to which languages are said to be either satellite-framed or path-framed. According to Talmy, satellite-framed languages, such as English, tend to code manner of motion in the verb and path of motion in an adverbial (particle) in self-motion constructions, i.e constructions in which it is the syntactic subject which moves, as in *He walked to work*. Path-framed languages, such as Spanish, tend to code path in the verb and manner, if at all, in an adverbial. In recent years this typology has been expanded to include so-called equipollent framing, found in various serial verb languages (Slobin 2006). The clear dichotomy proposed by Talmy has also been nuanced by scholars who point to the co-existence of several patterns of framing in one and the same language. Kopecka (2006) and Pourcel and Kopecka (2005), for example, propose such a hybrid situation for French.

In this chapter I take a fresh look at satellite- and path-framing in English and French in a comparative study of codings of self-motion predications

---

[1] I would like to thank the editors for inviting me to contribute to this volume in honour of Nils-Lennart. I would also like to thank two anonymous referees for helpful and insightful comments on my chapter.

How to cite this book chapter:
Egan, T. 2015. Motion to and Motion through: Evidence from a Multilingual Corpus. In: Shaw, P., Erman, B., Melchers, G. and Sundkvist, P. (eds) *From Clerks to Corpora: essays on the English language yesterday and today*. Pp. 285–302. Stockholm: Stockholm University Press. DOI: http://dx.doi.org/10.16993/bab.p License: CC-BY.

in which the path either traverses a space or area ('through-ness') or leads up to a goal ('to-ness'). The reason for choosing these two path types is that French in particular is said to avoid the use of manner verbs with telic actions in general (Aske 1989: 6) and actions involving boundary-crossing in particular (Cappelle 2012: 189). In order to carry out a comparison of types of predication in two languages one needs a reliable *tertium comparationis* (see Jaszczolt 2003, Johansson 2007: 39, Krzeszowski 1990: 15). Much earlier research into the ways in which languages code motion events made use of a *tertium comparationis* in the form of events in a picture book (such as the Frog story: see Berman & Slobin 1994) or in short video snippets, which are described by participants in the experiment. The Oslo Multilingual Corpus (OMC), provides the *tertium comparationis* for the present study, where expressions in a source language serve as grounds for the comparison of their translations into two or more languages (see Egan 2013, Egan & Rawoens 2013).

I take as my starting point Norwegian predications in the OMC of self-motion events containing two path prepositions, *til* (= to) and *gjennom* (= through), and compare the English and French translations of these predications. In section 2 I introduce the corpus and explain briefly why I consider such a corpus to be suitable for this sort of study. Sections 3 and 4 compare English and French renderings of the notion of 'through-ness' and 'to-ness', as these are coded by the Norwegian prepositions *gjennom* and *til*. The results of the investigation of the two sorts of path predications are compared in section 5. Finally, section 6 contains a summary and conclusion.

2. Multilingual corpora as sources of *tertia comparationis*

In a comparative study such as the present one, which is based on English and French translations of Norwegian predications, the *tertium comparationis* is given by the original Norwegian texts. This *tertium comparationis* can, of course, only be viewed as a guarantor of semantic equivalence between the English and French expressions to the extent that the translators have aimed to convey as much as possible of the meaning of the original texts. My own experience of working with translation corpora has led me to believe that professional translators try to convey as much as possible of the sense of the original text most of the time. One will inevitably come across instances of mistranslation or non-translation, but the former are very rare in the OMC in my experience, which in itself testifies to the quality of the translations in the corpus. More common than mis-translation is the complete omission by a translator of a predication in the original text. In cases where one of two translators whose texts are being compared omits to translate a predication in the source text, one has no grounds for comparing them. Both the translated and non-translated version of this item must accordingly be excluded from the comparative study.

The OMC was compiled under the direction of Stig Johansson (see Johansson 2007). The No-En-Fr-Ge part of the corpus contains texts in four languages, consisting of long extracts from five Norwegian novels translated into English, French and German. For the present study I only looked at the English and French translations. A multilingual corpus has at least two advantages over a bilingual translation corpus. In the first place it allows for the comparison of identical text types, in that both texts being compared are translations, whereas in working with a bilingual translation corpus one is comparing an original text with a translation. Given that translated texts differ from original texts along various parameters, it makes obvious sense to compare one translation to another translation. In the second place, the examination of comparable translations in a multilingual corpus allows us to estimate the overlap between equivalent expressions in the two languages being compared.

My *tertium comparationis* comprises all Norwegian predications of self-motion events containing the two path prepositions, *gjennom* and *til* in the OMC. I downloaded all tokens containing the two forms in the corpus, then extracted all tokens coding motion events and finally discarded tokens coding caused motion, by which I mean tokens containing an explicit causer who/which causes someone/something to move along a path (such as 'She drove him to work'). All predications of motion without an explicit causer, in other words all S-V-A sentences, were categorised as coding self-motion, irrespective of the degree of agentivity of the mover. A glance at a bilingual dictionary or contrastive grammar will show that Norwegian *gjennom* codes relations that may be rendered in English by *through* and in French by *à travers*, among other prepositions. Similarly, Norwegian *til* codes relations that may be rendered in English by *to* and in French by *à*. My primary interest, however, is not in the correspondences between the Norwegian original and its translations into the other two languages, but in the correspondences between the two sets of translations. To this end, having extracted all the occurrences in the OMC of Norwegian *gjennom* (110 tokens) and *til* (664 tokens) in self-motion predications, the Norwegian originals were set aside and comparisons drawn between the English and French renderings of these predications.

One point that should be made about the data is that Norwegian is a satellite-framed language like English but unlike French.[2] Moreover, all the original Norwegian tokens contain a path preposition. Slobin (2006: 70) claims that "in translations [...] manner salience follows patterns of the target, rather than source language". If he is correct, the fact that Norwegian is satellite-framed should not affect the results of the comparison, at least as far as coding of manner is concerned. This contention of Slobin's has, however, been disputed by Cappelle (2012), who maintains that translations of motion predications will tend to some extent to borrow the form of the original text, irrespective of typological differences between the two languages involved. One should bear this argument in mind in interpreting the data presented in the next two sections.

3. English and French strategies for coding 'through-ness'

As mentioned in the previous section, the *tertium comparationis* for my analysis of 'through-ness' consists of codings in Norwegian of this concept by means of the preposition/particle *gjennom*. The main definition of *gjennom* in *Norsk Ordbok*, the closest Norwegian equivalent to the *OED*, is:

> [U]sed about a movement or something perceived as motion which takes place in (within, surrounded by) that which is encoded by the landmark [i.e. the prepositional object] from one end or side all the way to the other, containing the whole landmark from start to finish; (in) from the one side or end and (out) to the other. (*Norsk Ordbok* 2002, my translation)[3]

---

[2] In fact Norwegian is rather more satellite-framed than English. As a result of the Norman conquest English contains path verbs such as *enter* and *descend*, where Norwegian has a combination of a verb and a particle. One reviewer points out that Old English already contained some path verbs of native origin such as *stigan* which can be used in the sense 'ascend'. This is certainly true, but it is also true of Old Norse, with the verb *stiga* being cognate with OE *stigan*, for instance. The point is that the number of such verbs in English increased in Middle English.

[3] The original definition reads: "**Gjennom** el **igjennom** prep, adv 1 a) brukt om rørsle el noko oppfatta som rørsle for å uttrykkja at ho går føre seg i (innanfor, omslutta av) det som styringa nemner frå den eine enden, den eine sida heilt ut til (på) den andre, at ho omfattar det som er uttrykt i styringa frå byrjing til slutt; (inn) frå den eine og (ut) til den andre sida el enden av". (*Norsk Ordbok* 2002)

This definition of Norwegian *gjennom* is very similar to standard definitions of the prototype of *through*, as described for example by Egan (2012: 44), Lee (2001: 49), Leech (1969: 181), Lindstromberg (1998: 31), and Tyler and Evans (2003: 219). The similarity in the prototypical senses of Norwegian *gjennom* and English *through* is reflected in the number of occurrences of *through* in the English translations, 81 of which (74%) contain the form. This prototypical sense of *through* is illustrated here by examples (1) and (2), with the path in italics.[4]

(1) a. We began to walk slowly *through the galleries*, and up to the first floor. (JG3TE)
   b. Nous déambulâmes un moment *à travers les salles*, puis montâmes au premier étage. (JG3TF)

(2) a. I suggested I could walk with him *through the Retiro Park*. (JG3TE)
   b. Je proposai de l'accompagner *à travers le Retiro*. (JG3TF)

The French versions of (1) and (2) both contain the preposition *à travers*. The prototypical sense of this preposition, according to the definition in *Dictionnaire de l'Académie française*, differs from its English counterpart in emphasising the central portion of the landmark, the space or area through which the path extends (often referred to as a 'container' in the literature), backgrounding the elements of entrance and exit.

À TRAVERS, AU TRAVERS DE, locative preposition. Going from one side to the other, crossing: À travers is mostly used to code an open or free passage; Au travers de on the other hand is used to code a passage made between obstacles, or crossing or penetrating an obstacle; however this distinction is not rigorously observed. *(Dictionnaire de l'Académie française*, 8ᵉ edition: my translation)[5]

---

[4] The English and French versions of all tokens are cited in the text itself. The first part of the code, 'JG3' in (1) for example, refers to the text in the OMC from which the example has been taken. 'TE' stands for translated text in English, 'TF' translated text in French. The corresponding Norwegian originals are listed in an appendix.

[5] The 8ᵗʰ rather than the 9ᵗʰ, and most recent, edition of the dictionary has been used, as the online version of the 9ᵗʰ edition had not reached the letter 't' at the time of writing. The original definition reads "À TRAVERS, AU TRAVERS DE, loc. prép. En allant d'un bord à l'autre, en traversant. *À travers* se dit principalement pour désigner un Passage vide, libre; *Au travers de* se dit plutôt, au contraire, pour désigner un Passage qu'on se fait entre des obstacles, ou en traversant, en pénétrant un obstacle; mais cette distinction n'est pas toujours rigoureusement observe" (Dictionnaire de l'Académie française, 8ᵉ edition).

Note that the French definition of *á travers*, although not *au travers de*, differs from its English and Norwegian counterparts in making no reference to either entry into nor exit from a container. It is perhaps therefore not surprising that there are only 22 tokens in the French translations (20%) in which path is coded by *à travers*. Indeed French translators actually prefer to employ prepositions other than *à travers* to code motion 'through-ness'. Moreover, while the basic sense of 'through-ness', as coded by Norwegian *gjennom*, is a path relation involving subcomponents of 'entrance to', 'crossing of' and 'exit from' an area or container, only the central portion of the path, denoting the crossing of the area or container, is salient in all tokens in Norwegian. (Note that in the translation of the definition of *gjennom* above, the prepositions *in* and *out* are enclosed in brackets.) In addition, many of the French translations contain a prepositional phrase coding the area or container within which the motion event takes place (the 'site') rather than the actual path taken through the site by the mover.[6] Such translations either code the path in the verb, as in (3b), or leave it up to the addressee to infer the extension of the path, as in (4b). There are 20 examples of the preposition *dans* in the French texts, as opposed to just two of *in* in the English ones.

(3) a. During the summer, Dina began wandering *about the house*. (HW2TE)
    b. Dina recommença à *circuler dans la maison* cet été-là. (HW2TF)

(4) a. When he walked *through town* ... (BHH1TE)
    b. Lorsqu'il déambulait *dans la ville* ... (BHH1TF)

In the English version of (3) the prepositional phrase codes similar information to the verb in the French version, that the path extends in a non-linear fashion throughout the space comprised by the dwelling. The prepositional phrase in the French version just denotes the locus (site) of movement. Similarly, in (4a) we are given to understand that the path extends from (near to) one side of the town to the other, while from (4b) we can merely surmise that the movement took place within the confines of the town.

---

[6] Note that there are no tokens in which site is encoded by a verb in the present study, since these would be analysed as predications of location rather than motion and as such would per definition have been excluded from the data under examination.

If an area to be crossed is very small, or even two-dimensional, the translator does not have the option of concentrating on the central portion of the path. Aurnague (2000) dubs such small areas "intrinsically medial spaces". In such cases French translators sometimes choose to code the path in the verb phrase and encode the point of boundary crossing by the preposition *par*, as in (5b) and (6b).

(5) a. Then crawled *through the open window*. (HW2TE)
    b. Elle *sortait* ensuite *par la fenêtre*. (HW2TF)

(6) a. One spring a duck *entered* the cookhouse *through the open door* (HW2TE)
    b. Une année, une mère eider *entra par la porte ouverte* du fournil ... (HW2TF)

There are 13 instances of *par* in the French texts, but not a single one of English *by*, although the use of the latter in (6a), in which the path is coded by the verb, would result in an idiomatic English utterance. It would not, however, be possible to substitute *by* for *through* in (5a), in which the verb codes manner, without changing the direction of motion.

In the French versions of examples (3), (5) and (6) the path is coded by the verb rather than, or in addition to, an adverbial. This option is chosen by the French translators in just over half of the tokens (57 of 110). By far the most popular verb is *traverser* (32 tokens), followed by *entrer* (6 tokens), *franchir* (5 tokens) and *passer* and *sortir* (3 tokens each).

Manner, like path, may also be coded by a verb, by an adverbial, or both. In example (1), for instance, manner is coded by the verb in both translations. In (7) and (8), on the other hand, in which the form coding manner is underlined and the form coding path in italics, manner is coded by the verb in English with path being coded in an adverbial, but in an adverbial in French with path being coded by the verb.

(7) a. Later I <u>slipped</u> *through the door* of the Grand Café ... (BHH1TE)
    b. Après quoi j'ai <u>discrètement</u> *franchi* la porte du Grand Café ... BHH1TF)

(8) a. She <u>ran</u> *through the rooms* wearing only pantalets ... (HW2TE)
    b. En pantalon, et <u>en courant</u>, elle *traversa* la pièce ... (HW2TF)

Figure 1 provides details of how often the two sets of translations code manner, path and site in verbs, adverbials or both of these.

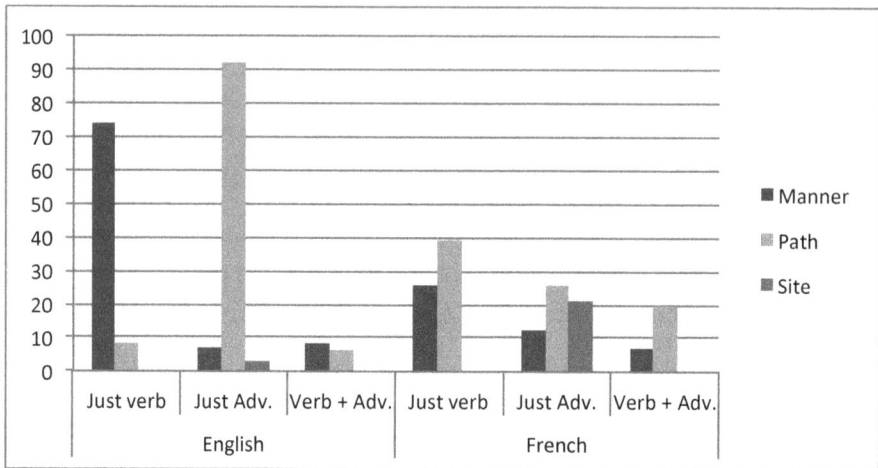

Figure 1. Manner, path and site in English and French codings of self-motion 'through-ness'.

We can see in Figure 1 that the English texts overwhelmingly code manner in the verb. Equally clear-cut is the tendency for path in English to be coded in an adverbial, rather than the verb. In other words, the evidence of the texts in the present study tends to confirm the view that English is indeed a satellite-framed language. The picture for French is more mixed with respect to Talmy's (2000: 221) typological distinction. The number of tokens coding path in the verb testify to it being path-framed to a much greater extent than English, but there is a sizable minority of tokens in which manner is coded in the verb, far more than one would have expected had French been a pure verb-framed language. Rather it appears to be predominantly verb-framed, but with a number of alternative possibilities for coding manner and path, as has been pointed out by Kopecka (2006) and Pourcel and Kopecka (2005).

4. English and French strategies for coding 'to-ness'

The *tertium comparationis* for my analysis of 'to-ness' consists of codings in Norwegian of self-motion predications by means of the preposition/particle *til*. The definition of *til* in *Norsk Riksmålsordbok* may be translated as follows[7]:

---

[7] The definition is taken from *Riksmålordbok* rather than *Den Norske ordboka* since the latter had not reached the letter 't' at the time of writing. The original definition reads: "brukt for å uttrykke at det styrte ord betegner bestemmelsessted, mål ell. sluttpunkt for en bevegelse, at det nevnte sted ell. område blir nådd ell. skal nås" (*Norsk Riksmålsordbok*: 1983)

used to express that the word governed codes a target-place, a goal or the endpoint of a movement, so that the place or area mentioned is reached or will be reached (Norsk Riksmålsordbok 1983: my translation)

This definition of Norwegian *til* is very similar to that of English *to* in the *OED* and French *à* in *Dictionnaire de l'Académie*.

> *To*: Expressing a spatial or local relation. Expressing motion directed towards and reaching: governing a n. denoting the place, thing, or person approached and reached. The opposite of *from*. (*OED*)

> *À* introduces a complement denoting a place: 1. The place towards which there is a movment, in the direction of which one is heading. (*Dictionnaire de l'Académie, neuvième édition*, my translation)[8]

Given the similarity between the definitions of *to* and *à* and that of *til*, it comes as no surprise that a large number of paths coded in Norwegian by the latter are coded in a similar fashion in both English and French. (9) and (10) may serve as typical examples.

(9) a. I ran up *to the window*... (BHH1TE)
   b. Je me suis précipité *à la fenêtre*... (BHH1TF)

(10) a. "Then they go *to church*!" Dina commented. (HW2TE)
   b. "Et après, elles courent *à l'église*!" fut le commentaire de Dina. (HW2TF)

There are as many as 552 English tokens containing *to* and 354 French tokens with *à*. The difference is partly due to a greater tendency for French to code path in the verb. However, in addition, the French translators tend to specify the extent to which the landmark has been actually reached (*jusqu'à*), as in (11), or whether the mover is still in the process of approaching the target (*vers*), as in (12).

(11) a. And calmly strolled across the room *to the window*! (HW2TE)
   b. Et traversait tranquillement la pièce *jusqu'à la fenêtre*! (HW2TF)

(12) a. Ana raced *to the jeep* and returned with a small video camera ... (JG3TE)

---

8 *À* introduit un complément désignant un lieu : ☆ 1. Le lieu vers lequel il y a mouvement, vers lequel on va. (*Dictionnaire de l'Académie*, neuvième édition.)

  b. Ana se précipita *vers la Jeep* et revint avec une caméra de poing... (JG3TF)

There are 40 French tokens containing the preposition *jusqu'à* and 90 with *vers*. In many of the latter there is actually no doubt that the target has been reached – thus in (12b) *Ana* could not have got hold of the camera if she had not reached the jeep – but the French translator, focussing on the process of the progress towards the jeep, chooses the more specific (and idiomatic) proposition *vers*. The English texts differ markedly in the extent to which they encode the mover's actual reaching the landmark (there are 24 tokens of *up to*) and mere progress in its direction (there are only 5 tokens of *towards*).

Both sets of translations contain tokens in which the path is coded by both verb and adverbial, as in (13), or verb alone, as in (14).

(13) a. I want you to *go to La Coste*, Ramon, and find De Sade. (NF1TE)
     b. Ramon, je veux que vous *alliez à La Coste* à la recherche de Sade (NF1TF1)

(14) a. Then Dagny and the boys *arrived*. (HW2TE)
     b. Ils *arrivèrent* alors, Dagny et les garçons. (HW2TF)

There are 160 constructions in English and 259 in French that resemble (13) in containing a double coding of path.[9] Moreover, the construction in (14) containing a single coding of path in the verb is much more common in French, with 113 tokens, compared to just 19 in English. A further difference worth noting is that 20 of these French tokens contain a purpose adverbial, the French translator substituting the aim of the mover in seeking out some goal for the actual goal itself. This sort of usage may be seen in (15).

(15) a. He *returned to Mother Karen*. (HW2TE)
     b. Il *retourna* voir Mère Karen. (HW2TF)

As for manner, underlined in the next three examples, this may also be coded by the verb, as in (16), in an adverbial, as in (17), or in both, as in (18).

---

[9] In (13) the verbs *go* and *aller* are categorised as path verbs since they are used deictically, to encode motion away from the speaker. More often they are categorised as neutral movement verbs, as are *come* and *venir*.

(16) a. Then she would be <u>running</u> past the horses *towards me*...
(NF1TE)
   b. Bientôt elle <u>trottinera</u> *vers moi* entre les croupes des chevaux
   ... (NF1TF)

(17) a. I'd be late if I went all the way *to Majorstua* <u>on foot</u>. (KF1TE)
   b. S'il fallait que j'aille <u>à pied</u> *jusqu'à Majorstuen*, j'arriverais
   trop tard. (KF1TF)

(18) a. It <u>leaped like a shaggy little animal</u> from person *to person*.
(HW2TE)
   b. Il <u>sautait</u> de l'un *à l'autre* <u>comme un petit animal velu</u>.
(HW2TF)

Double coding of manner as in (18) is much less common in both languages than double coding of path. There are just 16 tokens in English
and six in French. Nor is manner coding by an adverbial alone, as in
(17), frequent in either language, with 17 tokens in English and 27 in
French. More common is coding of manner by the verb alone, as in
(16), with 158 tokens in English and 64 in French.

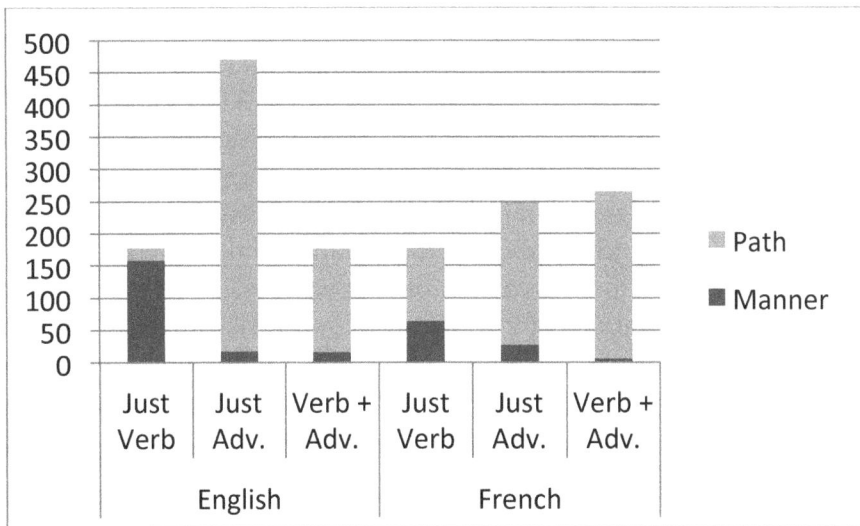

Figure 2. Coding of manner and path in English and French translations of
Norwegian 'to-ness' predications.

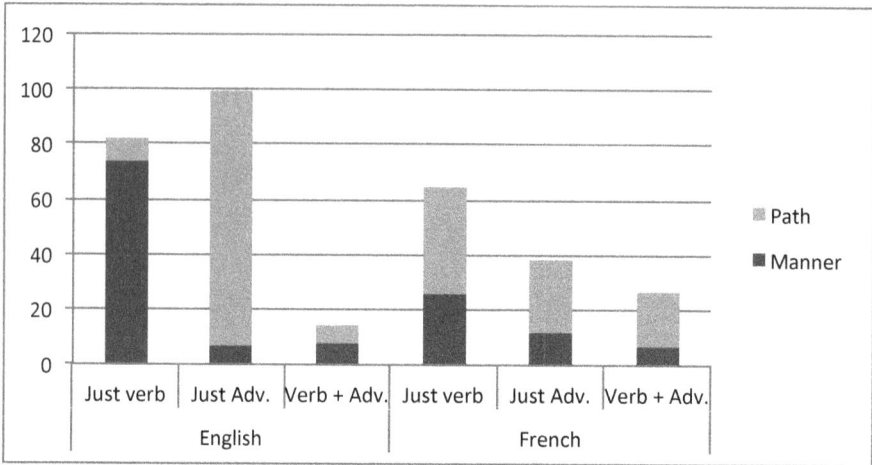

Figure 3. Coding of manner and path in English and French translations of Norwegian 'through-ness' predications.

5. Codings of 'through-ness' and 'to-ness' compared

This section contains a brief comparison of the English and French codings of 'to-ness' and 'through-ness' discussed in sections 3 and 4. In order to better facilitate the comparison of the two types of predication, the data for 'through-ness' in Figure 1 are reproduced in Figure 3, with the tokens coding site in an adverbial omitted.

Even a cursory glance at Figures 2 and 3 will suffice to reveal that the codings of the two different sorts of motion predication, one containing a path to a target, the other a path through some sort of container, resemble one another closely in both languages with respect to the coding of manner. As for the coding of path, there is a significant difference between the two sorts of predications in both languages. This difference is related to a greater tendency to code path twice, or to split the denotation of the path between verb and adverbial in predications of 'to-ness' compared to predications of 'through-ness'. This is related to the fact that predications of 'through-ness' just evoke a medial portion of the path, the 'route', whereas predications of 'to-ness' presuppose both a route and an end-point or goal. This double coding of path [to] is illustrated in (19) and (20) and may be compared to the single coding of path [through] in (21).

(19) a. But he did not *return to the dressing room.* (HW2TE)
     b. Mais il ne *retourna* pas *dans le cabinet.* (HW2TF)

(20) a. "Won't you *come down to this bad billygoat* of a man?"
(HW2TE)

b. "Ne peux-tu pas *descendre vers ce terrible bouc* de mari?"
(HW2TF)

(21) a. I suggested I could walk with him *through the Retiro Park*.
(JG3TE)_

b. Je proposai de l'accompagner *à travers le Retiro*. (JG3TF)

In (19) the verbs *return* and *retourna* code a path back to a previous location and the two prepositional phrases the end point of this path (*dans* here codes a path [into] rather than a site [in]). In (20a) the verb *come* codes path of motion towards the speaker, the particle *down* a horizontally descending path and the *to* phrase the end point of this path. In the corresponding French sentence it is the verb that codes the descending path, while the prepositional phrase codes the direction of the path towards its end point, rather than the end point itself. (21), on the other hand, contains only one coding of path, referring to the medial portion, with neither the starting nor end point being specified.

Another striking difference between the tokens coding 'to-ness' and those coding 'through-ness' is the number of verbs coding neutral movement, rather than either manner or path. Such verbs include *travel* and *voyager* and non-deictic *come, go, aller* and *venir* (the deictic readings of these four verbs code path of motion in the direction of, or away from, the focused participant). There are 265 neutral movement verbs in the English translations (43%) and 166 in the French translations (27%) of *til* compared to just 20 (17%) for English and 14 (12%) for French in the translations of *gjennom*.

In English, manner is far more likely to be coded in a verb than an adverbial and path more likely to be coded in an adverbial than a verb. Moreover, when path is coded in a verb, it is likely to be coded in an adverbial as well, especially in predications of 'to-ness'. English thus conforms largely to the prototype of satellite-framed languages. French is less likely than English to code manner, but if it does do so, it resembles English in so far as it is more likely to code it in the verb than an adverbial. Thus while French does conform to some extent to the prototype of the path-framed language by coding path in the verb, it diverges from it both in preferring to code manner, if at all, in the verb and in coding path in an adverbial in addition to the verb, especially in the case of 'to-ness'.

6. Summary and conclusions

In this chapter I compared codings of self-motion predications in which the path either traverses a container landmark ('through-ness') or leads up to a goal landmark ('to-ness'). The reason for choosing these two paths is that the former (potentially) involves the crossing of a boundary, while the latter does not do so. Given that French is commonly taken to avoid coding manner in the verb in boundary-crossing predications (see, for instance, Aske 1989, Cappelle 2012), one might have expected fewer such verbs in the translations of 'through-ness' predications. As we have seen in section 5, this is not in fact the case, there being no significant difference in the encoding of manner in the verb in French renderings of the two sorts of predication.

The data for the study were taken from the Oslo Multilingual Corpus and consist of codings in English and French of the concepts of 'through-ness' and 'to-ness' as these are instantiated in translations of the same Norwegian tokens all containing adverbials with the prepositions *gjennom* or *til*. With respect to predications of 'through-ness' the two languages differ in the frequency with which they employ the most frequent preposition in path adverbials. While *through* occurs in 83% of the English translations, *à travers* is only used in 20% of the French ones. In fact French translators often prefer to encode the landmark as the site within which an act of motion takes place, without specifying the nature of the path followed by the mover. Thus 15% of tokens contain the preposition *dans* used to encode a site (there are three tokens in which *dans* encodes a path, with the sense of English *into* rather than *in*). The English translators code manner in the verb and path in an adverbial in over half of all tokens (55%), whereas the French translators do so just 14% of the time. More common in French is double coding of path, with the verb coding the general direction of movement and the adverbial specifying this in greater detail. Also more common in French than in English are tokens in which the path is denoted by a verb such as *traverser* with the ground denoted by a direct object.

The translations of 'to-ness' predications differ from those of 'through-ness' in that a majority of tokens in both languages code path in an adverbial in the form of a preposition phrase containing the default prepositions *to* and *à*. There are more such tokens in English than in French, the difference being due to some extent to a greater tendency for French to code path in the verb, but also to a tendency on the part of the French translators to specify the extent to which the landmark has actually been reached (*jusqu'à*), or whether the mover is still in the process of approaching the target (*vers*). Both languages contain a large number of constructions with a double coding of path, with French again outnumbering English. On the other hand while there are also a large number of tokens in French containing a single coding of path in the verb, this sort of coding is comparatively rare in English. Finally one may note that French translators occasionally use a purpose adverbial in place of a path one, substituting the aim of the mover in seeking out some goal for the actual goal itself.

If we compare the two types of motion predications to one another, we see that there is no significant difference between codings of 'throughness' and 'to-ness' in either language with respect to the coding of manner. On the other hand, there is a significant difference between the two types of predications in both languages in the coding of path. Another striking difference is the number of verbs coding neutral movement, which are much more common in translations of 'to-ness' predications than 'through-ness' predications. This difference reflects a difference in the original Norwegian tokens. It appears that in goal-directed predications, both the original authors and the translators focussed more narrowly on the target landmark than on the manner of the mover's reaching it or the path along which the mover travelled. Having said that, there are far more Norwegian neutral movement verbs rendered by path verbs in French than there are in English.

Turning to the question of satellite- and path-framing, we have seen that in the case of both types of path predication English seems to conform largely to the satellite framed prototype, while the picture for French is more blurred. The English texts overwhelmingly code manner in the verb. Equally clear-cut is the tendency for path in English to be coded in an adverbial, rather than the verb. As for French the number of tokens coding path in the verb testify to it being path-framed to a greater extent than English, but there is a sizable minority of tokens in which manner is coded in the verb, far more than one would have expected had French been a pure verb-framed language. Rather, French appears to be predominantly verb-framed, but with a number of alternative possibilities for coding manner and path, as has been pointed out by Kopecka (2006) and Hickmann et al. (2009).

Appendix

(1) Vi begynte å gå langsomt gjennom galleriene, og opp i andre etasje. (JG3).

(2) Jeg foreslo at jeg kunne følge ham gjennom Retiro-parken. (JG3).

(3) Dina begynte å gå gjennom stuene denne sommeren. (HW2)

(4) Når han kom gående gjennom byen ... (BHH1)

(5) Og så klatre ut gjennom det åpne vinduet. (HW2)

(6) Et år kom ei ærfuglmor seg inn i eldhuset gjennom den åpne døra ... (HW2)

(7) Siden smøg jeg meg inn gjennom døren på Grand Kafé ... (BHH1)

(8) I bare mamelukkene sprang hun gjennom stuene ... (HW2)

(9) Jeg sprang til vinduet ... (BHH1)

(10) Siden fer de til kjerka! kommenterte Dina. (HW2)

(11) Og spaserte rolig over golvet og bort til vinduet! (HW2)

(12) Ana styrtet til jeepen og kom tilbake med et lite videokamera ... (JG3)

(13) Jeg vil at de skal reise til La Coste, Ramon, og finne de Sade. (NF1)

(14) Så kom de til, både Dagny og guttene. (HW2)

(15) Han gikk til Mor Karen enda en gang. (HW2)

(16) Snart småløper hun mellom hesterompene bort til meg. (NF1)

(17) Jeg ville komme for sent om jeg skulle ta meg helt ned til Majorstuen til fots. (KF1)

(18) Det hoppet som et lite loddent dyr, fra menneske til menneske. (HW2)

(19) Kan du ikke kom ned til dennan fryktelige bukken av en mann? (HW2)

(20) Men han gikk ikke til påkledningsværelset. (HW2)

(21) Jeg foreslo at jeg kunne følge ham gjennom Retiro-parken. (JG3)

References

Primary

Dictionnaire de l'Académie, huitième edition. http://artfl-project.uchicago.edu/content/dictionnaires-dautrefois

Dictionnaire de l'Académie, neuvième édition. http://atilf.atilf.fr/academie9.htm

Knudsen, T., Sommerfelt A. & Noreng H. (1983). Norsk Riksmålsordbok: Bind IV. Oslo: Kunnskapsforlaget.

Oslo Multilingual Corpus: http://www.hf.uio.no/ilos/english/services/omc/

Oxford English Dictionary: OED v4.0 on CD-Rom. Oxford: Oxford University Press.

Vikør, L. S. (ed.). 2002. *Norsk ordbok,* band IV [vol. 4]. Oslo: Det Norske Samlaget.

Secondary

Aske, J. (1989). Path predications in English and Spanish: a closer look. K. Hall, M. Meacham & R. Shapiro (eds) *Proceedings of the fifteenth annual meeting of the Berkeley Linguistics Society.* Berkeley: Berkeley Linguistics Society, 1–14.

Aurnague, M. (2000). Entrer par la petite porte, passer par des chemins de traverse: à propos de la preposition par et la notion de "trajet". *Carnets de grammaire.* Rapport no. 7. http://w3.erss.univ-tlse2.fr/textes/publications/CarnetsGrammaire/carnGram7.pdf

Berman, R. A., & Slobin, D. I. (1994). *Relating events in narrative: A cross-linguistic developmental study.* Hillsdale, NJ: Lawrence Erlbaum Associates.

Cappelle, B. (2012). English is less rich in manner-of-motion verbs when translated from French. *Across Languages and Cultures,* 13:2, 173–195.

Egan, T. (2012). *Through* seen through the looking glass of translation equivalence: a proposed method for determining closeness of word senses. S. Hoffman, P. Rayson & G. Leech (eds) *Corpus linguistics: Looking back – moving forward.* Amsterdam: Rodopi, 41–56.

———. (2013). *Tertia Comparationis* in Multilingual Corpora. K. Aijmer & B. Altenberg (eds) *Advances in corpus-based contrastive linguistics. Studies in honour of Stig Johansson.* Amsterdam: John Benjamins, 7–24 .

Egan, T. & Rawoens G. (2013). "Moving over in(to) English and French". *Languages in Contrast* 13:2, 193–211.

Filipović, L. & Jaszczolt K. M. (eds) (2012). *Space and Time in Languages and Cultures: Linguistic Diversity.* Amsterdam: John Benjamins.

Hickmann, M., & Robert S. (eds) (2006). *Space in Languages: Linguistic Systems and Cognitive Categories.* Amsterdam: John Benjamins.

Hickmann, M., Taranne P. & Bonnet P. (2009). Motion in first language acquisition: Manner and Path in French and English child language. *Journal of Child Language* 36, 705–741.

Jaszczolt, K. M. (2003). On translating what is said: *tertium comparationis* in contrastive semantics and pragmatics. K. M. Jaszczolt & K. Turner (eds) *Meaning Through Language Contrast. Vol. 2.* Amsterdam: John Benjamins, 441–462.

Johansson, S. (2007). *Seeing through Multilingual Corpora : On the use of corpora in contrastive studies*. Amsterdam: John Benjamins.

Kopecka, A. (2006). The semantic structure of motion verbs in French: Typological perspectives. M. Hickmann & S. Robert (eds) (2006), 59–81.

Krzeszowski, T.P. (1990). *Contrasting languages: the scope of contrastive linguistics*. Berlin: Mouton de Gruyter.

Lee, D. (2001). *Cognitive Linguistics: an Introduction*. Oxford: Oxford University Press.

Leech, G.N. (1969). *Towards a semantic description of English*. London: Longman.

Lindstromberg, S. (1998). *English Prepositions Explained*. Amsterdam: John Benjamins.

Pourcel, S. & Kopecka A. (2005). Motion expressions in French: Typological diversity. *Durham and Newcastle Working Papers in Linguistics* 11, 139–153.

Tyler, A. & Evans. V. (2007). *The Semantics of English Prepositions: Spatial scenes, embodied meaning and cognition*. Digitally printed (with corr.) ed. Cambridge: Cambridge University Press.

Slobin, D. (2006). What makes manner of motion salient? Explorations in linguistic typology, discourse and cognition. M. Hickmann & S. Robert (eds) (2006), 83–101.

Talmy, L. (1991). Path to realization: A typology of event conflation. L.A. Sutton, C. Johnson & R. Shields (eds) *Proceedings of the 17th Annual Meeting of the Berkeley Linguistics Society*. University of California at Berkeley, CA: Berkeley Linguistics Society, Inc. 480–519

Talmy, L. (2000). *Towards a Cognitive Semantics, Volume II: Typology and Process in Concept Structuring*. Cambridge MA: The MIT Press.

Viberg, Å. (1998). Contrasts in polysemy and differentiation: Running and putting in English and Swedish. S. Johansson & S. Oksefjell (eds) *Corpora and Cross-linguistic Research*. Amsterdam: Rodopi, 343–376.

————. (2003). The polysemy of the Swedish verb *komma* 'come': A view from translation corpora. K.M. Jaszczolt & K. Turner (eds) *Meaning through language contrast*. Vol. 2. Amsterdam: John Benjamins, 75–105.

————. (2013). Seeing the lexical profile of Swedish through multilingual corpora. The case of Swedish *åka* and other vehicle verbs. K. Aijmer & B. Altenberg (eds) *Advances in corpus-based contrastive linguistics. Studies in honour of Stig Johansson*. Amsterdam: John Benjamins, 25–56.

17 Using the World Wide Web to Research Spoken Varieties of English: The Case of Pulmonic Ingressive Speech

Peter Sundkvist
Stockholm University

1. Introduction

Undoubtedly, one of the most significant developments for human interaction and communication within the last thirty years or so is the internet. Its origins may be traced back to various experimental computer networks of the 1960s (Crystal 2013: 3). It has since grown by a phenomenal rate: between 2000 and 2012 the number of internet users increased by an average of 566.4% across the globe, and as of 2012 34.3% of the world's population was estimated to have access to the internet (Internet World Stats 2012). Partly as a result of its phenomenal growth the internet has also established itself as an important tool and source of information within the fields of linguistics and English studies. While much linguistically-oriented work has focused on features and developments related to the electronic medium of communication itself, inquiry has gradually extended into further domains, as researchers become more creative in exploring the full potential of the internet. In particular, the World Wide Web (WWW), defined as "the full collection of all the computers linked to the internet which hold documents that are mutually accessible through the use of a standard protocol (Hypertext transfer protocol, or HTTP)" (Crystal 2013: 13), has opened up a range of new possibilities with regard to linguistic research. Thus far, however, less attention has been devoted to its potential for research on spoken varieties of English. The aim of this paper, therefore, is to explore the World Wide Web as a source of evidence for a specific feature of spoken language. Drawing upon the fact that very large amounts of audio and video material have become available, through a diverse range of online resources, the aim is to

How to cite this book chapter:
Sundkvist, P. 2015. Using the World Wide Web to Research Spoken Varieties of English: The Case of Pulmonic Ingressive Speech. In: Shaw, P., Erman, B., Melchers, G. and Sundkvist, P. (eds) *From Clerks to Corpora: essays on the English language yesterday and today.* Pp. 303–321. Stockholm: Stockholm University Press. DOI: http://dx.doi.org/10.16993/bab.q License: CC-BY.

gather evidence for and provide documentation of a somewhat elusive paralinguistic feature within a set of regional Englishes, which has thus far proved challenging to study by means of more standard methods.

2. Pulmonic ingressive speech

Visitors to the Nordic countries are often struck by a curious feature in the speech of the locals. In conversation, Norwegians, Swedes and Danes can frequently be heard drawing their breath inwards, in a manner vaguely reminiscent of a sudden gasp. Although often erroneously interpreted by the uninitiated listener as a sign of sudden ill health or astonishment, this is in fact a well-established paralinguistic feature. The technical term for this phenomenon is 'pulmonic ingressive speech'. Most commonly of course, human speech occurs on an outward airstream, directed from the lungs towards the mouth. The phonetic term for this is pulmonic ('involving lungs') egressive ('outwards') speech. However, it is also perfectly possible to speak on a reverse, inward ('ingressive') airstream, by drawing air into the lungs while speaking. In the Nordic languages, this airstream mechanism is commonly used on short words for 'yes' and 'no', especially when provided as backchannel items in a conversation, when the listener wants to signal to the speaker that he or she is following what is being said. While the many anecdotes of befuddlement on part of newcomers may seem to imply that ingressive speech is restricted to the Nordic languages, it is becoming clear that the phenomenon in fact occurs in a much wider range of languages and language varieties, including several regional Englishes.

At present there is no consensus regarding the cross-linguistic distribution of pulmonic ingressive speech. According to one view it may be found in a wide range of languages, on all continents of the world. Based on an extensive review of various sources, Eklund (2007, 2008) suggests that it has simply gone unnoticed for many parts of the world, and that insufficient effort has been made to compile and compare reports from across the globe. In typological terms, pulmonic ingressive speech is thus seen as constituting a 'neglected universal' (Eklund 2007). However, an opposing view suggests that ingressive speech is geographically restricted. Clarke and Melchers (2005) argue that ingressive speech occurs primarily within a region stretching in the east from the Baltic countries (e.g. Estonia) and westwards over Scandinavia (peninsular as well as insular), northern parts of continental Europe (Germany, Austria), across some regions of the British

Isles, and finally into Maritime Canada and coastal New England. This pattern finds a ready historical explanation. Pulmonic ingressive speech, it is suggested, was first spread by Vikings from Scandinavia westwards to the British Isles and eastwards to the Baltic countries. Subsequently it was further transmitted across the North Atlantic by Irish and British migrants (Clarke & Melchers 2005; Shorrocks 2003). From this perspective, pulmonic ingressive speech is considered to be 'typologically highly marked' (Clarke & Melchers 2005).

While at first sight ingressive speech may merely seem as a quaint curiosity, it soon becomes clear that further investigation into the phenomenon is significant for several reasons. From a general viewpoint it is a feature whose typological status remains to be established. From the present perspective of English studies, its precise distribution among regional varieties of English remains an open question, in spite of the fact that it is reported in several areas. Further insight into the use of ingressive speech among such forms of English may furthermore reveal historical connections among relevant regions. What is more, pulmonic ingressive speech is commonly surrounded by popular mythology. For instance, where it occurs, locals often seem to believe that it is somewhat unique to them and their communities. This, as we will see, appears to be the case for some regional Englishes also.

3. Pulmonic ingressive speech in regional Englishes: A test case for the World Wide Web?

One problem which has stalled the study into ingressives is the lack of objective evidence. For many regions where it reportedly occurs there is very little documentation in such forms as audio or video recordings, and the sole evidence consists of informal observation. The absence of data is in many cases not attributable to a lack of trying but to various inherent challenges for data collection. While the most obvious method may seem to be to collect ingressives by recording interviews, such attempts have had rather mixed success. In many cases, the interview situation itself seems to militate against the occurrence of ingressives. It has been argued that pulmonic ingressive speech tends to be used primarily in relaxed, informal situations, and that a level of interpersonal affiliation between the speaker and listener is required (Clarke & Melchers 2005). Owing to such challenges facing anyone setting out to record ingressives through interviews, pre-existing data sets and corpora would seem like a suitable alternative, perhaps especially for such localities where the inquiry into ingressives is at an early stage and simply objectively supported instances would constitute an important step forward. Even for this approach, however, previous researchers report various difficulties, as ingressives seem poorly represented in certain types of existing recordings (cf. e.g. Thom 2005).

A major source of pre-existing recordings is of course audio and visual media. However, it has been suggested that the media may perhaps not be a very good resource for pulmonic ingressive speech. Thom remarks that ingressive speech is used especially by such sections of society which are not well represented in the media – which within this context means primarily elderly, rural speakers – and therefore is bound to be underrepresented in media-based corpora: "[...] it was difficult to find examples of [ingressive speech] in recorded material, either on radio or on television. This was because [ingressive speech] tends to be used in informal situations, and (as I discovered) mostly by groups of people who are rarely seen in the media." (Thom 2005: 28–9). In Swedish (and Finnish), the word *jo/ju* ('yes') is sometimes pronounced as a voiceless bilabial fricative or approximant, on a pulmonic ingressive airstream. The frequency of this feature appears to increase the further north in Sweden you go (Eklund 2008: 262–263), and it is popularly associated with northern parts. With regard to media, however, Hanell and Salö (2009: 19) claim that "You can actually spend hours among video clips on YouTube where [well-known people from the northern part of Sweden], such as Ingemar Stenmark and Maud Olofsson, go through interview after interview without making a single [*jo/ju*, bilabial fricative]" (author's translation).

In face of the difficulties in documenting ingressives through more standard methods, it is natural to consider what potential the World Wide Web may offer. Owing to its massive expansion, a wide range of audio and visual material is now available online. This includes not only news broadcasts, documentaries, entertainment etc. but also unedited material posted at sites such as YouTube. The aim of this paper is therefore to provide documentation of pulmonic ingressive speech in regional Englishes, and within the North Atlantic region more generally, based on material accessed through the World Wide Web. As far as has been possible, this is based on publicly available sources, for which URLs are provided; in some instances research data has been utilized as an additional source of information. Secondly, the aim is also to find illustrations of the popular mythology surrounding ingressives on the basis of material available through the WWW.

4. Documentation of pulmonic ingressive speech: Audio and video

The following section provides illustration of the use of pulmonic ingressive speech based on audio and visual data. The focus is on Englishes across the North Atlantic region for which relevant data has thus far been acquired. In addition, examples are offered from certain Scandinavian languages, as well as one speaker from western Canada. Brief extracts of conversations are transcribed and presented; in these, words spoken ingressively are underlined and in italics. Where available, URLs are stated, as well as the relevant time segment in the files.

4.1 Ireland

Illustration of Irish ingressives may be found in the speech of Paddy Malone, the piper of the Irish band The Chieftains, who hails from Dublin. Instances may for instance be heard in the brief documentary 'San Patricio – Behind the scenes', which portrays the making of the San Patricio album (2010), featuring the Chieftains and American guitarist Ry Cooder. The extract below comes from a conversation between Paddy Malone (PM) and Ry Cooder (RC), concerning the San Patricio battalion – a group of Irish volunteer soldiers who deserted the US army and fought on the Mexican side in the Mexican-American war (1846–1848).

(1) RC: It's a beautiful little song and the lyrics (…) are, if you flip it around, seems to me that (…) the same could be said for these poor Irish soldiers,   [who] are so far from home
    PM: [yeah]
    PM: That's right
    RC: Probably never going back
    PM: *Yeah* (ingressive)
    RC: Well,   [needless] to say
    PM: [Yeah]
    PM: *Yeah* (ingressive)
    RC: So for them it's also true
    RC: *Yeah* (ingressive), very much so
    RC: You know, Yeah. The diasporic person   [is] never gonna get back [there]
    PM: [Mmm]   [*Yeah* (ingressive)]

    Link: http://www.youtube.com/watch?v=54PDlicm_94
    Location in link: 7:22–7:41

4.2 England

It seems to be particularly difficult to find recorded instances of ingressives from England. However, instances occur in the audio recordings made by the Survey of English Dialects in Patterdale, Westmoreland, Northern England, in 1974. The recording consists of a conversation on the topic of gardening, work etc., between the fieldworker, linguist Clive Upton (CU), and the interviewee Edward Blamire (EB), born in 1903.

(2) CU: You do all sorts of other work, now, around the estate
    EB: Well, aye. I mow, I mow the la-, mow the lawns. Do fencing. And uh
    CU: [inaudible]
    EB: Anything what, anything what I can do
    CU: Hmm
    EB: Aye, *Aye* (ingressive)
    CU: Yeah, Hmhm
    EB: That's right
    CU: Yeah

   Link: http://sounds.bl.uk/Accents-and-dialects/
   Survey-of-English-dialects/021M-C0908X0005XX-0300V1
   Location in link: 4:10–4:30

4.3 Shetland

The Shetland Isles, situated in the North Sea, constitute the northernmost part of the UK. The presence of ingressives in Shetland has been documented more extensively (Sundkvist 2012a, 2012b). The extract below is from a conversation between the author (PS) and a Shetland man (LM) in his 80s, from Shetland's main town of Lerwick. The interview is part of a corpus collected by the author 2000–2003 for a study of Lerwick pronunciation, and the discussion concerns the microphone stand.

(3) LM: Yeah, you can't take the nut far enough, that's the thing, yeah
    PS: No. And then when you keep
    LM: You put a washer in, or something like that with
    PS: Yeah, I can put that but I [think] when I come home I need to take it
                                                              apart and [do]
    LM: [Yeah]
    [Yeah]
    PS: something with it
    LM: *Yeah* (ingressive)

   Link: Audio file not made available.

4.4 Orkney

The Orkney Isles are located just off the north coast of Scotland. The excerpt below is taken from data collected by Gunnel Melchers and Arne Kjell Foldvik between 1980 and 1985. The conversation involves one of the fieldworkers (Arne Kjell Foldvik, AKF) and a farmer from the isle of Westray (WM), whose age is estimated to be between 45 and 50 by Foldvik. The conversation takes place outdoors, and reflects a chance encounter with the local.

(4) AKF: But you got to have them inside all winter
    WM: [Oh, yes]
    AKF: [pass] the winter
    WM: Oh yes, they come in in November
    AKF: Umhm
    WM: and they're in 'til the first of May
    AKF: Silage? Is that [...]
    WM: [yes, mostly] silage, yes, that's right, *aye* (ingressive)

    Link: Audio file not made available.

4.5 Fair Isle

Fair Isle is a small island in the North Sea, situated halfway between the Orkney and Shetland Isles. Although it is officially part of Shetland, Fair Islanders display a strong local identity, often expressed as being distinct from that of the rest of Shetland. The presence of ingressives within the Fair Isle community was established in Sundkvist 2012a, b. The excerpt below is from an animated discussion between one local woman (FIF) and two local men (FIM1, FIM2). It was recorded in 1982 by Gunnel Melchers and Arne Kjell Foldvik. For simplicity, word forms and spelling have been adjusted to Standard English in the extract.

(5) FIM1: But someone, for the funeral, someone, someone who
          belonged to the body [=person] who was dead, they had to
          get around to every house, like
    FIM2: Invited every house [to the funeral]
    FIM1:   [(...) invite to the] funeral
    FIF: Yeah
    FIM1: *Yeah* (Ingressive)
    FIM2: Yeah

    Link: Audio file not made available.

4.6 Cape Breton

Turning the focus across the North Atlantic, instances of ingressives may also be found from North America. The example below is from a documentary about the Irish heritage of Cape Breton, Nova Scotia, Canada: 'The Irish in Cape Breton 1713–1990' (The Irish In Cape Breton 3 of 6, 1990, produced, directed and narrated by Kenneth Donovan). The interviewer is Kenneth Donovan (KD), a Parks Canada historian; the interviewee is Loretta Donovan (LD), an elderly lady.

(6) KD: And how many uh ... children were in your family, in your father and mother's family?
 LD: Nine, we had six boys and three girls
 KD: Six boys [and] three girls?
 LD: [Yes]
 LD: And I'm the only girl left, but I have two brothers in the States
 KD: Right
 LD: My older brother
 KD: Yeah
 LD: Not my older brother [name], _Yeah_ (ingressive), and one is 89 and the other is 84

 Link:http://www.youtube.com/watch?v=JsmyRknWUVo&feature=relmfu
 Location in link: 07.25–07:42

4.7 Newfoundland

As to Maritime Canada, examples of ingressives may be found for instance in the online archive of Memorial University of Newfoundland. The archives reveal the presence of ingressive speech in several locations within Newfoundland. The example presented below is from Lower Cove. The conversation took place between interviewer Lisa Wilson (LW) and interviewee Mamiellen Noseworthy (MN) on June 7, 2010, and concerns local craft.

(7) LW: Doreen just spent 'bout half an hour showing me, just a sample, how to do a pleat
 MN: Yeah
 LW: And, she's going quite fast [laughter], and there's no way I could do that without having to watch, a lot
 MN: Right
 LW: And then practice a lot
 MN: Yeah

LW: So, observe, observe, observe, and then practice, practice, practice
MN: *Yeah* (ingressive), yeah

Source: Noseworthy, Mamiellen. Lisa Wilson interviewing Mamiellen Noseworthy, June 7, 2010, Lower Cove, Newfoundland. Archive ID: ICHTS310
Link: http://collections.mun.ca/index.php
Location in link: 4:30–4:55

4.8 British Columbia

While previous sources have pointed towards the existence of ingressive speech in Maritime Canada, few have mentioned the possibility for the western parts of the country. The token below is from a young female from British Columbia. It occurs in an episode of the crime show '48 hours' titled 'Highway of Tears', which deals with a series of disappearances and homicides along a part of the Trans-Canada highway system supposedly known by some locals as the 'highway of tears'. However, only one ingressive token occurs in the material, on reported speech within a conversation between the reporter (R) and the female (Jordanne Bolduc, JB).

(8) R: What did she say to you?
JB: She was just like shocked, she's like: really? You're going? And I was like: *yeah* (ingressive), I'm going
JB: And [pause] she kinda begged me, and then I was just well you can come with us and she said 'no', She wanted to stay there with her tent, for it to be safe

Link: https://www.youtube.com/watch?v=xDQDQqDR8SI
Location in link: 13:30–13:45

4.9 The Nordic languages

The existence of ingressive speech is well documented for Swedish, Norwegian, and Danish. However, fewer samples appear to be easily available for Insular Scandinavian, such as Icelandic and Faroese. The following section thus presents examples concerning Icelandic and Faroese, as well as the Swedish word *jo/ju*, commented on earlier.

4.9.1 Icelandic

Icelandic ingressives are amply illustrated in the TV show Silfur Egils. In the excerpt below, the host Egill Helgason is talking to a book keeper,

Bragi Kristjónsson (aka Bragi bóksali). The conversation concerns a photographic book.

(9) BK: These are his parents.
    EH: Yes.
    BK: Haraldur Guðmundsson, master carpenter, and the mother.
    EH: *Yes* (ingressive).
    BK: And his brother Leifur who wrote the poem there "The young poets write verses…"
    EH: "…without being able to".
    BK: "…without being able to/ In the Public house[1] I get daily meals/ without eating them".
    EH: Yes, yes, *yes* (ingressive) Yes-yes.
    BK: But this brother of his, Magnús Haraldsson
    EH: *Yes* (ingressive).
    BK: he died in a car accident.

    Link: http://www.youtube.com/watch?v=5JMCuKGy-zM
    Location in link: 1:11–1:41

4.9.2 Faroese

Faroese ingressives may similarly be illustrated with material from a talk show. The interviewer below is journalist and show host Høgni í Jákupsstovu (speaking with a Tórshavn dialect); the interviewee is artist Tróndur Patursson (with a Kirkjubø dialect).

(10) HJ: Yes, welcome Tróndur Patursson.
    TP: Thank you.
    HJ: 40 years since you first were at the art museum (= Listasavn Føroya, National Gallery).
    TP: Yes, *yes* (ingressive).
    HJ: You do it like the queen, [hold] a 40 year anniversary?
    TP: Well, yes, yes-yes. I suppose it is. I suppose it is. *Yes* (ingressive)
    HJ: How was it to be back at the art museum, after that conflict [that you were a part of]?
    TP: Yes, yes, the art museum is a truly outstanding building (.)

    Link: http://www.youtube.com/
    watch?v=nqRqw8FyNRk&feature=relmfu
    Location in link: 3:05–3:30

---

[1] The word *Alþýðuhúsið* literally means 'the house of the public or the public house'. However this is not the same as a public house as abbreviated into 'pub' but rather a type of communal guesthouse (Friðrik Sólnes, p.c.).

4.9.3 Swedish 'jo'/'ju'

As pointed out previously, the word *jo/ju* ('yes') in Swedish may be spoken on a pulmonic ingressive airstream; in such instances it may be generally characterized as a voiceless bilabial fricative or approximant. This pronunciation is often associated with the northern parts of Sweden, and one individual commonly mentioned with regard to it is former alpine skier Ingemar Stenmark, whose laconic conversational style was popularly thought to fit well with the brief reply of a *jo/ju*. The discussion below occurs in an episode of the TV show 'Mästarnas mästare', whose participants are former top athletes. It concerns an annoying interview with a journalist who prematurely made the suggestion that Stenmark's career had come to an end. Stenmark (IS) is talking with Peter ("Pekka") Lindmark (PL), a former ice hockey goal keeper.

(11) PL: No, but really, it must be horrible to get a [expression meaning 'we thank you for the time you have been a skier'] and then you go on winning another 20
IS: Yeah
PL: Oh, [it] is like kicking the legs out from under you
IS: [Yeah]
IS: I really felt like, it would have been better to quit long, long before, before I had, just when I had reached the top
PL: Yes, because then you were, exactly, then you would have become immortal, but
IS: [Yes, then I would have]
PL: [But you]   really were outstanding, for very many years
IS: Yeah

Figure 1. Documentations of pulmonic ingressive speech in section 4.

PL: And won and won and won
IS: *Yeah* (Ingressive; bilabial fricative)

Link: http://www.youtube.com/watch?v=fHE9XgXNwfo&feature=related
Location in link: 8:57–9:21

4.10 Summary: Audio and video documentation within the North Atlantic region

The range of localities for which evidence of pulmonic ingressive speech, based on audio and visual material, has been presented in section 4 is summarized in Figure 1 below. A (red) dot in the map signifies that an illustration has been provided for the locality in question. Regarding access to relevant sound files, URLs are available and provided for Ireland, England, Cape Breton, Newfoundland, British Columbia; and also Icelandic, Faroese, and Swedish. For Shetland, Orkney, and Fair Isle no URLs are available. Further linguistic analysis of the ingressive tokens presented, including their discourse function, falls outside the scope of the present study. It should be noted, however, that all tokens in section 4 constitute expressions for 'yes' provided as feedback during a conversation.

5. Illustration of stereotypes, popular notions

Pulmonic ingressive speech is associated with a range of stereotypes and popular mythology. A common notion in localities where it occurs seems to be that it is unique to that particular area; general awareness of its wider distribution seems fairly limited. This self-perceived exclusivity, or at least typicality, applies not only to Swedes and Norwegians but also to several English-speaking localities. The following media clips illustrate the conception that it is unique to or at least characteristic of a particular region, that it may be misunderstood by outsiders, and that it consequently may need to be explained to them.

The part of North America which seems most commonly discussed with regard to ingressive speech is coastal Maine. In particular, it tends to be mentioned in conjunction with the word *ayuh* or *ayup* ('yes'). Similar anecdotes may be encountered for Maine as from Scandinavia, in which newcomers are bewildered and confused by the phenomenon. One such anecdote, illustrated in the link below, concerns a medical doctor from Kentucky, who was working in Down East Maine, a part of coastal north-eastern Maine which borders on Canada. The doctor asks a local patient if he is OK, to which he answers *ayuh* (pronounced as a voiced ingressive). The doctor is puzzled by the patient's apparent gasp and becomes concerned about his health, not realizing that it in fact represents a 'yes' to the question if he is OK.

Link: http://dailydevotions.org/index.php/infoDaily-Devotions/2012/09/1611
https://www.youtube.com/watch?v=hLU47YkclSM

A second case in point concerning coastal Maine is provided by humourist Tim Sample. This comes from a live stage show, based partly on an audio record: *How to Talk Yankee: A Downeast Foreign Language Record featuring Bob Bryan and Tim Sample.* During the show, Sample and Bryan discuss several local words and expressions, including 'ayuh'. As the conversation is fairly long, and digresses some-what at several points, only relevant parts are extracted below. Sample begins by suggesting to the audience that there are several ways of say-ing 'ayuh', including both egressive and ingressive variants. As to the more exotic ingressive variant, Sample discusses its use, implying that it forms part of a greeting, and provides explicit instruction and a drill to the audience on how to perform it. He starts:

(12) So I'll tell you one thing that will fool even a native occasionally. You can learn this, you can learn this even if you're driving a Volvo (…) (…) This is the 'Yankee reverse nod with inhalation'. This is how native Yankees communicate with each other on the road.

Sample goes on to give an instruction:

(13) Try this: you inhale like that, and throw your head back at the same time.

He finally illustrates its usage, as part of greeting a local:

(14) So you're driving down the road wishing you was from here. You see old Bert and his '67 Chevy pickup truck. (…). So, what you wanna do, you see Bert over the hill. You [Sample inhales and throws back his head, as instructed] like that. He does it too, see. And for a moment there, you're bonded.

Link: https://www.youtube.com/watch?v=hTz9LBxNai4
Location in link: 0:00–5:00; record also available for purchase (see list of references).

Reference to ingressive speech is also to be found in Maritime Canada. Some instances indicate that it is believed to be specific to the region.

As an example, a host at a local radio station on Prince Edward Island made the following call for listeners to phone in their 'islanderisms':

(15) Now, on to tonight's topic [...]. I have a favour to ask of you. I need you guys to call me in with your 'Islanderisms'. What I mean by that. 'Islanderism', definition = something that is specific to our native tongue. Example: 'slippy', as opposed to 'slippery'. The sound of an inhalation, as opposed to 'yes', and what I mean by that is: _yeah_ (ingressive). You know what I mean. Stuff like that. I want you guys to give me a call with your examples, and we can see just how many islanderisms there are.

   Link: http://www.youtube.com/watch?v=c65CxooxenA
   Location in link: 0:08–0:44

Turning to Norway, popular commentary on ingressive speech is fairly frequent. In a self-sarcastic manner, 'Song about integration' (as featured in the comedy show 'Sex og SingelSiv' broadcast on VGTV) plays on stereotypes of Norwegian culture and behaviour, with a focus on aspects that may be unfamiliar and seem peculiar to immigrants. Among the many stereotypes drawn upon is pulmonic ingressive speech:

(16) (...)
   And if you talk to strangers on the bus you are a jerk
   And when you say 'yes', so say it on ingressive speech

   Link: http://www.youtube.com/watch?v=rBvm3IpRzZ8

As mentioned, the Swedish word *jo/ju* ('yes') may be uttered as a voiceless bilabial fricative or approximant, on a pulmonic ingressive airstream. This feature appears to be more common in northern Sweden, and is stereotypically associated with it (Eklund 2008: 262–263). Popular commentary may be found online. One example is provided by former ice hockey player Jonas Bergqvist, who was born in southern Sweden (Ängelholm, Scania) but moved to a more northerly part (Leksand, Dalcarlia) to attend high school. He recalls that he adopted ingressive *jo/ju* among other features when moving north, and that it was overtly commented on when returning south, reflecting its distinct regional marking:

(17) (...) and that's how it was, when I moved there, then I had that real Scanian dialect, and said: "one and two and three" [Scanian accent] and "are you stupid?" and so on, and everyone said 'what?' all the time. So in some way it was only natural that I tried to make

myself understood, and then it started becoming "one and two and three."[clear standard]. Then sometimes a *jo/ju* (voiceless ingressive bilabial fricative) would enter [into my speech], and then they nearly split their sides laughing when I returned home in the summer.

Link: http://www.youtube.com/watch?v=9T-NTI5Ql7Y
Location in link: 17:40–18:03

6. Conclusion

Although pulmonic ingressive speech may initially admittedly seem like a fairly peripheral matter, upon further consideration the phenomenon is clearly significant in several ways. Its typological status remains a topic of debate, with proposals ranging from 'highly marked' to 'neglected universal'. Significantly for our purposes, its pattern of distribution among regional Englishes has not been sufficiently established; although it has been claimed to occur in a range of regions, there has been a glaring lack of objective evidence. What is more, it is a feature which may possibly reveal historical connections among Englishes across the North Atlantic region. Unfortunately, it has proved challenging to elicit and record pulmonic ingressive speech in many localities. In response, previous researchers have tried several alternatives to standard sociolinguistic methods, including observational methods (Peters 1981) and wide-scope searches of a broad range of written sources (Eklund 2008). In this paper we explored a further alternative, namely the World Wide Web and the many sources of information to which it provides access. Claims were reviewed that ingressives may be hard to study through the media, partly because relevant speaker groups are not well represented therein (Thom 2005; Salö & Hanell 2009). While this may be true to some extent, the massive expansion of the WWW has opened up new possibilities in this regard and necessitates a re-examination of the potential of the media, broadly defined. In this paper a collection of audio and video clips was presented; in addition excerpts from research data sets were provided. This contributed documentation for the existence of pulmonic ingressive speech in an additional set of Englishes. Despite the moderate total number of tokens, ingressive speech was illustrated for both genders, in each case on a brief 'yes' response. Furthermore, illustrations could also be found of the many popular notions surrounding ingressive speech.

Owing to the highly transient nature of the medium and technology involved, it is difficult to predict the future range of applications and benefits of the WWW for the study of spoken language (cf. Crystal 2013: 257, 273). At this stage, however, several possibilities as well as potential limitations are discernible. As to the many possibilities, while spoken language so far clearly is less well represented than written language on the WWW, there is reason to believe that both the amount and the proportion of video and sound material will increase as the WWW continues to grow and technology develops (Crystal 2013: 9; Ess & Consalvo 2011: 2). Since the expansion of the internet over the last ten years has been the greatest in Africa, the Middle East and Latin America, there is also reason to be hopeful that it may provide a source of evidence for pulmonic ingressive speech in these parts of the world, for which objective evidence is completely lacking. What is more, linguists are gradually beginning to realize the formidable, largely unexplored pedagogical potentials of the WWW with regard to spoken language. Squires and Queen (2011: 27) outline some of the benefits of media collections for the teaching of linguistics, which include the ability to illustrate particular features of spoken language.

A number of limitations are however apparent. The time factor is clearly significant. The set of clips presented in this paper was located through a combination of idle web surfing and purposeful, directed searches by the present author, sporadically as well as during more sustained intervals stretching over a total period of 3–4 years. Some were also obtained through kind suggestions by others. It must therefore be acknowledged that the compilation of even a relatively small collection of material is time-consuming, and perhaps best approached as a long-term project. A second serious limitation is the transience of the medium. URLs are notoriously short lived, and there is no guarantee that published web links will even be alive at the time of publication (Crystal 2013: 257; Squires & Queen 2011: 229). It is therefore of course preferable to save material onto more permanent storage, which, however, leads into other issues such as storage space and copyright (Crystal 2013: 273; Squires & Queen 2011: 229). In addition, it is also possible that in the future internet sites providing useful material to a greater extent will require their users to pay. On the whole, however, echoing Crystal's remark that "(…) the sheer scale of the present Internet, let alone its future telecosmic incarnations, has convinced me that we are on the brink of the biggest language revolution ever" (2013: 274–275), there is good reason to be optimistic that the World Wide Web will prove a useful tool for exploring a range of additional features of spoken English, reflecting the value of the internet in ways far beyond those originally envisaged.

Appendix: Excerpts in the original (Nordic languages)

Icelandic (example 9)

BK: Sko, þetta eru foreldrar hans.

EH: Já.

BK: Haraldur Guðmundsson trésmíðameistari og móðirin.

EH: **Já** (ingressive).

BK: Og Leifur bróðir hans sem orti þarna vísuna "Ungu skáldin yrkja kvæði...".

EH: "...án þess að geta það".

BK: "...án þess að geta það/ í Alþýðuhúsinu er ég í fæði/ án þess að éta það".

EH: Já, já, **já** (ingressive), jájá.

BK: En sko þessi bróðir hans, Magnús Haraldsson.

EH: **Já** (ingressive).

BK: Hann dó í bílslysi.

Faroese (example 10)

Hógni: Ja, vælkomin, Tróndur Patursson

Tróndur: Takk fyri tað

Hógni: 40 ár siðani tú fyrsti ferð vart á Listasavninum.

Tróndur: Ja, **ja** (ingressive).

Hógni: Tað er [tú gjert?] sum drottningin, 40 árs jubileum.

Tróndur: Ná, ja, jaja, tað er nakað um tað. Tað er nakað um tað. **Ja** (ingressive)

Hógni: Tú, hvussu tað at vera aftur, aftaná hetta her stíði hjá tykkum?

Tróndur: Ja, ja, Listasavnið er, er ein heilt einastandandi bygningur. (...)

Swedish (example 11)

PL: Nej, men alltså, det måste vara fan ruggigt att få ett tack för den tid som har varit ungefär och så vinner man 20 till

IS: Jo

PL: Åh, [det] är som att sparka undan bena

IS: [jo]

IS: Egentligen hade man ju lust, det hade varit bättre att sluta långt, långt innan, innan man hade, precis när man hade kommit upp på toppen

PL: Ja, för då va man, precis, då hade du varit odödlig, men

IS: [Ja, då hade jag]

PL: [men du] var ju hur bra som helst hur många år som helst

IS: Jo

PL: Och vann och vann och vann
IS: Jo (ingressive, bilabial fricative)

Norwegian (example 16)

Song about Integration: Norwegian lyrics:

(...)
Og snakker du med fremmede på bussen er du dust
Og når du sier "ja" så si det på innoverpust.
(...)

Orthographic transcription from: http://www.youtube.com/
watch?v=rBvm3IpRzZ8

Swedish (example 17)

[...] Och det var ju så när man flyttade dit, då hade jag den här riktigt skånska dialekten, va, och sa "itt och två och tre" och "e du dum i huvudet" och så där, och alla sa 'va' hela tiden, så då blev det liksom på nåt sätt att man försökte göra sig förstådd va, och då började det bli "ett och två och tre och'. Sen kom det in nåt *jo/ju* (ingressive) ibland och så där va, och då skattade de ihjäl sig när man kom hem på sommaren. [...]

Acknowledgements

I would like to thank several people who have provided useful comments and discussions on ingressive speech, translations, and in one case links to media clips; in particular I am grateful to Edit Bugge, Daniel Davis, Clelia LaMonica, Gunnel Melchers, and Friðrik Sólnes.

References

Clarke, S. & Melchers, G. (2005). Ingressive discourse particles across borders: Gender and discourse parallels across the North Atlantic. M. Filppula, J. Klemola, M. Palander & E. Pentitilä (eds) *Dialects across Borders: Selected papers from the 11th international conference on methods in dialectology (Methods XI), Joensuu, August 2002.* Amsterdam/Philadelphia: John Benjamins, 51–72.

Consalvo, M. & Ess, C. (eds) (2011). *The Handbook of Internet Studies.* Oxford: Blackwell Publishing Ltd.

Crystal, D. (2013). *Language and the Internet.* Cambridge Books Online. Cambridge: Cambridge University Press.

Donovan, K. (Producer, Director, Narrator) (1990). *The Irish in Cape Breton*

1713–1990 (part 3 of 6). Sydney, Nova Scotia, Canada: Irish Benevolent Society. Retrieved from: http://www.youtube.com/watch?v=JsmyRknWUVo

Eklund, R. (2007). Pulmonic ingressive speech: A neglected universal? *Proceedings of Fonetik 2007, Stockholm, TMH-QPSR, KTH*, 50, 21–24.

———. (2008). Pulmonic ingressive phonation: Diachronic and synchronic characteristics, distribution and function in animal and human sound production and in human speech. *Journal of the International Phonetic Association* 38, 235–324.

Ess, C. & Consalvo, M. (2011). Introduction: What is "Internet Studies"? M. Consalvo & C. Ess (eds) *The Handbook of Internet Studies*. Oxford: Blackwell Publishing Ltd, 1–8.

Hanell, L. & Salö, L. (2009, June). Säg jo och andas in – samtidigt. *Språktidningen* 3, 14–19.

Peters, F.J. (1981). *The Paralinguistic Sympathetic Ingressive Affirmative in English and the Scandinavian Languages*. (Unpublished doctoral dissertation). New York University, New York.

Pitschmann, L.A. (1987). The linguistic use of the ingressive air-stream in German and Scandinavian languages. *General Linguistics* 27, 153–161.

Sample, T. (1991). *How to Talk Yankee: A Downeast Foreign Language Record Featuring Bob Bryan and Tim Sample*. Down East Publisher.

Shorrocks, G. (2003). Pulmonic ingressive speech in Newfoundland English: A case of Irish-English influence? H.L.C. Tristram (ed.) *The Celtic Englishes III*. Heidelberg: Universitätsverlag Winter, 374–389.

Squires, L. & Queen, R. (2011). Media clips collection: Creation and application for the linguistics classroom. *American Speech* 86, 220–234.

Steinbergs, R. (1993). *The Use of the Paralinguistic Sympathetic Ingressive Affirmative in Speakers of English in the St. John's, Newfoundland Area*. (Unpublished master's dissertation). Memorial University, St. John's, Newfoundland, Canada.

Sundkvist, P. (2012a). Pulmonic ingressive speech in Shetland English. *World Englishes* 31, 434–448.

———. (2012b). Pulmonic ingressive speech in the Shetland Isles: Some observations on a potential Nordic relic feature. *Nordic Journal of English Studies* 11, 188–202.

Thom, E.J. (2005). *The Gaelic Gasp and its North Atlantic Cousins: A Study of Ingressive Pulmonic Speech in Scotland*. (Unpublished master's dissertation). University College London, London, UK.

18 Another Look at Preposition Stranding: English and Swedish Discourse Patterns

Francesco-Alessio Ursini
Stockholm University

1. Introduction: Basic Aspects of Preposition Stranding

Preposition Stranding (henceforth PS) is a syntactic construction that can be found across Germanic languages (Bolinger 1977, 1978). PS involves a non-canonical word order, in which a preposition and its object noun phrase (henceforth NP) are not adjacent, hence they appear to be "stranded". PS includes three sub-types of constructions: pseudo-passives, relative clauses and *wh*-constructions (Koopman 2000). The existence of PS in Southern and Western Germanic languages, such as German and Dutch, is considered a controversial matter (van Riemsdijk 1990, 1998; Maling & Zaenen 1985; Truswell 2009). However, PS is certainly attested in English and most Scandinavian languages including Swedish, Norwegian, Danish, and Icelandic (Åfarli 1992; Takami 1992; van Riemsdijk 1998; Law 2005; Klingvall 2012). Interestingly, some of these works observe that PS seems to be an uncommon construction in Swedish (Takami 1992; Klingvall 2012). For this reason, in this paper we concentrate on English and Swedish, in order to address whether this phenomenon can receive a unified account across both languages, regardless of its language-related frequency. We start by discussing some preliminary examples in (1)-(8)[1]:

(1) (This chair)$_i$ was sat on (NP)$_i$ (by Luigi)

(pseudo-passive)

(2) (The room)$_i$ that/Ø we went into (NP)$_i$ is occupied

(relative clause)

---

[1] The examples in (1)-(8) have been adapted from (corpora-based) examples found in previous literature, in particular Takami (1992) (Swedish), Truswell (2009) (English). The discourse-bound examples in (9)-(14) have been also tested with the help of native speakers of either language, which we thank for their patience.

How to cite this book chapter:
Ursini, F.-A. 2015. Another Look at Preposition Stranding: English and Swedish Discourse Patterns. In: Shaw, P., Erman, B., Melchers, G. and Sundkvist, P. (eds) *From Clerks to Corpora: essays on the English language yesterday and today*. Pp. 323–347. Stockholm: Stockholm University Press. DOI: http://dx.doi.org/10.16993/bab.r License: CC-BY.

(3) (Which apples)$_i$ are you talking about (NP)$_i$?

(wh-construction)

(4) *(De här sängarna)$_i$ har sovits i (NP)$_i$*

(pseudo-passive)

(The here beds)$_i$ have been slept in (NP)$_i$

'These beds have been slept in'

(5) *(De här sängarna)$_i$ har sovits i (NP)$_i$ av Jon*

(The here beds)$_i$ have been slept in (NP)$_i$ by John

'These beds have been slept in by John'

(6) *Dörr-en är målad av Jon*

(passive)

Door-ART is painted by John

'The door has been painted by John'

(7) *(Det rum)$_i$ som/(Ø) vi har betalat 300 kronor för (NP)$_i$ är ledigt*

(The room)$_i$ that/(Ø) we have paid 300 crowns for (NP)$_i$ is vacant

'The room that we have paid 300 crowns for is vacant'

(8) *(Vilk-a äpple-n)$_i$ pratar du om (NP)$_i$?*

(wh-construction)

(Which-PL apple-PL)$_i$ talk you about (NP)$_i$?

'which apples are you talking about?'

The "basic" position of the stranded NP is indicated via brackets; original and stranded NPs share the same index in order to highlight their structural relation. The English examples in (1)-(3) show that the NPs *this chair, the room* and *which apple* appear stranded from their governing prepositions, respectively *on, into* and *about*. Note: *that* in (2) can be omitted, a fact we represent via the symbol "Ø" to represent phonologically null/silent heads. The examples in (4)-(8) offer an illustration of PS in Swedish: pseudo-passives (i.e. (4)-(5)), standard passive constructions (i.e. (6)), relative clauses (7) and *wh*-constructions (i.e. (8)). These examples suggest that PS in Swedish follows similar but not identical patterns of distribution to English, principally centred on two properties.

First, Swedish pseudo-passive sentences cannot include the "passive" preposition *av* 'by', as examples (4)-(5) show[2]. Swedish passive sentences,

---

[2] There is an ongoing debate concerning which prepositions can occur in pseudo-passives (Abels 2003: ch.1-2). We gloss over this debate here, since it is orthogonal to our discussion.

on the other hand, can normally include *av*, like their English counterparts, and introduce the deep subject NP (*John*, in (6)). Second, Swedish pseudo-passives include the auxiliary verb *ha* 'to have', rather than *vara* 'to be', as their passive counterparts (Holmes & Hinchcliffe 2008: ch.3). Thus, Swedish pseudo-passive and passive sentences are not as closely related as their English counterparts. Examples (7)-(8), instead, show how relative clause and *wh*-constructions sub-types of PS are realized in Swedish. The relative pronoun *som* 'that' may be freely omitted, as in the case of English. In *wh*-constructions, the *wh*-pronoun *vilka* 'which' combines with the NP *äpplen* and agrees in number, as the glosses suggest.

As the examples seem to suggest, the PS patterns in both languages seem relatively clear. However, theoretical accounts of PS offer fairly different analyses of this phenomenon. Simplifying matters somewhat, classic and minimalist (transformational) proposals offer a movement-based analysis (Hornstein & Weinberg 1981; van Riemsdijk 1990, 1998; Maling & Zaenen 1985; Koopman 2000; Truswell 2009). According to these analyses, PS is an operation that targets NPs and moves them into sentence-initial position. In our examples, the bracketed and indexed NPs mark the starting position of the NPs that are moved in sentence-initial position. Within non-transformational theories, one analysis about PS exists within "Head-Driven Phrase Structure Grammar" (henceforth HPSG). The analysis found in Tseng (2000, 2004, 2005) suggests that PS involves two "copies" of the same NP, the two indexed NPs in our example. The sentence-initial copy, instead of the original copy, is the only phonologically realized copy in a sentence. *Qua* copies, both NPs must be identical in form; if they are not, PS cannot be licensed. Although other analyses of PS could certainly be formulated, this analysis represents the most prominent proposal, within this non-transformational framework.

Given these assumptions and the data in (1)-(8), it seems that both types of approaches can offer equally plausible, although theoretically different accounts of PS. Two questions that arise at this point, given this equilibrium among proposals, can be formulated as follows. A first more empirical question is whether we can discuss a broader set of data, in order to better understand the predictive power of these approaches. A second more theoretical question is whether we can offer a third, alternative analysis of this broader set of data that can perhaps improve upon previous analyses.

The goal of this paper is to offer an answer to this question by offering a "third way" analysis of PS. This analysis is couched in *Type-Logical*

Syntax, a formal, non-transformational approach to morpho-syntactic structures (Morryll 2011). Via this approach, we first offer a more flexible approach to the lexical properties of our NPs. Then, we sketch an analysis that shows how these properties are related to syntactic structures, and that a unified account of PS in English and Swedish is possible and could perhaps be seen as theory-neutral, to some extent. To offer this solution, we follow this plan. In section 2, we present the inter-sentential data; in section 3, we introduce our framework; in section 4, we offer our analysis, and compare it with previous analyses; in section 5, we offer some conclusions to the paper.

2. The Data: PS Licensing in Inter-Sentential Contexts

Standard theoretical analyses of PS tend to focus on intra-sentential data, as (1)-(8) show. However, descriptive works usually observe that PS is often licensed in certain inter-sentential contexts, as well. A common pattern is that when the stranded NP denotes a *specific, definite* referent in discourse, then PS can be licensed, although this is not a necessary condition. This often represents the preferred word order for a sentence (Huddlestone & Pullum 2002: 137-140; Holmes & Hinchcliffe 2008: 140; Ward & Birner 2012: 1938-1942). This can be the case, as PS can license the formation of *anaphoric relations* between a stranded NP and a possible antecedent, insofar as these NPs select the same referent in discourse. These anaphoric relations act as *ties* that establish the *cohesion* of a text, and can be established both as relations between (argument) NPs, but also via other devices (e.g. temporal relations). Since these factors play a key role in our discussion, we discuss cohesion and anaphoric relations in a compact but accurate manner, in the remainder of this section.

We start with cohesion, and define it as a syntactic property of sentences in a text to express information about the same topics and referents in discourse (Kehler 2011: 1964). One way to achieve cohesion is to have NPs referring to the same entities in sentence-initial position (the same chair, in ex. (9) below), in any sentence after the initial sentence. This is because the sentence-initial position is often reserved for topical noun phrases, which usually convey "old" information (Zeevat 2011: 956; Ward & Birner 2012: 1945-1948). Another way to achieve coherence is also by establishing precise temporal *and* causal relations among the events described by each sentence (Zeevat 2011: 957-958; Kehler 2011: 1965). A possibility that arises, then, is that PS may or may not uniquely determine whether a mini-discourse is cohesive: when the stranded NP conveys information about an "old" referent. I show these patterns in English via (9)-(11), in which I index the anaphorically related NPs via sub-scripts:

(9) I bought (this chair)$_i$/(a chair)$_j$ on the left. (The chair)$_{i/\#j}$ has been sat on

(10) (This room)$_i$ is free. (The room)$_i$/(a room)$_{\#j}$ that we went into is not

(11) A: (Which apples)$_i$ are you talking about?
      B: (The apples)$_i$/(some apples)$_{\#j}$ on the left side of the table

I concentrate on cases in which PS seems to be the key construction that allows the formation of anaphoric relations. In (9), sequence of tenses "simple past; present perfect" does not allow the formation of clear temporal relations. Thus, the event of buying the chair on the left and somebody sitting on it may be not causally "connected", but just occur in the past, with respect to the moment of utterance. The same reasoning can be applied to (10)-(11), although the sequence of tenses is different. In these cases, I would like to suggest that PS is the key syntactic construction that allows cohesion to be established. Since precise causal and perhaps temporal relations between the events that the sentences describe seem to be lacking, PS seems to be the key factor that licenses a cohesive mini-text[3]. The principle behind this relation can be described as follows.

If a first sentence introduces a definite *and* specific NP, such as *the chair*, then PS is licensed in a second sentence, as (9)-(11) suggest. If an indefinite, non-specific NP such as *a chair* is introduced, instead, the whole mini-text becomes incoherent, as the "#" and the lack of matching indexes display (*i* on *the chair*, *j* on *a chair*) in each example. This is because the sentence-initial NP matches in features (the combination of definiteness *and* specificity, in (9)-(11)) with the previous NP, otherwise they cannot possibly refer to the same entity in discourse: that is, be *anaphorically* related. Thus, it seems that when no other

---

[3] An important aspect is that other parts of speech can license the formation of temporal, anaphoric relations. An anonymous reviewer observes that the presence of sentence-final adverbs could render a mini-text involving an indefinite-definite NP sequence cohesive (*I bought a chair yesterday. The chair…*). In other words, PS may also involve non-matching NPs, but when other anaphoric relations allow cohesion to emerge. In these cases, the relation(s) between NPs are semantic in nature, hence beyond the scope our discussion. See however von Heusinger (2007); Zeevat (2011) and references therein, for discussion.

anaphoric relations can be established, an NP should be stranded from its preposition for a text to achieve cohesion. Furthermore, this stranding procedure seems to involve "feature-matching" as a condition that licenses anaphoric relations. Note that what is at stake in these cases is cohesion, not ungrammaticality. Each sentence in a mini-discourse can be perfectly grammatical, and yet the resulting text can fail to be cohesive, if no anaphoric relations are established.

This fact seems to hold for each of the three PS-type constructions, as examples (9)-(11) suggest. These examples also show that the stranded NPs are not formally identical to their anaphorically related NP. Consider (10), for instance: the two NPs *this room* and *the room* share the same values of specificity and definiteness, as a deictic phrase and a definite noun phrase, respectively (Heusinger 2007, 2011; Diessel 2012). Furthermore, the question in (11) contains a form of *wh*-construction PS, and can be answered only via an answer that also contains a definite and specific NP, in this case *the apple*, otherwise the answer is incohesive (cf. Krifka 2001, 2004). Thus, one type of anaphoric relation is established when two NPs carry matching morphological features, even if the NPs do not belong to exactly the same (syntactic) sub-type. Examples (12)-(14) show that a similar picture holds for Swedish, but with certain differences:

(12) *Jag köpte (stolen)$_i$/(någon stol)$_j$ till vänster.*
(Den här stolen)$_{i/\#j}$ var sutten på
I bought (chair-ART)i/(some chair)j to left-ART
(The here chair)$_{i/\#j}$ was sat on
'I bought the chair/a chair to the left. This chair was sat on'

(13) *(Detta rum)$_i$ är ledigt. (Det rum)$_i$/(något rum)$_{\#j}$ som vi gick in i*
är det inte
(This room)i is vacant. (The room)i/(some room)$_{\#j}$ that we went into is it not
'This room is vacant. The/a room that we went in is not'

(14) A: *(Vilk-a äpple-n)$_i$ pratar du om?*
(Which-PL apple-PL)$_i$ talk you about?
'Which apples are you talking about?'
B: *(Äpple-na)$_i$/(några äpple-n)$_{\#j}$ på vänster sida av bord-et*
(Apple-PL.ART)$_i$/(some apple-PL.ART)$_{\#j}$ on left-ART side of table-ART
'The apples/some apples on the left side of the table'

Example (12) shows that when the non-specific *någon stol* 'a chair' (lit. 'some chair') occurs in the first sentence, the NP *den här stol* 'this chair' does not find a suitable antecedent. This is the case, as *någon stol* is an antecedent NP that does not match the features that *Den här stolen* carries. The net effect is that the speaker appears to identify via the second sentence one chair that, however, was not mentioned in the first sentence. Thus, the mini-discourse appears incohesive, since no other anaphoric relations (e.g. temporal ones) are established. The same patterns emerge in (13)-(14), *modulo* the slightly different types of NPs and PS constructions involved[4]. Hence, both specificity and definiteness seem to play a role in the distribution of PS in discourse, as these features allow the establishment of cohesion (or lack thereof) in a text, when no other anaphoric relations can be established. Hence, an analysis of this phenomenon must include a treatment of the role of these features, and their relation to word order and cohesion.

One interesting dilemma that these data present consists in assessing the exact nature of this problem. From a theoretical perspective, specificity and definiteness are features that play a role at a morphological and semantic level of representation. The morphological values permit an anaphoric relation between two NPs to be established, and the related mini-text may become cohesive as a result. Both *the chair* and *this chair* are specific, definite NPs that can refer to a given chair. Hence, they can refer to the same chair in discourse, and license a discourse that is also semantically coherent (Kehler 2011; Zeevat 2011). As our data suggest, our problem regarding the nature of PS seems to involve a complex interplay between morphological, syntactic and semantic levels of representation.

As a consequence of this pin-pointing the nature of our PS dilemma, our empirical question can now receive a precise formulation. The extension of either current HPSG or minimalist analyses of PS to these data does not appear as a simple matter. One problem that both approaches share pertains to the feature values of anaphorically related NPs. The approach outlined in e.g. Tseng (2000: ch.4) includes an inter-sentential treatment of anaphoric phenomena that transformational approaches lack (Klingvall 2012), but the morpho-semantic

---

[4] We note here that this pattern emerges when indefinite *and* non-specific NPs such as *någon stol* are involved. Swedish differs from English in having a second indefinite article: *en* lit. 'one', ambiguous with respect to specificity. However, in PS constructions *en* can only have specific value (e.g. *en stol* 'one (specific) chair', in (12)). Our analysis can be extended to *en* as well, but the use of *någon* in our example better highlights the parallels between Swedish and English PS constructions.

problem of anaphora resolution would remain intact. This is the case, as this approach crucially relies on copied NPs and their phonologically realized counterparts to be formally identical. Our data in (9)-(14) suggest that this assumption is not tenable, at an inter-sentential level. Two NPs can be anaphorically related, license PS and a cohesive text, as long as they both carry the definiteness and specificity features. Therefore, a more flexible approach seems to be called for. Since both current analyses of PS seem to be problematic, we propose a third analysis in the next section.

3. The Proposal: An extended TL calculus

In this section our formal analysis is based on a framework known as *Type-Logical calculi* (henceforth TL, Jäger 2001, 2005; Moortgat 2010, 2011; Morryll 2011). Our variant of TL implements some assumptions from certain variants of minimalist syntax, notably Distributed Morphology (Embick & Noyer 2001; Harbour 2007; Harley 2012). However, the proposal I wish to make takes an inherently non-transformational perspective, in part closer to HPSG and other similar frameworks. I will spell out these assumptions, as we proceed in our presentation of the framework. We choose our variant of TL for two reasons. First, TL is a formally explicit framework that can treat morphological and syntactic data alike, without any supplementary assumptions specific to each domain. Second, it offers tools that allow one to easily analyse inter-sentential data, at least in our formulation. Here we offer a compact discussion; a more thorough presentation of this framework is found in previous work of the author (Ursini 2011, 2013 a, b, c, 2015 a, b; Ursini & Akagi 2013 a, b). I present some key assumptions of our TL analysis, then we move to our innovations.

First, parts of speech are mapped onto or assigned *types*, which can be considered as either being "complete" or "incomplete" bits of morpho-syntactic information. Complete types represent constituents that can stand as distinct, independent constituents (e.g. *np* for NPs such as *the girl*). Incomplete types represent constituents that must combine with other constituents to form a complete unit. An intransitive verb such as *runs* can be assigned type *np\s*, since it can combine with an *np*, *the girl*. The result is the sentence *the girl runs*, which is assigned the type *s* of sentences. Thus, types can also be used to represent the syntactic *valence* of lexical items, and possible restrictions on which types of arguments/phrases heads can take.

Second, we implement two connectives, "/" and "·", that are known as the *right division* (or just division) and the *product* connectives (Moortgat 2010: § 2; Morrill 2011: ch. 1). Both connectives are *binary* and *associative*, but product is also *non-commutative*. Products of types (e.g. *a·b*) are taken in this order. Third, we follow some TL calculi that take a psycholinguistic model of sentence production, and propose that sentences are derived in a top-down ("left-to-right", in linear terms) manner (Morryll 2011). This assumption is also found in psycholinguistics models such as Levelt (1989); Phillips (2006); Jarema & Libben (2007). More importantly, this assumption will turn out to be germane to our goals, since it allows us to treat anaphoric phenomena in a straightforward manner, as shown in section 4. The three assumptions represent innovations that I introduce with respect to standard TL calculi.

First, I leave aside other standard TL connectives, such as *left division* "\" and Jäger's (2001, 2005) connective "|" for anaphoric relations. In particular, I will suggest a way to treat anaphoric relations that exclusively rely on the interplay of division and product known as the *merge* schema, in part adumbrated in Jäger (2001: 78-81). I aim to show that, once we offer a formal analysis of the distributional properties of our lexical items, our basic combinatorial system will suffice to account for our data. Specifically, I aim to show that our PS data require a simple but precise analysis of the distribution of prepositions and nouns based on their morphological features.

Second, I take a more sophisticated view concerning types other than the one found in standard TL calculi, as we follow recent analyses on the nature of morpho-syntactic categories. Thus, I assume that lexical and functional categories are not primitive categories, but clusters of morphological features (Hale & Kayser 2002; Harbour 2007; Adger 2010; Acquaviva & Panagiotidis 2012). For instance, nouns include features such as gender and number while prepositions lack these features, but they may include a "spatial" feature or similar other non-nominal features. Hence, in our system morphemes correspond to *products* of features, which can then differ with respect to value they can carry (e.g. "male" or "female" for the gender feature). Here I follow proposals that assume the "separation hypothesis": vocabulary insertion occurs *after* morphological derivations (Levelt 1989; Embick & Noyer 2001). Thus, abstract morphological objects may lack an overt phonological exponent, or are realized by different exponents across languages (here, *that* vs. *som*: Embick & Noyer 2001). We return to this point in section 4.

Third, I assume the distributional properties of categories can be represented explicitly, via our type system. If transitive verbs (*loves*) and prepositions (e.g. *to*) act as heads with 2-valence, then their type should reflect this shared property. Hence, different categories and constituents (verbs, prepositions, phrases, sentences, and discourses) can be reduced to a handful of types. Depending on the valence of a constituent, one can determine the type *assigned* to this constituent. I capture this assumption by using only one basic type p, which is mnemonic for both "phrase" and "product of features". The rules for deriving other types are defined in (15):

(15) 1. p is a morphological type   (Lexical type)
2. If x is a type and y is a type, then x/y is a type (Type I.: Division)
3. If x is a type and y is a type, then $x \cdot y$ is a type (Type I.: Product)
4. If x/y is a type and y is a type, then $(x/y) \cdot y \vdash x$, $y \cdot (x/y) \vdash x$ (MI: For. A.)
5. If x/y is a type and y/z is a type, then $(x/y) \cdot (y/z) \vdash x/z$ (MI: Cut rule)
6. Nothing else is a type (Closure rule)

In words, rule 1 introduces our basic type p. Rule 2 says that two basic types combined via division (x, y) form a complex type, e.g. a head which can take one argument (here, x/y: a definite article taking an NP as an argument, as in *the car*). Rule 3 says that two basic types combined via product form a complex type that bundles information (i.e. $x \cdot y$). Rule 3 can also be used to introduce information (i.e. from x to $x \cdot y$), in a manner that we will discuss thoroughly in section 4. In this case, we take our basic type to represent single features, a move that we also fully motivate in section 4.

Rules 4 and 5 introduce two instances of *merge* schemas, rules that govern how (right) division and product types interact. Rule 4 is known as *forward application*. It says that the product of a complex (division) type and a simple type yields a certain output type, provided that the *input* type of the complex type (here, y) matches that of the simple type. Thus, rule 4 governs how a head can combine with an argument to form a more complex constituent such as a phrase, for instance. It also determines what the *output* of this phrase is (here, x), provided that the two input types "match". As rule 4 plays a crucial role in our analysis, we return to the specific details of its application when we discuss the data.

Rule 5 is a *merge* schema known as the *cut rule*, and says that two complex types sharing their "internal" type can be combined into a new type. This rule plays a key role for the analysis of our discourse data; we delay a more precise explanation to section 4. Rule 6 says that no other rules are necessary. In our system, the symbol "⊢" represents the *merge* schemas as ternary relations between the types of two input constituents and the type of their output, the constituent they form when merged together. If the NP *the girl* and the verb *runs* are assigned matching types, their merge will form the VP *the girl runs*. As a consequence, in our system rules 4 and 5 offer two formally precise schemas to "prove" that larger constituents can be formed, via our basic set of rules and types.

Overall, our minimal set of derivational rules allow us to generate complex type sets, intended as types that we can *assign* to our constituents. For our purposes, the set $TYPE=\{p \cdot p,\ p \cdot p/p \cdot p,\ p \cdot p/p \cdot p/p \cdot p\}$ will suffice to account for all the data at hand. This set respectively includes arguments taken as bundles of features, 1- and 2-valence heads. The precise nature of these types will become clear when we discuss how and why these types are assigned to our constituents, in the next section. However, before we introduce our analysis, we must discuss one last aspect of our formal apparatus. In order to capture the incremental nature of our derivations, we define a simple *pre-order* as the pair of an interval set *I*, and an addition operation "+", i.e. <*I*,+>. This pre-order represents an *index set*, which in turn allows the representation of all the steps in a derivation as sequential elements (e.g. *t*, *t+1*, *t+2*, etc.). We also implement two labels, *Lexical Selection* (LS) and *Merge Introduction*[5] (MI) in order to explicitly mark the introduction of a new element in a derivation, and the merge of two elements, respectively. With this formal apparatus at our disposal, we move to our data.

4. The Analysis: The Distribution of PS

The goal of this section is to offer our TL analysis of the data. We start by motivating our *type assignment* for our constituents, before moving to the derivations that illustrate how we can account for our data.

---

[5] In TL calculi, *merge* is an *elimination*, rather than *introduction* rule for division: It removes slashes in a structure. The label "introduction" stresses that morphemes are combined into more complex structures.

We start by motivating which categories are assigned the (product) type $p \cdot p$, which represents phrases that carry bundled morphological features. We assign this type to NPs *qua* phrasal arguments of a head. As our examples show, NPs carry (at least) the features p_{+f} or p_{-f}, for specificity, definiteness and similar other features. This simple fact seems to motivate the use of a product type for NPs. We then assume that *wh*-phrases *which apples* and *vilka äpplen* can be assigned the same type. We thus follow standard treatments of this category, although we choose a more coarse-grained perspective than standard analyses of *wh*-phrases (Alexiadou *et al.* 2000; Bianchi 2002a, b; Vermaat 2005). We represent this complex type as $p_{\pm spec}$, for simplicity, and leave the values for definiteness, (plural) number, pronominal and relative features implicit, in our analysis. Nothing crucial hinges on this notational simplification.

As our initial type assignment shows, we also assume that features can have different *values*, which can in turn determine whether an instance of *merge* is successful or not. Analyses of feature systems abound in the literature, in TL calculi and other frameworks (Johnson & Bayer 1995; Bernardi & Szabolcsi 2008; Tseng 2005; Adger 2010; Stabler 2013). As we only discuss cases in which the binary value(s) of features may determine the well-formedness or cohesion of a syntactic (or discourse) derivation, our analysis has an inherently theory-neutral perspective. However, the core aspects of our analysis are based on Johnson & Bayer (1995) and their proposal on *feature percolation*, as it will soon become clear.

We move to spatial prepositions, as we wish to offer an argument for assigning them the type $p \cdot p$ as well. Several minimalist analyses treat these prepositions as sequences of functional heads, which may or may not be phonologically realized. Thus, a non-stranded preposition such as *in* would be assigned the type $p \cdot p / p \cdot p / p \cdot p$ of heads, with its complement phrase being an NP. A stranded preposition would be assigned the same type, but it would also combine with a non-pronounced (silent) copy of the stranded NP (Koopman 2000; Truswell 2009; Svenonius 2006, 2010). Here we follow a different minimalist analysis of SPs, sometimes known as the "P-within-P" hypothesis (Hale & Kayser 2002; cf. also Emonds 1985; van Riemsdjik 1990, 1998). This analysis suggests that spatial prepositions involve a complex structure, in which a silent prepositional head takes another preposition as its specifier phrase[6]. Hence, a prepositional phrase such as *in the garden*

---

[6] TL calculi usually do not employ "silent" categories, although this assumption is not uniform (cf. Jäger 2005: ch. 2 vs Moortgat 2011 §2). This matter is not crucial, for our discussion.

would involve the phrase *in* (i.e. the "internal" preposition), a silent head "(P)", and the complement phrase *the garden*.

Via this assumption, our prepositions occurring in PS contexts are assigned the type $p{\cdot}p$, which is the same type they would receive in a non-stranded position. A minimal *proviso* is that when these prepositions occur in stranded positions, they act as complements of a verb, rather than specifiers of another preposition. Thus, prepositions such as *in* in *the room we went in* have a particle-like distribution, as complements of the verb (here, *went*: Åfarli 1992; Abels 2003). Importantly, although spatial prepositions and NPs are assigned type $p{\cdot}p$, they differ in the values of the features they carry as phrases. For instance, prepositions seem not to carry the feature value $_{p\pm spec}$ of NPs, a minimal morphological difference that suffices to distinguish these two categories. Both categories, though, can act as arguments of relational heads, something we represent via the general use of product types for phrases.

We move to our analysis of heads: verbs, prepositions introducing pseudo-passive constructions and complementizers. We assign the type $p{\cdot}p/p{\cdot}p/p{\cdot}p$ of 2-valence heads to these three categories, although with some minimal differences. First, verbs carry a "voice" feature, thus either a passive or active value on their output type. They can only merge with a preposition that matches these features, such as passive prepositions. For the sake of simplicity, we treat compound verbs as forming a single lexical unit: both *har sovits* 'have been slept' and *has been sat* receive this type, *qua* verbs. We thus assign type $p{\cdot}p_{+spec}/p{\cdot}p_{\pm pass}/p{\cdot}p$ to each verb[7], depending on whether it has active or passive voice. Note that since temporal features do not play a crucial role in the analysis of our examples, we omit them. However, a more thorough analysis of PS patterns could be offered, by adding a discussion of these features and their role in forming cohesive texts. We leave such an extension aside, for the time being.

Second, we also assign the type $p{\cdot}p_{pass}/p{\cdot}p/p{\cdot}p$ to passive prepositions (*by*, *av*) as heads, for a simple reason. Standard analyses of passive sentences suggest that these prepositions take the deep subject NP (*Luigi* in (1)) and the passive verb phrase (e.g. *this chair has been sat on* in (1)) as arguments (Abels 2003; Gehrke & Grillo 2009; Ishizuka 2010). Thus, their specifier input type must carry a passive feature value. Third, we also assign this relational type to complementizers, as heads

---

[7] For simplicity, rather than for necessity, we also assume that our heads always take a specific (specifier) input type $p{\cdot}p_{+spec}$, since all our examples involve specific NPs.

introducing relative clauses (*that*, *som*), in line with standard assumptions (Alexiadou *et al.* 2000; Bianchi 2002a; Vermaat 2005). We thus assign the type $p \cdot p_{+spec}/p \cdot p_{rel}/p \cdot p$ to this category. Before we show how these types can be combined together to form our sentences, we summarize our type assignment in (16):

(16) a. $p \cdot p$={*this chair, de här sängarna, up, i, which apples, vilka äpplen*}

b. $p \cdot p/p \cdot p/p \cdot p$={*was sat, by, av, that, som*}

From this type assignment and the rules in (15), we can offer an account of how our examples are derived, starting from pseudo-passives. We repeat (1) as (17a) to illustrate our account. We use simplified notations for types (e.g. p_+ for p_{spec}, p' for p_{pass}, p'' for p_{rel}) and shortened lexical entries in our derivations (e.g. *this* for *this chair*) for reasons of space:

(17) a. This chair was sat on by Luigi

$\quad$ b. t. $\quad$ [this chair$_{p \cdot p+}$] $\hfill$ (LS)

$\quad\quad$ t+1. [was sat$_{p \cdot p+/p \cdot p'/p \cdot p}$] $\hfill$ (LS)

$\quad\quad$ t+2. [this chair$_{p \cdot p+}$]·[was sat$_{p \cdot p+/p \cdot pp'/p \cdot p}$]⊢

$\quad\quad\quad$ [$_{p \cdot p'/p \cdot p}$[this chair$_{p \cdot p+}$] was sat$_{p \cdot p+/p \cdot p'/p \cdot p}$] $\hfill$ (MI)

$\quad\quad$ t+3. [on$_{p \cdot p}$] $\hfill$ (LS)

$\quad\quad$ t+4. [$_{p \cdot p'/p \cdot p}$[this chair$_{p \cdot p+}$] was sat$_{p \cdot p+/p \cdot p'/p \cdot p}$]·[on$_{p \cdot p}$]⊢

$\quad\quad\quad$ [$_{p \cdot p'}$[this chair$_{p \cdot p+}$] was sat$_{p \cdot p+/p \cdot p'/p \cdot p}$ [on$_{p \cdot p}$]] $\hfill$ (MI)

$\quad\quad$ t+5. [by $_{p \cdot p'/p \cdot p/p \cdot p}$] $\hfill$ (LS)

$\quad\quad$ t+6. [$_{p \cdot p'}$[this chair$_{p \cdot p+}$] was sat$_{p \cdot p/p \cdot p'/p \cdot p}$ [on$_{p \cdot p}$]]·[by$_{p \cdot p'/p \cdot p/p \cdot p}$]⊢

$\quad\quad\quad$ [$_{p \cdot p/p \cdot p}$[$_{p \cdot p'}$[this$_{p \cdot p+}$] was sat$_{p \cdot p+/p \cdot p'/p \cdot p}$[on$_{p \cdot p}$]] by$_{p \cdot p'/p \cdot p/p \cdot p}$] (MI)

$\quad\quad$ t+8. [Luigi$_{p \cdot p}$] $\hfill$ (LS)

$\quad\quad$ t+9. [$_{p \cdot p/p \cdot p}$[$_{p \cdot p'}$[this$_{p \cdot p+}$] was$_{p \cdot p+/p \cdot p'/p \cdot p}$[on$_{p \cdot p}$]] by$_{p \cdot p'/p \cdot p/p \cdot p}$]·[Luigi$_{p \cdot p}$]⊢

$\quad\quad\quad$ [$_{p \cdot p}$[$_{p \cdot p}$[this$_{p \cdot p+}$] was$_{p \cdot p+/p \cdot p'/p \cdot p}$[on$_{p \cdot p}$]] by$_{p \cdot p'/p \cdot p/p \cdot p}$[Luigi$_{p \cdot p}$]] (MI)

Our derivation reads as follows. The NP denoting the object, *this chair*, merges with the passive verb *was sat*. The result of this operation merges with the spatial preposition *on*, thus deriving the VP *this chair was sat on* (steps *t* to *t*+4). The preposition *by* carries passive features, and merges with the passive VP *this chair was sat on*. This is the case, as the passive feature values of the two merged constituents match (step *t*+6). The deep subject NP *Luigi* is then merged, and (17a) is derived accordingly (steps *t*+7 to *t*+9). An important result of this derivation, then, is that the word order in a sentence involving PS can be derived *without* assuming silent or copied NPs in the sentence-final position. Thus, we can explain how English pseudo-passives are derived as complete sentences without resorting to assumptions involving copied/

moved constituents. Since we have also shown how a grammatical pseu-do-passive sentence is derived, we can now show how an ungrammat-ical sentence is instead blocked. We do so by offering a "compressed" derivation for our Swedish example (5), repeated as (18a):

(18) a. *De här sängarna har sovits i av Jon

b. $t+6$. $[_{p\cdot p}[$De här sängarna$_{p\cdot p+}]$har sovits$_{p\cdot p/p\cdot p/p\cdot p}[$ i$_{p\cdot p}]]\cdot[$ av$_{p\cdot p'/p\cdot p/p\cdot p}]$
⊢*

(Feature mismatch, derivation crashes)

We focus on the derivational step at which the derivation blocks or "crashes", $t+6$. The merge of a clausal phrase that lacks a passive feature (*de här sängarna har sovits i* 'these beds have been slept in') and passive preposition results in a mismatch of features. Recall now that Swedish pseudo-passives differ from "true" passives by having *ha* 'to have' as the main auxiliary verb, hence being closer to active forms. This fact suggests that *har sovits* carries the opposite voice feature val-ues of *av*. As we have established via rule 4, if two merged units do not match in type/feature value, then a derivation is blocked. Thus, (18b) suggests that our analysis *predicts* the ungrammaticality of (18a) as a feature mismatch case. This basic aspect of *merge*, together with the type assignment for our English and Swedish lexical items, seems to suffice to explain this datum. Via this result, other data can now also be accounted for, a fact that we show by focusing on relative clause PS patterns in both languages. Recall that the difference between English and Swedish pertains to the exponent that realizes the complementizer head: *that* and *som*. If the exponents differ, but the lexical items that are merged are the same, then the same type of derivation can generate the structures of both English and Swedish relative PS sentences. We show this derivational symmetry in (19)-(20):

(19) a. The room that we went into is occupied

b. $t.$ $[$ the room$_{p\cdot p+}]$ (LS)

$t+1.$ $[$ that$_{p\cdot p+/p\cdot''/p\cdot p}]$ (LS)

$t+2.$ $[$ the room$_{p\cdot p+}]\cdot[$ that$_{p\cdot p+/p\cdot p''/p\cdot p}]\vdash$
$[_{p\cdot p''/p\cdot p}[$ the room$_{p\cdot p+}]$ that$_{p\cdot p+/p\cdot p''/p\cdot p}]$ (MI)

$t+3.$ $[$ we went into$_{p\cdot p}]$ (LS)

$t+4.$ $[_{p\cdot p''/p\cdot p}[$ the room$_{p\cdot p+}]$ that$_{p\cdot p+/p\cdot p/p\cdot p}]\cdot[$ we went into$_{p\cdot p}]\vdash$
$[_{p\cdot p''}[$ the room$_{p\cdot p+}]$ that$_{p\cdot p+/p\cdot p/p\cdot p}[$ we went into$_{p\cdot p}]]$ (MI)

(20) a. *Det rum som vi har betalat 300 kronor för är ledigt*

b. $t.$ $[$ det rum$_{p\cdot p+}]$ (LS)

$t+1.$ [som$_{p·p+/p·p"/p·p}$] (LS)
$t+2.$ [det rum$_{p·p+}$]·[som$_{p·p+/p·p"/p·p}$]⊢
$\quad$ [$_{p·p/p·p}$ [det rum$_{p·p+}$] som$_{p·p+/p·p"/p·p}$] (MI)
$t+3.$ [vi har betalat för$_{p·p}$] (LS)
$t+4.$ [$_{p·p"/p·p}$ [det rum$_{p·p+}$] som$_{p·p+/p·p"/p·p}$]·[vi har betalat för$_{p·p}$]⊢
$\quad$ [$_{p·p"}$ [det rum$_{p·p+}$] som$_{p·p/p·p/p·p"/p·p}$ [vi har betalat för$_{p·p}$]] (MI)

These derivations suggest that our subject relative clauses, such as *the room that we went in*, can include the stranded NP, in this case *the room*. Our type assignment and our derivational rules show that this subject relative clause is well-formed and can be merged with the rest of the sentence as a phrase (argument). Thus, our analysis of PS, when also applied to this type of PS constructions, seems to offer a parsimonious but overall accurate analysis of how the observed word order can be derived.

Before we move to *wh*-constructions, we discuss the optional/obligatory realizations of complementizers. Recall now that *som* and *that* may be omitted (cf. (2), (7)), a phenomenon that is "post-syntactic" in our account (Embick & Noyer 2001). That is, it pertains to which vocabulary exponents are inserted in a derivation, not to the morpho-syntactic objects that are merged together. Thus, it can be based on language-specific *ellipsis* rules, which usually target specific feature values that elided categories can carry (Merchant 2001: ch. 1-2, 2004). Since we distinguish between morpho-syntactic derivations and phonological operations, language-specific operations are a natural consequence of our approach, one example being relative clauses in PS contexts. Once we have this second piece of our PS puzzle in its correct place, we can offer an analysis of *wh*-pronoun PS constructions, which builds on the results obtained so far. We repeat (3) and (8) as (21a) and (22a), to show this fact:

(21) a. Which apples are you talking about?
$\quad$ b. $t.$ $\quad$ [which apples$_{p·p+}$] (LS)
$\quad\quad$ $t+1.$ [are you talking$_{p·p+/p·p/p·p}$] (LS)
$\quad\quad$ $t+2.$ [which apples$_{p·p+}$]·[are you talking$_{p·p+/p·p/p·p}$]⊢
$\quad\quad\quad$ [$_{p·p/p·p}$ [which apples$_{p·p+}$] are you talking$_{p·p+/p·p/p·p}$] (MI)

(22) a. *Vilka äpplen pratar du om?*
$\quad$ b. $t.$ $\quad$ [Vilka äpplen$_{p·p+}$] (LS)
$\quad\quad$ $t+1.$ [pratar du$_{p·p+/p·p/p·p}$] (LS)
$\quad\quad$ $t+2.$ [Vilka äpplen$_{p·p+}$]·[pratar du$_{p·p+/p·p/p·p}$]⊢
$\quad\quad\quad$ [$_{p·p/p·p}$ [Vilka äpplen$_{p·p+}$] pratar du$_{p·p+/p·p/p·p}$] (MI)

The partial derivations in (21b) and (22b) read as follows. For the sake of simplicity, we treat both *you* and *du* as part of the verbal head, hence treating these pronouns as clitic-like elements (cf. Koopman 2000; Jäger 2005). These verbs merge with the relative NPs *which apples* and *vilka äpplen* 'which apples', which also carry a specificity feature. Since we do not explicitly represent other feature values, these derivations appear equivalent to those we offered in examples (18b)-(20b). Since our type assignment for relative NPs and our derivational analyses prove that silent NPs must be merged into our sentences, we can extend our parsimonious analysis to this PS sub-type, too[8].

We now have an account of each of the three sub-types of PS constructions in intra-sentential examples found in (1)-(8). Thanks to this result, we are in a position to also sketch an account for our inter-sentential examples in (9)-(14). For this purpose, I build on Jäger's (2001: 84-86) implementation of TL calculi to derive discourse structures. Differently from his proposal, however, we do not employ a special type for sentences as part of discourses (his type *D*). In our system, we assign type *p* to sentences *qua* complete syntactic objects, as our derivations show. Thus, I sketch an approach in which the same logical analysis can be applied to different levels of structure, and *merge* can act as a schema that combines sentences into discourses.

We must now account for two important problems that arise at this level of analysis: inter-sentential anaphoric relations and, consequently, discourse cohesion. Since anaphoric relations can define the cohesion of discourses (Kehler 2011; Reuland 2011), their analysis can permit us to sketch a preliminary syntax of discourse that can also account for PS. For this purpose, I take the fairly standard assumption that a system of feature percolation is active (Adger 2010: 188-195; Tseng 2005; Stabler 2013). The theory-neutral assumption is that the features of constituents making up sentences can percolate at a sentence level, and constrain how anaphoric relations can be established. Insofar as at least one set of features can license the formation of anaphoric relations, then cohesion is obtained. Thus, PS can potentially permit the formation of a cohesive text, in cases when no other anaphoric relations can be established (i.e.

---

[8] We must offer one *caveat*. We partly deviate from standard analyses of questions, including TL-based ones (Vermaat 2005), since we are concerned with offering an account of PS. While standard accounts of questions assign a type close to *p/p*, here we treat these types of sentences as if they were simple declarative sentences, of type *p*. This is a simplification, although a non-problematic one.

our (9)-(14)). In order to capture these facts, however, we must capture how feature percolations systems work, in the first place.

For this purpose, I follow feature percolation systems found in TL calculi (Johnson & Bayer 1995; cf. also Bernardi & Szabolcsi 2008). I assume that percolation involves the "duplication" of the feature types of an argument NP to the VP that contains this NP, as per rule 3 (type formation: product). Since we are discussing PS and its contribution to cohesion, we can restrict this assumption to the features that NPs contribute to a sentence. Hence, I assume that the features that allow the formation of an anaphoric relations are those that the stranded NP in the second sentence, and its non-stranded counterpart in the first sentence contribute. Thus, if p represents the type of a VP such as (17a), $p \cdot p_{+spec}$ can represent[9] the type of this sentence, made ready to be merged with another sentence taking this type as an input[10]. Once these features are percolated, an anaphoric relation can be established, and the two sentences that include these NPs form a cohesive discourse. In order to show how our analysis works, I repeat (9) as (23a) and offer its two simplified derivations in (23b-c)[11]:

(23) a. I bought the chair/a chair on the left. This chair was sat on
      by Luigi

   b. t. [...the chair on$_{p \cdot p+}$]   (LS)

     $t+1$. [This chair...$_{p \cdot p+}$]   (LS)

     $t+2$. [...the chair on.$_{p \cdot p+}$]·[This chair...$_{p \cdot p+}$]⊢

         [$_{p \cdot p}$ [...the chair on$_{p \cdot p+}$ .This chair$_{p \cdot +p}$]]   (MI: cut rule)

   c. t. [...a chair on$_{p \cdot p-}$]   (LS)

     $t+1$. [This chair...$_{p \cdot p+}$]   (LS)

     $t+2$. [...a chair on$_{p \cdot p-}$]·[This chair...$_{p \cdot p+}$]⊢*   (Der. crashes)

In words, the two sentences *I bought the chair on the left* and *this chair...* are both assigned the type $p \cdot p_{+spec}$. This is the type assigned to

---

[9] This type minimally differs from the type assigned to NPs by the specific value assigned to p, since it may represent sentence types, rather than nominal types. Again, I do not explicitly represent this distinction, for mere reasons of space.

[10] In this case, we *assume* rather than *prove* that our mechanism of feature percolation derives the results we discuss. See Bernardi & Szabolcsi (2008: § 1-2) for discussion. Note also that we implement product types, although the standard definition of the cut rule we offer is better suited for functional types.

[11] Our system could offer an incremental account of how these mini-discourses are derived, not unlike other related proposals in the literature (e.g. Asher & Lascarides 2003). Here we only merge two fully formed sentences, in order to sketch how our apparatus works.

sentences that receive the relevant features from one of their argument NPs via feature percolation. Via the cut rule, a *merge* schema and rule 5 in our set of rules, we can establish an anaphoric relation between NPs across sentences. In doing so, we also establish one form of cohesion between the sentences that contain them, as a reflection of the "matching" component of merge. In this way, we can offer a proof on how to derive our discourse example. Hence, our analysis can derive anaphoric relations that emerge in PS constructions, as instances of our general type-matching mechanism that is part of merge.

One important *caveat* is that our examples highlight the possible role of PS as one cohesion-building construction, but certainly as not the only construction to do so. Recall from section 2 that the verbs in our examples lack temporal features that permit to establish anaphoric relations between sentences. For instance, the event of buying a chair and that of someone sitting on this chair, described by the mini-text in (23), are not necessarily related. In this case, PS seems to reflect the fact that the only features that can percolate, and allow cohesion to be established, are those that the stranded NP carries. Consequently, the derivation in (23c) shows that when not even this anaphoric relation can be established, a mini-discourse becomes incohesive. The cut rule cannot merge two sentences that lack matching types, so a cohesive mini-discourse cannot be formed. Therefore, we can now capture the fact that PS can allow the formation of cohesive discourses, especially when no other constructions can do so.

Two other results that we obtain via our analysis are the following. First, we can now predict a preference for PS constructions in inter-sentential examples. This can be seen as a strategy that allows for an easy resolution of anaphoric relations, via cross-sentential feature-matching (Reuland 2011; Ward & Birner 2012). Second, we can indirectly predict that, when other features can percolate at a sentential level, cohesion may be established even if a stranded NP does not match the features of its anaphoric counterpart. If the events described by each sentence are anaphorically related via e.g. temporal morphology on verbs and/or adverbs, then we could expect that *some chair* could occur in (23a), and the mini-discourse be cohesive. If cohesion emerges insofar as the types of two sentences match on one feature (value), e.g. p_{+tense}, then PS does not univocally determine the cohesion of a discourse. Once more, however, our examples suggest that it may play this role, given the more general mechanisms that govern cohesion. Thus, an extension of our analysis could ideally account for these data, as well.

342 From Clerks to Corpora

Given these two results, we have now shown how our non-transformational analysis can now derive all the examples in (1)-(14) in a principled and parsimonious way. As we have reached our main goal, we can move to the conclusions.

5. Conclusions

In this paper we have offered an account of Preposition Stranding (PS) and its three sub-types (pseudo-passives, *wh*-constructions, relative clauses) in English and Swedish. We have suggested that the three assumptions on which our account rests upon can offer an empirically broader and theoretically parsimonious analysis of this phenomenon. Our first assumption is that, if we treat morphological features as "bits" of information, then we can successfully account for how (and when) stranded constituents are inserted (merged) in a sentence. Our second assumption is that, if we pursue a top-down ("left-to-right") derivational approach to sentences, then we do not need copying/movement analyses to account for word order in PS constructions. Our third assumption is that the feature-matching aspect of *merge* suffices to capture the anaphoric relations that arise between sentences when PS constructions are involved, and that can create discourse cohesion. This is obtained via a very simple system of feature percolation that simply copies "old" morphological information at the level of discourse (here, the specificity and definiteness of NPs).

Thus, our account seems to be successful in explaining our data, and seems to sketch an alternative analysis to both minimalist proposals (Truswell 2009) and HPSG-based proposals (e.g. Tseng 2000). However, nothing prevents that feature-based proposals can be offered within these frameworks, that can cover our data and perhaps broader sets, in a similarly accurate manner. I would like to suggest that the current analysis can indeed be seen as complementing and enriching previous analyses, as well as our understanding of PS as a syntactic construction and its relation to discourse structure and cohesion (cf. Ward & Birner 2012).

It is goes without saying that we have not exhausted the discussion on PS. For one thing, we have focused on a specific sub-set of data, and left aside the possibility that PS can interact with other syntactic constructions, and partake in a fairly complex interaction between feature percolation and cohesion phenomena. This has been a necessary choice, given our limits of space and the complexity of PS as a general phenomenon. We also have left aside a discussion of other Scandinavian languages, such as Norwegian or Icelandic, in which PS seems to be a more common, but also a more complex phenomenon. Also, we conjecture that this approach can also potentially offer a morpho-syntactic counterpart of the semantic treatments of anaphoric relations (Elbourne 2005; Kamp, van Genabith & Reyle 2011). Furthermore, our work sketches the possibility that our Type-Logical analysis can be extended to a more sophisticated theory of discourse structure, as discussed in the literature (Asher & Lascarides 2003). However, we leave such theoretical problems for future work.

References

Abels, K. (2003). Successive cyclicity, anti-locality and adposition stranding. Ph.D. dissertation, University of Connecticut.

Acquaviva, P. & Panagiotidis, P. (2012). Lexical Decomposition meets conceptual atomism. *Lingue e Linguaggio XI*:2, 165–180.

Adger, D. (2010). A minimalist theory of feature structure. A. Kibort & C. Greville (eds) *Features: Perspectives on a Key Notion in Linguistics*. Oxford: Oxford University Press, 185–218.

Åfarli, T. (1992). *The Syntax of Norwegian Passive Constructions*. Philadelphia: John Benjamins.

Alexiadou, A., Law, P., Meinunger, A. & Wilder, C. (eds) (2000). *The Syntax of Relative Clauses*. Amsterdam: John Benjamins.

Asher, N. & Lascarides, A. (2003). *Logics of Conversation*. Cambridge: Cambridge University Press.

Bernardi, R. & Szabolcsi, A. (2008). Optionality, scope, and licensing: an application of partially ordered categories. *Journal of Logic, Language and Computation* 17:3, 237–289.

Bianchi, V. (2002a). Headed relative clauses in generative syntax: Part I. *Glot International* 6:7, 118–130.

———. (2002b). Headed relative clauses in generative syntax: Part II. *Glot International* 6:8, 235–247.

Bolinger, D. (1977). Transitivity and spatiality: The passive of prepositional verbs. A. Makkai, V. B. Makkai, & L. Heilmann (eds) *Linguistics at the Crossroads*. Lake Bluff, IL: Jupiter Press, 57–78.

———. (1978). Passive and transitivity again. *Forum Linguisticum* 3, 25–28.

Diessel, H. (2012). Deixis and demonstratives. C. Maienborn, K. von Heusinger

& P. Portner (eds) *An International Handbook of Natural Language Meaning* (Vol. 3). Berlin: Mouton de Gruyter, 2407–2431.

Embick, D. & Noyer, R. (2001). Movement operations after syntax. *Linguistic Inquiry* 32:4, 555–595.

Elbourne, P. (2005). *Situations and Individuals*. Cambridge, MA: The MIT Press.

Emonds, J. (1985). *A Unified Theory of Syntactic Categories*. Dordrecht: Foris Publications.

Gehrke, B. & Grillo, N. (2009). How to become passive. K. Grohmann (ed.) *Exploration of Phase Theory: Features, Arguments, and Interpretation at the Interfaces*. Berlin: De Gruyter, 213–268.

Hale, K. & Keyser, S. J. (2002). *Prolegomenona to a Theory of Argument Structure*. Cambridge, MA: MIT Press.

Harbour, D. (2007). *Morphosemantic Number: From Kiowa Noun Classes to UG Number Features*. Dordrecht: Springer.

Harley, H. (2012). Semantics in distributed morphology. K. von Heusinger, C. Maierborn & P. Portner (eds) *Semantics: An International Handbook of Natural Language Meaning*. Amsterdam: De Gruyter, 688–709.

Heusinger, K. von (2007). Accessibility and definite noun phrases. M. Schwarz-Friesel, M. Consten & M. Knees (eds) *Anaphors in Text: Cognitive, Formal and Applied Approaches to Anaphoric Reference*. Amsterdam: Benjamins, 123–144.

———. (2011). Specificity. K. von Heusinger, C. Maienborn & P. Portner (eds) *Semantics: An International Handbook of Natural Language Meaning, Volume 2* Berlin: de Gruyter, 1024–1057.

Holmes, P. & Hinchliffe, I. (2008). *Swedish: An Essential Grammar*. Routledge: New York.

Hornstein, N., & Weinberg, A. (1981). Case theory and preposition stranding. *Linguistic Inquiry* 12:1, 55–91.

Huddleston, R. & Pullum, G.K. (2002). *The Cambridge Grammar of the English Language*. Cambridge: Cambridge University Press.

Ishizuka, T. (2010). *Towards a Unified Analysis of Passive in Japanese: A Cartographic Minimalist Approach*. Ph.D. Dissertation, UCLA.

Jäger, G. (2001). Anaphora and quantification in Categorial Grammar. M.J. Moortgat (ed.) *Logical Aspects of Computational Linguistics, Springer Lecture notes in Artiificial Intelligence* 2014. Springer:Dordrecht, 70–90.

———. (2005). *Anaphora and Type Logical Grammar*. Springer: Dordrecht.

Jarema, G. & Libben, G. (eds) (2007). *The Mental Lexicon: Core Perspectives.* Amsterdam: Elsevier.

Johnson, M & Bayer, S. (1995). Features and agreement in Lambek Categorial Grammar. *Formal Grammar. Proceedings of the Conference of the European Summer School in Logic, Language and Information, Barcelona,* 122–127.

Kamp, H., van Genabith, J. & Reyle, U. (2011). Discourse representation theory. *Handbook of Philosophical Logic 15.* Dordrecht: Kluwer, 125–394.

Kehler, A. (2011). Cohesion and coherence. C. Maienborn, K. von Heusinger & P. Portner (eds) *Semantics: An International Handbook of Natural Language Meaning* (vol. 2). Berlin: Morton de Gruyter, 1963–1987.

Klingvall, E. (2012). Topics in pseudo-passives. C. Platzack (ed.) *Working papers in Scandinavian Syntax* 90, 53–80.

Koopman, H. (2000). Prepositions, postpositions, circumpositions, and particles. Koopman, H. (ed.) *The Syntax of Specifiers and Heads.* London: Routledge, 204–260.

Krifka, M. (2001). For a structured meaning account of questions and answers. C. Fery, & W. Sternefeld (eds) *Audiatur Vox Sapientia. A Festschrift for Arnim von Stechow. Berlin: Akademie Verlag,* 287–319.

———. (2004). The semantics of questions and the focusation of answers. C. Lee, M. Gordon & D. Büring (eds) *Topic and Focus: A Cross-Linguistic Perspective.* Dordrecht: Kluwer Academic Publishers, 139–151.

Law, P. (2005). Preposition stranding. M. Everaert & H. van Riemsdijk (ed.) *The Blackwell Companion to Syntax, Volume III.* Malden, MA: Blackwell, 631–684.

Levelt, W.J.M. (1989). *Speaking: From Intention to Articulation.* Cambridge (Mass.): The MIT Press.

Maling, J. & Zaenen, A. (1985). Preposition-stranding and passive. *Nordic Journal of Linguistics* 8:2, 197–209.

Merchant, J. (2001). The Syntax of Silence. Oxford: Oxford University Press.

———. (2004). *Fragments and ellipsis. Linguistics and Philosophy,* 27:6, 661–738.

Moortgat, M.J. (2010). Typelogical grammar. E.N. Zalta (ed.) *The Stanford Encyclopedia of Philosophy* (Winter 2010 Edition). Stanford.

———. (2011). Categorial type logics. J. van Benthem & A. ter Meulen (eds) *Handbook of Logic and Language. (2nd ed.).* Amsterdam: Elsevier, 95–179.

Morrill, G. (2011). *Categorial Grammar: Logical Syntax, Semantics, and Processing.* Oxford: Oxford University Press.

Phillips, C. (2006). The real-time status of island phenomena. *Language 82:5,* *795–823.*

Reuland, E. (2011). *Anaphora and Language Design.* Cambridge, MA: The MIT press.

Riemsdijk, H. van (1990). Functional prepositions. H. Pinkster & I. Genee (ed.) *Unity in Diversity.* Dordrecht: Foris, 229–241.

Riemsdijk, H. van. (1998). Head movement and adjacency. *Natural Language and Linguistic Theory* 16:5, 633–378.

Stabler, E. (2013). Two models of minimalist, incremental syntactic analysis. *Topics in Cognitive Science* 5:3, 611–633.

Svenonius, P. (2006). The emergence of axial parts. *Nordlyd, Tromsø University Working Papers in Language and Linguistics,* 33:1, 49–77.

———. (2010). Spatial P in English. G. Cinque & L. Rizzi (eds) *The Cartography of syntactic Structures:* (vol. 6) Oxford: Oxford University Press, 127–160.

Takami, K. (1992). *Preposition Stranding. From Syntactic to Functional Analyses.* Berlin and New York: Mouton de Gruyter.

Tseng, J. (2000). *The Representation and Selection of Prepositions.* Edinburgh: Ph.D. Dissertation.

———. (2004). Directionality and the complementation of Dutch prepositions. H. Cuyckens, W. De Mulder & T. Mortelmans (eds) *Adpositions of movement. Belgian Journal of Linguistics* 18, 167–194.

Tseng, J. (2005). Prepositions and complement selection. A. Villavicencio & V. Kordoni)(eds) *Proceedings of the* 2nd *ACL-SIGSEM Workshop on the linguistic dimensions of prepositions and their use in computational linguistics formalisms and applications.* Colchester: Essex University, 11–19.

Truswell, R. (2009). Preposition-stranding, passivisation, and extraction from adjuncts in Germanic. J. van Craenenbroeck & J. Rooryck (ed.) *Linguistic variation yearbook 8.* Amsterdam: John Benjamins, 131–177.

Ursini, F.-A. (2011). On the syntax and semantics of "Ser" and "Estar". *Lingue & Linguaggio* 9:1, 57–87.

———. (2013a). On the syntax and semantics of "Tener" and "Haber". *Lingue & Linguaggio* 11:1, 89–120.

———. (2013b). Esse and Sta: Auxiliary selection in the Aquilan dialect. *Dialectologia* 10:1, 107–134.

———. (2013b). Another look at spatial prepositions and the modification problem. *Iberia: An International Journal of Theoretical Linguistics* 5:2, 38–84.

———. (2013c). On the syntax and semantics of spatial Ps in Spanish. *Borealis: An International Journal about Hispanic Linguistics* 2:1, 117–166.

———. (2015a). The morphology of spatial P: Is a unitary perspective possible? G. Boyes et al. (eds) *Proceedings of Les Decembrettes 8*. Toulouse: Mirail, 1–20.

———. (2015b). On the syntax and semantics of Italian spatial prepositions. *Acta Linguistica Hungarica* 63:1, 3–57.

Ursini, F.-A. & Akagi, N. (2013a). On the distributed morphology and semantics of spatial Ps. I.-J. Lee & U. Dolgormaa (eds) *Proceedings of the 15th Seoul International Conference on Generative Grammar (SICOGG 15)*. Seoul: Hankuk University Press, 447–468.

Vermaat, W. (2005). *The Logic of Variation: A Cross-linguistic Account of Wh-question Formation*. Doctoral Dissertation, Utrecht.

Ward, G. & Birner, M. (2012). Discourse effects of word order variation. C. Maienborn, K. von Heusinger & P. Portner (eds) *Semantics: An International Handbook of Natural Language Meaning* (vol. 2). Berlin: Mouton de Gruyter, 1934–1963.

Zeevat, H. (2011). Discourse relations. C. Maienborn, K. von Heusinger & P. Portner (eds) *Semantics: An International Handbook of Natural Language Meaning, Volume 1*. Berlin: Mouton de Gruyter, 946–972

19 There is Nothing Like Native Speech: A Comparison of Native and Very Advanced Non-Native Speech

Britt Erman & Margareta Lewis
Stockholm University

"I've been here for 8 ½ years, my English should be more fluent than this. Yes … sometimes I really stumble on the words...on the words"

1. Introduction

The above quote shows that finding words can be hard even for someone who has lived and worked in the L2 community for a considerable time. Vocabulary is an area of L2 acquisition that has received increasing attention in the last couple of decades. The present study is part of the research program "High-level proficiency in L2 use"[1]. The program seeks to provide answers to questions pertaining to what characterizes the very advanced L2 user, and involves several language departments at a Swedish university. This study compares vocabulary of different frequencies in the oral production of two groups of speakers of English, one non-native Swedish group and one native English-speaking group as a control. The non-native Swedish group has lived and worked in the UK (London) for an average of 7.3 years. The main aim of the study is to establish the rate of high-frequency and low-frequency words in the spoken data of these two groups. The material is made up of a recorded semi-structured interview. In order to establish lexical variation the present study, in contrast to several earlier studies, includes results not only from frequencies of tokens but also frequencies of types and T/T

[1] Thanks for generous grants are due to The Bank of Sweden Tercentenary Foundation.

How to cite this book chapter:
Erman, B. and Lewis, M. 2015. There is Nothing Like Native Speech: A Comparison of Native and Very Advanced Non-Native Speech. In: Shaw, P., Erman, B., Melchers, G. and Sundkvist, P. (eds) *From Clerks to Corpora: essays on the English language yesterday and today*. Pp. 349–366. Stockholm: Stockholm University Press. DOI: http://dx.doi.org/10.16993/bab.s License: CC-BY.

ratios, (cf. Lindqvist 2010, Lindqvist et al. 2011; Bardel et al. 2012; Lindqvist et al. 2013; Forsberg Lundell and Lindqvist 2012). Including types in the study will give indications regarding variation, which is assumed to distinguish native from non-native speech. Lindqvist (2010) found in her study of L2 French that the advanced learners used more general words to refer to key objects in a video film clip compared to a native control group.

The interview is one of three tasks carried out with the same participants. The results from two earlier studies, one on vocabulary and one on multiword structures (formulaic language), both involving two other tasks, a role play (dialogic) and an online retelling task (monologic), showed that in the role play the results of the London Swedes (LS) were like the natives in both studies, whereas the retelling task revealed significant differences between the NS and LS groups (Erman & Lewis 2011; 2013; Erman et al. 2014). Some of the questions asked in the interview concerned the Swedish participants' knowledge of languages and in particular their knowledge of English. Questions relating to English included for example the age at which they started learning English at school (in Sweden), whether they found speaking English difficult when they arrived in England, and the extent to which they used English also at home when in the UK. It is worth noting that all the Swedish speakers used English at work, and most of them had English-speaking partners at the time of the recording. Reading through the transcribed interviews it became apparent that the interviewees had rather varied perceptions of their knowledge of English, as the extracts below show. However, the general impression from these extracts is that the interviewees believe that their English is quite good, some even to the extent that English has taken over at the expense of their mother tongue, Swedish.

- An easy ride when it comes to languages. Watched English TV a lot when little. Always speak English with my English partner.
- It's much more natural to use English when speaking about music. I just can't find the Swedish word...
- English was one of my worst subjects in Sweden. Wasn't good at English at first (was very shy) but then just started speaking to people.
- I was fluent when arriving in England.
- Sometimes I feel when I go back, I become so conscious about my Swedish. And obviously I can still speak Swedish...it's no problem, but ...
- ... sometimes I could have difficulty of swinging back into ...into fluent Swedish. I mean, when it comes to the more advanced

Swedish, I think. Because, I think, my Swedish stopped developing when I was 22 and I came here. And...and here I don't ...I don't associate that much with Swedes.

- English is ...what I realize with English is [after living in France]... it got a lot more words than French. French is, I think, if you're good in French, you use grammar to show that you are educated.

In this last extract there is a hint that English is perceived as having a large vocabulary.

The aim of the present study is not to establish whether the London Swedes' own perceptions of their knowledge of English has a bearing on the results but to find out how the two groups differ in their use of vocabulary in this task, more specifically across two main frequency ranges to be explained below.

We start by accounting for earlier research on vocabulary with a focus on advanced L2 speakers' spoken production (2). After presentations of aims (2.1), and material and method (3), we discuss the notion of frequency in relation to L2 acquisition (4). A description of the 1–2000 frequency range (4.1) is followed by a display of the results from this range (4.2), a description of the frequency range beyond 2000 words as this is applied in the present study (4.3), and the results of this frequency range (4.4). Finally, since the 1–2000 frequency range also includes high-frequency words typical of spoken discourse, we introduce a selection of sequences involving words from the 1000 most frequent words functioning as pragmatic markers (4.5) and present results from their distribution across the participant groups (4.6). Apart from offering some general insights to be drawn from the results, section 5 discusses the main contribution of the study. Section 6 winds up by presenting some more voices from the London Swedes in light of the results.

2. Earlier research

Establishing methods that relate vocabulary knowledge to different proficiency levels in L2 production has in the last few years been a major concern (Daller et al. 2007; Milton 2007; Tidball and Treffers-Daller 2007; Lindqvist 2010; Lindqvist et al. 2011; Bardel et al. 2012; Lindqvist et al. 2013). One method used is the Lexical Frequency Profile developed by Laufer and Nation (1995). A basic assumption behind most studies of vocabulary in relation to frequency is that frequency of input will affect output, so that the more frequent a word is the more likely it is to appear in an L2 speaker's production (Cobb and Horst 2004; Vermeer 2004). There is also evidence to prove that frequency plays an important role in L2 acquisition, implying that high-frequency words are shared by more L2 users than low-frequency words (Tidball and Treffers-Daller 2007). The higher the percentage of words beyond the 2000 most frequent words is in an L2 user's production, the more advanced is this person's vocabulary (Laufer 1995).The proportion of low-frequency words is also commonly referred to as lexical richness in the literature. The results from studies of lexical richness have shown that the quantity of lemma tokens of different frequencies distinguishes not only native from non-native speakers but also L2 speakers at different proficiency levels (Bardel et al. 2012). Some advanced non-native speakers of L2 French have been shown to reach nativelike levels in their use of low-frequency lemma tokens. But if some of these were removed from the list containing many low-frequency words (i.e. the 'Off-list'; see section 3), such as thematic words occurring in teaching materials and words that are similar in L1 and L2 (and some others), no non-native speaker of either L2 French or L2 Italian reached native-like levels (Bardel et al. 2012).

2.1 Aims and research questions

In the aforementioned studies of multiword structures (MWSs) and vocabulary with the same participants in two tasks (see Introduction) it was found that the London Swedes behaved like the natives in the role play, but differed significantly from the native speakers on both vocabulary and MWSs in the online retelling of a film clip that was unfamiliar to them. On the basis of these results it is hypothesized that the London Swedes, being immersed in an English-speaking community, will come close to the native speakers in the interview, since this task is connected to a situation that is believed to be familiar, notably answering questions about themselves. As mentioned, two main frequency ranges are examined: the first two thousand words (1–2000 frequency range, i.e. words of high frequency), and those outside the first two thousand words (the 2000+ frequency range, i.e. low-frequency words). Our main aim is to compare the LS group with the NS group with regard to T/T ratios, and quantity of types and tokens in these two frequency ranges.

Another aspect closely related to vocabulary is the use of pragmatic markers, which are assumed to vary with text type (Simon-Vandenbergen

2000). Based on this it is hypothesized that an interaction involving a description of self such as in an interview will generate a considerable number of pragmatic markers. Furthermore, pragmatic markers have been found to distinguish native from non-native speech (Altenberg 1997; Denke 2009; Fant & Hancock 2014). These facts lead to our second aim, which is to establish how the LS group compares with the NS group on a selection of frequent pragmatic markers.

3. Material and method

Table 1 provides some more information about the participants.

The method used involves sorting the transcribed texts into frequency ranges by using the Lexical Frequency Profile (LFP), which is accessible via LexTutor[2]. By feeding in the transcribed texts in this program we get not only different frequency lists (see below) but also the total number of words, which distributes as follows over the two groups (Table 2).

Lexical frequency profiles are available in LexTutor via the program Vocabprofile. In Vocabprofile all the words are registered alphabetically in terms of type and token frequency; this makes the data easily accessible and allows various kinds of analyses. The words have not been lemmatized, which means that type frequencies are indicated in terms of 'word forms'; for example, *museum, museums,* and *call, calls,*

Table 1. Participants.

Informants	Time with English	Average age
10 Native speakers	Life	32
10 London Swedes	9 years at school and an average of 7.3 years' residency in London	32

Table 2. Number of words over the native speakers (NS), and London Swedes (LS).

Tasks/Participants	NS	LS	Total
Interview	23061	25184	48245

---

[2] LexTutor is accessible at: www.lextutor.ca

called, calling are all registered as six separate types, while representing two lemmas. The LFP program maps the word forms onto their lemmatized forms (i.e. 'call' and 'museum' for the six word forms above) in four categories (or lists): the first most frequent 1000 words, the second most frequent 1000 words, and the Academic Word List (AWL; Coxhead 2000). The fourth category is a separate list, called the Off-list, comprising any word (or item see 4.2) outside the 2000 most frequent words and the words in the AWL list.

It should be mentioned that although some types, especially in the high-frequency 1–1000 list, are inflections of one and the same lemma as in the examples above the majority belong to different lemmas (see 4.1). The further we move away on a scale from high-frequency words towards low-frequency words the more likely it is that type equates lemma type, and is thus unique (see 4.1).

4. Analysis and results

As mentioned, the results are divided into two main groups, the 1–2000 words frequency range and words beyond 2000, the 2000+ frequency range. The words (i.e. tokens) in the first 2000 word span constitute the major part of the present material and cover between 88% and 90% of the texts (see Table 3 below). These figures are above the average for written text, which is 80% for the first 2000 words;[3] this discrepancy may be explained by the rather informal character of the text type studied here, and by the fact that the present material constitutes spoken production.

In the present study the 2000+ frequency range is made up of the words in the AWL list and a pruned version of the words in the Off-list (see 4.3). The words in AWL make up the smallest proportion of the words for both groups, covering between 1% and 2% of the texts. It is common in the literature for calculations only to include number of lemma tokens (Bardel and Gudmundson 2012; Lindqvist et al. 2013; Forsberg, Lundell and Lindqvist 2012), but, as mentioned, in the present study it was relevant also to include the number of types. For instance, on some measurements the LS group is nativelike on the number of tokens, whereas they are non-nativelike on the number of types, which is an indication that this group recycles their types more often, implying less diversity. Although her own study only includes

---

[3] See http://www.lextutor.ca/research/Cobb

lemma tokens, Lindqvist (2010: 415) emphasizes the importance of also including types in studies on vocabulary.

4.1 Description of the 1-2000 frequency range

The 1–2000 frequency range apparently holds the most frequent content words and among the first thousand words we find many grammatical words needed to ensure structure and coherence, such as determiners, pronouns, conjunctions, etc. Words of high frequency by necessity come out in different word forms (i.e. types in LexTutor), some of which are based on the same lemma. In order to provide more exact relations between LexTutor (LT) type and lemma type we lemmatized all the LT types to find out the proportions over the frequency ranges. In the 1–2000 frequency range it was found that the proportions of different lemmas to LT types in the two groups are: NS 79.4% and LS 79.5%, and for the AWL lists: NS 92.6% and LS 93.0%. At the other end of the scale are the Off-list words where it was found that for NS 98.1% and LS 97.6% of the LT types belong to different lemmas. In other words, the vast majority of word forms (LT types) in the interview belong to different lemmas with average percentages for NS 86.7% and LS 85.8%.

Lexical frequency profiles with their focus on words are obviously independent of syntax and text type. It is not within the scope of the present study to evaluate the vocabulary produced, i.e. either to establish whether the words are syntactically, semantically or pragmatically appropriate, or their functions.

We start by accounting for the T/T ratios, and types and tokens per hundred words pertaining to the 1–2000 frequency range (Table 3) followed by a corresponding account of the results from the 2000+ frequency range (Table 4). Finally, we present and discuss results from searches targeting specific sequences (*you know, I think, sort of*) – which are among the 50 most frequent collocations according to Shin and Nation (2008) – and their distribution over the two groups.

The NS group functions as benchmark, and the threshold for significance is set at $p < .05$.[4]

---

[4] The chi-square test has been used throughout the study. We wish to thank Nils-Lennart for drawing our attention to this website: http://www.quantpsy.org/chisq/chisq.htm.

Table 3. T/T ratios, types and tokens/100 words in 1–2000 range in the Interview.

Interview	Type/Token	T/T ratios	p	Type/100 wds	p	Token/100 wds	p
NS	1416/20470	0.07		6.1		88.76	
LS	1366/22712	0.06	.000	5.4	.001	90.20	0.23

4.2 Results for the 1–2000 frequency range

Words belonging in the 1–2000 frequency range cover a large part of the texts as can be seen in the number of tokens per 100 words (Table 3). We also observe that the results in Table 3 are all based on LT results, since lemma types and LT types per 100 words yielded the same result, both showing that the difference between the NS and LS groups is highly significant (for lemma types per 100 words $p <. 000$). For this reason, *types* refers to LT types throughout the study.

Our hypothesis that the LS group would be nativelike on measurements pertaining to this task given its everyday character is only partly supported. While the LS group is nativelike on tokens per hundred words, they use significantly fewer types compared to the NS group. This result gives support for the inclusion of types in vocabulary studies. The highly significant difference in T/T ratio in the LS group compared to the NS group indicates that they recycle more words in this frequency range.

4.3 Description of the 2000+ range

In the present study the 2000+ frequency range is composed of a pruned version of the words in the Off-list combined with the words in the AWL list. The LexTutor Off-list is a heterogeneous group of items, low-frequency words as well as very informal high-frequency words and voiced pausing. In order to avoid a situation where words, because they are outside the frequency bands of the first 2000 words, would unduly be considered advanced or low-frequency, the Off-list was scrutinized and certain items were removed (cf. Lindqvist 2010; Lindqvist et al. 2013). As a consequence, all the items in the LexTutor Off-list that were deemed as not being part of a language's vocabulary, such as voiced pausing and word fragments, were removed. Indeed, equating the Off-list words with lexical richness can be misleading (Lindqvist 2010: 415).

The following types of items in the Off-lists have also been removed: **names** (of people, regions, places, continents, countries (including languages and nationalities, many of which are similar in Swedish and English, therefore more readily accessible; cf. Horst and Collins 2006; Milton 2007; Lindqvist et al. 2013)), **feedback** words (*yea, yeah, ok, huh, mm*), **foreign words** (*cher*), **contractions** (*wanna, gonna, gotta, coz*), **swear words** (*fucking*), **slang words** (*kids, guys, crap, ass*), and **voiced pausing** (*eh, uh/uhm/um(m)*), and, finally, **fragments** of words (*Thur, archi*, etc.).

Table 4 below shows the results for T/T ratios and types and tokens /100 words in the 2000+ word range.

4.4 Results for the 2000+ range

While the LS group is nativelike on T/T ratios, they significantly differ from the NS group on types and tokens per 100 words in the 2000+ frequency range (Table 4).

Our hypothesis that the LS group would be nativelike also in the 2000+ frequency range in view of the everyday character of this task was not confirmed by the results. The number of tokens per 100 words is significantly lower compared to the NS group, and the difference between the groups in the number of types per 100 words is highly significant, the *p*-value being close to zero. One possible explanation for this result is that the NSs use more specific vocabulary compared to the NNSs, which is in line with the results from several earlier studies (Ovtcharov et al. 2006; Lindqvist 2010; Erman & Lewis 2011).

It is worth noting that a comparison of T/T ratios between the three tasks targeting the LS and NS groups, i.e. the interview in the present study and the role play and the retelling task in Erman & Lewis (2013), shows that the interview is the task that demonstrates the highest T/T

Table 4. T/T ratios, types and tokens/100 words in 2000+ range (incl. AWL) in the Interview.

Interview	Type/Token	T/T ratios	p	Type/100 wds	p	Token/100 wds	p
NS	627/1077	0.58		2.7		4.7	
LS	537/1041	0.52	0.09	2.1	.000	4.1	.005

ratio in this frequency range. This is apparently the task where these speakers display the most diversity.

Summing up, while the non-natives reached nativelike levels in number of tokens in the 1–2000 frequency range, it is in the number of types in both frequency ranges that differences between natives and non-natives become visible. In light of the fact that the 1–2000 frequency range covers between 80% and 90% of all spoken texts, and to judge by the results of the present study, variation in this frequency range obviously is a nativelike feature, which distinguishes native and advanced non-native speakers. It is proposed in the present study that reaching a nativelike level in types in the first 2000 frequency range should be included in what is considered advanced vocabulary. In other words, showing variation among the 2000 most common words should be a skill worth aiming for also for advanced non-native speakers.

On the basis of the results presented in this study it seems reasonable to suggest that a contributing factor to divergences shown between the LS and NS groups is the difference in exposure, which has an effect also on types of high-frequency words as well as in the range of productive vocabulary at large.

4.5 Combinations of high-frequency words

LexTutor provides not only statistics, and alphabetical lists of words item per item in the frequency lists, but also the entire texts with each word marked for frequency and identifiable in the text. Depending on the query one can do either a search in the texts proper or in the word lists. If we are interested in specific *combinations* of words we apply the search command to the entire texts.

Since our results show that there are significant differences between the NS and LS groups in both frequency ranges, a sub-study involving particular, frequent combinations of high-frequency words, the majority functioning as pragmatic markers, was carried out.

The use of pragmatic markers has been shown to distinguish NN and N speakers of English (Denke 2009), and very advanced NN and N speakers of French and Spanish (Hancock & Kirchmeyer 2009; Hancock 2012; Fant & Hancock 2014). English pragmatic markers which have been shown to be used differently by NN and N speakers include *you know* (Denke 2009) and *sort of* (De Cock 2004). Denke (2009) found that not only is the pragmatic marker *you know* significantly more frequent in NS than in NNS speech, but the marker is also used differently, the NS speakers using the marker to organize discourse, i.e. as a discourse marker, and the NNS group as an editing marker in connection with stalling and repair. De Cock (2004) found that pragmatic markers of vagueness (*sort of, kind of*) are underrepresented in NNS compared to NS speech. Another English pragmatic marker, which, along with *you know* and *sort of*, belongs to the 50 most common 'collocations' in the 10 million word spoken part of the British National Corpus is *I think* (Shin and Nation 2008). This pragmatic marker has been shown to be overused by NN speakers in both speech (Altenberg 1997) and writing (Aijmer 2001). The results from the study of these collocations with a potential function as pragmatic markers will be shown below. It should be noted that this study is purely quantitative.

4.6 Results for pragmatic markers

The results show that in total figures the NS group has twice the number of pragmatic markers compared to the LS group (525 vs. 226). Numerically the LS group comes the closest to the NS group in their use of *you know*. Although the difference is statistically significant ($p < .03$), it is close to the threshold ($p < .05$).

The difference between the LS and NS groups for *sort of* is highly significant, the LS group using approximately one sixth (1/6) of the number used by the NS group. The significantly higher figure for *I think* in the LS group confirms results from earlier studies showing that there is a general tendency for non-natives to overuse this marker in both speech (Altenberg 1997; de Cock et al. 1998) and writing (Granger 1998; Ringbom 1998; Aijmer 2001). *I think* is a versatile marker and can signal a tentative attitude as well as authoritative deliberation

Table 5. Collocations (pragmatic markers) over the NS and LS groups in the interview.

Sequences Groups	you know	p	sort of	p	I think	p	Total
NS	162		235		128		525
/100 wds	0.7		1.0		0.55		2.27
LS	138		36		203		226
/100 wds	0.55	0.03	0.14	.000	0.8	.000	0.9

(Simon-Vandenbergen 2000; Aijmer 2001), but, as mentioned, the present study does not take qualitative aspects of these markers into account. It is worth noting that the *p*-values for *sort of* and *I think* are close to zero. This result strongly diverges from the LS results for *you know* which in comparison differ marginally from the NS group. One tentative explanation for the overuse of *I think* is that there are formally similar phrases in Swedish ('jag tycker', 'jag tror', 'jag tänker') with partly overlapping meanings and functions with the English phrase. The formal similarity and shared semantics between the English phrase and the three Swedish phrases may thus explain an overuse on the part of the Swedish L2 English users. This contrasts with the underuse of *sort of* which has no formal correspondence in Swedish. Swedish uses other downtoning items.

In sum, results from earlier studies of *sort of* being significantly underrepresented and *I think* significantly overrepresented in non-native compared to native speech have been confirmed in the present study. Nevertheless, it is worth noting that the significant overuse of *I think* in the LS group compared to the NS group does not compensate for a significant underuse by the LS group of all three pragmatic markers when collapsed compared to NS group (*p*-value < .000).

5. Conclusion and discussion

As is clear from our results, our hypothesis, that the LS group living and working in the L2 country would be nativelike on both frequency ranges studied in view of the fact that the participants are invited to talk about themselves, was in the main contradicted by the results. In only two out of six measurements (one for each frequency range) did the LS group score like the NS group. More specifically, they produced a nativelike number of tokens per 100 words in the high frequency range (1–2000), and were nativelike on the T/T ratio in the frequency range beyond 2000 (2000+). The most interesting result cutting across the two frequency ranges is that the LS group produced significantly fewer types compared to the NS group. However, the result for high-frequency tokens (the 1–2000 frequency range) for the LS group is in line with the general assumption that frequency plays an important role in L2 acquisition (Tidball and Treffers-Daller 2007).

The most important insight gained from the results of the present study is that when studying vocabulary it is important to analyze tokens as well as types, since they may yield divergent results. In other words, it is with regard to types that there is room for further development for

L2 users in the high-frequency as well as the low-frequency range. The results of this study suggest that displaying variation in the first 2000 frequency range is as much a native feature as showing variation in the beyond 2000 frequency range.

Furthermore, results from many earlier studies suggesting that the use of pragmatic markers is one area that distinguishes NSs and NNSs are supported in the present study, notably through significantly fewer occurrences of *you know* and *sort of*, and significantly more occurrences of *I think* in the LS group compared to the NS group. The quantity as well as proportion of pragmatic markers is thus what distinguishes the two groups. It is also worth noting that the significant overuse of *I think* in the LS group compared to the NS group does not compensate for a significant underuse by the LS group of all three pragmatic markers when collapsed compared to NS group (*p*-value < .000). One plausible explanation for this result is that although the pragmatic markers are known by the NN speakers, they have not become routinized. This would be in accordance with Bialystok (1993) who sees state of knowledge and control of knowledge as two separate processes. In other words, although the LS group obviously knows these pragmatic markers and may know when to use them, they might not have automatic control of them, which in turn can be explained by constraints related to real-time task performance.

The overall results suggest that native speakers have more immediate access not only to high-frequency and low-frequency words, but also to productive vocabulary more generally, including pragmatic markers. This can only be explained by differences in exposure and degree of more or less immediate access to items relevant for the situation.

6. Winding up

Against the backdrop of the results let us contemplate some more voices from the London Swedes regarding their beliefs about their knowledge of English. According to one of them, British English is difficult because of the rate at which it is spoken, and it is worth noting that this view persists after several years in the country.

> It's sometimes difficult to actively participate in the social environment. They...it's uh...British English is difficult, I think. It's spoken very, very fast... very quickly and you really have to ...to listen to understand. Uh...and sometimes you just don't understand what ...what they're talking about. I was taken aback by that.

We observe that understanding rapid speech can be an obstacle even at high levels of proficiency. From the introduction we recall the words of another participant concluding that English comes more naturally when speaking about certain topics (repeated here):

> It's much more natural to use English when speaking about music. I just can't find the Swedish word...

And below is one more extract along similar lines:

> And I would say that my English now has come to a point...and... uh... and at work, some topics at work, I feel more confident in English.

As a linguist it is easy to agree with these two speakers, linguistics being one of the many domains dominated by English.

> I think for certain things my English is better and for other things my Italian. For the job English is far better, but if I'm talking, I think, emotionally or generally, then I would be more comfortable in Italian than...than in English, I think.

Some acknowledge that English is difficult, but also that practice helps, as in this quote from the introduction, repeated here.

> English was one of my worst subjects in Sweden. Wasn't good at English at first (was very shy) but then just started speaking to people.

This view is shared by another speaker who, like the former speaker, eventually realized that participating in conversations is essential in everyday life.

> I always struggled with languages. That was never my strong subject in school. I'm a physicist. I'm a mathematician and... and I can't learn anything by heart. I need to have, you know, I need to understand why it is this way. But I realized that if I don't say anything, this is gonna be really, really boring and a bit useless so .. and I just kind of started speaking.

A couple of speakers comment on their Swedish accent when speaking English. In the second extract the speaker apparently considers her Swedish accent part of her identity.

> When I speak Swedish, it sounds like I'm singing. But when I speak English, I think my voice sounds really...uh ... monotone, do you see

that? I heard some people say they thought I was Irish which was for me very, very strange.

> I have a Swedish accent but, yeah, and I don't think I'm trying to get away from that.

Whether or not you have an accent is of no importance according to another speaker.

In England no one cares if you have got an accent.

Finally, two of the ten Swedes comment on English vocabulary and the limitations they often sense when speaking the language, which provides a clear link to the results of the present study. In fact, these quotes neatly summarize the overall results from the present study.

> Actually, I was surprised. I often find myself using English expressions but with Swedish words. And that's also funny because if you migrate away from what you're used to, you casually speak to someone about something else, you realize how poor your vocabulary actually is.

> I've been here for 8 ½ years, my English should be more fluent than this. Yes, sometimes I really stumble on the words...on the words. (We recall this quote from the beginning of the article.)

Of the three vocabulary tasks administered to these two groups (the interview in the present study, a role play and a retelling task (Erman & Lewis 2013), the interview was the task in which the London Swedes were the furthest away from the native group. Furthermore, this was the task in which the natives showed the most diversity in regard to low-frequency as well as high-frequency words. The fact that the native speakers distinguish themselves from the non-native speakers by having significantly higher numbers of types in both frequency ranges in this task may be explained by the interviewee being able to talk freely about anything that comes to mind in answering the questions asked by the interviewer. All in all, the results have shown that the native speakers had more immediate access to words across the board. Indeed, the most important insight gained through this study is that it is *frequent* word *types*, i.e. those within the 1–2000 range, that require practice in order to approach the quantity of native speakers. Infrequent words are presumably less important for general communication. Finally, the results of this study should encourage more research involving word types as well as tokens, and on larger corpora of different types of spoken production.

References

Aijmer, K. (ed.). (2001). *A Wealth of English: Studies in Honour of Göran Kjellmer.* Gothenburg Studies in English 81. Acta Universitatis Gothoburgensis, Gothenburg University.

———. (2001). *I think* as a marker of discourse style in argumentative student writing. K. Aijmer (ed.), 247–257.

Altenberg, B. (1997). Exploring the Swedish component of the International Corpus of Learner English. B. Lewandowska-Tomaszcyk & P. J. Melia (eds) *Proceedings of PALC'97: Practical Applications in Language Corpora.* Lódz: Lódz University Press, 119–132.

Bardel, C., Gudmundson, A. & Lindqvist, C. (2012). Aspects of lexical sophistication in advanced learners' oral production: vocabulary acquisition and use in L2 French and Italian. N. Abrahamsson & K. Hyltenstam (eds) *High-level L2 Acquisition, Learning and Use.* Thematic issue of *Studies in Second Language Acquisition,* 34:2, 269–290.

Bialystok, E. (1993). Symbolic representation and attentional control in pragmatic competence. G. Kasper & S. Blum-Kulka (eds) *Interlanguage Pragmatics.* Oxford: Oxford University Press, 43–59.

Cobb, H., & Horst M. (2004). Is there room for an academic word list in French? P. Bogaards, & B. Laufer (eds) *Vocabulary in a Second Language: Selection, Acquisition, and Testing.* Amsterdam: Benjamins, 15–38.

Coxhead, A. (2000). A new academic word list. *TESOL Quarterly,* 34:2, 213–238.

Daller, H., van Hout, R. & Treffers-Daller, J. (2003). Lexical richness in spontaneous speech of bilinguals. *Applied Linguistics,* 24:2, 197–222.

Daller, H., Milton, J., & Treffers-Daller, J. (eds) (2007). *Modelling and Assessing Vocabulary Knowledge.* Cambridge: Cambridge University Press.

De Cock, S., Granger, S., Leech, G. & McEnery, T. (1998). An automated approach to the phrasicon of EFL learners. S. Granger (ed.) *Learner English on Computer.* London & New York: Longman, 67–79.

De Cock, S. (2004). Preferred sequences of words in NS and NNS speech. *Belgian Journal of English language and literatures (BELL) New Series,* 2, 225–246.

Denke, A. (2009). *Nativelike Performance: A Corpus Study of Pragmatic Markers, Repair and Repetition in Native and Non-native English Speech.* Saarbrücken: VDM Verlag.

Erman, B. & Lewis, M. (2011). Multiword structures in the speech of non-native and native speakers of English. Paper presented at EUROSLA 21, 21st annual conference of the European second language association, 8–10 September.

Erman, B. & Lewis, M. (2013). Vocabulary in advanced L2 English speech. N.-L. Johannesson, G. Melchers & B. Björkman (eds) *Of Butterflies and Birds, Dialects and Genres*. Stockholm Studies in English 104. Acta Universitatis Stockholmiensis, 93–108.

Erman, B., Denke, A., Fant, L. & Forsberg Lundell, F. (2014). Nativelike expression in the speech of long-residency L2 users: A study of multiword structures in L2 English, French and Spanish. *International Journal of Applied Linguistics* 24, doi: 10.1111/ijal.12061 2014.

Fant, L. & Hancock, V. (2014). Marqueurs discursifs connectifs chez des locuteurs de L2 très avancés: le cas de *alors* et *donc* en français et de *entonces* en espagnol. M. Borreguero Zuloaga & S. Gómez-Jordana Ferary (eds) *Marqueurs du discours dans les langues romanes: une approche contrastive*. Limoges: Lambert Lucas, 317–335.

Forsberg Lundell, F. & Lindqvist, C. (2012). Vocabulary development in advanced L2 French: do formulaic sequences and lexical richness develop at the same rate? *Language, Interaction, Acquisition (LIA)*, 3:1, 73–92.

Granger, S. (1998). Prefabricated patterns in advanced EFL writing: collocations and formulae. A.P. Cowie (ed.) *Phraseology, Theory, Analysis and Applications*, 145–160.

Hancock, V. & Kirchmeyer, N. (2009). Étude du marqueur polyfonctionnel *vraiment*. *L'information grammaticale*, 120, 14–23.

Hancock, V. (2012). Pragmatic use of temporal adverbs in L1 and L2 French: Functions and syntactic positions of textual markers in a spoken corpus. C. Lindqvist & C. Bardel (eds) *The Acquisition of French as a Second Language: New Developmental Perspectives*. Special issue of *Language, Interaction and Acquisition*, 3:1, 29–51.

Laufer, B. (1995). Beyond 2000: A measure of productive lexicon in a second language. L. Eubank, L. Selinker, & M. Sharwood Smith (eds) *The Current State of Interlanguage: Studies in Honor of William E. Rutherford*. Amsterdam: Benjamins, 265–272.

Laufer, B. & Nation, P. (1995). Vocabulary size and use: Lexical richness in L2 written production. *Applied Linguistics*, 16, 307–322.

Lindqvist, C. (2010). La richesse lexicale dans la production orale de l'apprenant avancé de français. *La revue Canadienne des Langues Vivantes/The Canadian Modern Language Review*, 66:3, 393–420.

Lindqvist, C., Bardel, C., & Gudmundson, A. (2011). Lexical richness in the advanced learner's oral production of French and Italian L2. *International Review of Applied Linguistics (IRAL)*, 49, 221–240.

Lindqvist, C., Gudmundson, A., & Bardel, C. (2013). A new approach to measuring lexical sophistication in L2 oral production. *Eurosla Monographs Series*, 2, 109–126.

McCarthy, P. M., & Jarvis, S. (2007). Vocd: A theoretical and empirical evaluation. *Language Testing*, 24:4, 459–488.

Milton, J. (2007). Lexical profiles, learning styles and the construct validity of lexical size tests. H. Daller, J. Milton, & J. Treffers-Daller (eds) *Modelling and Assessing Vocabulary Knowledge*. Cambridge: Cambridge University Press, 133–149.

Ringbom, H. (1998). Vocabulary frequencies in advanced learner English: a cross-linguistic approach. S. Granger (ed.) *Learner English on Computer.* London & New York: Longman.

Shin, D. & Nation, P. (2008). Beyond single words: The most frequent collocations in spoken English. *ELT Journal*, 62:4, 339–348.

Simon-Vandenbergen, A.-M. (2000). The functions of *I think* in political discourse. *International Journal of Applied Linguistics*, 10:1, 41–63.

Tidball, F., & Treffers-Daller, J. (2007). Exploring measures of vocabulary richness in semi-spontaneous French speech. H. Daller, J. Milton, & J. Treffers-Daller (eds) *Modelling and Assessing Vocabulary Knowledge*. Cambridge: Cambridge University Press, 133–149.

Vermeer, A. (2004). The relation between lexical richness and vocabulary size in Dutch L1 and L2 children. P. Bogaards, & B. Laufer (eds) *Vocabulary in a Second Language: Selection, Acquisition, and Testing*. Amsterdam: Benjamins, 15–38.

20 "Bachelor Means Nothing Without Husband and Father"[1] : What Collocations Reveal about a Cognitive Category

Christina Alm-Arvius (1945–2013)

Stockholm University. Based on an unfinished manuscript, posthumously edited by Cecilia Ovesdotter Alm.

1. Introduction

This study combines recent insights into the interpretation of language in cognitive linguistics with the examination of syntagmatic patterns, or collocations, in English language use. The focus is on collocations involving the English lexeme *bachelor*. To further our science, the aim must be to try to integrate information from different theoretical perspectives to get as comprehensive and profound a view as possible of semantic questions (cf. Alm-Arvius 1999). It is hardly possible to discuss meaning in natural human languages without making use of such basic notions as reference, denotation, sense, and syntagmatic and paradigmatic sense relations. Significantly enough, different versions of the cognitive semantic school have in many respects developed through critical reactions to these earlier semantic paradigms.

The sense or senses of the lexeme *bachelor* have been described in different ways, and often the sense descriptions given are straightforwardly connected with the theoretical standpoint of the linguist(s) producing them regarding semantic questions in general. In particular we can note that cognitive semantics has been critical of what it calls classical categorization. In short, it insists that classical categorization overlooks certain crucial observations concerning how speakers of English really understand and use, for instance, the noun *bachelor*. In this study I shall look into the semantics of this English lexeme, and

---

[1] From the *British National Corpus*.

How to cite this book chapter:
Alm-Arvius, C. 2015. "Bachelor Means Nothing Without Husband and Father": What Collocations Reveal about a Cognitive Category. In: Shaw, P., Erman, B., Melchers, G. and Sundkvist, P. (eds) *From Clerks to Corpora: essays on the English language yesterday and today*. Pp. 367–386. Stockholm: Stockholm University Press. DOI: http://dx.doi.org/10.16993/bab.t License: CC-BY.

use it as a touchstone as well as a steppingstone for gaining insight into general semantic questions and the contributions that different types of theories can be expected to give to linguistic semantics in general. The empirical material consists of *bachelor* occurrences in *The Times* and *The Sunday Times* 1995 and examples in the *British National Corpus*. Below, *T* and *ST* are abbreviations of *The Times* and *The Sunday Times* respectively, and *BNC* is short for the *British National Corpus*.[2]

The discussion will consider certain explanatory models within the cognitive linguistic paradigm, examining their usefulness and descriptive validity when trying to explain the meaning(s) conveyed by *bachelor*.

Cognitive science is the result of work in a number of related disciplines, including linguistics and philosophy, but in many ways it has been particularly influenced by findings in cognitive psychology and, more recently, neurobiology (see e.g. Lakoff 1987; Lakoff & Johnson 1999). More specifically, the concept of prototype is a central one in cognitive semantics. It was introduced by Eleanor Rosch and her co-workers in the 1970s in their studies into the nature of ordinary human categorization (Rosch 1978,1977,1975; Rosch & Mervis 1975).

Fillmore's notion of frames has proved quite influential in cognitively oriented research on language meaning(s). It is somewhat loose and open to partly variant understandings. Sometimes it must be taken to stand for a fairly specific type of situation, not unlike the propositional structures outlined by a predicator and its argument(s) in predicate logic. However, there are also said to be complex frames, a more comprehensive scenario supposed to constitute a common ground for the more specific conceptual figures represented by individual words. This is reminiscent of lexical fields or sense relations in structuralist semantics, but according to Fillmore and other adherents of the frame theory it is the conceptual frames which are basic, and words are only understood and related to each other via their grounding in such experiential schematizations (Fillmore 1985).

A fundamental fact about lexical words in English is that they are used together in linear sequences according to more general and

---

[2] Even if the *bachelor* occurrences in these British texts cannot be taken to exemplify the average way of using *bachelor* in English at large, they nonetheless show how native speakers of the language can use the word for different kinds of communicative purposes.

recursive syntactic patterns. Lexical co-occurrence is however restricted not only by the syntactic properties of words but also by more specific lexico-semantic selectional tendencies. Some syntagmatic connections are quite fixed or "frozen" constructions (idioms) whose meanings are sometimes idiosyncratic and not calculable from the individual words used in them. On the whole, it seems however more common that lexical items occur together in more variable combinations or collocations. These are also idiomatic or language specific in a great many cases and often constitute difficulties both for language learners and in translation work. Prototype analyses of lexical senses have not paid much attention to the collocational behaviour of individual lexemes like *bachelor*.

2. The lexicon and the grammar

Examining *bachelor* allows exploration of how cognition, in a wider sense, and structural conventions in the English language are important for how it can be used and understood in syntagmatic sequences. The relationship between the lexicon and the grammar of a human language is a central question in linguistics. It concerns the character of lexemes, word formation, collocations, and syntactic structures, and their relationships.

Arguably, syntagmatic sense relations are more basic than paradigmatic or substitutional ones; language is usually realized in compositional linear strings moulded on recurring, and thus conventionalized, constructional patterns. The collocations of lexical items within syntactic structures are in principle variable, even if they are also restricted. In fact, the intuitions among proficient speakers concerning lexical co-occurrence potentials are often intricate, as they involve, for instance, the possibility for creative figurative extensions of lexical senses. As a result, it has in many cases proved difficult to unravel them analytically and describe them in a satisfactory way (cf. Cruse 2000: 229–234).

The combination of a premodifier and a nominal head, as in *eligible bachelor*, *poor bachelor* and *wealthy spinster*, is a two-lexeme collocation and part of a noun phrase, but lexical words – or rather specific morphosyntactic forms of lexical words – are of course usually strung together in longer and more complex syntagms which often also include function words. An example of this would be the combination of words in the main declarative clause *A poor bachelor wants to marry a wealthy spinster.*

As I exemplify below, *bachelor* can either be treated as a kind of civil legal term or as a general language word. In the first function it has a well-defined sense distinguishing it from other terms within the terminological field dealing with marriage or being single like *husband*, *wife*, *spinster*, and *divorcee*. Its use in the general language overlaps ordinarily with this technical application to a considerable extent, but it is more variable and open to changes as to what associations are foregrounded on a particular occasion of use.

3. Collocations: co-occurrence potentials of words in syntactic strings

The term *collocation* was introduced by J R Firth (1957: 194–196). It concerns the semantic significance of the co-occurrence of words within language sequences. Firth does not provide a more exact description of this concept, however.

> "Meaning by collocation is an abstraction at the syntagmatic level and is not directly concerned with the conceptual or idea approach to the meaning of words. One of the meanings of *night* is its collocability with *dark*, and of *dark*, of course, collocation with *night*. This kind of mutuality may be paralleled in most languages and has resulted in similarities of poetic diction in literatures sharing common classical sources." (1957: 196)

In the passage quoted above, which occurs towards the end of his brief outline of the notion of collocation, Firth appears, firstly, to distinguish between the conceptual meaning of a word and its collocability. The former is presumably the meaning it has also when it is uttered quite on its own, without the company of other words in a composite syntactic string. A word's collocability with another word is said to be a separable kind of meaning, or perhaps we should rather take it to be another aspect of its meaning. At any rate, Firth can be taken to claim that the collocability of a word is not directly reflected in, or does not straight-forwardly follow from, its conceptual content.[3]

Quite generally speaking, collocability seems to be connected with semantic compatibility. More specifically, empirical observations of collocates in syntactic strings suggest that they can occur together

i)   because they represent **conceptual contents** that **intersect** to a certain degree

ii) and often also because of established habits within the speech community.

In other words, words' collocational behaviour is part of the **idiomaticity** of the language, and this would appear to account for the perceived arbitrariness of certain collocational preferences and restrictions – also in factually oriented descriptions. Why are for instance both *a high building* and *a tall building* possible – and synonymous – while we only talk of *a tall man?*

3.1 Collocations involving bachelor

We can note that the extent to which the sense of a possible collocate is integrated into the sense of a lexeme apparently varies. A potential collocate is not reflected so directly in the general understanding of a word, but all the same it can be said to specify the character of a property that will be found in the members of a given sense category. *Be of a certain age* is an inalienable characteristic of material phenomena, including living creatures like human beings. Since the

---

[3] Cruse (2000: 221f) suggests two types of co-occurrence preferences in language: selectional preferences which inescapably follow from the propositional content of a string, and collocational preferences which do not have the same kind of inescapable logico-factual basis, and that violation of selectional preferences is more serious. It will result in a paradox or even outright incongruity. Instead I would suggest that the terms **collocability** or **collocational restrictions** and **preferences** are used in a broad sense about syntagmatic co-occurrence in general between the words in various actual or conceivable phrases, clauses, and sentences within a given language system. In English we can, for instance, both *ride a horse* and *ride a bicycle/motorcycle*, but the Swedish cognate verb *rida* is only used in the translation of the first predication: *rida en häst*, while another verb must be used in collocation with *cykel* and *motorcykel*, the translation equivalents of *bicycle* and *motorcycle*: *åka cykel/ motorcykel* – in spite of the obvious etymological relation between these Swedish and English words. Similarly, drivers or passengers can *ride in a vehicle* like *a bus/a cab/a car/a limousine/a taxi* in English, but *rida* would again not be possible in the corresponding Swedish expressions: *åka bil/buss/limousin/taxi*.

primary sense of *bachelor* denotes *unmarried adult human males*, the adjectives *old* and *young* are both natural collocates: *an old/a young bachelor*. Similarly, we can talk about, for instance, *an aged* or *ageing bachelor*, *a forty-year-old bachelor*, or *a bachelor in his early thirties* (cf. Cruse 1986: 214ff). Indeed, *bachelor* is comparatively frequently found in collocation with words that say something about how long a man has been a bachelor. This is connected with the fact that a man's bachelor days are over as soon as he marries. Comparing the antonyms *bachelor* and *husband*, the sense relation between them tends to involve a temporal aspect: a man is typically a bachelor before he becomes a husband, although some remain bachelors all their lives. Consequently, it is hardly surprising that the sentential formulation *X remained a bachelor* is often seen in obituaries, sometimes with minor variations. Instances of this kind of formulaic sentence occur in *The Times* and *The Sunday*. *Still a bachelor* is another idiomatic expression that is linked with the temporal aspect of bachelor status in these newspaper texts. They also contain instances of the collocation *lifelong bachelor*.

(1)   He remained a bachelor. (*T*11/10,19), (*T*1/9,19), (*T*31/8,17)

(2)   Tubby Broomhall remained a bachelor all his life. (*T*17/1,19)

(3)   Having remained a bachelor until he was well into his seventies, Cramrose married in 1986 Princess Joan Aly Khan. (*T*16/2,21)

(4)   Still a bachelor, he is content with doting on his nephews in Scotland and has little interest in having children of his own. (*ST*29/10,SP/4)

(5)   Anyone who's been a bachelor for as long as me, and there are very few of those around who aren't gay, can knock up the odd this and that. (*ST*22/10,9/15)

To sum up, observations indicate that the collocational potential of a lexical item typically reflects both the conceptual intersection between the senses of collocates and established idiomatic practices in the language in question. This means that collocations tend to be the result of **language specific** combinatory relations between word senses, idiosyncratic conventions within a particular speech community. When translated into other languages, they must commonly be translated as wholes and be calculated in a more global way, involving idiomatic constructional patterns and stylistic norms by language (for instance, consider the common English collocation *eligible bachelor* vs. a Swedish translation equivalent).[4]

It is clear that collocations cannot generally be explained by referring to factual or general conceptual knowledge. From a strictly informative point of view *marriageable bachelor* would appear an appropriate collocation, but it is not a normal collocational choice in English. *Eligible bachelor* is, on the other hand, an idiomatic collocation conveying the same sort of meaning. Collocations are thus commonly habitual or idiomatic combinations of words, and there is no strict distinction between what should be considered a compound or a multi-word expression/idiom and an idiomatic collocation.

Furthermore, regarding collocation and syntactic structure, lexical words are necessarily integrated in the grammar of a language and predisposed to function in particular syntactic slots. As a result, it is arguable that co-occurrence relations between words – be they lexical or grammatical – are limited to items which are syntactically related in a string.

3.2 Types of collocational connections

It is possible – or even necessary in some cases – to distinguish between different types of collocational connections, depending on what kind of syntactic relation exists between a 'collocational focus' and its collocate(s). In a noun phrase the head appears to be the collocational focus, while the modifiers are dependent collocates, adding specifying information about it. Similarly, the subject will be the collocational focus in a clause in relation to predicative items like a verb predicator or a subject complement, and a transitive verb will be collocationally dependent on both its subject and its object(s). In other words, a collocational

---

[4] Strings that deal with hypothetical situations – or combinations or blends of situational scenarios that are at least partly hypothetical – as well as strings which simply negate or question a description of the real world may contain lexical collocations that would appear anomalous in an affirmative assertion describing some event or circumstance in the real world (cf. Alm-Arvius 1993: 26–28; Fauconnier 1997: 14–18, 99ff, 93f, 156ff).

(1) *Bachelors are married/female.
(2) If bachelors were married/female …
(3) Are bachelors married/female?
(4) Bachelors are not married/female.

focus typically has a more independent and weightier denotational or referential status compared to its collocate(s). It tends to be the referential hub in such a combination, a basic link with the extralinguistic thing described. As a result, its meaning will be more directly influenced by the things referred to, and the reading of a collocate will in its turn be adjusted to the understanding of the focus. Accordingly, the distinction between a collocational focus and its collocate(s) is important for the direction of 'collocational tailoring', as the interpretation of a dependent collocate is commonly adjusted to fit the character of a collocational focus rather than the other way round.

Interestingly enough, the direction of collocational selection seems largely the opposite. A modifier, for instance, links on to or selects a phrasal head because, as it were, the contents of this head provide it with an adequate carrier of the characteristic that it represents. In the collocation *old bachelor* the noun head *bachelor* will stand for a person that exhibits the quality described by *old*.

4. Regular vs. occasional features of *bachelor*

4.1 Regularly incorporated aspects of the meaning of bachelor

So-called analytic sentences tell us something about our experience of the world and how cognitive categories are represented. Analytic sentences contain a specific, more unusual type of collocation, as they spell out sense relations between lexical units which are regularly incorporated within the sense of the semantically defined subject constituent, a bachelor, such as a bachelor being *human*, *male*, *adult*, and *unmarried*. If we make the sentences synthetic in (6) through (9) by replacing an initial indefinite article with the definite article or a demonstrative pronoun, these strings appear odd – it is difficult to think of a communicative situation in which they occur. There is usually no need explicitly to add meaning aspects to an instance of a lexical item by means of a collocate if these qualities are already regularly incorporated in its sense – unless one wants to explain the sense in question by using an analytic sentence.

(6) ?The/This/That bachelor is (a) human
(7) ?The/This/That bachelor is (a) male.
(8) ?The/This/That bachelor is (an) adult.
(9) ?The/This/That bachelor is unmarried.

Admittedly, it is often difficult to decide whether a general sentential description of the contents of word – or part of it – is strictly speaking an analytic sentence or whether it is instead largely synthetic. Clearly, the difficulty to draw an absolute boundary between analytic and synthetic sentences is directly related to the often cumbersome distinction between what can be said to be strictly entailed by a propositional statement and meaning features that seem merely to be regularly presupposed or even just commonly expected in the use of certain lexical and grammatical constructs.

Arguably, the following two statements, which essentially express the same claim, are not unconditional analytic sentences, because even if they would be true of most men who can be included in the primary sense of *bachelor* category, they need not be true of all of them. In other words, being a bachelor does not entail living in circumstances that make it possible to enter into the state of matrimony. Instead this quality is just **expected** in most cases, although it need not be part of the characterization of each and every bachelor.

(10)   A bachelor can marry.
(11)   If a man is a bachelor, he is free to marry.

Such observations directly support a **prototype**-centred analysis of lexical senses. Indeed, individual bachelors necessarily exhibit a host of characteristics which are not regularly or even commonly shared by all the members of this category. This is directly relevant for the impression that this sense category – like most others – does not have strict conceptual boundaries. Bachelors come in many different shapes or forms, as it were. They are men that are old enough to marry, but each of them also has a great many other qualities, and they all participate in a considerable range of social scenarios, although some of them are more associated with the status of bachelorhood than others. These unavoidable experiential facts cannot be disregarded when we consider and try to describe how users of English understand this term within or even out of specific language contexts.

Cognitive semantics allows us to consider also such merely occasional characteristics of, for instance, bachelors. By comparison, earlier – or classical – types of sense analyses normally aimed at identifying a skeletal and finite set of supposedly necessary or at least criterial features, but this proved difficult in many cases for a number of reasons. Our general experience of what can be included in a category like *bachelor* is many-sided and even partly variable, and our cognitive grasp of word senses also allows imaginative, unpredictable variations, many of which are logically and factually impossible. All the same, they occur and provide food for speculative thought as well as for figurative extensions of sense categories (cf. Alm-Arvius 1999). In addition, language habits sometimes impose arbitrary-like preferences or even restrictions on the use of lexical items or longer expressions, for instance as regards what words or word forms can naturally collocate in a given language (cf. Cruse 1986: 281f).

4.2 Occasional collocates of bachelor

Examining the semantic relation between a lexical item like *bachelor* and its lexical collocates or collocational foci, we can first observe that generally recognized analytic sentences, used to explain the primary sense of bachelor are exceptional in containing collocates that only stand for senses that are just regularly incorporated parts of this other, typically more specific, lexical sense – or cognitive category, if we instead use the terminology of cognitive semantics. But if the purpose of the utterance is not to explain this particular word sense, such a collocation will appear tautological or pleonastic (cf. Cruse 2000: 45, 223f, 227–229). Importantly enough, this appears to be true of constructions that contain the entailed predicative quality *unmarried* as well as those that explicitly attribute the regularly presupposed features *human*, *male*, and *adult* to the referent of a particular *bachelor* instance.

The following two examples show that *male* and *unmarried* have been used as premodifying collocates of *bachelor* also in non-analytic constructions. These two premodifiers might have been added to these particular examples of *bachelor* functioning as noun phrase heads as semantic emphasis markers.

> (12) How, then, can this zeitgeisty little lifestyle development for the heterosexual male bachelor be on the way out, ... (*ST*23/4,9/4)
>
> (13) ... a revenge drama about an unmarried bachelor who likes to razor off people's ears to avenge his deaf brother. (*ST*8/1,10/49)

However, normally the collocates of a lexical item with a particular sense like *bachelor* add merely **occasional** features to it. This is in fact why they are informative. The premodifiers *posh*, *young*, *kindly*, *old*, *taciturn*, *painfully shy*, *American*, *millionaire*[5], and *middle-aged*, as well

---

[5] *American millionaire* in (18) could well be regarded as one composite modifier consisting of a phrase in which *millionaire* is the head and *American* is a premodifier.

as the postmodifiers *in his fifties* and *farming alone* ... in the examples below are all possible but by no means regular features of members of the *bachelor* category. In other words, these senses are compatible with the primary sense of *bachelor*, but not regularly incorporated in it.

(14)   ... a posh young bachelor ... (*T31/3,2*)
(15)   ... the kindly old bachelor ... (*ST26/11,7/7*)
(16)   Mr Cassidy, a taciturn bachelor, ... (*T6/11,4*)
(17)   ... the duke, a painfully shy bachelor, ... (*T24/7,15*)
(18)   ... , American millionaire bachelor, ... (*BNC,AP7(762)*)
(19)   ... a bachelor in his fifties ... (*BNC,AFC(1644)*)
(20)   ... a middle-aged bachelor farming alone after his mother dies, ... (*BNC,A36(270)*)

The observation that the dependent collocates of a particular lexical word typically add occasional but by no means regular features to its collocational focus helps us to understand the character of lexical senses or categories. It shows us that they are semantically flexible, as they have the potential to take on certain additional meaning aspects temporarily, in specific language sequences and as a result of the actual or would-be referents or reference situations described by particular uses of a lexical sense. Indeed this observation agrees well with proto-type analysis of lexical meanings.

Even quite common collocates of, for instance, *bachelor* which occur in synthetic sentences rather than in analytic ones – like *eligible*, *confirmed*, or phrases and words that say something about the age of a bachelor – represent additional, non-core features of their colloca-tional focus. Common collocations like *eligible bachelor* and *confirmed bachelor* ought to have some kind of lexical status, even if they cannot be considered compounds (cf. ALD 1989: 72; Longman 1987: 63). This kind of linguistic mental imprint must, however, be quite intricate and involve possible variations in the realizations of a collocational pattern. When used in actual syntactic structures in utterances, these colloc-ations must accordingly be realized as parts of whole noun phrases. *Eligible* in *eligible bachelor* is then often, but not necessarily, found in its superlative form, *most eligible*, with a preceding geographical term in the genitive case. In addition, such a noun phrase appears often to be the complement of the preposition *of* in a partitive construction: *one of X's most eligible bachelors*.

The regular features of a lexical sense constitute its core, while the occasional features added by dependent collocates are merely various kinds of conceivable but not generally incorporated sense attributes. In other words, in the case of *bachelor* collocational meaning additions will be semantic aspects that are quite compatible with being a bachelor, even if a man can also very well be a bachelor without being associated with them either just transiently or more permanently. Most importantly, it is clear that in addition to shared, regular features of this category (see above), every bachelor must also have a host of other, either more stable or just incidental, or even just potential characteristics. Speakers of English are naturally aware of this, and it is debatable whether they ever think of bachelors as simply having the skeletal set of attributes that I have called regular, incorporated sense features. Instead it seems likely that their conceptions of bachelors tend to be both richer and somewhat variable through the inclusion of merely occasional sense attributes.

More specifically, occasional attributes with *bachelor* understandings in actual language use can clearly be placed along a continuum from usually **expected** ones over those that are just **possible** but not ordinarily expected to more unique, **individual** qualities of particular bachelors like *farming alone ...* in (20) (cf. Cruse 1986).

> Continuum of **occasional** features of *bachelor*:
> **expected** -------- **possible** -------- **individual**

It seems somewhat problematic to try to sketch a general prototype of the primary sense of *bachelor* without considering special types of circumstances or language contexts, but it appears reasonable to suggest that the **regular** and typically **expected** features of bachelors together form a loose kind of prototypical conception of the sense category we speak of as *bachelor*. In particular, it should be noted that this explanatory model of the semantics of this lexical item makes a distinction between regularly presupposed and usually expected qualities. Only the former will be felt to be criterial enough to be regularly incorporated in the primary sense of *bachelor*.

> **regular features: entailed – presupposed**
> **occasional features: expected** -------- **possible** -------- **individual**

Furthermore, it seems as though it would normally be wrong to consider occasional collocates accidental or selectionally arbitrary, since apparently they can co-occur with, or select, the collocational focus because the two somehow share a semantic quality. This semantic affinity need not be the result of the actual character of the kind of phenomena represented by a collocational focus. It could just be a cultural and cognitive construct, and thus an indication of how speakers of a given language, or a variety of it, conceive of something part of their life experience. Actually, also regular sense features can depend on cultural conceptions and conventions. This applies to the fourth core feature regardless of whether it can be paraphrased as (a man who) has never been married or just as (an) unmarried (man). The institution of marriage is a cultural construct, and the sense of bachelor is directly dependent on it.

We have now discussed how the meaning of a collocational focus, bachelor, can be made more specific by in particular modifying collocates. However, bachelor appears also to be fairly frequently used itself as a dependent collocate, that is as an adjectivalized premodifier or as a predicative complement. In turning to such bachelor occurrences, it is relevant to recall that dependent collocates are often semantically tailored, that is adjusted, to the meaning of their collocational focus. In other words, the reading of a collocate can also be influenced by a collocational relationship, or sometimes perhaps mainly as a result of the extralinguistic character of the thing(s) described.

All the "bachelor plus noun" combinations exemplified below are used in my empirical material, and especially bachelor pad seems so common that it may be appropriate to consider it a compound noun rather than a collocation.[6]

> (21)   The first time Mathias and Christa make love is in a cheesy bachelor pad, complete with mirrored ceiling. (ST5/2,7/12)

---

[6] *Bachelor* appears also to be quite frequently used as the head of a noun phrase functioning as a subject complement. I would suggest that such an instance is typically not as closely integrated semantically with the subject element it adds information about as many premodifier instances of *bachelor* and their head nouns. A premodifier and its head are parts of the same noun phrase and will function together also semantically within such referring or predicative expressions. By comparison, a subject and its subject complement do not belong to the same syntactic phrase, just to the same clause. A complement makes up a phrase of its own, which is furthermore syntactically more directly related to the copular predicate verb than to the subject, as it is first tied to this verb through its complement status. It is then syntactically related to the subject through it, as an element of the predicate constituent. The syntactic relationship between a dependent collocate and its collocational focus appears to be relevant for how much the latter can dominate or mould the reading of the former.

(5) Charles had been a bachelor for thirty-two years. (BNC,A7H(445))

(6) Gary Bond remained a bachelor. (T14/10,23)

(7) Fortunately, too, most of the men are bachelors and so are spared the withering remarks of bored spouses. (T24/6,SP/2)

(22)   I was pursing a bachelor life with almost no downside. (*ST*15/10,9/13)

(23)   It was one of the first recipes that my husband attempted in his bachelor days. (*BNC*, ABB(864))

(24)   "You mean, he had them under the bed in his old bachelor flat in Wimbledon, ..." (*ST*24/2,5/7)

(25)   Heuston lived the life of a bachelor don with rooms in college for the next 15 years. (*T*27/12, 9)

(26)   She met Ernest Weekly, a bachelor lecturer from Nottingham University, when she was 18 and he was 33, and they embarked on a loveless, dessicated marriage, ... (*ST*25/6,7/3)

(27)   ... since Wendy and Tom Witherington had two young children upon whom their bachelor uncle doted. (*BNC*, AOD(2559))

(28)   Or, as he sang back in 1962, "until then I'll be your bachelor boy and that's the way I'll stay, happy to be a bachelor boy until my dying day." (*ST*18/6,3/2)

5. Two types of occasional features or collocates

Within the class of occasional *bachelor* attributes which occur as premodifying collocates of this noun we can in fact distinguish two different groups depending on what regular features in *bachelor* they can be used to comment on. The first group consists of premodifiers that can also be found with the superordinate *man*. Such *bachelor* instances can be replaced by *man* without affecting the reading of the premodifier, although such a noun phrase would of course have a less specific meaning, since *bachelor* contains the additional information that we can spell out as *has never been married* or *is unmarried*. The strings from (29) to (31) contain examples of such premodifying collocates of *bachelor*.

(29)   Starkie, an American bachelor, regularly accompanies the duchess on charity trips to eastern Europe, ... (*ST*18/6,1/7)

(30)   He is Marc Andreessen, a large, loose-limbed 24-year-old bachelor from the Midwest, who appears to live for nothing but computers and junk food. (*ST*13/8,3/8)

(31)   He was an old, stooping, emaciated bachelor,aghast at the facts of life; he never smiled but glowered defensively at the world from under his eyebrows, ... (BNC,ABW(240))

The second group is illustrated below. The collocates *eligible*, *confirmed*, *incorrigible*, *entrenched*, and *lifelong* must be taken necessarily to associate to the entailed *unmarried* feature of the head *bachelor*. In all these cases the combination of the premodifying collocate and *bachelor* is semantically quite cohesive, and an instance of *man* could not be substituted for *bachelor* in any these phrases, as the choice of these particular premodifiers would then no longer make sense, at least not in these specific contexts. Not even *unmarried man* would seem a possible alternative, because it is not normally used in collocation with these premodifying adjectives to convey the same sense as *bachelor*.

As I have outlined, *bachelor* seems to be associated with a rich and variable set of characteristics, and this is no doubt directly connected with its use in so many different collocations and wider contexts depicting scenarios involving bachelors and aspects of bachelorhood. There are likely to be differences between individual speakers as regards what occasional features tend to come to mind when they hear this lexical item mentioned, especially out of a specifying context, but speakers are prepared for variation in the use of the noun. This is presumably a result of their linguistic experience; the many times they have heard *bachelor* being used or used it themselves. Their extralinguistic experiences of bachelors and their way of life must, as usual, interact with their language competence and practices, for instance their recognition of both frequent and apparently conventionalized collocations and other collocations considered possible.

(32) John Fitzgerald Kennedy, 34-year-old son of the slain President, is variously known as "the hunk", "the sexiest man alive", and America's most eligible bachelor. (T12/9,15)

(33) ... he had the slightly panicky look of a confirmed bachelor who has just walked into a maternity ward of bawling babies, ... (ST26/2,10/7)

(34) He had long seemed an incorrigible bachelor but in 1971 he surprised his friends with marriage. (T2/10,23)

(35) ... verses aimed at turning the thoughts of entrenched bachelors to the comforts of matrimony ... (ST12/2,5/7)

(36) A lifelong bachelor, Paul Hogan leaves no survivors. (T18/3,21)

(37) Often dubbed Britain's most eligible bachelor, the late duke was linked with a series of glamorous women ... (T1/11,1)

(38) One Fleet Street columnist after another claimed her wedding to one of the world's most eligible bachelors was an appalling mistake. (ST19/11,1/5)

(39) ... he was an international champion golfer and one of the most eligible young bachelors in the London society of the early 1930s. (BNC,K5J(2175))

(40)   As a youth Richard was red-haired, high, wide and handsome, and considered the most eligible bachelor in Christendom. (*ST*8/1,3/1)

(41)   Thus Andrew Davies has Mrs Bennet's initial announcement to her husband that an eligible bachelor has taken the tenancy of Netherfield Hall take place most incongruously as the family hurries home from church. (*T*6/10,39)

(42)   But while some women complain that eligible black bachelors are hard to find, others play solitaire by choice. (*ST*19/12,9/8)

(43)   Housman, a confirmed bachelor, was born in 1859 and had a stifling Victorian upbringing. (*T*23/9,5)

(44)   Sadly, most seem to be confirmed bachelors. (*ST*30/4,9/14)

(45)   ... a retired businessman and confirmed bachelor with bald head and circular spectacles, dressed in old-fashioned tights and gaiters. (*BNC*,Boy(981))

6. Figurative shifts and irregular features

As an interesting contrast, in the next two examples *bachelor* is used as a premodifier of the noun phrase heads *Mother* and *queen*. These collocational foci stand for women, and accordingly they force a suppression of the regular sense quality *male* in the primary sense of the collocate *bachelor*. This collocational tailoring of the both syntactically and semantically dependent item *bachelor* is necessary if they are to function together to convey the intended meaning.

(46)   Notable among her films during the period were the comedy Bachelor Mother (1939), with David Niven, as a shopgirl who finds an abandoned baby, and the drama Kitty Foyle (1948), ... (*T*26/4,19)

(47)   Queen Christina, directed by Rouben Mamoulian, takes liberties with history, telling how Sweden's 17th-century bachelor queen abjures her love for the Spanish ambassador (John Gilbert) in the higher interests of the state. (*T*8/4,SP/4)

In short, such a figurative, or more specifically metaphorical shift in the reading of *bachelor* is connected with the introduction of an **irregular** feature in the understanding of this lexical item within a specific collocation, and I would suggest that this is commonly the case in figurative uses. A lexical word like *bachelor* can be semantically influenced by its companion. If *bachelor* is the collocational focus, its collocate can decisively add a specifying feature to its semantic contents, but if it is itself a more dependent collocate, it can be collocationally tailored by the focus. The semantic characteristics that can explicitly be spelt out in a collocational companion are of three different, general types. **Regular** features are only added to a word in specific cases, usually to explain its meaning in an analytic sentence, while **occasional** semantic attributes highlight possible but not regular features of a particular lexicalized sense. Finally, **irregular** attributes trigger a figurative shift of some kind in the reading of a lexical item.

regular -------- occasional -------- irregular

However, *bachelor* instances like the two in (46) and (47) share other, both regular and merely occasional attributes of the sense category *bachelor*. Actually, more unstable but still common occasional *bachelor* features like *independent* or *fending for oneself* appear to be important for the use of *bachelor* in such cases. Obviously, *spinster* cannot be used to convey the complex meanings expressed by presumably incidental combinations like *bachelor mother* and *bachelor queen*, because it is not typically associated with such positive meaning aspects.[7]

Adding to the above, in the kind of similarly metaphorical *bachelor* application exemplified below, it is instead primarily the regular semantic attribute *human* in *bachelor* that is suppressed. And since animals do not marry, although the relations between the sexes among mammals and birds are similar to what we find in human societies, the *unmarried* or *has-not-married* feature cannot be taken at face value either in such contexts. Actually, this is a good example of the insistent impression that our interpretations of words and compositional verbal strings are typically many-sided, **holistic** complexes rather than some kind of simplistic adding-up of discrete sense aspects.

(48) Any sedge warblers that are still singing at midsummer will be bachelors, just warbling on hopefully. (*T29/4,WE/12*)

(49) A minority of the males accomplish most of the mating; and many males die bachelors. (*BNC,GUB(2048)*)

(50) Large groups of dolphins are mixed in age and sex, but smaller groups generally are of three types: a nuclear group, comprising a single adult male and female; a nursery group, with a number of adult females and young; and a bachelor group, with adult and young males. (*BNC,ABC(440)*)

---

[7] *Bachelor girl* seems, on the other hand, to be a lexicalised compound (*ALD* 1989: 72).

(51)   Gelada baboons often move in large herds; individual harems move separately and the 'bachelor' males are found in their own discrete and coherent social units. (*BNC*,AMG(1433))

Furthermore, there is probably a difference between the systematic status of the types of figurative *bachelor* uses exemplified above. The use of *bachelor* to denote animal males without a female partner can be regarded as a lexicalised secondary sense of this lexeme, while it is questionable whether the use of *bachelor* in combinations like *bachelor girl* and *bachelor queen* has the same more independent applicatory status. Both commonly occur as premodifying collocates, but *bachelor* as a synonym of *male animal without a female partner* can clearly also be used as a noun phrase head that on its own serves to pick out referents in the extralinguistic universe of discourse.

7. Conclusion

This study of the collocational range and the textual environment of the English lexeme *bachelor* suggests that its meaning potential is quite complex and variable. Even if we look just at the primary sense of *bachelor*, it is clear that its meaning potential is in certain respects far richer, or more multifaceted and variable, than what was assumed in different attempts at a classical kind of categorization, which would simply claim that the noun had a fixed and clearly delimited content that could be paraphrased as *unmarried man*, or *man who has never been married*. Together with ordinarily expected features like *able/free to marry*, the regular, incorporated features summed up in these paraphrases appear to make up a kind of general sense prototype for speakers of English. The collocational potential of *bachelor* makes it quite clear, however, that the understanding of this lexical item can be associated with a wide range of merely occasional but still possible meaning features. In other words, the more peripheral range of this sense category is variable and rich in possible associations or attributes. There are bachelors of many different sorts of personalities and characteristics, all with unique life stories, and speakers of English may differ as to how typical they feel that a given representative of the category *bachelor* is. We build up our understanding of words, including our assessment of their collocational potential in compositional grammatical string, through active interaction with our environment. In short, the experiences that help form our conception of how a lexical item like *bachelor* can be used in English are both extralinguistic and verbal.

References

Alm-Arvius, C. (1999). Metaphor and Metonymy as Meaning Generalisations Comparable to Hyponymy and Meronymy Respectively. S.-K. Tanskanen & B. Wårvik (eds) *Proceedings from the 7th Nordic Conference for English Studies*. Anglicana Turkuensia No 20. Turku, Finland: University of Turku, 35–46.

Alm-Arvius, C. (1993). (Photocopy version in 1991) *The English Verb* See*: A Study in Multiple Meaning*. Gothenburg Studies in English 64. Göteborg, Sweden: Acta Universitatis Gothoburgensis.

Cruse, D. A. (1986). *Lexical Semantics*. Cambridge Textbooks in Linguistics. Cambridge, UK: Cambridge University Press.

———. (2000). *Meaning in Language*. Oxford & New York: Oxford University Press.

Fauconnier, G. (1997). *Mappings in Thought and Language*. Cambridge, UK: Cambridge University Press.

Fillmore, C. J. (1985). Frames and the Semantics of Understanding. *Quaderni di Semantica*, 6:2, 222–254.

———. (1982). Towards a Descriptive Framework for Spatial Deixis. R. J. Jarvella & W. Klein (eds) *Speech, Place and Action*. Chichester, New York: John Wiley & Sons Ltd, 31–59.

Firth, J. R. (1957). Modes of Meaning. *Papers in Linguistics 1934–1951*. London, New York & Toronto: Oxford University Press.

Lakoff, G. (1987). *Women, Fire, and Dangerous Things*. Chicago & London: The University of Chicago Press.

Lakoff, G. & Johnson, M. (1999). *Philosophy in the Flesh*. New York: Basic Books.

Longman Dictionary of Contemporary English 1987. (2nd ed.). Burnt Mill, Harlow, Essex: Longman. (*Longman*).

Oxford Advanced Learner's Dictionary 1989. (4th ed.). Oxford, New York, etc: Oxford University Press. (*ALD*).

Rosch, E. (1975). Cognitive Reference Points. *Cognitive Psychology*, 7(4), 532-547.

————. (1977). Human Categorisation. N. Warren (ed.) *Studies in Cross-cultural Psychology* Volume 1. London, New York & San Francisco: Academic Press, 1–49.

————. (1978). Principles of Categorization. E. Rosch & B. B. Lloyd (eds) *Cognition and Categorization*. Hillsdale, N.J.: Lawrence Erlbaum, 27–48.

Rosch, E. & Mervis, C. B. (1975). Family Resemblances: Studies in the Internal Structure of Categories. *Cognitive Psychology*, 7(4), 573-605.

About the Authors

Editors

Philip Shaw is a professor in the English Department at Stockholm University. He has published within a wide range of areas including historical linguistics and, more recently, World Englishes, applied linguistics, particularly with a focus on academic and business English, and vocabulary learning among advanced students. With Gunnel Melchers he has published a textbook on World Englishes (see above), and his recent articles have appeared in such journals as *Journal of Second Language Writing*, *TESOL Quarterly*, and *Journal of Pragmatics*. ORCID: 0000-0002-8301-3960

Britt Erman has retired from a post as associate professor in the English Department at Stockholm University. Her earlier research focused on pragmatics and communication. More recently she has published within the areas of cognitive linguistics and L2 acquisition, the latter focusing on academic writing, formulaic language, vocabulary and syntactic complexity among high-level learners of English. Her recent work has appeared in journals such as *International Journal of Corpus Linguistics, Journal of Pragmatics* and *English Language and Linguistics (ELL)*. ORCID: 0000-0002-5009-440X

Gunnel Melchers is Professor Emerita in the English Department at Stockholm University. Her research has been devoted to regional and social variation, with special reference to the north of England and Scotland's Northern Isles. Among her many publications within these areas are such books as *World Englishes*, with Philip Shaw, (Hodder, 2011 2nd ed.), *Writing in Nonstandard English*, co-edited with Irma Taavitsainen and Päivi Pahta (Benjamins, 1999), *Studies in Anglistics* (1995; co-edited with Beatrice Warren), and *Nonstandard Varieties of English* (1994; co-edited with Nils-Lennart Johannesson). ORCID: 0000-0001-8231-2400

Peter Sundkvist is an associate professor in the English Department at Stockholm University. His research interests concern phonology, phonetics, and dialectology, relating to varieties of English and Germanic languages more generally. Most of his empirical work has focused on the Shetland Islands and such topics as Shetland Scots and Scottish Standard English. His work has appeared in journals such as *English World-Wide* and *World Englishes*. ORCID: 0000-0001-7870-6351

Contributors

Karin Aijmer is Professor Emerita in English Linguistics at the University of Gothenburg. Her research has focused on pragmatics and discourse, including such topics as modality, pragmatic markers, conversational routines, and fixed expressions. Her recent publications include *Understanding Pragmatic Markers: A Variational Pragmatic Approach* (Edinburgh University Press, 2013), a special issue of *Functions of Language* on "Discourse linguistics: Theory and practice" (Benjamins, 2014, co-edited with Anita Fetzer)and the chapter on pragmatics in *The Routledge Companion to English Studies* (Routledge, 2014). ORCID: 0000-0001-8461-4437

Christina Alm-Arvius, who passed away in 2013, was an associate professor in the English Department at Stockholm University. Her main area of research was semantics, in particular lexical semantics. Many of her studies focused on aspects of polysemy and involved such related fields as word formation, idiomaticity, the concept of construction, discourse and text analysis. Her publications include *Introduction to Semantics* (Studentlitteratur, 1998) and *Figures of Speech* (Studentlitteratur, 2003).

Cecilia Ovesdotter Alm is an assistant professor in the Department of English at the Rochester Institute of Technology. Her specialism is computational linguistics. Her research has involved interdisciplinary research in this field. Recent publications include the book *Affect in Text and Speech* (VDM Verlag, 2009) and 'The Role of affect in the computational modelling of natural language' (*Language and Linguistic Compass: Computational and Mathematical*, 2012). ORCID: 0000-0002-8730-0916

Javier Calle-Martin is a tenured senior lecturer in the Department of English at the University of Málaga (Spain). His research interests are within historical linguistics and manuscript studies, focusing on early English documents. He is also the leading researcher of a project for the electronic edition of hitherto unedited late Middle English and early Modern English *Fachliteratur*. He is the editor of *The Middle English Version of De viribus herbarum* (2012) and *A Late Middle English Remedybook in MS Wellcome 542* (2013). ORCID: 0000-0003-1040-5979

Marcelle Cole is an assistant professor in the English department at the University of Utrecht. Her most recent book is *Verbal Morphosyntax in Old Northumbrian and the (Northern) Subject Rule*. NOWELE Supplement Series (Benjamins, 2014). ORCID: 0000-0003-4255-7686

Östen Dahl is Professor Emeritus in General Linguistics at Stockholm University. His fields of research include linguistic typology and he has published extensively on tense and aspect, negation, definiteness and grammaticalization. Among his monographs are *Logic in Linguistics*, with J. Allwood and L-G Andersson (Cambridge University Press, 1977), *Tense and Aspect Systems* (Blackwell, 1985), and *The Growth and Maintenance of Linguistic Complexity* (Benjamins, 2004). ORCID: 0000-0001-8914-7129

Marina Dossena is Professor of English Language at the University of Bergamo, Italy. Her research interests focus on Scots and Scottish English and the history of specialized discourse. Her many publications include *Insights into Late Modern English,* co-edited with Charles Jones (Peter Lang, 2003), *Methods and Data in English Historical Dialectology*, co-edited with Roger Lass (Peter Lang, 2005), and the monograph *Scotticisms in Grammar and Vocabulary* (John Donald, 2005). ORCID: 0000-0002-8025-6086

Thomas Egan is Professor of English Linguistics at Hedmark University College in Hamar, Norway. His research interests encompass topics within the areas of corpus linguistics, contrastive linguistics, cognitive linguistics and historical linguistics, including grammaticalisation. He is the author of a monograph on complementation, entitled *Non-finite Complementation: A Usage-based Study of Infinitive and –ing Clauses in English* (Rodopi, 2008). ORCID: 0000-0002-8826-5972

Christine Johansson is a senior lecturer in the English department at Uppsala University. Her fields of research include syntax, diachronic syntax, corpus linguistics and learner English. Her publications include 'Relativizers in 19th-century English' in *Nineteenth-century English:*

Stability and Change (Cambridge, 2006) and 'Relativization in Early Modern English: Written versus speech-related genres' in *Historical Linguistics of English,* (Mouton, 2012). ORCID: 0000-0002-9440-9215

Maria Kuteeva is a professor and Director of the Centre for Academic English in the English Department at Stockholm University. Her main research interests lie in the field of applied linguistics, with a particular focus on academic uses of English across disciplines. Her recent work has appeared in such journals as *Applied Linguistics, Journal of English for Academic Purposes* and *Journal of Second Language Writing.* ORCID: 0000-0003-2942-1426

Merja Kytö is Professor of English Language at Uppsala University. Her research focuses on variation in English (synchronic and diachronic), corpus linguistics, historical pragmatics and early manuscript studies. Among her publications are *English Corpus Linguistics: Crossing Paths* (Rodopi, 2012), *Testifying to Language and Life in Early Modern England*, with Peter J. Grund and Terry Walker (Benjamins, 2011), and *Early Modern English Dialogues: Spoken Interaction as Writing*, with Jonathan Culpeper (Cambridge University Press, 2010).

Margareta Lewis is affiliated with the English Department at Stockholm University through the large-scale project "High-Level L2 Proficiency and Use" involving several language departments. At present Lewis holds a position as senior lecturer in L2 English within adult education. Recent publications include 'Multiword structures in different materials and with different goals and methodologies', with Britt Erman, *Yearbook of Corpus Linguistics and Pragmatics 2013* (Springer). ORCID: 0000-0001-9123-116x

David Minugh recently retired from a post as foreign lecturer in the English Department at Stockholm University. His research has primarily concerned corpus linguistics and idiom research, and American English, but also includes work on a number of dictionaries. His recent publications include a chapter in *Corpus Linguistics 25 Years on* (Rodopi, 2007), and his compilation PhD thesis *Studies in Corpora and Idioms: Getting the Cat Out of the Bag.* 2014. Stockholm: Stockholm University. ORCID: 0000-0002-6481-1975

David Moreno Olalla is a lecturer at the University of Málaga. Most of his work deals with Middle English Scientific *Fachliteratur* and manuscript studies, which he alternates with dialectological research. He has published of late on the textual transmission of a hitherto unknown

northern ME translation of Macer Floridus's *De Viribus Herbarum*.
ORCID: 0000-0002-9772-8959

Erik Smitterberg is an associate professor and a senior lecturer in English Linguistics, at Uppsala University. His main fields of research concern Late Modern English, from a corpus-based perspective. Among his publications are the books *The Progressive in 19th-century English: A Process of Integration* (Rodopi, 2005), and *Spotting the Error: A Problem-based Workbook on English Grammar and Usage* (Studentlitteratur, 2007). ORCID: 0000-0001-9596-7406

Gjertrud F. Stenbrenden is an associate professor of English in the Department of Literature, Area Studies, and European Languages at the University of Oslo. Her main interests are phonology, dialectology, diachronic linguistics, linguistic variation and change. Recent publications include 'The diphthongisation of ME *ū* : The spelling evidence'. *Language and Computers* 2013, and *Academic Writing in English,* with Per Lysvåg, (Cappelen Damm, 2014). ORCID: 0000-0003-3094-7900

Gunnel Tottie is Professor Emerita at the Department of English, University of Zurich. She has published widely within such fields as syntax and pragmatics. Her most recent book is *An Introduction to American English* (Blackwell). ORCID: 0000-0001-6994-9829

Francesco-Alessio Ursini is a lecturer in the English Department at Stockholm University. Recent publications include 'The interpretation of spatial *At*: An Experimental Study', *Journal of Cognitive Science* 2013. ORCID: 0000-0001-7042-3576

Laura Wright is a Reader in English Language at the Faculty of English, University of Cambridge. Her most recent book is *Code-Switching in Early English,* co-edited with Herbert Schendl (Mouton de Gruyter, 2011). ORCID: 0000-0002-9953-6483

Arne Zettersten is Professor Emeritus of English at the University of Copenhagen. His scholarly contributions cover a broad range of areas, including grammar, semantics, lexicography, etymology, and medieval textual studies. He has made important contributions to work on J.R.R. Tolkien. Among Zettersten's many works is his monograph on Tolkien: *Tolkien – min vän Ronald och hans världar* (Atlantis, 2008) (later translated into *J.R.R. Tolkien's Double Worlds and Creative Process* (Palgrave McMillan, 2011)). ORCID: 0000-0003-3393-1330